ADVANCE PRAISE FOR *Envoy for Christ*

"Like it or not, apologetics is a major apostolic need of the Church today. Patrick Madrid is an example to us all of the courage, sharpness of mind, and patience of soul that it requires."

—*Aidan Nichols, O.P., Blackfriars, Cambridge*

"The Church has been blessed with the fine scholarly work of Mr. Patrick Madrid, and his books deserve a place on every Catholic person's bookshelf. The New Evangelization requires a new apologetics to announce the Gospel message with confidence and cogency. For a quarter of a century, Patrick Madrid has been an outstanding apostle of the new evangelization. He is a man of deep faith, who opens himself daily to the power of conversion and transformation of the Lord.

"It was almost twenty-five years ago that Patrick Madrid came to visit me in my first diocese as bishop in the United States Virgin Islands. His clear exposition of the Catholic Faith and the powerful witness of our doctrines and traditions made a huge impact on Catholics and non-Catholics alike. I have followed his trajectory with admiration and gratitude. Hopefully his memoirs will inspire others to follow the same path with the same energy and zeal."

—*Sean Cardinal O'Malley, Archbishop of Boston*

"With his customary good cheer, Madrid debates with Jehovah's Witnesses, Seventh-Day Adventists, Mormon missionaries, and more. This book is a veritable introduction to apologetics in the contemporary American religious scene, with Scripture at the center."

—*Matthew Levering, Ph.D., professor of theology, University of Dayton, coeditor,*
Nova et Vetera

"All of Patrick Madrid's books are very good and rock solid, but this one, *Envoy for Christ,* is unique. While reading it, I was reminded of the old saying: 'People don't care how much you know, until they know how much you care.' Patrick's intellectual energy and communication skills have always impressed me, but even more his virtually unlimited capacity for friendship, which he has extended to many different people, in many different ways, including me. This book is a powerful testimony to how our Lord is using this gifted apologist not only to bless the Church—for over a quarter century now—but also to gradually transform him from being a good man (a godly husband and father of eleven) into a saint."

—Scott Hahn, bestselling author, speaker, and professor of theology and Scripture, Franciscan University

"I can think of no more engaging and persuasive 'envoy for Christ' than Patrick Madrid. This captivating new book makes apologetics accessible, personal and downright inspiring. Peppered with personal anecdotes and witness, *Envoy for Christ* will undoubtedly bring new readers to Patrick's work and, God willing, fulfill Patrick's great mission of bringing them, as well, to Christ."

—Deacon Greg Kandra, blogger, "The Deacon's Bench"

ENVOY
FOR
CHRIST

. . . .

25 Years as a Catholic Apologist

Patrick Madrid

SERVANT
BOOKS

PUBLISHED BY FRANCISCAN MEDIA
Cincinnati, Ohio

Cover and book design by Mark Sullivan
Cover image © Kim Linder

LIBRARY OF CONGRESS CATALOGING-IN-PUBLICATION DATA
Madrid, Patrick, 1960-
Envoy for Christ : 25 years as a Catholic apologist / Patrick Madrid.
p. cm.
Includes bibliographical references (p.   ) and index.
ISBN 978-1-61636-484-7 (alk. paper)
1. Catholic Church—Apologetic works. 2. Theology. 3. Madrid, Patrick, 1960- I. Title.
BX1752.M238 2012
230'.2—dc23
2012025630

Published by Servant Books, an imprint of Franciscan Media.
28 W. Liberty St.
Cincinnati, OH 45202
www.FranciscanMedia.org
www.ServantBooks.org

Printed in the United States of America.
Printed on acid-free paper.
12 13 14 15 16   5 4 3 2 1

Contents

Foreword

||||||||||||||||||||||||||||||||||||

NOT LONG MARRIED, MY WIFE AND I were making our first joint visit to her native Japan. I had been practicing law for three years, so she introduced me to her family and friends as a *bengoshi* or barrister. Japan models its legal system after Britain's, so, unlike in America, there are very few attorneys in the country. Back then, there were more attorneys in our hometown of San Diego than in the whole of Japan. In America attorneys may be less than a dime a dozen, but in Japan to be a bengoshi is to be somebody. (My wife didn't reveal that I had a solo practice that provided for us so meagerly that she was forced to work outside the home.)

Nine years after that visit I managed to ease out of the practice of law and became a full-time Catholic apologist. This was a step up in terms of my interests but a step down socially. In Japan, the term "Catholic apologist" carries no meaning. Most Japanese know a smidgen about Christianity but nothing about Catholic distinctives. When my wife introduced me as a Catholic apologist, the response was a polite "That's nice." There was no understanding of what an apologist might be.

Often that's true on this side of the Pacific too, among both Catholics and Protestants. There are times, when I am in a puckish mood, that I open a talk before a mixed audience by saying I think I should offer a definition: "A Catholic apologist is someone who goes around the country apologizing for being a Catholic." Catholics in the audience look startled. (Did he just say what we think he said?) Evangelicals and fundamentalists momentarily nod in grateful satisfaction that I confirmed what they always thought. But after a few seconds everyone breaks out with smiles, realizing it has been a joke, and I go on to explain what an apologist really is and what *apologetics* does and doesn't mean.

Much of the definition I learned by engaging in apologetics. This is true of every Catholic apologist. He may begin with the dictionary definition, but that doesn't take him far. He fleshes out the definition through years-long intellectual engagement with people on both sides of the religious divide. If he pays attention, he discovers that it is one thing to be an apologist but another to be an effective apologist.

An effective apologist will have developed several attributes. He will have a broad knowledge of the faith, of course, but he also will have a willingness to say, "I don't know—but I'll look it up and get back to you." The important part of that reply is the second part. No one can know everything about the faith, and no questioner expects an apologist to know everything, but some apologists fear to acknowledge their own ignorance. This is a mistake, and it is equally a mistake to acknowledge ignorance while trying to change the subject. The effective apologist will hit the books and bring his newfound knowledge back to his questioner. Both will profit.

In apologetics, there is no equivalent to Athena being born fully-formed from the forehead of Zeus. An apologist learns the trade one issue or one question at a time. Early on, even long before he can be considered an apologist, he makes a confidence-building discovery. He has known that the attacks on the Church and on Catholic beliefs are ill-founded, but he never has had the wits about him to counter an attack effectively.

One day, after idly studying some disputed topic, he finds himself being questioned by a non-Catholic who recites a litany of the Church's "errors." Half way through, up pops the very topic the Catholic has been studying, and he manages to give a reasonable and perhaps even compelling defense of the Catholic position. His interlocutor is surprised and momentarily silenced; he might even leave thinking he has more to think about. Some good has been done him, but more good has been done the Catholic—he has developed a sense of confidence. He sees that if he can work up the answer to one question, he can work up the answers to ten. If he can work up ten, he can work up a hundred—or a thousand.

This is a thrilling realization, and it dawns on him that, some months or years down the road (depending on how diligently he studies), he might be able to "do apologetics" all day, every day, perhaps even making a living from it. He makes plans to go public at a propitious moment, not realizing that, given his personality, he might do the Church a greater favor if he keeps his new knowledge to himself.

It isn't enough to know the propositions of the faith or even how to syllogize with them, at least not if one's aim is to bring others away from their misunderstandings and toward an acceptance of Catholic teachings. Knowledge must be married to technique. Over the years I have come across self-styled apologists whose main goal has been winning an argument rather than winning a mind. To aim for the former is to miss the latter. These apologists, almost to a man (and they always are men; female apologists—yes, there are a few of them—never seem to have this failing), are missing another key attribute, good humor, and its close ally, self-deprecation. Without those, the craft of apologetics stumbles.

Whenever Patrick Madrid and I meet up—which is not often enough, now that we live half a continent apart—we reminisce about our early years together in apologetics, and always we recollect a speaking engagement we had at a Midwestern parish that was named in honor of Our Lady of Fatima. Outside the rectory was a stature of the Virgin Mary, and at her feet were statues of the three kneeling children. As I steered our rental car to the curb, Pat turned to me and said, "What a great religion we have, Karl. Not only can we worship statues, but our statues can worship statues!"

It was an iconic wisecrack. It illustrated the silliness of what some people have been brought up to believe about the Catholic faith by seeming to affirm it. Of course, Pat's joke was not something he could use in most public settings because, human impenetrability being what it is, there likely would be a few people in the audience who would think he was affirming their worst fears. (One of the consequences of the Fall is that some people have no discoverable sense of humor.)

In the following pages Pat has refreshed my memory on many incidents from our joint work in apologetics, those eight years or so that we worked together at Catholic Answers. But he has done more than take me for a pleasing stroll down memory lane. He has reminded me, chapter by chapter, of what it takes to engage in effective apologetics, of how one forms an argument that convinces, of why our mutual vocation of apologetics is important in a world that has become unreasonable and needs to be shown reasons for the hope that is within us—and that ought to be in everyone.

—Karl Keating

Acknowledgments

TO BORROW A (SLIGHTLY REVISED) LINE FROM a popular 1967 song: How do you thank someone who has taken you from crayons to publishing? It isn't easy, but I'll try.

I owe unpayable debts of gratitude to the innumerable people who have helped, guided, taught, encouraged, and prayed for me over my lifetime, beginning with my parents, Bernie and Gretchen Madrid, who gave me the two greatest possible gifts: my life and the Catholic Faith. Any success I may have achieved over the last thirty-one years would have been impossible without the patience and support of my lovely wife, Nancy (we'll celebrate thirty-two years on February 7, 2013!).

Without doubt, the fervent prayers of my dear friend Sister Judith Zuñiga, O.C.D., Fr. Luke Tancrell, O.P., and many others, have helped me write straight with crooked lines. I am most grateful to all of them.

This book would not be complete without a heartfelt word of thanks to all my friends, colleagues, and benefactors in the world of Catholic apologetics who, over the years, have helped me in ways small and large, seen and unseen. I cannot give a comprehensive list of their names because, were every one of them to be written, I suppose that the world itself could not contain the books that would be written. But a few deserve special mention here, including Karl Keating, Fr. Bud Pelletier, Bishop Robert J. Baker, Scott Hahn, Archbishop Charles Chaput, O.F.M., C.A.P, Fr. Ron Tacelli, S.J., Mary Merrill Russell, Michael

Dubruiel (R.I.P.), John Barger, Deacon Michael Ross, Fr. Mitch Pacwa, s.j., Marcus Grodi, Steve Wood, Ken Davison, Martha Fernández-Sardina, Doug Sherman, Tom Peterson, Doug Keck, Bob Salmon, Brian Linder, Chris Aubert, and Dan Wood. There are many others, but I have to stop somewhere.

I also offer my sincere gratitude to all the folks at Franciscan Media for their professional, enthusiastic, and welcoming collaboration with me on this, my third title with the Servant Books imprint—in particular, my editors Louise Paré and Claudia Volkman, as well as Barbara Baker, Matt Wielgos, Lindsey Simmons, Chris Holmes, Ron Riegler, Jennifer Scroggins, Judy Zarick, and Katie Carroll.

Thank you! May God reward you all.

Introduction

‖‖

I HAVE A KALEIDOSCOPE OF MEMORIES OF the past twenty-five years that span my career as a full-time Catholic apologist. They are memories of the countless fascinating people I have met along the way, the varied and far-flung places I have been privileged to visit, and the challenging, personally fulfilling, intensely interesting, and sometimes daunting debates, books, speaking engagements, and other projects I have undertaken over these years. I treasure these memories and don't take any of them for granted. In truth, I thank God every day for his gift of allowing me to have a very minor role to play in the vast drama of the Church Militant's sojourn on earth during my lifetime.

"Apologetics" refers to the art of giving a reasoned defense for something—in this case, the Catholic Faith, its doctrines and customs. An "apologist" is one who practices that art. Apologetics does not mean offering an *apology* for something you regret. It means that you do your best to lay out the rational, biblical, and historical facts in support of your position. Properly done, apologetics is not "arguing" with people; it is not "triumphalistic," nor is it "pre–Vatican II."

Indeed, in several places, the documents of Vatican II specifically urge lay Catholics to "defend" the Faith—in other words, to engage in apologetics. Apologetics was quite common and widely acceptable in the Catholic Church in the United States for as long as Catholics have been in the United States. But after the Council, it fell sharply out of favor and was widely regarded, especially by priests who were trained in the seminary during the 1960s and 1970s to see apologetics in a decidedly negative light, as something "reactionary" and "anti-ecumenical," and thus something to be avoided and discouraged.

This may help you understand what a complete wasteland the situation was in the 1980s when apologetics started to make a comeback. Not only was it something the average lay Catholic had never heard of, the typical parish priest back then was suspicious of apologetics and not inclined to foster it at the parish level. Back when I began my work in this field, apologetics wasn't "cool" and there really was very little apologetics material to speak of. Talk about starting at "ground zero." That's where I found myself at the start of my career as an apologist. The only way to go was up.

What I share with you in *Envoy for Christ* is a series of "written depictions" of these memories—not only of the people, places, and things that have made up the world of apologetics I inhabit, but also (and more importantly) the doctrines, concepts, ideas, conflicts, and friendships that have, for me, given the last quarter century its texture, depth, contours, light, and meaning. Reading back through the essays and articles I have selected for this book was both nostalgic and, here and there, a reminder of how I have grown and matured during this phase of my life, not only personally but in my style of writing, tone, and ability to communicate the great truths of the Faith I grew up with as a cradle Catholic as well as the ones I learned along the way.

"You Can Catch More Flies With Honey Than With Vinegar"

To be candid, I must admit that I winced now and then at the unnecessarily sharp tone of a few things I wrote years ago. Although I have never been a bellicose or pugnacious person (as my wife, family, and friends will tell you), when I was young I sometimes wrote in a more aggressive style than I would today. I attribute my occasional sharpness of tone back then to two things: the testosterone-fueled "fighting spirit" that is natural to men, especially young men, and the fact that I was writing for an audience—Catholic and non-Catholic—that sometimes saw apologetics more in terms of personal combat than for what it really is and always should be: a calm, rational, and always charitable defense of the truth.

The older I get, the more clearly I have come to see how bellicosity is antithetical to authentic apologetics. Or, in the words of St. Peter, we must "always be prepared to make a defense to anyone who calls you to account for the hope that is in you," but we must also engage in this defense "with gentleness and respect" (1 Peter 3:15–16). This is a very important lesson for all who seek to explain and defend the Faith. I guess you could say that I myself learned it in the school of hard knocks.

Bottom line: A cheerful, winsome presentation of the Truth will always do more good for souls than one that is caustic or peremptory, plus it has a far better chance of "getting through" to the other guy. As tempting as it may be to think of yourself as an apologetics gladiator (I have seen *many* people fall prey to this folly, especially among the current crop of Protestant pop apologists who love nothing more than to "do battle" with Catholics), if you really want to fight the good fight, strive to be polite, respectful, and kind even as you seek to vigorously and compellingly present the truth. Take it from me. As someone who had to learn this lesson firsthand, it really works.

And now, some of the more memorable memories that stand out in my mind...

A Phone Call That Changed My Life

I wrote this essay in 2009, nearly fourteen years after I had left my position as vice president at Catholic Answers to pursue a career as an author, and about twenty-three years since I first got to know Karl Keating back in early 1987. The subtext to this anecdote was the painful and tumultuous "reconversion" to Christ that I experienced in 1987, an ordeal lasting for nearly a year.

I had been trying in vain to "be Catholic" and, at the same time, dabble in worldly pleasures and pursuits that are antithetical to being Catholic. I went to Mass every Sunday without fail, said grace before every meal, etc., and in many ways was, at least exteriorly, a thoroughly committed Catholic. But my conscience bothered me so much that eventually everything coalesced into a crisis of conscience that brought me to my knees in prayer and repentance. I decisively turned my back on all things and attitudes that I knew were keeping me from knowing, loving, and serving God in this life.

I became deeply convinced that God wanted me to do something different with my life—I was already married with a few children at that time, so it clearly was not a change in that sense. Rather, I had become certain that God wanted me to work in a different field, though I had no idea what it could be. I had a good job, and with a wife and children, a mortgage payment, and all the financial demands every young family faces, I did not have the luxury of picking and choosing a new career. I had to keep making money without interruption or my family wouldn't eat and we'd have no place to live. But God did have other plans for me, as you shall see in this essay.

I got to know Karl Keating in the spring of 1987, back when he was still practicing law full-time and dabbling in apologetics part-time.

Catholic Answers was, in those days, simply a part-time tract and newsletter apostolate Karl had operated for several years from his home, writing new materials in his spare time.

We made contact as the result of an article I happened across in our diocesan newspaper, a brief, blasé squib about a public debate on the papacy that Karl had engaged in with an itinerant Baptist minister who ran an anti-Catholic organization aimed solely at converting Catholics to the "truth." That caught my attention.

I was excited to see someone else involved in apologetics, something I had developed a deep love for, doing it also in my spare time (I had a full-time career in sales). For some time I had assumed I was alone in the world in my love for apologetics, and it was energizing to see another Catholic out there mixing it up with critics of the Church.

I put down the paper and reached for the phone. The article had provided no contact information for Keating or Catholic Answers, so I doubted I'd be able to reach him, but just for a lark I decided to check with directory information.

To my surprise, presto, I had a phone number for Catholic Answers. But since it was after 9:00 P.M., I knew no one would be at the office, so I called, intending to just leave a message. After a couple of rings, a voice answered:

"Hello, Catholic Answers."

"Um…hello," I said, surprised that someone was actually answering the phone this late. "I realize I'm calling after hours, but I wanted to leave a message for Karl Keating."

"This is Karl Keating," the voice on the other end said.

"Wow," I exclaimed. "I didn't expect you to answer the phone," and then I told him I had read the article and that I was happy to hear about the apologetics work he was doing.

An hour later, we finished our phone conversation, and I had a new friend.

Karl and I had talked enthusiastically about our common love for apologetics, and I was impressed with all the good work he had undertaken, single-handedly, to answer critics of the Church. He told me about the tracts he had written, the monthly *Catholic Answers* apologetics newsletter he produced, and the debates he was engaging in. All of this was very exciting to me, and over the next several months, Karl and I spoke frequently by phone, comparing notes and discussing various apologetics issues.

Fast-forward now to early December 1987. Through a lot of prayer and reflection, I had come to realize that God was calling me to do something for him, something other than the secular work in sales I was doing at that time. The problem was, although I sensed he wanted something in particular from me, I had no idea what it might be.

For a solid month, in addition to praying the rosary every day for this special intention, I spent my lunch hours at a Catholic parish near my office on my knees in front of the Blessed Sacrament, praying and asking the Lord to show me what he wanted me to do with my life. I knew he was calling me to something, but I simply couldn't discern what that something was.

So, deciding to "step out in faith," I resigned from my job, determined to force the issue and find the new career I felt God was calling me to. That weekend, after I quit my job, Karl called. During the course of our conversation, I asked him to keep me in his prayers as I figured out what career direction I'd be headed in.

"Sure, I'll pray for you," he said. "But I can do something else. I've recently decided to shut down my law practice and open an office for Catholic Answers. I'm going to turn it into a full-time venture. Why don't you come work with me at Catholic Answers and we'll build it into something big?"

Without hesitating, I said, "No, thanks. I appreciate the offer, but whatever it is God wants me to be doing with my life, I'm sure it's not apologetics." Working in Catholic apologetics had never even remotely occurred to me as an option. It never entered my mind that I could make a living and support my growing family as an apologist.

But Karl was persistent. He reiterated his offer for me to come work with him and help establish the full-time Catholic Answers operation. Though I tried to demur, I can see now that God was working through him. For the next twenty minutes we discussed the idea, and our call ended with my agreeing to give it a try. After all, he reminded me, what did I have to lose?

That phone call changed my life. Only months later, as I looked back on how it all happened, did it finally dawn on me that my prayers for God's guidance had been answered. The Lord had shown me what he wanted from me. I was too blind to see it at first. I realized that this—being an apologist—was Christ's answer to my prayers.

I had the privilege of working with Karl and the many other great people at Catholic Answers for eight years. When I became vice president of Catholic Answers, a few years into my employment there, I had the best seat in the house from which to watch the organization unfold from a part-time apostolate to the major institution it is today.

I thank God for the opportunity to have been a part of such a thing. During my time at Catholic Answers, I saw close-up the dizzying rise of Catholic apologetics: the flood of tapes and books, the seminars and debates, countless new converts, and now the once unheard of luxuries such as Catholic apologetics radio programs, websites, and the plethora of excellent apologetics television programs on EWTN.

Working with Karl, back in those early days before apologetics had caught on—well, before being an apologist was acceptable, much less "cool" —was a wonderful and extremely enriching experience for me, personally, spiritually, and professionally. I learned a lot and had an immense amount of fun along the way, helping to "blaze the trail."

I thank God every day for that privilege. I also thank my friend, Karl Keating, for inviting me to join him on the adventure.

The Early Days

During this early phase of Catholic Answers' full-time incarnation, there was plenty to do, though little of it then resembled the work the apostolate does today. Back then, there was no *Catholic Answers Live* radio show (that was still many years away and not even on our radar screen then), no seminars or conferences, no books or tapes or CDs (digital downloads were also years away then), no catholic.com website, nothing. In fact, back in early 1988, Karl's landmark bestselling book, *Catholicism and Fundamentalism*, had not yet been printed by Ignatius Press. In May, we received several dozen cases of the book which we scurried to ship out to the hundreds of subscribers who had pre-ordered their copies, but in the months leading up to that day, Karl, Charlie, and I, as well as a couple of dedicated local volunteers had our hands full with packing and shipping tracts, the newsletter, answering the ever-growing influx of correspondence, and planning what new projects we wanted to tackle, going forward.

We had no idea, no idea whatsoever, how big Catholic Answers was going to become, how huge its reach would someday be, and how many souls it would assist on their journeys into the Catholic Church. As I write this, I am truly staggered by the immensity of the impact that Catholic Answers grew to have. I was only there for the first eight years. The really big things happened after I left. I am content and happy, though, to know that I had a role to play in getting things off the ground early on. For me, it was something like being Orville Wright to Karl's Wilbur. Or better yet, given our height disparity, I was Robin to his Batman. Or something like that.

Early 1989—Karl informed me that we'd soon be interviewing Mark Brumley, a convert from Protestantism who lived in St. Louis whom Karl had invited to join the Catholic Answers' staff to do the same kind of work I did as a writer and public speaker. I discovered that Mark and I were almost exactly the same age. Not yet twenty-nine years old, we had no inkling of how things would unfold for us, along two different paths that converged for a time at Catholic Answers. Today, Mark is the president of Ignatius Press, one of the premiere Catholic publishing houses in the United States. He worked for Catholic Answers for only two or three years but still played an important role back in those early days helping shape the fundamental structures of that apostolate that would propel it (and our respective post-Catholic Answers careers) forward, well into the twenty-first century.

Summer 1989—I'm plowing through a stack of papers with the names and contact info of people around the country who were given a gift subscription to the *Catholic Answers* newsletter but, for some reason, were not receiving them in the mail. My task—oh yes, Catholic apologetics was *such* a glamorous job back then—was to call each person and figure out if we had the wrong mailing address or what.

Halfway through the stack, I dialed a number in the 815 area code (Joliet, Illinois).

"Hello?" a man answers.

"Uh, hi. This is Patrick Madrid from Catholic Answers, and I'm calling for, uh, for Scott Hahn. Is this Mr. Hahn?"

"Why, yes. This is Scott Hahn."

"Ah, well, Mr. Hahn—may I call you Scott?—I was just calling because a friend of yours recently purchased a gift subscription on the *Catholic Answers* newsletter and, from what she told us, it seems that you haven't been receiving it in the mail, so I'm checking to see if we have your correct mailing address."

"No, I haven't gotten it yet, but it sounds interesting. *'Catholic Answers?'* Tell me more, please."

"No problem! Catholic Answers is a Catholic apologetics organization that specializes in helping Catholics learn how to answer challenges from Protestants, Mormons, Jehovah's Witnesses, and other non-Catholics. Tell me, do you..."

"Oh *really?* Well, now I'm *very* interested. I used to be a Protestant minister, and I converted to the Catholic Church three years ago!"

Now it was my turn to be very interested. What ensued was a lively two-hour conversation in which I did little talking and Scott explained in mesmerizing detail the saga of how he had once been a deeply anti-Catholic Protestant who, by God's grace and a truly astonishing series of unexpected events, very reluctantly studied his way into the Catholic Church—the very Church he had previously denounced as the "Whore of Babylon."

After about two hours on the phone with Scott, Karl Keating happened to walk past my desk. I put my hand over the receiver.

"*Karl!* You have *got* to talk to this guy! His name is Scott Hahn, and he's an ex-Protestant minister convert to the Church. His story is mind-blowing!"

"Nah," Karl said, as he kept walking. "I'm busy right now."

"No, really, you have to talk to him."

"No, really. I'm busy."

"No, *really*. I'm serious. You have to talk to him. Just do it. You'll see."

Karl rolled his eyes and gave me an exasperated look that meant, "All right, but this better not be a waste of time." He walked to his office, picked up his extension, and I made the introductions: "Karl Keating, meet Scott Hahn. Scott, meet Karl." Then I said good-bye and hung up, my head spinning at the conversation Scott and I had just had.

Two more hours went by.

Karl walked over to my desk with a look on his face that confirms that I was right: he needed to take that call.

We were both impressed by what a great guy Scott was, by his powerful conversion story, by his extensive knowledge of Scripture, and by the new and exciting possibilities for apologetics collaboration with him that began to dance like sugarplums before our eyes.

Little did either of us know—how could we have possibly foreseen it?—what a dramatic impact Scott Hahn, at that time an as yet obscure, unknown assistant theology professor at the then College of St. Francis in Joliet, would make on the Catholic Church in the United States. All of that still lie ahead. All Karl and I knew then was that we had encountered a kindred spirit in Scott, someone who not only "got" what we were trying to do at Catholic Answers, but in many ways, knew how to do it better than we did. And thus began an extraordinary friendship and collaboration that has lasted all these years, producing untold good fruit for the Church and for souls. *Deo gratias.*

August 1989—I walked into Karl's office with an idea.

"Hey, Karl. I've been thinking about Scott Hahn's background as a minister, and I think we should set up a seminar for him, out here in California, so he can tell his story. We can record it and sell the tapes. What do you think?"

"What parish could we get him in to on short notice?" Karl asked.

"How about my parish? I'll bet my pastor would say 'yes' if I asked him."

"Go ahead. Sounds like a good idea. Let me know what Scott says about it."

Within the week, I had secured both Scott's and my pastor's approval to move forward with setting up this event. Getting the priest's permission, however, wasn't easy at first. When I broached the subject, he wasn't enthusiastic about bringing a completely unknown speaker to the parish.

"Do you know this fellow personally?" he asked me.

"Yes. He's a good man with an astonishing background, and he's really well-spoken."

"Have you ever heard him speak in public?" he asked, eyebrow arched.

"Uh…no, not in public. But I'm sure he will do fine. Really."

Father didn't seem mollified.

"Well, I've never heard of him before," he said. "How can I be sure that he won't preach some kind of error or say something controversial about the Catholic Church? I won't stand for that, you know."

"Yes, Father, I know. I can assure you that Scott won't say anything heterodox."

"Well, all right. He'd better not. And if he does, I am holding *you* responsible!"

We advertised Scott's conversion testimony as a Catholic Answers seminar, though neither Karl nor I would be the speaker. An unknown former Protestant minister by the name of Scott Hahn would be the draw. Turns out—if you can believe this—Scott proved to be no draw at all. The night of the seminar, a mere thirty-five people turned out to hear him speak. Those three-dozen men and women had no earthly idea that they were witnessing an important moment in Catholic apologetics history. I didn't either.

What I was sure of, though, is that although not a single person in the parish hall that evening had ever heard the name "Scott Hahn" before, they were all there because of the novelty of his being a former Protestant minister who would tell his story of conversion. And tell it he did. With gusto. With dramatic flair. With all the human drama and theological struggle one could imagine, and then some.

Five minutes into Scott's talk, my pastor turned around in his front-row seat and craned his neck to look at me sitting in the back of the room. With a big grin and a hearty "thumbs-up," he let me know I was off the hook. Scott had won him (and the rest of the audience) over within just the first few minutes of his powerful conversion account.

That talk was titled "The Conversion of a Former Protestant Minister." It went on to outsell any other Catholic tape at that time, with literally millions of copies produced and distributed, often for free and quite often in lots of hundreds and even thousands. There is simply no way to account for all the good that Scott's conversion story tape did for souls (not to mention the hundreds of other teaching tapes he went on to produce). Many converts I have met subsequently have told me, sometimes with breathless excitement, how their hearing that tape was the beginning of their journey into the Catholic Church. This humble little seminar had such massive and far-reaching effects that I simply can't exaggerate how incongruous the smallness and obscurity of the event itself was compared to the colossal, grace-filled impact that it had on the Church and the world.

Barnstorming

Early 1988 through 1995—Catholic Answers was always a bootstrap operation. Sure, the sales of books, tracts, and subscriptions to the newsletter were important parts of the company's revenues, but they weren't enough to "float the boat." To do that, Karl and I early on started barnstorming around southern California conducting parish seminars. My being fluent in Spanish was a help. It enabled us to add Spanish-language seminars to the already bulging speaking calendar that we both worked hard to keep well-stocked with a backlog of events. These seminars generated revenue in the form of the collections we took up at each event (the more people who attended, the larger the collections, so we did everything we could to advertise them), as well as book sales of Karl's book, our tracts, and other materials we made available on the book table.

For the first few years, it was not uncommon for Karl and me to be on the road speaking at a different Southland parish two or even three nights a week, for weeks and months on end. I am so very grateful to my lovely wife Nancy for her patience and understanding. The incessant travel to speaking engagements was tough for both of us, but probably tougher for her, because she was holding the fort and taking care of kids, while I was having the time of my life, loving every opportunity to explain and defend the Faith before public audiences, not all of whom were friendly to the Catholic Church.

I can recall more than a few seminars where the first pew was entirely filled with the evangelical Protestant pastor of the local Calvary Chapel and a dozen of his members. Or several Mormon missionaries. Or, at times, a hootenanny fundamentalist preacher who, with well-worn King James Bible in hand, would suddenly leap to his feet in the middle of our talk and start rebuking us for preaching error. Believe me, I have seen it all. As they say, "Been there, done that." And I loved every single second of it.

This Rock Magazine

January 1990—As the close of 1989 drew near, Karl decided that we should transition the newsletter to a magazine format. We spent a lot of time discussing, planning, and designing the new magazine. Coming up with a catchy name wasn't an easy process. We sifted through dozens of possible titles. One name idea that I championed was *Envoy Magazine*, though Karl does not find it as compelling and catchy as *This Rock,* referring to Christ's words to Simon Peter in Matthew 16: "Upon this rock I will build my Church." That became the title, and we debuted it with a bang!

At that time there were no other Catholic magazines like it. Filled with "red meat" apologetics articles on a wide variety of subjects, it caught fire quickly and became our flagship publication, a way to further extend Catholic Answers' growing presence in the Church in the US and Canada.

I remember all too well an angry phone call that Karl took in his office on February 28, 1990, just before we were leaving to drive from San Diego to Long Beach, California, to conduct our first major apologetics conference, a three-day symposium featuring several up-and-coming Catholic speakers, including Scott Hahn. The caller was a staff member of the Christian Research Institute, a Protestant apologetics organization based in Orange County, California. I had written a negative review of a book written by this Protestant staffer, and he was upset. I don't remember now what Karl told him, but it seemed to calm things down. That review would be an example of the more aggressive edge that sometimes surfaced in my writings back then, something I am happy to say has abated a great deal, if not entirely.

Mormonism

A great deal of my apologetics energies were expended in those early years on the subject of Mormonism. I wrote many articles and gave countless seminars on the subject, trying to help my fellow Catholics from being syphoned out of the Church by door-to-door Mormon missionaries with their slick presentations and heartstring-tugging testimonies about the truth of their religion. Only two of the many articles I wrote in those years on the subject of Mormonism appear in *Envoy for Christ,* and that is primarily due to space constraints. I have a new book coming out in the near future on that subject.

During the eight years I worked at Catholic Answers, I visited the Mormon Church's headquarters in Salt Lake City several times, once even having a sit-down private meeting with one of their Twelve Apostles, Elder David B. Haight. I was surprised and slightly disconcerted when his assistant handed Haight a manila file containing papers that guided some of our discussion. Apparently, that was the "Patrick Madrid" file. Weird to think that a file on *me* might exist in a filing cabinet in the Mormon Church's high-rise headquarters.

The more I studied Mormon doctrine and history, the more engrossed in it I became. I had two public debates with official Mormon spokesmen, the first in 1990 with Gary Coleman in Hacienda Heights, California (Los Angeles area), and the second in 1992 with Frank Bradshaw in Orange, California. The first debate, conducted before an audience of over five hundred Mormons and Catholics, was on the subject of the Mormon doctrine of a total apostasy of the Church and on the Trinity (contrasted with the Mormon teaching on the plurality of Gods—i.e., polytheism). In the second debate, Frank Bradshaw and I discussed the question of whether the Book of Mormon is truly inspired Scripture and also whether the pope or the Mormon prophet held the "keys" of authority (cf. Matthew 16:18–19).[1]

I had the opportunity[2] to tour three different "MTCs," or "Missionary Training Centers"—the main one in Provo, Utah; one in Tokyo, Japan; and one in London, England. I was allowed to sit in a classroom with a group of eight or ten missionaries and watch them learn how to give their "missionary lessons" in various languages. It was a very eye-opening education for me, and I learned a tremendous amount, up-close and firsthand, about this group.

As a related side note, I did something similar regarding my efforts to become more knowledgeable about Jehovah's Witnesses and Islam. On several occasions, I visited the local Kingdom Hall and sat in on the Wednesday evening training sessions Witnesses go through in which they practice assiduously on how to go door-to-door and lure Catholics out of the Church with their arguments against, for example, the Trinity and the Divinity of Christ. My innumerable up-close discussions with Jehovah's Witnesses really helped me understand how to refute their arguments against the Faith.

Similarly, in the early 1990s, I started visiting a mosque in a city near where I lived in an effort to learn what Islam teaches *and* how Muslims argue against Christianity. After visiting three or four times and having long discussions with the imam and congregants about God, Christianity, Jesus, etc., one of them took me aside and asked in all seriousness if I were an FBI agent. They just couldn't figure out why I was so friendly and kept coming back. My "Columbo" routine of playing dumb and bumbling along seemed to have worked. But some of them were suspicious of my true motives. Was I trying to infiltrate the mosque?

"No, I'm not an FBI agent." I dismissed his question with a chuckle. "I'm really just someone who wants to learn."

And so, to allay their apprehensions, I did what anyone would do in that situation. I enrolled in Arabic classes. Well, that lasted for only a few weeks until I realized that they really were not very keen on my coming around to the mosque and trying to evangelize *them*. You see, that's how things had progressed. I was at first trying to give them the impression that I was really quite ignorant of Islam, although I never ever lied about anything. I was always honest with them, though I didn't mind at all that my "Columbo" routine made them think I was more of an ignoramus than I really was.

Debates

The 1990s—I was invited to participate in about a dozen formal, public debates with Protestant ministers, usually at Protestant churches, before large audiences that were primarily Protestant and not the least bit friendly to the Catholic Church's teachings. I described one of these debates in detail in my 1993 *This Rock* article "The White Man's Burden." Although, again due to space constraints, that article is not included in this book, it is easily available at my website, www.patrickmadrid.com/articles. In it I recap the debate I had with Protestant apologist James White (our second debate, on Mary and the Communion of Saints, was held on Long Island in 2002) and elaborate on some of the issues that came out in that exchange. Many times over the years since then, former Protestants have written to me or told me in person how that debate helped them a great deal to see that *sola Scriptura* is biblically indefensible, and many Catholics have similarly told me that they have found that studying that debate has really helped them to effectively evangelize their Protestant friends and family.[3]

But I won't get ahead of myself. As you will see, *Envoy for Christ* has a lengthy section on the issue of *sola Scriptura*. In addition to what you read here, I encourage anyone who is interested in my "Does the Bible Teach *Sola Scriptura?*" debate with James White to download the MP3 version available at www.patrickmadrid.com and read my follow-up article "The White Man's Burden."

I honestly do not enjoy public debates, nor have I ever sought them out. But as emotionally and intellectually draining as they can be, when properly done, they have a valid and even necessary place in the world of Catholic apologetics. The chroniclers of St. Augustine, for example, mention his various public debates with the proponents of heresy in his day. That was an era when, in certain localities at least, defending the Catholic Faith in a public debate could result in martyrdom! I reckon that if the early Catholics were willing to do this, then we today should be just as ready and willing to speak out in defense of our Faith, especially since it is unlikely (at least for the moment) that we might be faced with martyrdom for our trouble.

One debate, held in San Diego sometime around 1992 or 1993, was a tag-team event in which Mark Brumley and I debated *sola Scriptura* with two Protestants: the prominent "moderate Calvinist" author and apologist Dr. Norman Geisler[4] and Evangelical Ralph MacKenzie. Geisler happens to be a very pleasant fellow whom I had gotten to know at a couple of social events. This made the debate much more relaxed and, as far as I'm concerned, more productive, because there was no spirit of combat at work, but a serious theological discussion between Catholics and Protestants who knew and respected one another.

This particular debate was held in a San Diego-area Protestant church in front of a smallish audience of about 150 people. One thing about the exchange that I remember quite clearly is, oddly enough, the quip I used in my opening remarks. I mentioned how I felt when, as my wife and I got out of the car and walked up the street toward the church (I in my suit and tie, my Bible in one hand and a briefcase in the other, and she in high heels and a dress) it occurred to me that we looked very much like two Jehovah's Witnesses prowling the neighborhood. Feeling self-conscious, I sheepishly wondered if I should reassure the people we walked past that, *no*, we were not JWs. The debate audience of Catholics and Protestants had a good chuckle at that. To this day, though, I still can't pinpoint exactly why it was so funny.

And then there was a debate in 1993 sponsored by the New Wine Christian Fellowship near Riverside, California. I remember the name of the place only because it became useful to me as a debating point. My opponent, Lloyd, an ex-Catholic, was a member of that church and, as I recall, we were debating whether or not Catholics are truly Christian; my thesis being that evening that, yes, not only are Catholics Christians, they are the *original* Christians, and the Catholic Church is the fullness of Christianity. During my concluding remarks, I pointed out to the audience that the pastor of the New Wine Christian Fellowship had started that church several years earlier because of a disagreement he had with the pastor of his previous church over how that minister interpreted the Bible on some doctrine or another. I wanted to demonstrate the folly of the Protestant notion that the Bible is formally sufficient (*sola Scriptura*) *and* show that, just because someone quotes the Bible in support of his beliefs, that does not guarantee that he is correct in his interpretation of the passages he's quoting.

"The church we're present in this evening, the New Wine Christian Fellowship, was started by a dispute over how to interpret the Bible" I reminded the audience.

"What's to prevent one of you here, if you should decide that the biblical interpretation of *this* pastor in *this* church is incorrect, from hiving off and starting your own church called the *Newer* New Wine Christian Fellowship?"

I hoped the audience had gotten my point. Years later, I discovered that at least one of them did when he told me that the debate had had an effect on him. That person was Lloyd, the ex-Catholic fellow I had debated. A decade after that debate, he e-mailed me out of the blue to inform me that, after years of pondering the case for the Catholic Church he encountered in books, CDs, and, yes, in our debate, he had returned to the Catholic Church of his upbringing.

I give thanks and praise to God for his work of grace in Lloyd's heart. I often marvel at how, so often, it is the seemingly inconsequential elements of apologetics that God makes use of to accomplish his purposes, things like debates, in which people show up more out of a desire to cheer for their team's champion than to really grapple with the evidence.

In 1993, Karl and I were invited ("challenged" would be more like it) to debate two Baptist ministers, Bill Jackson (founder of Christians Evangelizing Catholics) and Ron Nemec, on the subject of *sola Scriptura*. The event was sponsored by a large Baptist church in the Denver suburb of Lakewood, Colorado. What a night that was!

There must have been almost seven hundred people in the audience that evening, and the atmosphere crackled with the electricity of their anticipation. Most of them were Baptist, though several Catholics came up beforehand to let us know they were praying for us. Turns out, their prayers worked. This debate—known subsequently as "The Denver 'Bible Only?' Debate"—did not turn out at all the way the Baptist organizers hoped (and expected) it would. In fact, much to his credit, Bill Jackson publicly admitted in his ministry newsletter that he felt the Catholic side had carried the day. He certainly didn't say he was convinced by our arguments, far from it, but I admire his willingness to acknowledge that he and his debate partner failed to make their case and failed to effectively refute ours. Nearly twenty years later, Bill Jackson, if he is still alive today, must be quite old by now, probably well into his eighties. I have prayed for him often over the years that he too, like Lloyd, will come home to the Catholic Church. I hope to bump into him someday in heaven, where we can look back on our debate with a whole new perspective.

One final debate I'd like to mention took place in January 1995, at Lake Avenue Church in Pasadena, California. A few months earlier, in the fall of 1994, a Protestant apologist named Michael Horton, then president of a Protestant apologetics organization called C.U.R.E. (Christians United for Reformation) invited me to join him and two of his Protestant colleagues on their "White Horse Inn" radio show to discuss the question of justification. In the one or two hours the show lasted, we were able to dig into several biblical passages dealing with how sinners are justified. Our three-on-one discussion focused on the differences between the Catholic teaching on justification as explained by the Council of Trent (1545–1563) and the Protestant principle of *sola fide* (Latin: "[justification] by faith alone").

A week later, Horton called my office at Catholic Answers.

"We've had such positive listener response to our discussion on last week's show," he said, "that we're interested in setting up something more formal, something like a debate, in which we could discuss these issues in more depth. Would you be willing to do join us as the Catholic participant?"

"Would I?" I exclaimed. "Yes! I'd be delighted to participate."

And with that, plans got underway for what would become the much-heralded, heavily attended "What Still Divides Us?" Catholic/Protestant debate at Lake Avenue Church. Rather than a one-on-one debate between Horton and myself, C.U.R.E. suggested we make it a three-on-three exchange. Personally, I would have preferred to debate Horton solo, but for whatever reason, he preferred the team approach. A key part of our agreement was that I would receive a duplicate master copy of the audio and video recording of the event with full rights to make use of them as I wished.

The Catholic team I led included William Marshner[5] and Bob Sungenis. The Protestant debate team featured Calvinist ministers Michael Horton and Robert Godfrey[6] and Lutheran theologian Rod Rosenbladt.[7] The format called for two multi-hour exchanges over two days, the first day focusing on the Reformation principle of *sola Scriptura* and second on *sola fide*. The questions to be debated were: "Is Scripture alone sufficient?" and "Are we justified by faith alone?"

Given the massive promotional campaign that C.U.R.E. undertook in the weeks leading up to the debate, I assumed there would be a good-sized audience, but I was not prepared for what I saw when I arrived at Lake Avenue Church that first day.

Well over an hour before the debate was to start, at least six hundred people were already seated in the cavernous room. I noticed several professional video cameras and lighting systems strategically placed to record the events for posterity. This was serious business.

I admit, I had a few "pre-game" jitters, but I knew that I and my team were well-prepared for this debate, we knew the relevant subject matter thoroughly, inside and out, forward and backward, our side and theirs, etc., so I did my best to stay calm, cool, and collected.

Ten minutes before the debate was to start, I stepped out of room behind the sanctuary to see how large the crowd had grown. The church's main level was completely full, and there were at many others seated above in the mezzanine level. And people were still streaming in through the front doors.

I asked one of the C.U.R.E. staff members how many attendees they estimated were there. (I was starting to understand how Daniel might have felt as he entered the lions' den.)

"About twelve to thirteen hundred so far, I'd guess," he said with a satisfied smile. "Maybe a more. Hard to say."

"Any idea how many of them are *Catholic?*" I asked?

"Maybe two hundred. Hard to say."

My adrenaline started pumping. Faced with a capacity crowd composed mainly of Protestants—pastors, seminary students, and other folks who were definitely expecting to see the Protestant team mop the floor with the Catholic Church (i.e., with *my team*)—my mind began to play a sickening what-if newsreel of the Hindenburg crashing and burning as the cameras rolled.

"Oh, the humanity!" I could just hear the Catholics in the audience lamenting in my mind's ear should the Catholic team perform poorly.

Once the debate started, though, my fears vanished. I realized that there was nothing to worry about. The Protestant team was very good—polished, articulate, and definitely in command of their arguments. They delivered a rhetorically impressive defense of *sola Scriptura,* but the essence of their argument in defense of the formal sufficiency of Scripture was, in my view, woefully insufficient. They simply had no compelling biblical argument to vindicate the notion that *"the only infallible rule of interpretation of Scripture is the Scripture itself."*[8]

One of my favorite moments that first day was when Robert Godfrey proudly proclaimed that he was a Calvinist because "the Bible *teaches* Calvinism."

"Oh?" I responded wryly. "The Bible teaches *Calvinism?*" Gesturing toward his teammate, Rod Rosenbladt, I declared that I'd very much like to know whether *he,* a committed Lutheran, would agree that "the Bible teaches Calvinism."

The hearty chuckle this elicited from the audience told me my question was well-placed. Maybe this was not quite the verbal *estocada*[9] or knock-out blow I would have liked to have landed, but it would do. A lot of meaning was attached to Godfrey's little blunder, and the audience knew it. The theological incongruity between the two men on the same side of the debate, one a Calvinist and the other a Lutheran, was clear and indisputable. They would disagree on key aspects of the gospel, such as the effects of baptism,[10] and yet both would claim that *his* understanding of Scripture was the correct one. Both the Calvinist and the Lutheran were defending the notion that the Bible is sufficiently clear (perspicacious) and sufficient in itself for establishing correct Christian doctrine and yet, as I pointed out with my "The Bible teaches *Calvinism?*" retort to Godfrey, these two men strongly disagreed between themselves as to what exactly the Bible does teach.

The following day, we reconvened to debate *sola fide.* In my estimation, the Protestant side performed considerably better on this subject than they had on *sola Scriptura* and, if anything, the Catholic side performed less well than we had the first day. Not by much, but I did notice a tilt in energy and momentum toward the Protestant side as the debate crescendoed toward the finale of closing remarks.[11]

When it was all over, I was pleased but exhausted. Thanking my teammates and shaking hands with the members of the other team, I gathered my notes, found my wife, and headed across the parking lot toward our car. We were intercepted by a young woman who walked up and introduced herself as Annie, a Calvinist Protestant who had attended both days of the debate. I'll say more about our conversation later in the book.

My *Bible Answer Man* Days

Long before I starting working as a full-time apologist at Catholic Answers, I was an avid listener to *The Bible Answer Man* radio broadcast. The host was one Walter R. Martin, a savvy, articulate, and glib Evangelical apologist who founded the Christian Research Institute as a Protestant bulwark against "the cults." Mormonism, Jehovah's Witnesses, Scientology, Seventh-Day Adventism, and similar groups bore the brunt of Martin's interesting, energetic, and always entertaining apologetics critiques, and it was pure joy to me whenever a member of one of these religions would call in to take him on. It usually didn't end well for them, mainly because Martin knew more than they did about their own religions, or at least that's how it seemed. His punchy style of confronting callers with challenges about their beliefs was something I never tired of listening to.

Occasionally, a Protestant caller would ask Martin to comment on the Catholic Church. When this happened, my amusement usually gave way to bemusement as he would take a few whacks at Catholicism with about the same accuracy as a blindfolded man might swing at a piñata. Sure, he'd land a few blows here and there, but for the most part, Martin's criticisms of the Catholic Church were just far enough off the mark to frustrate me.

In those years, *The Bible Answer Man* show aired two hours a day, Monday through Friday. My job as an outside salesman enabled me to listen in my car, and that enabled me to assimilate a *lot* of Walter Martin's brand of apologetics. This was both good and bad.

On the plus side, listening to his show helped me ramp up much faster on the learning curve of understanding Mormonism, Jehovah's Witnesses, etc.

On the negative side, I was also imbibing a steady stream of Martin's combative style of apologetics, something I had to work hard to curb and eventually eradicate as I matured personally and as an apologist.

Those several years of daily listening to *The Bible Answer Man* and absorbing the major themes and methods of Protestant-style apologetics—the techniques, the biblical proof-texts, and the (not always accurate) historical arguments— provided me with a unique and extremely useful storehouse of knowledge from which to draw once I entered the full-time work of apologetics. Reading Walter Martin's book, *The Kingdom of the Cults,* also helped, though I had to filter out a certain degree of his faulty arguments and incorrect theology.[12]

When I started working at Catholic Answers, a natural division of labor presented itself. In parish talks and in writing articles for the *Catholic Answers* newsletter, Karl tended to handle the "Protestant Desk" while I tackled the "Mormon and JW Desk." But by the end of 1988, I was routinely handling parish seminars on all three of these groups. The more seminars I presented, the more proficient I became. The freewheeling question-and-answer sessions especially were very formative. I'd spend an hour or more fielding questions and challenges from the audience, some of whom were non-Catholic. These sessions were an invaluable trial-by-fire for me as a cub apologist. Years of frontline experience inevitably turned me into a seasoned veteran.

A nondescript donut shop in the grocery store plaza near my house was the scene of an unusual apologetics ritual I engaged in several times over the next few years, usually on Sunday mornings when we'd stop in to buy a dozen donuts after Mass. I confess that it irked me to see, Sunday after Sunday, one particular Jehovah's Witness fellow standing right outside the front door with copies of *Watchtower* and *Awake!* magazines in hand. No one could go in or out of the shop without that man trying to engage him in conversation and hand out a copy of his *Watchtower* literature.

After a few Sundays of ignoring the man as I passed by to buy donuts, I had had enough. Grabbing a few copies of *This Rock* magazine from my car, I stood right next to the Jehovah's Witness, mimicking his stance and his come-on to passers by. He was clearly bugged by that, but not nearly as bugged as he was when I would butt in to any conversation he managed to strike up with someone. As soon as he had buttonholed someone and began discoursing on why the Trinity was "unbiblical" and how Jesus is not really God, I became his third wheel. It was actually kind of fun to watch the reactions of the people walking by as I stood there with my Catholic magazines, streetcorner debating with the Jehovah's Witness. More than a few times someone would walk past us and cheer me on with an "Amen!" or a "Jesus is Lord!" word of encouragement.

I admit, this was rather odd, but for me it wasn't some kind of eccentric apologetics stunt. I just didn't like the idea of someone preaching publicly against the Trinity and the divinity of Jesus Christ. But because that sort of thing is a perfectly legal and protected form of free speech, there was nothing I could do about it . . . except take up my station right next door and exercise *my* right to free speech in response to what the other guy was saying. I guess it was my way of putting into practice the old saying, "If you can't beat 'em, join 'em."

Back in 1986 or 1987, I was flipping the channels on the TV and chanced upon a Protestant show featuring a young Jesuit priest named Fr. Mitch Pacwa. He was debating Catholic teaching with none other than Walter Martin! The venue for their debate was the Protestant apologetics *John Ankerberg Show*. As I watched the exchange, I was impressed with how ably Fr. Pacwa held his own against Martin and Ankerberg. Later, after we had become friends, Fr. Mitch told me how irritated he was when the show's producers deceptively edited the *substance* of his debate with Martin such that the expurgated version they aired on TV did not include those parts of the discussion when the priest had decisively refuted Martin's arguments. *Those* bits all wound up on the cutting room floor.

I don't blame Martin personally for that underhanded tactic, as it's unlikely he had any say in the final edit. But it did teach me something about how these things can go if you're not careful. I myself experienced this kind of thing at the hands of two different non-Catholic apologetics organizations which promised to provide me with the unedited, unexpurgated video of debates I did with them. One simply refused to honor its promise to release the videos to me once the debates were complete. The other claimed that an unforeseen "technical error" was responsible for a major gap in the video during a pivotal part of our debate. Luckily, the audio survived intact.

Before I leave Walter Martin, let me tell you how Walter Martin left us.

In May 1989, Fr. Pacwa had arranged for Karl and me to visit the Christian Research Institute's headquarters. (He and Martin had become good friends subsequent to the Ankerberg debate). It was a fascinating day. We took an extended tour of the facilities, including the *Bible Answer Man* studio. We even had a private working lunch and a friendly theological discussion with several of the key CRI staffers, including Hank Hanegraaff, who would very soon become Walter Martin's successor, though none of us had any inkling of what would happen to bring that about.

Martin wasn't in the office that day, but I happened to be invited back again the following week for another meeting with Fr. Pacwa. Just as we were about to leave, as we were walking down the hallway toward the front entrance who should step out of his office and greet us with a big smile, but Walter Ralston Martin! We shook hands and chatted for maybe five minutes. When I told Martin how much and for how long I had enjoyed listening to his radio show, he invited me to return to CRI so I could sit in the studio and watch the show. Our brief discussion ended with a quick prayer. We bowed our heads and Martin offered a gracious prayer for us. Then, he gave me a bear hug and a handshake and promised he'd soon come down to San Diego to visit Catholic Answers. We said good-bye and left.

I mentioned to Fr. Pacwa that I was surprised at how friendly Martin had been to us. "I figured he would have been less welcoming to Catholics," I said.

"On the contrary," Fr. Pacwa responded. He explained that, after their debate on the Ankerberg show, he and Martin had become personal friends. He said that Martin's attitude toward the Catholic Church had grown increasingly open and even conciliatory. Who knows? With enough prayer and discussion, even someone as set in his opinions as Walter Martin could become Catholic, right?

Several weeks later, on June 26, a CRI staff member and his wife happened to be over at our house for a backyard barbecue. Someone called asking urgently for him and delivered the shocking news that Walter Martin had just died suddenly of a massive heart attack at the age of sixty. May he rest in peace.

Since that day, I've prayed for the repose of Walter Martin's soul countless times at Mass and in my daily rosary. I hope to see him in heaven someday. If I do, I'll be sure to return the bear hug.

Surprised by Truth

A hugely significant "life event" happened to me in 1994—something that would radically alter the course of my future work in apologetics in ways I did not expect. It was the release of my first book, *Surprised by Truth: 11 Men and Women Give the Biblical and Historical Reasons for Becoming Catholic*, the first volume in a series of three books by that title.[13] Truth be told, as I look back on it from a distance of eighteen years, I am astonished at how this book also changed the lives of countless other people too. It would not be an exaggeration to say that, in those eighteen years, I have received literally hundreds of e-mails, handwritten letters, and personal comments from men and women across the country and around the world expressing gratitude for the *Surprised by Truth* books.

If they are grateful to me personally, then their gratitude is somewhat misplaced. Although my name is on the cover as editor and coauthor, it is really the unique and powerful testimonies of the people who tell their conversion stories that make these books so life-changing.

Innumerable people have shared with me the astonishing details of their conversions and reconversions to the Catholic Church as a result of reading these books.

There was the U.S. Air Force officer who e-mailed me from his base in Saudi Arabia in 1996 describing how he had been away from the Catholic Church and far from God since graduating from high school. Utterly bored one day, he came across a purple book lying on a table in a rec room. The title, *Surprised by Truth* intrigued him and, since he had nothing better to do, he sat down and started reading it. He read it for hours straight through. When he was finished, he put the book down, went directly to the Catholic chaplain's office, and made a good sacramental confession, then and there. The next thing he did was to call his mom to let her know that her prodigal son had returned to the Church. He described her reaction as being "beside herself" with joy.

Another time, a Baptist man in northern Ohio whom I'll call "John" called me at Catholic Answers asking for help with several biblical questions he had about the Catholic Church. In the course of our conversation he explained that his wife, who was also Baptist, was getting very angry with him for exploring the Catholic Church. She had even threatened to divorce him and take the children if he became Catholic. It was a difficult and delicate predicament for him. John felt drawn the Church but he was also terrified of losing his wife and children over it. So, when I offered to send him some Catholic apologetics tapes and a copy of *Surprised by Truth,* he said "yes" but only on the condition that the materials be sent in a plain, brown box with no indication of any kind that it was coming from a Catholic source. If his wife were to discover it, he assured me, she would have a conniption fit.

I sent the box just as he requested. Within a week, John called back and told me the most amazing story. Sure enough, as God's providence would have it, the UPS truck happened to arrive at his house to deliver that box just minutes after John had left to run some errands.

His wife signed for the delivery. Suspicious, she wondered what was in the "mystery box" addressed to her husband.

A moment later, when her curiosity had gotten the better of her, John's prediction came true. She flipped out in anger. Taking the box with her into the bedroom, she locked the door. When John got home, his wife screamed at him through the locked door that she was going to end the marriage. She couldn't stay with him and be "unequally yoked" with a *Catholic,* someone who believed a "different gospel" and worshipped a "different Jesus." Nothing John said could coax her out of the bedroom. He slept on the couch that night, fearful of what the next day would bring.

Early that morning, while it was still dark, John's wife woke him up and tearfully apologized to him for her anger and unwillingness to tolerate his growing interest in the Catholic Church. Bewildered, he asked what had changed her mind.

"This did," she said, holding up a purple book—*Surprised by Truth*.

After she had locked herself in the bedroom, she started angrily thumbing through it. Before long, she was engrossed in the conversion testimonies and couldn't stop reading until she had finished the last story. Miraculously, reading the book not only cleared away many of her emotional and theological barriers to the Catholic Faith, it piqued her own interest in learning more.

As John related this dramatic story by phone, he got choked up. How amazing it is, we both agreed, that God's grace can penetrate and change the heart of someone as adamantly opposed to the Church as his wife was and do it literally in the twinkling of an eye. I give God thanks and all the credit for whatever good these books have done for folks.

One final quick story: I was conducting a parish seminar recently at a parish in Los Lunas, New Mexico, south of Albuquerque. During an intermission a fortyish woman asked me to sign a few books, and as I did so, she pointed to a copy of *Surprised by Truth 2* on the table, saying, *"That* book brought me back to the Catholic Church after having been gone for a long, long time." She explained how she stopped going to church, stopped praying, and had slid into a life devoted to worldly pleasures and pursuits.

"Fantastic!" I said, happy to hear yet another first-person account of the effect these books have on people. "What happened?"

Her story was remarkable even by *Surprised by Truth* standards of remarkableness. She had been vacationing in a remote and sparsely populated area of northern Minnesota and happened into a tiny, one-room country post office to mail some postcards. As she was buying stamps and chatting with the postal clerk, somehow, improbably, she let slip that she was an ex-Catholic. That's all it took. The clerk reached under the counter and took out a copy of *Surprised by Truth 2*.

"Here you go. If you're an ex-Catholic, you really should read this book."

"Oh, I couldn't take your copy," she responded, thanking him.

"No, really. Go ahead," he encouraged her. "I have a stack of them I give out to people all the time—people who used to be Catholic, just like you!"

In a bit of a daze at this odd happenstance, she accepted the book. That evening, she started reading it. As she described to me what happened, I couldn't help but marvel at the power and mystery of God's grace. She soon after made a sacramental confession and returned wholeheartedly to God and the Catholic Church.

And all because she just happened to stop at a rinky-dink post office in the middle of nowhere to buy some stamps!

There is no space here to explain further the wonderful consequences and truly miraculous conversions that have followed in the wake of the *Surprised by Truth* books. If you want a fuller account of how I came to write them and how I chose the name (hint: it was a riff on C.S. Lewis's great *Surprised by Joy*), I'd invite you to read my introduction to *Surprised by Truth 2* wherein I explain the whole thing. For now, though, I'll just say that if it were not for the release of that first volume, I may never have tried my hand at writing books at all. My career would have gone down a different path, and you would not be reading *this* book now either.

Envoy

In the summer of 1995, after seven and a half great years working at Catholic Answers, I was getting a bit restless. *Surprised by Truth* had been out for about a year and was selling well. My oldest son, Jonathon, was going to go off to the Legion of Christ "apostolic school" in New Hampshire for high school, and I was feeling unsettled by the fact that one of my children was leaving home at such an early age. I didn't want to wake up one day at age fifty-five or sixty filled with regrets for not having spent more time with my family.

I sensed that the Lord might be nudging me to strike out in a new direction. I figured that with one book under my belt, maybe I could write another one and, who knows? Maybe I could make a living as an author. That idea appealed to me, especially since it would allow me to work from home and be with my family 24/7.

After weeks of intense prayer, soul-searching, and long talks with my wife, I decided that I would take a literal leap of faith and resign my position at Catholic Answers. I would no longer be "Robin" to Karl's "Batman." That made me melancholy, but I still felt that the time had come for me to see if I could blaze my own trail.

In early November, I decided to act. My conversation about this with Karl was not a happy one. Both of us were calm and our discussion about my leaving Catholic Answers was friendly, if tense. I was sad, and I think Karl must have been somewhat hurt, or at least feeling let down by my decision to leave. But he was gracious and understanding, and we agreed that I'd wrap things up on December 31.

It was the weirdest feeling to not report back to the Catholic Answers offices on January 2, 1996. I was a now a free agent. I had to make my own way as an apologist now. Game time. Paint or get off the ladder. Sink or swim.

I let a few months go by. That spring, I had a conversation with Matthew Pinto, one of my friends who had also worked at Catholic Answers for a couple of years. We were both very interested in doing something "apostolic" in the field of Catholic apologetics, and we concocted a plan for launching a new magazine, one that would not compete with *This Rock*. We were adamant about two things. First, we did not want to attempt to duplicate the good work Catholic Answers was already doing with *This Rock*. And two, we wanted to try our hand at producing a magazine that would be completely different from anything else out there in the Catholic world. It took awhile to hit on a good name, but eventually we settled on *Envoy*, the name I had proposed unsuccessfully for what became *This Rock*.

After many planning and strategy sessions, we began putting the first issue together. We had assembled a superbly gifted team of graphic artists and writers, in particular the hugely talented Kinsey Caruth and his wife Suzy, who undertook the layout and design of the magazine. Kinsey was flat-out a *wizard* when it came to concepting and creating eye-popping graphics for

Envoy's covers and article layouts. Matt handled the business side of things, and I oversaw the editorial department.

Amazingly, even with an extraordinarily naïve and amusingly optimistic business plan combined with virtually no money on hand to launch this venture, it did launch. And *Envoy* lived up to our hopes of being something completely different from what people were accustomed to seeing in the Catholic world. We designed *Envoy* to accomplish three objectives: to help our readers learn how to explain their Catholic Faith more intelligently, defend it more charitably, and share it more effectively.

Before long, *Envoy* was winning national journalism awards. We even took the prestigious first-place award in the Catholic Press Association's "General Excellence" category two years running, beating out a slew of established, well-funded Catholic magazines such as *Commonweal, U.S. Catholic,* and *America.* After a couple of years, Matt left *Envoy* to work on other projects, and I ran the company solo, changing it to a nonprofit in early 2000. Eventually, Kinsey phased out too, and another ace creative director, the immensely talented Ted Schluenderfritz, stepped into his place and kept *Envoy* rolling along with the same high artistic standards and production values.

Since our debut in 1996, the magazine saw about sixty editions issued, even with having to take a hiatus from printing new issues between 2004 and 2007 due to a lack of funds. I launched the Envoy Institute in the spring of 2007 with assistance from Belmont Abbey College, an arrangement that concluded at the end of 2011, again due to a lack of funds. In the meantime, the Envoy Institute revived the publication of *Envoy* magazine and also accomplished several important initiatives, such as sponsoring some high-powered multi-day conferences responding to moral relativism and atheism. It was also during this time that I launched a new and successful program of Envoy Institute apologetics summer camps for young Catholics aged fifteen to nineteen.

Envoy has been a major part of my work in apologetics since 1996, and I am deeply grateful to all those writers, editors, artists, and of course subscribers who helped make it the success that it was for all those years. Now, though it seems that *Envoy* magazine has likely run its course and may not appear again (due mainly to the now prohibitive printing and mailing costs involved with publishing such a periodical), the Envoy Institute plans to "keep on keepin' on" with its work of training Catholics of all ages to better explain, defend, and share the Faith.

EWTN

One of the other important facets of my work in apologetics has been my association with EWTN, a global Catholic television and radio network based in the Birmingham, Alabama, suburb of Irondale. The storied apostolate, founded in 1980 by Mother Angelica, a Poor Clare nun who had a mere pittance of a few hundred dollars to start with, has become a global colossus of Catholic television and radio programming.[14] It has been one of the singular privileges of my life to be associated with EWTN as a TV and radio host.

The first invitation I ever received to be on an EWTN television program came in 1990 from Msgr. Patrick Brankin, now a pastor in the Diocese of Tulsa, Oklahoma. At that time, he was the publisher of *Catholic Extension* magazine, headquartered in downtown Chicago. He and the head of the Extension Society, Msgr. Edward Slattery (bishop of Tulsa since 1993), were filming some shows at EWTN and kindly invited me to participate. My wife even got to be on one of the shows, interviewed on the subject of parenting and family life.

That same summer, I was speaking at an apologetics conference at Franciscan University of Steubenville (where I now teach as an adjunct professor of theology). There I met the vivacious and energetic television host, Johnnette Benkovic,[15] who was also speaking at the conference. Over lunch, Johnnette invited me to do a few interviews for her show. She had a set and camera crew at the ready in the university's own television studio. We taped two or three segments on Mormonism and other apologetics topics, which aired later that year. It was the beginning of a long and warm friendship with Johnnette.

Over the next few years, I became friends with Jeff Cavins and Marcus Grodi, both of whom soon went on to host major EWTN television shows: *Life on the Rock* and *The Journey Home* programs respectively. Marcus had me on his show several times to discuss the dynamics of conversion and what role apologetics can play in that process. Even though it was all business on camera, there were a few uproariously funny behind-the-scenes incidents that Marcus and I still laugh about. One had to do with a hilarious joke involving a certain funny facial expression that Marcus told me about an hour before we were to start the live show. We laughed till we cried—it was that funny.

Later, *while we were doing the show*, Marcus decided to relive the excitement. At one point, when the live cameras were trained on me, probably in close-up for all I know, and Marcus was off camera, he looked at me with a straight face and then made that facial expression. The next thirty seconds were agonizing for me as I summoned all my powers of concentration to keep a straight face. Thankfully, I made it through intact and without even cracking a smile, and no one, except for Marcus, was the wiser.

In the early 2000s I was invited by EWTN to write and record some new sixteen-part television series, most notably "Search and Rescue," "Pope Fiction," and "Where Is That in the Bible?" I'm grateful that these series have been running more or less continually (sometimes in the wee hours of the morning) ever since.

In late 2006, Marcus called to tell me that he was going to step aside from hosting the Thursday edition of EWTN Radio's "Open Line" broadcast so that he could launch a new show for the network called "Deep in Scripture." He asked if I'd be willing to step in as his replacement. It took about a nanosecond for my response: "Yes!"

We did a few shows together so I could get the hang of it, and by January 2007, I was flying solo. Hosting the "Open Line" Thursday show all the years since then has been another gigantic blessing for me. It's a chance to spend two solid hours fielding calls and comments from listeners across the country and around the world. Best of all, since a good number of the callers are not Catholic and sometimes let fly some pretty challenging questions, hosting "Open Line" allows me the opportunity to keep growing and learning as an apologist.

One brief, final reminiscence I'd like to share with you has to do with the Carmelite Sisters of the Most Sacred Heart of Los Angeles, headquartered in Los Angeles. This wonderful congregation of nuns first came into my life in January of 1990 when I was speaking at a clergy and religious conference in Los Angeles. Many of these Carmelite sisters were in attendance, and I had a chance to strike up a conversation with a few of them. We stayed in touch.

When it came time to plan our Catholic Answers apologetics conference, held in Long Beach, California, March 1–3, I saw that we would have plenty of room, and so I asked Karl if we could invite the Carmelite sisters to attend at no charge. He agreed.

My liaison with Carmelites was Sister Judith Zuñiga, O.C.D., a joyful, vibrant, and deeply compassionate sister who was tasked with working with me over the phone on the logistics for the event. The first morning of the conference, I met Sister Judith in person for the first time, and we soon became fast friends. Ever since, she and the whole community of Carmelite sisters have been faithful friends and an indispensable help to me by their prayers for me, my family, and my work.

During my many foreign travels around the world on apologetics-related activities—England, Germany, Italy, Switzerland, France, Austria, Israel, Panama, India, the Philippines, Malaysia, Japan, South Korea, Australia, New Zealand, Mexico, Spain, and everywhere else I've been privileged to visit over the years—these good nuns have helped me tremendously with the spiritual "fire power" of their prayers, rosaries, and Mass intentions on my behalf.

Truly, for the last twenty-five years, while I have been traveling hither and yon as a Catholic apologist trying to do carry out what little, modest part I have played in the Church's grand battle for souls, my dear friend Sister Judith and her army of smiling Carmelite prayer warriors have given me the "air cover" I've needed, and then some. For that and for their solid-gold friendship in the Lord, I am deeply and eternally grateful because I'm convinced that, without their prayers, none of this would have been possible.

SECTION ONE
Sola Scriptura

DURING THE TWENTY-FIVE-PLUS YEARS THAT I have been active in Catholic apologetics with Protestants, no single subject has dominated discussion more than *sola Scriptura,* the Reformation slogan in Latin meaning "Scripture alone." The principle that Scripture is not just materially but formally sufficient for Christian doctrine and practice (a concept I will explain in detail in this section's essays) has spawned innumerable debates between Catholics and Protestants in the five hundred years since the phenomenon we know as Protestantism began. For my own part, I have participated in many such debates, oral and written, public and private, on the radio and on many a dais in front of live audiences.

What these many interactions with Protestants (ministers and scholars especially) have taught me is that this linchpin issue, because it is so fundamental to the Protestant position, is also by far its weakest and least defensible theological component. In fact, I don't think it would be any exaggeration to say that countless opportunities I have had to discuss and debate *sola Scriptura* with those who ardently defend it has served consistently to confirm and strengthen beyond measure my certitude that the Catholic Church has the biblically and historically correct answer in this discussion and Protestantism does not.

In spite of my own deficiencies as a debater (I have many), in spite of my missteps, mistakes, omissions, and similar failings in exchanges I have participated in, I have never once seen *sola Scriptura* vindicated in a debate. In fact, time after time, I have been happily surprised to see Protestants convert to the Catholic Faith after finally being exposed to both the Catholic response to Protestant arguments against Tradition, traditions, and the Magisterium (the first and last of these three being integral components of the authentic model of biblical authority) and hearing the Catholic critique of the Protestant principle of *sola Scriptura*. Several such converts, folks who once were absolutely convinced that *sola Scriptura* is true and the Catholic Church is false have become lifelong friends of mine. One of them is Annie Witz (née McHargue). She attended my "What Still Divides Us?" debate on *sola Scriptura* and *sola fide* (justification by faith alone) at Lake Avenue Church in Pasadena, California, in January 1995.[16] As an Evangelical Protestant, she was so intent on seeing the Catholic Church vanquished in this debate that took place before an audience of some 1500 people that she made sure to bring a carload of her Catholic friends so that they would become convinced that *sola Scriptura* is true. Things didn't work out as she planned. Not only did her Catholic friends come away from that debate stronger and more convinced in their Catholic Faith (as Annie herself told me), Annie wound up converting to the Catholic Church! All these years later, she is still in touch, continuing to send me the occasional e-mail, like the one about how she shared a set of the debate CDs with a Baptist minister she had met. "Guess what!" she wrote with true joy. "He's decided to become Catholic and will be entering the Church on the next Easter Vigil."

Another person who comes to mind is Heidi Reeves, a former staunch Baptist whose husband, Doug, is an equally staunch Catholic. When it was announced that I would debate James White on the question "Does the Bible Teach *Sola Scriptura*?" at an Orthodox Presbyterian Church in Chula Vista in September 1993, Heidi wanted Doug to go so he would "see the light" and leave the Catholic Church. And Doug wanted her to go for the same, though opposite, reason. Doug tells the story of what happened in detail in his excellent new book, *The Victory of the Battle Maiden.* In it he recounts how that debate had a profound effect on Heidi and led—rather quickly, it turns out—to her conversion to the Catholic Church.

I attribute none of this to myself. Rather, the truth of the Catholic Faith is attractive and beautiful, having a powerful gravitational pull of its own that draws people to itself. That is what is at work in these kinds of conversions—that and God's grace. I have always seen myself as an irrigation ditch and nothing more. If God can make use of my meager knowledge and abilities to let his grace flow through me through a debate or a book or a lecture, then I am perfectly happy to fulfill that role for him!

As I try to demonstrate throughout the essays and written debates you'll find in this section, no Catholic should be worried or fearful in the face of *sola Scriptura* claims. This principle is simply not taught by the Bible; it was not taught by Jesus Christ or the apostles, it was not believed in the early and medieval Church (not, at least, in any way resembling the Protestant sense of the term), and it should not be believed by Christians today. And in this next collection of articles, I will lay out for you my reasons for making these claims.

Sola Scriptura: A Blueprint for Anarchy

LET'S SAY I'M AN EVANGELICAL. WHEN I find out you're Catholic, I'm going to hammer you with Bible verses that I believe demonstrate that the Catholic Church's teachings on issues such as purgatory, Mary, the papacy, and the Eucharist are unbiblical. "The Bible alone provides the totality of God's revealed truth that's necessary for the Church to have. Forget about all those manmade Catholic traditions (traditions which, by the way, are condemned by Christ in Matthew 15:3–9 and Mark 7:6–8). Just go by the Bible alone," I'll argue.

Let's say you're hip to this argument. You know that the Protestant principle of the Bible alone—*sola Scriptura* as the Reformers called it—is untrue. But you don't know how to demonstrate that *sola Scriptura* is not what Christ taught, it's not what the apostles and Church Fathers taught and, most ironically, it's not what the Bible itself teaches.

Catholics need to realize just how untenable *sola Scriptura* is and simply ask that it be proven from the Bible. Instead of allowing himself to be put on the defensive when purgatory, the Real Presence, or some other Catholic doctrine is challenged by a demand that it be proven from Scripture, the Catholic should ask, "Where does the Bible teach *sola Scriptura?*" Scriptural evidence, whether explicit or implicit, can indeed be adduced for these Catholic teachings, but those apologetics discussions are not our focus here and must be left for other articles.

The Catholic case against *sola Scriptura* may be summarized by saying that *sola Scriptura* is unhistorical, unbiblical, and unworkable. This article will examine each of these points, without claiming to offer an exhaustive historical and biblical critique of the doctrine (there are a number of books and tape sets which do that). Nevertheless, I hope the essential elements of the Catholic case will be clear.

Sola Scriptura Is Unhistorical

First, let's consider *sola Scriptura* from the vantage point of history. If the notion of the absolute sufficiency of Scripture were indeed part of "the faith that was once for all handed on to the saints" (Jude 3), we would expect to find it everywhere taught and practiced in the early Church. We would expect to see the ancient Christian liturgical life dominated and shaped by the rule of *sola Scriptura*. But we don't see anything of the sort. The fact is, the writings of the Church Fathers and the councils, both regional and ecumenical, reveal that *sola Scriptura* was completely alien to the thought and life of the early Church. Mind you, the early Church placed an exceedingly great emphasis on the importance and authority of Scripture to guide and govern the life of the Church, and Scripture was employed constantly by the Fathers in their doctrinal treatises and pastoral directives. But Scripture was never regarded (or used) by the Church Fathers as something that stands alone, self-sufficient and entirely independent of Sacred Tradition and the Magisterium. In the distinct, formal sense that Protestants advocate, over against the Catholic position of the "material sufficiency" of Scripture, which will be discussed later in this article.

Sometimes Protestant apologists try to bolster their case for *sola Scriptura* by using highly selective quotes from Church Fathers such as Athanasius, John Chrysostom, Cyril of Jerusalem, Augustine, and Basil of Caesarea. This is due, I believe, to the recent dramatic rise in apologetics works against *sola Scriptura* by Catholics. These quotes, isolated from the rest of what the Father in question wrote about church authority, Tradition and Scripture, can give the appearance that these Fathers were hard-core Evangelicals who promoted an unvarnished *sola Scriptura* principle that would have done John Calvin proud. But this is merely a chimera. In order for the selective "pro-*sola Scriptura*" quotes from the Fathers to be of value to a Protestant apologist, his audience must have little or no firsthand knowledge of what these Fathers wrote. By considering the patristic evidence on the subject of Scriptural authority in context, a very different picture emerges. A few examples will suffice to demonstrate what I mean.

Basil of Caesarea provides Evangelical polemicists with what they think is a "smoking gun" quote upholding *sola Scriptura*: "Therefore, let God-inspired Scripture decide between us; and on whichever side be found doctrines in harmony with the Word of God, in favor of that side will be cast the vote of truth" (*Epistle ad Eustathius*). This, they think, means that Basil would have been comfortable with the Calvinist notion that "All things in Scripture are not alike plain in themselves, nor alike clear unto all; yet those things which are necessary to be known, believed, and observed, for salvation, are so clearly propounded and opened in some place of Scripture or other, that not only the learned, but the unlearned, in a due use of the ordinary means, may attain unto a sufficient understanding of them."[17] Yet if Basil's quote is to be of any use to the Protestant apologist, the rest of Basil's writings must be shown to be consistent and compatible with *sola Scriptura*. But watch what happens to Basil's alleged position when we look at other statements of his:

> Of the beliefs and practices whether generally accepted or enjoined which are preserved in the Church, some we possess derived from written teaching; others we have delivered to us in a mystery by the apostles by the tradition of the apostles; and both of these in relation to true religion have the same force.[18]

> In answer to the objection that the doxology in the form 'with the Spirit' has no written authority, we maintain that if there is not another instance of that which is unwritten, then this must not be received [as authoritative]. But if the great number of our mysteries are admitted into our constitution without [the] written authority [of Scripture],

then, in company with many others, let us receive this one. For I hold it apostolic to abide by the unwritten traditions. "I praise you," it is said [by Paul in 1 Corinthians 11:1] "that you remember me in all things and keep the traditions just as I handed them on to you," and "Hold fast to the traditions that you were taught whether by an oral statement or by a letter of ours" [2 Thessalonians 2:15]. One of these traditions is the practice which is now before us [under consideration], which they who ordained from the beginning, rooted firmly in the churches, delivering it to their successors, and its use through long custom advances pace by pace with time.[19]

Such talk hardly fits with the principle that Scripture is formally sufficient for all matters of Christian doctrine. This type of appeal to a body of unwritten apostolic Tradition within the Church as being authoritative is frequent in Basil's writings.

Protestant apologists often quote two particular passages from St. Athanasius: "The holy and inspired Scriptures are sufficient of themselves for the preaching of the truth"[20] and "These books [of canonical Scripture] are the fountains of salvation, so that he who thirsts may be satisfied with the oracles contained in them. In these alone the school of piety preaches the Gospel. Let no man add to these or take away from them."[21] But in neither place is Athanasius teaching *sola Scriptura*.

First, in the case of the *Festal Letter*, he was instructing his churches as to what could and could not be read at Church as "Scripture." The context of the epistle makes it clear that he was laying down a liturgical directive for his flock.

Second, as in the case of Basil and the other Fathers Protestants attempt to press into service, Athanasius's writings show no signs of *sola Scriptura*, but rather of his staunchly orthodox Catholicism. Athanasius, for example, wrote:

The confession arrived at Nicaea was, we say more, sufficient and enough by itself for the subversion of all irreligious heresy and for the security and furtherance of the doctrine of the Church.[22]

And:

> [T]he very tradition, teaching, and faith of the Catholic Church from the beginning was preached by the Apostles and preserved by the Fathers. On this the Church was founded; and if anyone departs from this, he neither is nor any longer ought to be called a Christian.[23]

And consider this quote from Cyril of Jerusalem's *Catechetical Lectures*, a favorite among the *nouveau* Protestant apologists:

> In regard to the divine and holy mysteries of the Faith, not the least part may be handed on without the Holy Scriptures. Do not be led astray by winning words and clever arguments. Even to me, who tell you these things, do not give ready belief, unless you receive from the Holy Scriptures the proof of the things which I announce. The salvation which we believe is not proved from clever reasoning, but from the Holy Scriptures.[24]

How should we understand this? Catholic patristic scholars would point out that such language as Cyril uses here is consistent with his and the other Fathers' high view of Scripture's authority and with what is sometimes called its material sufficiency (more on that shortly).

This language, while perhaps more rigorously biblical than some modern Catholics are used to, nonetheless conveys an accurate sense of Catholic teaching on the importance of Scripture. Even taken at face value, Cyril's admonition poses no problem for the Catholic. But it does, ironically, for the Protestant.

The proponent of *sola Scriptura* is faced with a dilemma when he attempts to use Cyril's quote. Option One: If Cyril was in fact teaching *sola Scriptura*, Protestants have a big problem. Cyril's *Catechetical Lectures* are filled with his forceful teachings on the infallible teaching office of the Catholic Church (18:23), the Mass as a sacrifice (23:6–8), the concept of purgatory and the efficacy of expiatory prayers for the dead (23:10), the Real Presence of Christ in the Eucharist (19:7; 21:3; 22:1–9), the theology of sacraments (1:3), the intercession of the saints (23:9), holy orders (23:2), the importance of frequent Communion (23:23), baptismal regeneration (1:1–3; 3:10–12; 21:3–4), indeed a staggering array of specifically "Catholic" doctrines.

These are the same Catholic doctrines that Protestants claim are not found in Scripture. So, if Cyril really held to the notion of *sola Scriptura*, he certainly believed he had found those Catholic doctrines in Scripture. One would then have to posit that Cyril was badly mistaken in his exegesis of Scripture, but this tack, of course, leads nowhere for Protestants, for it would of necessity impugn Cyril's exegetical credibility as well as his claim to find *sola Scriptura* in Scripture.

Option Two: Cyril did not teach *sola Scriptura*; the Protestant understanding of this passage is incorrect. That means an attempt to hijack this quote to support *sola Scriptura* is futile (if not dishonest), since it would require a hopelessly incorrect understanding of Cyril's method of systematic theology, the doctrinal schema he sets forth in Catechetical Lectures, and his view of the authority of Scripture. Obviously, neither of these options is palatable to the Protestant apologist.

Were there time and space to cycle through each of the patristic quotes proffered by Protestants arguing for *sola Scriptura*, we could demonstrate in each case that the Fathers are being quoted out of context and without regard to the rest of their statements on the authority of Scripture, Tradition and the Magisterium. It will suffice for now, though, to remind Catholics that the Fathers did not teach *sola Scriptura*, and no amount of clever "cut-and-paste" work by defenders of *sola Scriptura* can demonstrate otherwise.

Sola Scriptura Is Unbiblical

Consider the Old Testament. The principle of *sola Scriptura* is utterly alien to the way in which God dealt with his people before Christ. Besides the fact that no Scripture of any sort was available before Moses's time [apart from occasional, terrifying incidents of direct revelation en masse, commands were mediated to his people through prophets and patriarchs). No Israelite was free to practice private interpretation of the Law, deciding for himself how he believed the text should be interpreted. Imagine someone telling Moses, "Look, I read Genesis

17 differently. I think God was speaking about circumcision here figuratively. He wasn't literally telling Abraham to take a knife and start cutting things." The Old Testament contains no hint of *sola Scriptura*.

The New Testament is the same. Not only does Christ institute a teaching Church (Matthew 28:19–20), endowed with his own authority (Luke 10:16; Matthew 16:18; 18:18), we nowhere see the notion of "Scripture alone" in the teachings of any of the apostles or any of their successors. In fact, we even see examples of a preference for imparting teachings orally and not in writing: "Though I have much to write to you, I would rather not use paper and ink, but I hope to come to see you and talk with you face to face, so that our joy may be complete" (2 John 12; see 3 John 13).

The fatal flaw of *sola Scriptura* then is that it is itself not taught in Scripture. *The Westminster Confession of Faith* says: "The whole counsel of God, concerning all things necessary for his own glory, man's salvation, faith, and life, is either expressly set down in Scripture, or by good and necessary consequence may be deduced from Scripture: unto which nothing at any time is to be added, whether by new revelations of the Spirit, or traditions of men."[25] If this statement is true, then the doctrine of *sola Scriptura* must itself be "expressly set down in Scripture, or…deduced from Scripture."

And that's the rub. By asserting *sola Scriptura*, Protestants are making the concomitant assertion that all divine revelation necessary for the Church to possess comes down to us in Scripture alone. The Anglican Reformers put it this way: "The Holy Scripture containeth all things necessary to salvation: so that whatsoever is not read therein, nor may be proved thereby, is not to be required of any man that it should be believed as an article of the Faith, or be thought requisite or necessary to salvation."[26]

More specifically, as *The Westminster Confession of Faith* explains, to be divinely revealed, a doctrine must be explicitly expressed or logically implied in Scripture. And that leads us to the question of formal and material sufficiency.

Many eminent Catholic theologians and doctors down through the centuries, including most of the Church Fathers, have taught that Scripture is materially sufficient.[27]

A thorough discussion of the meaning of formal and material sufficiency with regard to the claims of the classical Protestant definitions of *sola Scriptura* is found in Yves M.J. Congar's *Tradition and Traditions.*[28] Protestants who object to the categories formal and material with regard to Scriptural sufficiency would do well to read Congar's treatment before they reject them as "improperly imposed" by Catholic apologists.[29]

The problem is that Evangelical Protestants who venture into patristic literature in pursuit of ammunition for their position come away with a faulty understanding of what the Fathers meant. Newman observed this problem in a letter to an Anglican friend: "You have made a collection of these passages from the Fathers, as witnesses in behalf of your doctrines that the whole Christian Faith is contained in Scripture, as if, in your sense of my words, Catholics contradicted you here."[30]

We must make a distinction here in order to understand the critical difference between the material sufficiency of Scripture taught by the Fathers and the Reformers' much narrower notion of formal sufficiency. At certain levels, the Catholic position intersects with the Protestant formula of *sola Scriptura*. But the fundamental difference is this: The Catholic Church holds that in order for the meaning of Sacred Scripture to be properly understood, the Church must have recourse to its living Tradition—i.e., the infallible interpretation of the apostolic *depositum fidei* (see *Dei Verbum*, 10). And this interpretation is guaranteed by an infallible Magisterium.

The Reformation creeds, while paying an ostensible limited respect to Tradition, Church councils and the Fathers, nonetheless refuse to accord them infallibility. Protestants claim that Scripture is sufficient *in se* and, ultimately, does not require an infallible Tradition or Magisterium in order to be authentically interpreted. In contrast, the Catholic model for authority is tripartite: Scripture, Tradition, and the Magisterium are distinct yet mutually interdependent.[31] *Scriptura, Traditio,* and *Magisterium* may be summarized in this way: Scriptura is the object of the Church's interpretation; Traditio is the Church's lived interpretation of Scripture; and Magisterium is the organ of the Church that does the interpreting.

But the Protestant understanding of Scriptural sufficiency pushes beyond mere material sufficiency into the province of formal sufficiency. Formal sufficiency means that all revelation necessary for the Church to possess is presented formally in the pages of Scripture, with nothing else needed—no Tradition or Magisterium. This nuance—and make no mistake, it's a very important nuance—is where the failure of *sola Scriptura* occurs.

Another problem for *sola Scriptura* is the canon of the New Testament. There's no "inspired table of contents" in Scripture that tells us which books belong and which ones don't. That information comes to us from outside Scripture. Our knowledge of which books comprise the canon of the New Testament must be infallible; if not, there's no way to know for sure if the books we regard as inspired really are inspired. It must be binding; otherwise folks would be free to have their own customized canon containing those books they take a fancy to and lacking the ones they don't. And it must be part of divine revelation; if it's not it's merely a tradition of men, and if that were so, Protestants would be forced into the intolerable position of championing a canon of purely human origin.

These facts don't square with the classic Protestant creeds—for example, *The Westminster Confession*, asserts that:

> The authority of the Holy Scripture, for which it ought to be believed and obeyed, dependeth not upon the testimony of any man or church, but wholly upon God (who is truth itself), the author thereof; and therefore it is to be received, because it is the Word of God. We may be moved and induced by the testimony of the Church to a high and reverent esteem for the Holy Scripture…yet, notwithstanding, our full persuasion and assurance of the infallible truth and divine authority thereof, is from the inward work of the Holy Spirit, bearing witness by and with the Word in our hearts.

This is pure Mormonism—the old "I know it's inspired because I feel in my heart that it's inspired" line that Mormon missionaries use. As a proof for the inspiration of Scripture, this bromide is useless.

Sola Scriptura becomes "canon" fodder as soon as the Catholic asks the Protestant to explain how the books of the Bible got into the Bible. Under the *sola Scriptura* rubric, Scripture exists in an absolute epistemological vacuum, since it and the veracity of its contents "dependeth not upon the testimony of any man or church." If that's true, how then can anyone know with certitude what belongs in Scripture in the first place?

The answer is, you can't.

Without recognizing the trustworthiness of the Magisterium, endowed with Christ's own teaching authority (see Matthew 16:18–19; 18:18; Luke 10:16) guided by the Holy Spirit (John 14:25–26; 16:13), and the living apostolic Tradition of the Church (1 Corinthians 11:1; 2 Thessalonians 2:15; 2 Timothy 2:2), there is no way to know for certain which books belong in Scripture and which do not.

As soon as Protestants begin to appeal to the canons drawn up by this or that Father, or this or that council, they immediately concede defeat, since they are forced to appeal to the very "testimony of man and Church" that they claim to not need.

It's important here to say a few words about some of the Scriptural arguments raised by Protestants in defense of *sola Scriptura*. The verse most often raised is 2 Timothy 3:16–17, yet this passage is a minefield of difficulties for *sola Scriptura*. Here Paul tells his young episcopal protégé, Timothy, "All scripture is inspired by God [Greek: *theopneustos* = "God breathed"] and is useful for teaching, for refutation, for correction, and for training in righteousness, so that the man of God may be competent, equipped for every good work." The conclusion drawn is that 2 Timothy 3:16–17 teaches that the Bible is sufficient in all matters of Christian doctrine and practice because it will make the man of God equipped for "every good work."

But notice the Greek, *pasa graphé theopneustos*. This means "each" or "every" Scripture is inspired. This complicates matters further for Protestants. For if Paul is pointing to sufficiency in this passage, he's designated each book of Scripture as sufficient in itself for the task he goes on to outline. But that of course is not what Paul is saying.

In one of my public debates on *sola Scriptura*, "Does the Bible Teach *Sola Scriptura?*" a Protestant apologist attempted to make his case for the formal sufficiency of Scripture by using an analogy of a bike shop. He argued that just as the bike shop contains all the necessary accouterments for bike riding and can fully equip a bike rider, so too Scripture is sufficient to "fully equip" the man of God. Unfortunately for his case, this analogy, although superficially plausible, is faulty. The bike shop may provide all the necessary equipment, but the customer must first know how to ride a bike to make use of that equipment. This is analogous to the Christian knowing how to correctly use Scripture. Bike shops can certainly equip their customer with all the necessary paraphernalia, but don't teach him how to ride.

My debate opponent tried to get around this by countering that 2 Timothy 3:17 says that the "man of God" is made fully equipped by Scripture, so there is no question that he'll know how to use Scripture correctly. But the problem with this argument is that it provides no sure way to determine who is a "man of God" and who isn't. Protestantism is so divided over central doctrinal issues (e.g. infant baptism, baptismal regeneration, the nature of justification, salvation, divorce and remarriage, etc.), that this "man of God" argument only begs the question.

All Protestants believe that they have embraced the "correct" interpretation of Scripture, but doing so includes the implicit assertion that all the other denominations don't have the correct interpretation on all things. If they did, why the need for denominations?

The answer to the Protestant claims of formal sufficiency in this passage is that Paul is not trying to establish Scripture as the sole, sufficient thing that renders the man of God fit for these tasks. Rather, he is reminding Timothy of several things that, combined with God's grace and Timothy's faithful diligence, will make him so equipped.

There's also the lexical argument based on the Greek of 2 Timothy, which argues that because Scripture will make the man of God "*ártios*" (suitable) and "*exartizo*" (thoroughly furnished), it therefore is sufficient. But this argument fails for several reasons.

First, with regard to what Scripture says about itself, 2 Timothy 3:16–17 merely says that Scripture is *ophelímos*, which means "useful" or "profitable." Paul's use of the Greek terms *ártios* ("suitable" or "correct") and *exartisménos* ("having been furnished") does not imply the sufficiency of Scripture, on purely lexical grounds. Although some Greek scholars note that *ártios* and *exartizo* could mean sufficient, we must do our best to understand their actual meaning based on the context of the passage.

A telling fact is that no major Bible translation, not even those produced by the most ardent supporters of *sola Scriptura*, renders either *ártios* or *exartisménos* "sufficient." Furthermore, the "sufficiency" hermeneutic Protestants use in 2 Timothy 3:16–17 fails when applied to similar passages.

For example, in 2 Timothy 2:19–21, Paul exhorts Timothy to cleanse himself from all that is not holy and virtuous, saying that doing so will make him "ready for every good work" (v. 21). The exact same Greek phrase is used here as in 2 Timothy 3:16: *pan ergon agathon* ("for every good work"). Under the "sufficiency" hermeneutic used by Protestants to defend *sola Scriptura* in 2 Timothy 3:16, Paul would here be made to say that one's personal efforts to become purified from sin are "sufficient." But this is an absurd conclusion.

We can see the same absurdity in the Protestant argument arise when it is applied to James 1:4: "And let [your] perseverance be perfect [*téleion*], so that you may be perfect [*téleioi*] and complete [*holóklepoi*], lacking in nothing [*en meden" leipómenoi*]." This passage uses far stronger language than that found in 2 Timothy 3:16–17, and goes far beyond the mere implication of sufficiency Protestants want to see in this verse, by the explicit statement that perseverance will make you "perfect and complete, lacking in nothing."

If any verse in the Bible could be used to argue for "sufficiency" James 1:4 would be it. Under the hermeneutic employed by the proponents of *sola Scriptura*, in this passage James would be saying that all one needs is perseverance (the context is perseverance in suffering and good works!).

This would mean that mere perseverance is sufficient, and such things as faith, grace, prayer, repentance, even Scripture, are unnecessary. Again, an absurd proposition, but that's what this form of Protestant argumentation leads to, not only here in James 1:4, but also in 2 Timothy 3:16–17.

Some Protestants wind up committing a lexical fallacy in their attempt to ward off the obvious implication of James 1:4 and 2 Timothy 2:19–21. They claim that because the word *téleios* is used in James 1 (not *ártios*), the two passages cannot be compared. But in fact, the primary meaning of *téleios* is "complete" or "perfect."

It's a much more forceful word for indicating perfection or completion than is *ártios*, which primarily means merely "suitable" or "fit."[32] Delling gives the meanings of *ártios* as: "right," "faultless," "normal," "meeting demands," and "proper."[33] Of *exartizo* he says, "At 2 Timothy 3:17 [it] means to bring to a suitable state for Christian moral action."

And if the *ártios/exartizo* argument proves anything, it proves too much. 2 Timothy 3:16–17 shows that *ártios* and *exartizo* modify "the man of God" (*ho tou theou ánthropos*) not "Scripture" (*graphê*).

Scripture does not claim sufficiency for itself here. It says it completes and makes fit the man of God. So, at best, this argument proves only that Scripture makes the man of God sufficient.

The context of this epistle is Paul's general instructions to Timothy on how to be a holy and pastorally effective bishop. Besides Scripture, Paul appeals to oral tradition (as he does in other epistles) as a source for apostolic doctrine "what you have heard from me before many witnesses entrust to faithful men who will be able to teach others also" (2:2; see 1 Corinthians 11:2; 2 Thessalonians 2:15).

He alludes to this oral teaching two verses earlier: "But you, remain faithful to what you have learned and believed, because you know from whom you learned it" (3:14). In 2 Timothy 2:15 Paul advises Timothy to "rightly divide the word of truth." Contrary to the common Protestant assumption, the phrase "word of truth" is not restricted to Scripture alone, but includes oral tradition as well.

For example, in Ephesians 1:13 and Colossians 1:5 "the word of truth" refers specifically to Apostolic Tradition, not Scripture. There are many other Scriptural arguments Protestants use, but in the interest of space, we'll simply discuss a few briefly.

Matthew 4:1–11 is the passage where Jesus rebukes the devil with the phrase "It is written," referring to Scripture. Protestants see in this and other "It is written" passages a vindication of *sola Scriptura.* "See!" they say, "Jesus did not appeal to Tradition or the Church or anything else, but to Scripture. That means that Scripture is sufficient to settle all issues." But that's not at all what this verse means. Notice first of all that in this same passage Jesus reminds the devil of the passage, "Man shall live by every word that proceeds from the mouth of God." Not all of God's words are contained in Scripture. Besides Christ who is the Word of God (John 1:1, 14), some of God's words come down to us in oral fashion (see Acts 20:27; Galatians 1:11–12, 15–16; 1 Thessalonians 2:13; 2 Timothy 2:2).

Christ does not say nor does he imply a "Scripture alone" approach to truth in this passage. Rather, he reminds us that we are to cling to and live by every word that he speaks, not just the written words contained in Scripture. Notice too the implicit warning here. The mere quoting of Scripture is not enough to establish one's truth claims, since here we see the devil himself (mis) quoting Scripture! That's why Peter warned, "In [Paul's epistles] there are some things hard to understand that the ignorant and unstable distort to their own destruction, just as they do the other Scriptures" (2 Peter 3:16).

In the year 434, St. Vincent of Lerins reflected on this problem:

If one should ask one of the heretics who gives you this advice, 'How do you prove [your assertion]? What ground have you for saying that I ought to cast away the universal and ancient faith of the Catholic Church?' He has the answer ready: 'For it is written.' And forthwith he produces a thousand examples, a thousand authorities from the Law, from the Psalms, from the apostles, from the prophets, by means of which, interpreted on a new and wrong principle, the unhappy soul may be precipitated from the height of Catholic truth to the lowest abyss of heresy....

Do heretics appeal to Scripture? They do indeed, and with a vengeance. For you may see them scamper through every single book of Holy Scripture....Whether among their own people or among strangers, in private or in public, in speaking or in writing, at convivial meetings or in the streets, hardly ever do they bring forward anything of their own which they do not endeavor to shelter under the words of Scripture....

You will see an infinite heap of instances, hardly a single page, which does not bristle with plausible quotations from the New Testament or the Old.[34]

Another passage Protestants use is Acts 17:10–11 which says, "Upon arrival they went to the synagogue of the Jews. These Jews were more noble than those in Thessalonica, for they received the word with all willingness and examined the Scriptures daily to determine whether these things were so." This passage is appealed to as evidence that it is more "noble" to go by what Scripture says, than by what even apostles themselves preach orally. But this is not so. First, remember that these Jews were called noble mainly because they did not riot upon hearing Paul's claims for Christ's divinity, as did the Jews of Thessalonica (see Acts 17:1–8). The Berean Jews were docile and willing to check to see if Paul's claims squared with Scripture. After all, he was preaching the Gospel to the Jews, and urging them to check these things out for themselves in what had by then become the "Old" Testament (see 17:2–3).

Using Scripture was certainly appropriate when dealing with Jews, who revered and believed in Scripture, though it was futile to use when preaching to Gentiles, who had no appreciation for Scripture. That's why we *don't* see Paul or the other Apostles typically using Scripture in their apostolic work among the Gentiles, and sometimes we see an appeal even to pagan writings to make a point, when necessary! (see Acts 17:22–32). Besides, the apostles were charged with teaching the Gospel to all creatures (Matthew 28:19–20), and this magisterial office included the task of interpreting Scripture. When the apostles taught, whether in writing or orally, God was teaching through them (Luke 10:16; 1 Thessalonians 2:13). Revelation 22:18–19: "I warn everyone who hears the prophetic words in this book; if anyone adds to them, God will add to him the plagues described in this book, and if anyone takes away from the words in this book, God will take away his share in the tree of life and in the holy City described in this book."

Protestants argue that Catholic Tradition is "adding" to Scripture. But this passage refers to the book of Revelation itself, not Scripture in general. After all, Scripture, compiled definitively as a single volume, would not be known by the Church until the councils of Hippo (393) and Carthage (397, 419).

There's also a problem for this argument in light of Deuteronomy 4:2, 12:32, where the Israelites are warned to neither add nor subtract anything from the teachings contained therein. The same warning in Revelation 22 is found in Deuteronomy, yet any Protestant will admit that it doesn't prohibit the adding of all the books of the Old Testament that follow Deuteronomy and all of the New Testament to the canon of Scripture.

It's Unworkable

We've reached that point where the "rubber" of *sola Scriptura* meets the "road" of everyday life. The final question that should be asked of the Protestant is, "Can you show where in history *sola Scriptura* has worked?" In other words, where, throughout Protestantism's relatively brief life span, can we find examples (just one will do) of *sola Scriptura* actually working—functioning in such a way that it brings about doctrinal certitude and unity of doctrine among Christians?

The answer is: "Nowhere."

As a rule of faith that, without recourse to Sacred Tradition and an infallible Magisterium, promises doctrinal certitude and a unity of faith, *sola Scriptura* fails miserably. The best evidence of this is Protestantism itself. There are today, according to one recent study, hundreds of distinct Protestant denominations in the world, each of which claims to go by the "Bible alone," yet no two of them agree on what exactly the Bible teaches.

Ironically, the blueprint for the doctrinal chaos that is Protestantism is laid out in *The Westminster Confession of Faith*:

> The whole counsel of God, concerning all things necessary for his own glory, man's salvation, faith, and life, is either expressly set down in Scripture, or by good and necessary consequence may be deduced from Scripture: unto which nothing at any time is to be added, whether by new revelations of the Spirit, or traditions of men....
>
> All things in Scripture are not alike plain in themselves, nor alike clear unto all; yet those things which are necessary to be known, believed, and observed, for salvation, are so clearly propounded and opened in some place of Scripture or other, that not only the learned, but the unlearned, in a due use of the ordinary means, may attain unto a sufficient understanding of them....
>
> The infallible rule of interpretation of Scripture, is the Scripture itself; and therefore, when there is a question about the true and full sense of any scripture (which is not manifold, but one), it may be searched and known by other places that speak more clearly. The Supreme Judge, by which all controversies of religion are to be determined, and all decrees of councils, opinions of ancient writers, doctrines of men, and private spirits, are to be examined, and in whose sentence we are to rest, can be no other but the Holy Spirit speaking in the Scripture.[35]

All of that sounds fine at first glance, but upon inspection, this framework collapses. First, if "the whole counsel of God...is either expressly set down in Scripture, or by good and necessary consequence may be deduced from Scripture," then *sola Scriptura* must itself appear somewhere in Scripture, but it does not.

And thus, under the terms set forth in all the classical Protestant creeds, it is a self-refuting proposition. Second, if "those things which are necessary to be known, believed, and observed, for salvation, are so clearly propounded and opened in some place of Scripture or other, that not only the learned, but the unlearned, in a due use of the ordinary means, may attain unto a sufficient understanding of them," then we have another problem.

What are we to do with such things "necessary to be known, believed, and observed for salvation" as the doctrine that the Persons of the Trinity are *homoousios*, that in Christ there are two wills, the Hypostatic Union, the cessation of divine revelation upon the death of the last apostle, the canon of Scripture, whether or not infants should be baptized, and a whole host of key issues that bear directly upon the core of the Christian faith.

Scripture alone—Scripture forced to stand apart from the infallible teaching magisterium that has been given Christ's own authority to accurately interpret Scripture, and Sacred Tradition, which is the Church's living interpretation of those written words—is unstable and leads to the myriad of conflicting, erroneous, and sometimes spiritually fatal "human traditions" (see Matthew 15:3–9; Mark 7:6–7) that lead people away from Christ.

Scripture alone, as the tragic history of Protestantism has shown, becomes the private play toy of any self-styled "exegete" who wishes to interpret God's Word to suit his own views. The history of Protestantism, laboring under *sola Scriptura*, is an unending kaleidoscope of fragmentation and splintering.

It cannot provide any sort of doctrinal certitude for the Christian, because it is built on the shifting sand of mere human opinion—what the individual pastor thinks Scripture means. Even Martin Luther saw the inescapable principle of fragmentation and disunity that lies at the heart of *sola Scriptura*. In a letter to Ulrich Zwingli, he complained bitterly about the doctrinal anarchy that was even then rampant among Protestants:

"If the world lasts, it will be necessary, on account of the differing interpretations of Scripture which now exist, that to preserve the unity of faith, we should receive the [Catholic] councils and decrees and fly to them for refuge." Catholics should not flinch when confronted with alleged "biblical" and "historical" arguments for *sola Scriptura*. They fall apart. Scripture and history are the two best apologetics tools for effective evangelization in discussions with Protestants about *sola Scriptura*.

I know firsthand the importance of discussing *sola Scriptura* with Protestants. Having engaged in a number of live debates with Protestant ministers on this subject, I've seen Protestants become flummoxed (some, even converted to Catholicism) when they discover that *sola Scriptura* is simply indefensible.

So, go ahead and jerk their chain. *Sola Scriptura* is by far and away the weakest link.

Catholic Dossier *magazine, March/April 1996*

Going Beyond

||||||||||||||||||||||||||||||||||||||||||||||||||||

RECENTLY, A BAPTIST MINISTER WROTE US A letter. He'd heard a Catholic Answers staffer being interviewed on an Evangelical radio station say, "There is not even a single verse in the Bible which supports the Protestant doctrine of *sola Scriptura*." The minister disagreed, expressing his conviction that 1 Corinthians 4:6 fits the bill: "I have applied these things to myself and Apollos for your benefit, brothers, so that you may learn from us not to go beyond what is written." He asked how Catholics could deny that this verse teaches *sola Scriptura*.

For reasons which will soon become obvious, proponents of *sola Scriptura* don't often turn to 1 Corinthians 4:6. But since it does come up from time to time, Catholics should know how to refute the misuse of this verse. (This article will not address any of the other arguments Protestants use in support of *sola Scriptura*; it will look only at 1 Corinthians 4:6.)

There are several ways to demonstrate that 1 Corinthians 4:6 can't rescue *sola Scriptura* from the realm of myth. First, notice that none of the Reformers attempted to use this verse to vindicate *sola Scriptura*. In fact, John Calvin says Paul's use of the phrase "what is written" is probably either a reference to the Old Testament verses he quotes within his epistle or to the epistle itself.[36] Not only did Calvin not see in 1 Corinthians any support for *sola Scriptura*, a theory he vociferously promoted, he regarded the verse as obscure at best and of negligible value in the effort to vindicate Protestantism.

Some commentators see in 1 Corinthians 4:6 an allusion to "what is written" in the Book of Life (Exodus 32:32–33, Revelation 20:12). This is quite possibly what Paul had in mind, since the context of 1 Corinthians 4:1–5 is divine judgment (when the Book of Life will be opened and scrutinized). He admonishes the Corinthians against speculating about how people will be judged, leaving it up to "what has been written" in the Book of Life. Although that interpretation of the text is a possibility, being consistent with the rest of Scripture, it is by no means certain.

What is certain is that Paul, in saying, "do not go beyond what is written," was not teaching *sola Scriptura*. If he had, he would have been advocating one of four principles, which are inconsistent with the rest of his theology: (1) Accept as authoritative only the Old Testament writings; (2) accept as authoritative only the Old Testament writings and the New Testament writings penned as of the date Paul wrote 1 Corinthians (circa A.D. 56); (3) accept as authoritative orally transmitted doctrine only until it has been reduced to writing (scripture) and only while the apostles are alive, then disregard all oral tradition and adhere only to what is written; or (4) the most extreme position, accept as authoritative only doctrine reduced to writing.

The difficulties with these options are immediately clear. No Protestant would agree with option one, that the Old Testament is a sufficient authority in matters of doctrine. Nor would he accept option two, for this would mean all New Testament books written after the year 56 would not qualify under the 1 Corinthians 4:6 guideline. Hence, John's Gospel, Acts, Romans, 2 Corinthians, Galatians, Ephesians, Philippians, Colossians, Philemon, Titus, 1 and 2 Timothy, Hebrews, James, 1 and 2 Peter, 1, 2, and 3 John, Jude, and Revelation would all have to be jettisoned as non-authoritative.

Option three fails because in order for *sola Scriptura* to be a "biblical" doctrine there must be, by definition, at least one Bible verse which says Scripture is sufficient, or that oral Tradition is to be disregarded once Scripture has supplanted it, or that Scripture is superior to oral Tradition. But there are no such verses, and as we'll see, 1 Corinthians 4:6 is no exception.

Option four is likewise untenable because it contradicts Paul's express command to "Stand fast and hold firm to the traditions that you were taught, either by an oral statement or by a letter of ours" (2 Thessalonians 2:15). Thus, for 1 Corinthians 4:6 to support the theory of *sola Scriptura*, Paul would have been talking out of both sides of his mouth, on one side demanding adherence to the written word only, and on the other urging fastidious adherence to both written and oral tradition.

And then there's that small matter of the unity of doctrine among the apostles. If Paul had been promulgating *sola Scriptura* in 1 Corinthians 4, he would have been in conflict with the practice of the rest of the apostles. Most of the apostles never wrote a single line of Scripture; instead they transmitted the deposit of faith orally. Did their oral teachings carry any less weight of authority than the written teachings of Paul or Peter or John?

None of the other apostles taught *sola Scriptura*. In fact, John said, "I have much to write to you, but I do not wish to write with pen and ink. Instead, I hope to see you soon when we can talk face to face" (3 John 13). Why would the apostle emphasize his preference for oral Tradition over written Tradition (a preference he reiterates in 2 John 12) if, as proponents of *sola Scriptura* assert, Scripture is superior to oral Tradition?

The already flimsy case for *sola Scriptura* is further weakened by Paul's comments in 1 Corinthians 11:2 where he praises the Christians in Corinth for holding fast to the traditions just as he had handed them on to them. It's clear from the context that he was referring to oral Tradition because the Corinthians had as yet no New Testament Scriptures, 1 Corinthians being the very first letter Paul had sent them. Prior to this letter all his teaching had been oral.

The same is true in the case of the Ephesians to whom Paul said, "I did not shrink from proclaiming to you the entire plan of God" (Acts 20:27). This statement undercuts *sola Scriptura*. Paul remained in Ephesus for over two years teaching the faith so diligently that "all the inhabitants of the province of Asia heard the word of the Lord" (Acts 19:10), yet his epistle to the Ephesians is a scant four or five pages and could not even begin to touch upon all the doctrines he taught them orally.

What's more, if Paul had included *sola Scriptura* among the doctrines which comprised "the entire plan of God"—especially in the sense of option three— why didn't he simply say so? Why didn't he tell the Ephesians, "Now that I've written you this letter, you can disregard my two years worth of oral teachings and consider this document to be your sole authority"? Nowhere in his epistles does Paul even hint at such a thing.

An examination of first- , second- , and third-century Church writings shows the early Christians did not believe in *sola Scriptura*. In fact Irenaeus of Lyons (A.D. 140–202) delivered a withering attack on the notion in *Against Heresies*, as did Vincent of Lerins in *Commonitoria* (435). It was not a subject of discussion in any early Church councils, nor was it mentioned in any of the many creeds formulated by the early Church.

Sola Scriptura is the Reformation version of the emperor's new clothes. In their attempt to evade the biblical and historical evidence of the Church's magisterial authority the Reformers insisted on seeing in the Bible a doctrine that simply isn't there.

Don't Touch That Bible!

||||||||||||||||||||||||||||||||||||||||||||||||||||||||||||||||||||||||||||||||||||||||||||||||||||

SOME PROTESTANTS BELIEVE THE CATHOLIC CHURCH USED to forbid its members to read the Bible. The Church couldn't risk letting the average Catholic read the Bible for himself. If that happened, the poor papist would realize he'd been duped by Rome.

"What?" he'd cry upon sneaking a furtive glance at the Good Book. "The Bible disagrees with the Catholic Church! There's no mention here of priests or popes or Mass, much less rosaries or Mary worship. No wonder they wouldn't let me have a close look at it!"

The late Loraine Boettner, in his well-known anti-Catholic handbook, *Roman Catholicism*, perpetuates the myth of the enmity between the Catholic Church and the Bible:

> Up until the time of the Reformation the Bible had been a book for priests only. It was written in Latin, and the Roman Church refused to allow it to be translated into the language of the common people. But when the Reformers came on the scene all of that was changed. Luther translated the entire Bible into German for the people of his native land, and within 25 years of its appearance one hundred editions of the German Bible came off the press. It was also soon translated into most of the vernacular tongues of Europe, and wherever the light of the Reformation went it became the book of the common people. Decrees of popes and church councils gave way to the Word of Life.[37]

Let's examine the facts. Before Luther's translation (1530) there were already at least thirty-three printed German translations, many of them translated from the original Greek and Hebrew, including Fust's at Metz in 1462 and Bemler's at Augsburg in 1467—plus others at Augsburg and Nuremburg in 1477; at Leipzig in 1466 (reprinted at least sixteen times by 1522); at Wittenburg in 1470, 1483, and 1490; at Augsburg in 1518; at Lubeck in 1494; at Cutna in 1498; at Venice in 1506 and 1511.

In fifteenth-century Poland the Bible was translated into the vernacular at the behest of the Catholic Queen Hedwig; a second version was translated soon after by Andrew Jassowitz. In Spain, King Alfonso the Wise (1221–1284) also a Catholic, commissioned the Bible to be translated into Castilian, and Vincent Boniface Ferrier translated it into the Valencian dialect in 1405.

In France, at least sixteen translations were known to be extant before 1547. Archbishop Giacomo of Genoa translated the Bible into Italian around 1220. A Swedish translation was made as early as the mid-fourteenth century, and Iceland had its own translation by 1279. (The monk Nicolo Malerimi's Italian translation had been reprinted at least thirteen times before the "light of the Reformation" had ignited Europe into a conflagration of dissension.)

In addition to European languages, the Bible was being translated under the direction of the Catholic Church in Rome into Arabic, Syriac, Ethiopian, Armenian, Chinese, and Hindi while the Reformation was getting underway.

A common assertion is that there were no Bibles in English until John Wycliffe—touted by Protestants as the "morning star of the Reformation"— came along in 1382. Wycliffe, a Catholic priest and leading Oxford philosopher and theologian, got himself into hot water by his radical ideas on social issues. Later he went into open rebellion against the Church when he attacked the sacrament of penance and the validity of tradition, denied the Real Presence of Jesus in the Eucharist, taught the heretical doctrine of *sola Scriptura*, and railed against the papacy as being the "institution of the Antichrist."

When Wycliffe and his followers the Lollards (a pejorative term meaning "mumblers") issued their own English translation of the Bible, the Church condemned it not because it had been translated into the vernacular—that had been done in the past with the encouragement of the Catholic Church—but because of its source (which in itself was quite enough of a reason to condemn it) and because of its doctrinal errors.

St. Thomas More (1478–1535), Lord Chancellor of England and martyr under Henry VIII, explained the issue: "Wycliffe, whereas the whole Bible was long before his days, by virtuous and well learned men, translated into the English tongue, and by good and godley people with devotion and soberness, well and reverently read, took upon him a malicious purpose to translate it of new."[38]

The 1408 Council of Oxford explained why illicit translations were condemned by the Church:

> It is dangerous, as St. Jerome declares, to translate the text of the Holy Scripture out of one idiom into another since it is not easy, in translating, to preserve exactly the same meaning in all things. We therefore command and ordain that henceforth no one translate any passages of Holy Scripture into English or any other language, in a book or booklet or tract of this kind lately made in the time of the said John Wycliffe or since, or that hereafter may be made either in part or wholly, either publicly or privately, under pain of excommunication, until such translation shall have been approved and allowed by the diocesan bishop of the place or (if need be) by the provincial council.

St. Thomas More evoked the spirit of the Council of Oxford in his condemnation of Wycliffe's translation and in his rebuttal to the Protestant claim that the Church had a history of officially forbidding vernacular translations:

> [The Catholic Church] neither forbiddeth the translations to be read, that were always done of old before Wycliffe's days, nor damneth his because it was new, but because it was nought; nor prohibiteth new

[translations] to be made, but provideth that they shall not be made amiss, till they be, by good examination, amended.[39]

Let's take an extended quotation from Fr. Paul Stenhouse's booklet *Catholic Answers to "Bible" Christians*:

St. Thomas More says, in essence, that the Church, far from forbidding translations, simply believed that standards of translation should be strict. Quality control is taken for granted in all aspects of daily life these days. The Church still expects that Sacred Scripture should be given at least the same respect we pay the food we eat, the homes we inhabit, or the cars we drive!

In 1844, the Rev. S.R. Maitland, librarian to the Archbishop of Canterbury, published a book entitled *The Dark Ages*, in which he demolished, one should have thought forever, the myth that no Catholic (in pre-Reformation England) ever knew his Bible well. None of the facts collected by Maitland, a non-Catholic historian, supports the Fundamentalist claims.

Thus, in 705 St. Adhelm is reported to have bought a Bible from a ship that entered Dover Harbor and presented it to the Abbey of Malmsbury; King Offa, king of the Mercians, presented a Bible to the church at Worcester in 780; Paul, abbot of St. Alban's, in 1077 presented two Bibles, adorned with gold and silver and precious stones, to the church there; his successor, Abbot Walter, donated a "golden text of the Gospels."

Maitland quotes a letter of one monk to another written about 1170: "A monastery without a library is like a castle without an armory. See to it, therefore, that in your armory of defense, the greatest defense of all others is not wanting. That defense is the Holy Bible."

Maitland confesses that in the course of his research he came across not a single instance in which the Bible was treated disrespectfully, and no instance of its being kept from the people. Nor did he discover any hint that the Bible was regarded simply as a valuable piece of furniture, hardly used at all, or simply by the monks themselves. Many of the Bibles to which Maitland refers would have been in Latin, but the author makes frequent reference to copies in Anglo-Saxon.[40]

The Catholic Church is frequently accused of keeping the Bible in Latin so the common man couldn't understand it for himself. Not true. The fact is that the Church encouraged vernacular translations so long as they were (1) faithful to the original texts (or the Latin Vulgate—itself faithful to the original texts) and (2) not translated in an ambiguous way that would promote doctrinal error.

Two points are often missed by both Catholics and Protestants. The first is that until the late Renaissance most Europeans were illiterate. The clergy and the nobility were lettered, but rarely was the common man. The second point is that for those who could read, Latin posed no obstacle. For over a thousand years Latin had been the lingua franca of Europe. One key reason the Church made the Latin Vulgate the official Bible of Christendom was precisely because anyone who could read could read Latin. But what about the poor fellow who couldn't read the Bible? The Bible was read to him.

Very early on, the Bible became increasingly accessible to the average European in his native idiom. Archbishop James Ussher (1581–1656), the Protestant bishop of Armagh, Ireland, and a staunch foe of Roman Catholicism, gives the date for the first English translation of the Bible as 1290 (a century before Wycliffe). But Ussher didn't go back nearly far enough. The Venerable Bede (672–735) translated the entire Bible into Saxon (the precursor of English) so it would be understandable to his flock in England—virtually none of whom yet knew Latin. In 734 he wrote to Egbert, the Archbishop of York, instructing him to preach to the people from the translated Bible, especially from the Pauline epistles.

In 747, at the Council of Cloveshoe, England, the bishops emphasized the importance of reading the Bible in the vernacular, something not easily done if there were no vernacular translations extant. The council further required that the Creed, the Our Father, and the administration of the sacraments should be in the vernacular in order that the people's spiritual benefit might be greater.

In 1109 Pope Innocent III wrote:

> The Bishop of Metz has told us...that many laymen and women too, led by a desire, mainly of understanding the Bible, have translated for themselves the Gospels, the Epistles of St. Paul, [and] the Psalms. Their aim is that with the help of this translation, made at their own discretion—and we could wish that it had been made prudently—laymen and women could expound such matters and preach to each other. Now, the desire to understand the Bible is something to be praised, not condemned. Yet it seems that here certain lay people have justly merited criticism; for they hold meetings in secret and usurp the function of preaching.[41]

In the same way that Protestant ministers would admonish their parishioners not to use the Jehovah's Witnesses defective Bible version—the New World Translation—because of its many errors and misleading footnotes, the Catholic Church also warned (and warns) Catholics to avoid Bible translations that have similar problems. Contrary to the claims made by Loraine Boettner and other non-Catholic writers who want us to believe otherwise, the Catholic Church did not and does not "hide" the Holy Bible from the faithful, but it does take seriously its obligation to shield Christians from inaccurate translations and heretical interpretations of the Bible.

Catholic Answers, *1988*

Those "Extra" Books in the Bible

ONE OF THE HALLMARKS OF PROTESTANTISM IS its rejection of seven Deuterocanonical (second canon) books of the Bible: Tobit, Judith, Wisdom, Ecclesiasticus, Baruch, and 1 and 2 Maccabees, as well as sections of Daniel (3:24–90 and chapters 13 and 14) and of Esther (10:14 to 16:24).

These books have always been accepted by the Church as canonical, and it wasn't until the sixteenth century that the Protestant Reformers removed them from their Bibles. Since they don't contain these seven books, Protestant Bibles are incomplete. This biblical deficiency is particularly ironic because Protestants have long and loudly trumpeted their claim of championing "Biblical Christianity."

The question of which books constitute the canon of Scripture is an especially thorny problem for Protestants when it's juxtaposed against their doctrine of *sola Scriptura* because the very Bible they hold forth as the sole rule of faith is itself incomplete. Those who disagree with the Catholic position that these seven books do belong in the Bible attempt to impugn the integrity of the books claiming, that they "couldn't be canonical because they contain 'unbiblical' doctrines."

For example, Martin Luther, in his effort to refute the Catholic doctrine of purgatory, repudiated the two books of Maccabees mainly because of 2 Maccabees 12:46: "It is a holy and wholesome thought to pray for the dead that they may be loosed from their sins." Luther insisted that since purgatory is an unbiblical doctrine, prayers for the dead are meaningless because those in heaven don't need them and those in hell can't benefit by them, and any book that teaches prayers for the dead is unbiblical and should be removed from the canon. Luther also wanted to delete the Epistle of James (which he called "an epistle of straw"), as well as other books, but was dissuaded by his followers from doing so. Luther's error here was calling a doctrine unbiblical only because, after he removed the offending book from the lineup, he couldn't find the doctrine in the Bible.

Evangelical author Josh McDowell's bestselling book *Evidence That Demands a Verdict* levels the standard Protestant argument against the inspiration of Tobit and Judith.

The problem as McDowell sees it is that major (and holy) figures in both of these books are found to have lied. In the case of Tobit, Raphael deliberately lied to Tobias by claiming to be a man when, in reality, he was an angel (Tobit 5:4–5).

In Judith, the Jewish heroine asked God to bless her lies against the enemy king Holofernes (Judith 9:9–13). McDowell claims that Tobit and Judith are disqualified from the canon because Raphael, as an angel, wouldn't lie, and Judith, if she really was holy, wouldn't defy biblical prohibitions against lying in Exodus 20:16, Proverbs 6:16–19, and Proverbs 12:22.

The problem with this argument is that although God doesn't approve of lying per se, the mere incident of deception doesn't automatically disqualify a book from being canonical. If it did, Protestants would have to reject many other books that they accept as inspired. In the Old Testament angels passed themselves off as human beings. Take, for example, the three "men" who appeared to Abraham by the oaks of Mamre (Genesis 18:1). Two of them were angels (Genesis 19:1), and the third man seems to have been a theophany—a pre-Incarnation appearance of Christ.

There's also the incident of Jacob wrestling with an angel who pretended to be a man (Genesis 32:22–32). In Genesis 12:10–20 and 20:1–18 both Abraham and Sarah lied to Pharaoh and later to King Abimelech by claiming to be brother and sister. In Genesis 27:1–39, Jacob, the future patriarch Israel, deliberately deceived his blind father Isaac and stole Esau's birthright. In Judges 4:19–20 we read of Sisera instructing Jael to lie to anyone asking if he is in her tent (she agreed, but later, when he was asleep, drove a tent peg through his head). James 2:25 tells us that "Rahab the harlot also was justified" when she deceived her countrymen by hiding Jewish spies and helping them escape from Jericho (see Joshua 2:1–21).

In Hebrews 13:2 Paul says, "Do not neglect to show hospitality to strangers, for by this some have entertained angels without knowing it." Paul's words imply that angels have disguised themselves as human beings. It would be to harsh to call that lying, but at the very least it is a deliberate deception. Christ himself disguised his identity from the two disciples on the road to Emmaus, giving them the impression he was a fellow traveler who was unaware of the events in Jerusalem (Luke 24:13–31).

The fact that he did so deliberately is demonstrated by verse 16: "Their eyes were prevented from recognizing him." It seems Jesus was having a bit of sport with the two men because in addition to disguising his identity "he gave them the impression he was going on farther" (verse 28). John 7:8–10 relates that Jesus told his disciples he wasn't going to go up to the feast, and then later did. The Gospel goes so far as to say that Jesus "himself also went up, not openly but [as it were] in secret."

Did Jesus deceive the disciples? It would appear that he did, although not in a sinful way. The question is: If one accepts the Protestant charge that Tobit and Judith are uncanonical because they contain "unbiblical" examples of lying, what do we do with the books of Genesis, Joshua, Judges, John, Hebrews, James, and the other canonical books which contain similar accounts of deliberate deception?

Catholic Answers, *December 1989*

A Catholic/Protestant Debate on *Sola Scriptura* Between Patrick Madrid and Douglas Jones

||||||||||||||||||||||||||||||||||||||||||||||||||||||||||||||||||||||||||||||||||||||||||||||||||||||||||||||||||||||||||||||||||

This written debate on *sola Scriptura* between Patrick Madrid, editor of *Envoy Magazine* and Douglas Jones, editor of *Credenda/Agenda,* a Reformed Evangelical Protestant journal, appeared recently in *Credenda/Agenda* (1996). It was agreed that Doug would select and frame the debate theme, he would have the first *and* last comment in the exchange, and each response would be limited to no more than 115 words.

DEBATE THEME (selected and framed by Doug Jones)

What is the relationship between Scripture and the Church? Is Scripture or the Church the supreme and infallible judge of truth?

DJ: Many modern evangelicals and Roman Catholics haggle over the Anabaptistic notion of *solo* rather than *sola Scriptura.* The classical Protestant notion of that doctrine was never intended as a condemnation of tradition or a denigration of the authority of the Church. Both Scripture and the Church are genuinely authoritative norms, not mere advisory boards. Protestants maintain that Scripture is the ultimate authority, with the Church serving as a subordinate, though real, authority. In practice, conservative Roman Catholicism reverses this hierarchy, necessitating an infallible Church. The debate with Rome over *sola Scriptura* really turns on the question of Rome's claim to infallibility. If it can't justify that claim, then *sola Scriptura* takes the day rather easily.

PM: Since you concede that the Church is "genuinely authoritative," not a mere advisory board, I have this debate already half won. The other half will be to demonstrate that this means Scripture is not sufficient *in se* for all matters of doctrine. For if, to be correctly interpreted, Scripture needs a magisterial Church (as I believe Christ intended), then *sola Scriptura*, as promulgated by *The Westminster Confession of Faith*, is an erroneous concept. "Geneva" asserts:

"The only infallible rule of interpretation of Scripture is the Scripture itself."[42] Rome responds: "Tradition, Sacred Scripture and the teaching authority of the Church…are so linked and joined together that one cannot stand without the others."[43]

DJ: Notice, though, what you do here. You have to treat the classical Protestant teaching on the genuine authority of the Church *(potestas ordinis)* as though it were a modern "concession." But classical Protestants never held to such Anabaptistic views as you suppose. Connected to this, your third sentence assumes that genuine spiritual authority requires infallibility. This is clearly false, though. We would agree that parents have genuine spiritual authority without being infallible. Isn't it a *non sequitur,* then, for Rome to insist the Church must be infallible to be authoritative? If you want to undermine the classical view, you need to criticize, not sole sufficiency, but the claim that Scripture alone is the ultimate and infallible norm.

PM: Stop flailing at the poor Anabaptists. It remains for you to make good the *WCF's* claim that "the only infallible rule of interpretation of Scripture is the Scripture itself." Where does the Bible teach that? Which pre-Reformation Church council or creed taught that? Scripture doesn't and the Church never did. (Historically, the "classical" view is Rome's, not Geneva's.) The "parent/ child" analogy doesn't obtain. One needn't assume the need for an infallible Church. I recognize this as Christ's intention (vis. the historical and Scriptural evidence). And you've just demonstrated why Scripture requires an infallible Church, by claiming the Anabaptist view is "incorrect." The Anabaptists sure think it's what Scripture teaches. Who decides? Aren't they just being consistent with the *WCF* claim?

DJ: Flailing Anabaptists must remain an important hobby, especially since Rome tries to force everyone into an individualistic mold. For example, you read your cite of the *WCF* as claiming that only individuals can infallibly interpret Scripture, a position rejected by the Westminster divines and the Reformers. The Church has genuine interpretive authority like a supreme court, but Rome's novelty is to insist that this authority must be infallible.

That runs contrary to Scriptural descriptions of an authoritative Church which in abnormal times may teach falsehood (Jeremiah 6:13; 14:14; Isaiah 29:10; Ezekiel 22:25; 2 Peter 2:2; Acts 20:29; 1 Timothy 4:1). You ask, "Who decides?" The answer does require authority, but how does it require infallibility?

PM: I'm simply trying to force you to defend the *WCF* claim, but you seem unwilling to do so. You haven't explained how Scripture can be its own "infallible interpreter," where Scripture claims this, and when Scripture ever actually functioned as such. These elements must be proven if you're to vindicate the *WCF* version of *sola Scriptura*. I contend that you can't prove them since your position is epistemologically untenable. The "who decides?" dilemma pivots on the a priori question: "Which 'church' is the Church?" Under the *WCF* rubric, you can't even determine that with certitude; just as you can't be completely certain the Anabaptist or any view (Rome's, for example) is incorrect. That certainty requires infallibility, otherwise, you're simply guessing.

DJ: Actually, I've defended that *WCF* claim in each of my previous paragraphs; it's just another aspect of the teaching that Scripture is the "supreme judge" (I, X). If Scripture alone is ultimate and infallible, then it certainly doesn't contradict itself (I, IX). So, for our discussion, anything showing the infallibility of Scripture and the fallibility of the Church is an argument for *sola Scriptura*. I've supplied passages pointing to the Church's fallibility. I now argue by challenge that Rome's exegetical arguments for infallibility are simple non-sequiturs. Moreover, your epistemological argument for infallibility starts an infinite regress: if we need infallibility to interpret Scripture, then we'll need it to interpret the Church, and so on. What help is that?

PM: Please furnish even one example of Scripture interpreting itself. I reject your interpretation of the verses you cited and your premise that "Scripture alone is…infallible." On the contrary, Christ's Church is infallible (see Matthew 10:40, 16:18, 18:18, 28:20; Luke 10:16; John 14:25–26,16:13; 1 Thessalonians 2:13; 2 Timothy 3:15). Your argument entails the conclusion that the dogmas promulgated by Nicaea I, Ephesus, and Chalcedon were merely fallible, as was the Church's determination of the NT canon. (If this is true, we're all in big trouble!) Your syllogism is flawed, and it's no non sequitur to claim that Scripture requires an infallible Church (see 2 Peter 1:20–21; 3:15–16). And this debate is your perfect opportunity to prove otherwise: Please demonstrate how Scripture can "infallibly interpret itself" so as to solve this particular standoff.

DJ: Your ongoing concern about self-interpretation is really not particularly relevant to *sola Scriptura*. "Interpreting itself" is just another way of saying that clearer passages shed light upon the less clear. Every ultimate norm, including yours, does that (see John 10:35). More to the point are your proofs for Church infallibility. First, regarding councils, you again assume that fallibility entails falsehood. Must parents and courts always judge falsely? Second, the passages cited prove too much or too little. Those speaking of leading the Church into "all truth" clearly go beyond Rome's very narrow subset of infallible truths. Why preclude science and economics? Others cited speak of preserving the Church, but something can be preserved without being infallible. Infallibility simply doesn't follow.

PM: Actually, the claim that "the only infallible rule of interpretation of Scripture is the Scripture itself" lies at the very heart of this disputation. Can Scripture "decide" which passages are clear and which are unclear? (Matthew 16:18–19 seems quite clear to me.) Of course not, but the Church can, and before the Reformation the Church consistently taught the Catholic model of authority, not *sola Scriptura*. Since you've admitted the Church has real authority, why don't you adhere to its historic teaching? Or is this authority merely a convenient prop? Finally, fallibility entails the possibility not the necessity of error. Under your "fallible Church" rubric, you can never be certain which Scriptural interpretations are erroneous and which aren't.

DJ: Careful. Your challenge, "Can Scripture decide?" again works only against *solo* not *sola Scriptura*. We both agree that, along with classical Protestants and the WCF, the Church alone should decide authoritatively. She weighs passages for clarity, allowing one passage to clarify another. This model is far more historic than Rome's late novelties, and I gladly adhere to it. And if an infallible Church provides the certainty you demand, why is Rome still debating the meaning of

Trent? Subjectivism can't just stop with Scripture. You have yet to show how my arguments against Roman infallibility fail. But can we at least agree that if the Church is fallible, then only Scripture can be ultimate and infallible?

PM: We agree that the Church weighs passages, but notice that it has always done considerably more than that. The aforementioned councils show that since apostolic times the magisterium saw itself as teaching infallibly, imposing its interpretation of Scripture as dogmatic (see Acts 15:28, 1 Thessalonians 2:13). St. Athanasius explained in *De Decretis* that First Nicaea's definition of Christ as *homoousious* with the Father was not a merely fallible interpretation. This is hardly a "Roman novelty," as you allege. (The nascent Catholic model is visible in Acts 15:15–35, 16:4.) And remember, Orthodoxy also rejects *sola Scriptura*. Like the Catholic Church, they have preserved the ancient Christian teaching that the Church, at least in its ecumenical councils, teaches infallibly. Historically, *sola Scriptura* is the novelty.

DJ: There is simply no such thing as the historic view on these matters. Several competing views always existed side by side (though not the solo view). Even by the late medieval period, the Church still struggled to clarify notions of tradition and Scripture. And Athanasius's *De Decretis* is a particularly weak buttress for Rome, since Athanasius appeals to countless Scriptures to justify Nicaea's language. Why not just cite the council and cease all disputing, as Rome's notion entails? And Eastern Orthodoxy openly rejects Rome's sweeping claims about definitive conciliar infallibility. But quite apart from these concerns, you still haven't provided any rebuttal to the arguments against Roman infallibility. If that fails, then *sola Scriptura* follows easily.

PM: Your dismissal of *De Decretis* as "weak" evidence boggles the mind. Athanasius composed it precisely to refute the Arian claim that the Church teaches fallibly and erroneously. He did appeal "just to the council" to quell the dispute (as Orthodoxy does): "The Confession arrived at Nicaea was, we should say, more sufficient and enough by itself for the subversion of all religious heresies and for the security and furtherance of the doctrine of the Church."[44] Earlier, you mentioned, "Rome's very narrow subset of infallible truths." Now you decry "Rome's sweeping claims about…infallibility." You're dodging here. Ultimately, to vindicate *sola Scriptura*, you must explain how Scripture infallibly interprets itself. So far you haven't.

DJ: You'll find the explanation of self-interpretation in my fourth through sixth paragraphs. My "sweeping" and "narrow" describe different features. Interestingly, you don't cite *De Decretis* itself. There's nothing in it or *Ad Afros* contrary to a classical Protestant view. Sufficiency is far from Roman infallibility. I suspect you're still pursuing Anabaptist ghosts. Elsewhere Athanasius actually understates conciliar authority more than I would, claiming, "Vainly do they run about with the pretext that they have demanded councils for the faith's sake; for divine Scripture is sufficient above all things."[45] I'm sincerely curious why you haven't rebutted my criticism that your case proves too much and too little. Without a response, doesn't my syllogism stand uncontested?

PM: Remember, fallibility entails the possibility, not the inevitability, of teaching error. This possibility creates your dilemma. Under *sola Scriptura*, you can't know with certitude if Scripture is being interpreted correctly. Agreeing with an interpretation is vastly different from knowing it's true. This is why your criticisms and syllogism fail. The passages cited here cannot, in 115 words, be adequately analyzed, but I have indeed rebutted your understanding of them repeatedly, showing that epistemologically, historically, and practically, *sola Scriptura* is a paper tiger. It's not taught in Scripture (you've provided no direct evidence), it's alien to historic Christian teaching and praxis, and it simply doesn't work. If it did, why doesn't Scripture infallibly resolve this standoff?

DJ: Why doesn't Roman infallibility resolve this standoff? In the end, all your epistemological and practical objections apply equally against your own position. Similarly, if fallibility always precluded "certitude," then unless we had infallible civil courts, we could never have justice with certitude. But that's absurd (Ezekiel 45:9). Throughout, my argument has been: (1) Either Scripture or the Church alone is infallible and ultimate; (2) It's not the case that the Church alone is infallible and ultimate (my paragraphs three and five); (3) Scripture alone is infallible and ultimate. With this, the Church is a genuinely authoritative, sufficient (as with Athanasius), anti-individualistic, and reformable Court. Both Rome and modern evangelicalism join arms in rejecting these ancient truths.

Well, Patrick, we have to stop somewhere. We both have more to say. I've wanted to have this little chat for some time. And you have been, as always, a gentleman and an honorable opponent. I wish we could be on the same side. You have my sincere thanks.

Credenda/Agenda *magazine 1996*

Post Script: Even though more than a few of my Catholic friends and colleagues complained that the structure of this written debate with Doug Jones was "unfair" (i.e., he got to frame the debate and he got the first and last comments, etc.), I didn't mind a bit. It was a good opportunity to get some Catholic responses and challenges in front of an almost exclusively Calvinist Protestant readership who might never otherwise have encountered them. For that reason alone, I didn't mind the lopsided nature to this written debate.

—Patrick Madrid, 2012

The Madrid/Jones Dialogue on
Scripture and the Church

Catholic writer Patrick Madrid and Reformed writer Douglas Jones were invited to ask each other a question for this dialogue on Scripture and the Church and then given the opportunity to reply to the original essays.

Patrick Madrid's Question:

The Westminster Confession of Faith asserts, "The only infallible rule of interpretation of Scripture is the Scripture itself." I contend that this proposition is unworkable. Given the substantive doctrinal divisions among Protestant denominations that adhere to *sola Scriptura*, can you explain how Scripture infallibly interprets itself and show post-Reformation examples of this?

Doug Jones's Response:

We should always find ourselves with some sorrow when entering into these sorts of discussions. Many things beautiful in medieval Christendom have been lost, and both Rome and Protestantism share the blame. But the issues surrounding the authority of Scripture and the church are not light or dismissible, for they are stained with martyrs' blood and marked out by ancient covenantal threats.

Most of the differences between classical Protestantism on one side and Rome and Constantinople on the other stem from a background clash between Hebraism and Hellenism. The Reformation was one of the fruits of the late medieval period's attempt to throw off the shackles of Hellenism and revive Hebraic, covenantal thinking. When classical Protestants, especially those of us in the Reformed tradition, gaze at the issues that separate these groups (redemption, authority, worship), many of us cannot help but see that Rome and the East have not yet extricated themselves from the dark labyrinths of Plato and Aristotle.

Thematically, Protestants carried forth Athanasius's praise of the demise of Greek philosophy—"not only does the wisdom of the Greeks no longer make any progress, but that which used to be is disappearing." But the battle has been longer than he expected.

My friend Patrick Madrid, whom I greatly respect, asks a question above about *sola Scriptura* which shows some of this Hellenistic/Hebraic conflict. One of the biggest contemporary confusions about the Protestant doctrine is that between *sola* and what can be called "*solo Scriptura*." These two notions are really worlds apart. The former (*sola*) is the classical Protestant view with deep medieval and patristic roots, namely the teaching that Scripture is the only infallible and supreme *criterion of* truth.

Whereas the latter view (*solo*) is the more Anabaptistic, individualistic, evangelical view that Scripture is the only *location* of truth and authority. The difference between the two views is akin to the difference between a constitution as the *highest* law of the land over an authoritative court, on one side, and a constitution as the *only* law of the land without any courts. Tragically, the Anabaptistic view has clearly taken the field in modern evangelicalism.

Richard Muller has noted that the Reformation arguments "against the idea of a co-equal authority of Scripture, tradition, and church, typically summarized by the phrase *sola Scriptura*, must never be taken as a condemnation of tradition or a denigration of the authority of the church.... The Reformation took as its point of departure the late medieval debate over the relation of Scripture to tradition and assumed that tradition stood as a subordinate norm under the authority of Scripture and derived its authority from Scripture."

Patrick's question misses the heart of the debate, since all sides invoke self-interpretation. All "self-interpretation" means is that there is no higher epistemological appeal; the highest norm must be consistent with itself. I suspect Patrick is personifying "self-interpretation" and reading it as making the constitution also the court itself, but that is the Anabaptistic position. Elsewhere the *WCF* teaches that the church holds the power of interpretation. Chrysostom expresses self-interpretation well: "Sacred Scripture whenever it wants to teach us something like this, gives its own interpretation, and doesn't let the reader go astray.... So, I beg you, block your ears against all distractions of that kind, and let us follow the norm of Sacred Scripture."[46] Historical examples of this can be found at just about every ecclesiastical council, pre- and post-Reformation.

Since we share a commitment to the infallibility of Scripture, the heart of the debate with Rome over *sola Scriptura* really turns on the question of the church's infallibility. If Rome can't justify that claim, then *sola Scriptura* prevails rather easily. *Sola Scriptura* maintains that the church has genuine interpretive authority like a supreme court, but Rome's novelty is to insist that this authority must be infallible. That, however, runs contrary to Scriptural descriptions of an authoritative church that in abnormal times may teach falsehood (see Jeremiah 6:13; Isaiah 29:10; Ezekiel 22:25; 2 Peter 2:2; Acts 20:29; 1 Timothy 4:1). Moreover, Rome's positive exegetical arguments for infallibility are simple *non-sequiturs*. None of the appeals to the church's perseverance or "leading into all truth" entail infallibility. And the stated need for an infallible Church creates a vicious infinite regress: if we need infallibility to interpret Scripture with "certitude," then we'll need it to interpret the church with "certitude," and so on. What help is that?

Now when critics deny that the early church held to *sola Scriptura*, they have to have the Anabaptistic notion in mind. You certainly won't find the Anabaptistic notion in the early church or Scripture, but that's no great victory since you won't find the *solo* doctrine among the classical Protestants either. Among the Fathers, though, we can often hear early forms of the *sola* notion, as in Basil's *Moralia:* "The hearers who are instructed in the Scripture should examine what is said by the teachers, receiving what is in conformity with Scripture and rejecting what is opposed to them."

Now, this is a bit too individualistic for classical Protestants, but it's a start. Yet the common reply to this claim is to take us immediately to Basil's famous statements about unwritten traditions. But notice how that reply misfires. It works only against the Anabaptistic notion concerned with location of truth; unwritten tradition doesn't count at all against Scripture as the ultimate criterion of truth. If we aren't confusing *solo* for *sola*, then we can easily find the classical Protestant teaching throughout the Fathers.

But then the howls start, since admittedly and shamefully, modern evangelicalism's fragmentation bears little resemblance to the unity of the church in the Fathers' time. One answer to that is that modern evangelicalism has abandoned *sola* for *solo Scriptura*. In addition, "Protestant fragmentation" is only an objection against *sola Scriptura* if we have a very un-Hebraic view of the church. From Abraham's time on, the church has faced both institutional unity and fragmentation, yet the church persevered even during apostasy and exile. The Jewish Sanhedrin in the first century had much more institutional unity than the early Christians, but it was apostate. In the Hebraic mindset, institutional unity is no guarantee of covenantal faithfulness. The Apostle Paul raised covenantal threats similar to those of Moses: "If God did not spare the natural branches, he may not spare you either" (Romans 11:21).

Many of the Fathers had a far more Hebraic understanding of the church than does Rome. Jerome tells us that, "The church does not consist in walls, but in the truth of her doctrines. The church is there, where true faith is. But fifteen or twenty years ago heretics possessed all walls here, for twenty years ago heretics possessed all the churches here; the church however was where true faith was."

Similarly, Hilary teaches us, "I warn you of one thing: beware of Antichrist, for the love of walls has taken you badly; you venerate the church of God badly in houses and buildings.... Is it doubtful that Antichrist will have his seat in these?" Unity is sometimes a veneer for apostasy and fragmentation the scar of faithfulness.

Contemporary Protestant fragmentation won't stay with us forever. The Enlightenment joke is growing more stale by the minute. By the Spirit's work in fulfillment of divine promises, the Protestant Church will one day be both faithful and institutionally united. Until then, we have to imitate Elijah's patience. But we ought not reject the ancient doctrine of *sola Scriptura* for dangerous Roman novelties.

Doug Jones's Question:

The debate over *sola Scriptura* is at base a debate over the nature of the church. We both agree that the church has real authority, but why do you think the church must be infallible?

Patrick Madrid's Response:

Which "church" do you mean? One of the Eastern Orthodox Churches? The Catholic Church? What about the Lutherans, Anglicans, Orthodox Presbyterians, Church of Christ, Calvary Chapel, or the Reformed Baptists? Is it the Presbyterian Church in America or the independent, "Bible-believing" fellowship down the street? The twin fallacies of ambiguity and of begging the question lurk at the heart of your question. Before you can deny the infallibility of the "church," you must first define which church you mean.

You accord "real authority" to the Church, but what does this mean? Where exactly is this authority located? Who exercises it? When and how is it used? What are its limits? The Catholic Church has concrete answers to these questions and can furnish sixteen centuries of pre-Reformation evidence that its model of authority (Scripture, Tradition, and Magisterium) works. For *sola Scriptura* to be more than a mere slogan, it must be demonstrable in practice. Can you show us where *sola Scriptura* has actually worked?

This debate is not about the Church, but about the nature of the Scriptures that the Church recognizes as canonical. *Sola Scriptura* entails formal sufficiency— that all revelation necessary for the Church to possess is presented formally in Scripture. Catholics and Eastern Orthodox reject this. Vatican II said, "Tradition, Sacred Scripture and the teaching authority of the Church...are so linked and joined together that one cannot stand without the others."[47]

St. Athanasius wrote: "The very tradition, teaching, and faith of the Catholic Church from the beginning was preached by the apostles and preserved by the Fathers. On this the Church was founded; and if anyone departs from this, he neither is nor any longer ought to be called a Christian."[48]

A major disproof of *sola Scriptura* is the New Testament canon. There's no "inspired table of contents" in Scripture listing the canonical books. This divinely revealed information comes to us from outside Scripture, through the

Church. If Christ's Church is not infallible, then you can have no certainty that the books in your Bible belong there.

But Christ's Church indeed teaches with his infallible authority: "He who listens to you, listens to me; and he who rejects you rejects me" (Luke 10:16; see Matthew 10:40, 16:18, 18:18, 28:20, John 14:25–26, 16:13, 1 Thessalonians 2:13; 1 Timothy 3:15). Christian orthodoxy has always been measured by adherence to the Church's doctrinal interpretations of Scripture.

In contrast, the *Westminster Confession of Faith* declares: "The only infallible rule of interpretation of Scripture is the Scripture itself." But where does Scripture teach this? The *Westminster Catechism* says: "The whole counsel of God, concerning all things necessary for his own glory, man's salvation, faith, and life is either expressly set down in Scripture, or by good and necessary consequence may be deduced from Scripture." For this to be true, *sola Scriptura* itself must be "expressly set down in Scripture, or...deduced from Scripture."

But where does Scripture teach *sola Scriptura?* What pre-Reformation creed or council taught it? If *sola Scriptura* were part of "the faith once for all handed on to the saints" (Jude 3), we'd expect to find it everywhere in the early Church. But we don't. The patristic testimony alone leaves *sola Scriptura* squashed flat.

For example, the early Church taught the doctrine of baptismal regeneration, a doctrine you reject. Conversely, it did not teach *sola Scriptura*, a doctrine you embrace. So if we can at least agree that "the Church: equates with the Church Saints Athanasius and Augustine wrote about, isn't it safe to say that you are doctrinally at odds with that Church, at least on baptismal regeneration? And if so, why do you claim that the Church has "real authority," if you are not bound by it? Or is this authority merely just a convenient prop?

St. Cyril of Jerusalem wrote that the Church "is called Catholic, then, because it extends over the whole world, from end to end of the earth, and because it teaches universally and infallibly each and every doctrine which must come to the knowledge of men, concerning things visible and invisible, heavenly and earthly and because it brings every race of men into subjection to godliness."[49]

The *Catechetical Lectures* are packed with Catholic doctrines: the Mass, the efficacy of prayers for the dead, the Real Presence of Christ in the Eucharist, the intercession of the saints, holy orders, baptismal regeneration, and many other doctrines Protestants reject as "unscriptural."

The First Council of Constantinople proclaimed the Church's belief in "baptism for the remission of sins" and warned it would "anathematize every heresy which is not of the same mind of the holy, Catholic, and apostolic Church of God" (Canon 7, A.D. 381).

As a Reformed Christian, you *don't* believe in baptism for the remission of sins, basing your position on Scripture. *Sola Scriptura* has put you at odds with the Church you admit has authority over you.

St. Augustine defined orthodoxy as the assent to all the doctrines taught by the Church: "It is in fact that the Church is called 'Catholic' because it truly embraces the whole of that truth, some particles of which may be found even in various heresies."[50]

This "whole truth" didn't include *sola Scriptura*, nor was it transmitted according to the *sola Scriptura* model. St. Basil of Caesarea expressly denied *sola Scriptura:* "Of the beliefs and practices whether generally accepted or enjoined which are preserved in the Church, some we possess derived from written teaching; others we have delivered to us in a mystery by the apostles by the tradition of the apostles; and both of these in relation to true religion have the same force."[51]

St. Vincent of Lerins said:

> I have often then inquired earnestly and attentively of very many men eminent for sanctity and learning, how and by what sure and so to speak universal rule I may be able to distinguish the truth of Catholic Faith from the falsehood of heretical depravity; and I have always, and in almost every instance, received an answer to this effect: that whether I or anyone else should wish to detect the frauds and avoid the snares of heretics as they rise, and to continue sound and complete in the Catholic Faith, we must, the Lord helping, fortify our own belief in two ways: first, by the authority of the Divine Law [Scripture],

and then by the Tradition of the Catholic Church. But here some one perhaps will ask, 'Since the canon of Scripture is complete, and sufficient of itself for everything, and more than sufficient, what need is there to join with it the authority of the Church's interpretation?' For this reason: Because, owing to the depth of Holy Scripture, all do not accept it in one and the same sense, but one understands its words in one way, another in another, so that it seems to be capable of as many interpretations as there are men.... therefore, it is very necessary, on account of so great intricacies of such various error, that the rule for the right understanding of the prophets and apostles should be framed in accordance with the standard of ecclesiastical and Catholic interpretation.[52]

That standard never included *sola Scriptura*.

Sola Scriptura is a paper tiger. It's not taught in Scripture, it's alien to historic Christian teaching and practice, and it simply doesn't work.

Doug Jones's Follow-up:

I sincerely wish my always-honorable friend Patrick and I could be on the same side of these issues, but alas, we'll just have to keep talking and hoping for now.

The sum of Patrick's answer to my initial question is that without an infallible church, Christians can have no certainty. He didn't elaborate on this, but as it stands it's rather problematic. Consider how this conflicts with our views of other authorities, such as civil courts and parents.

Both of these are intimately involved in applying standards of justice, and yet both are fallible authorities. But on Patrick's view, we could never be sure about any questions of justice. In fact, we could never know what justice is.

Even more problematic is the infinite regress produced by Patrick's infallibility claim. If an infallible Scripture is so cursed by subjectivity that we need an infallible interpreter, then we can't stop there. We will also need an unending row of infallible interpreters at each subsequent stage. We end up in an almost postmodern subjectivism.

As to Patrick's scriptural proofs, notice that they prove too much or too little.

They prove too much because they are so general as to include everything the church would say, but Rome severely narrows what it will count as infallible. They prove too little because they are wonderful exhortations to faithfulness and perseverance, but neither of these entails infallibility. And remember that the rub about the claim to church infallibility is that if it's false, then *sola Scriptura* follows rather quickly, since Scripture would be the only infallible authority left.

Patrick's other criticisms apply only against the *solo* location view. Note that even that favorite "major disproof" regarding the canon assumes the *solo* view—that is, no table of contents "in Scripture." And even if that criticism could be transformed to apply against the classical Protestant view, it would also prove that the Old Covenant Church never had authoritative revelation.

Patrick's other challenges about the definition of the church, patristic testimony, and pre-Reformation councils were already discussed in my opening essay. And as much as all sides of this issue long for the wonderful truths expressed by Vincent of Lerins, none of us can legitimately hold it up while the East and West remain divided. In the end, the most interesting part of this discussion for me is that continuing background conflict between Hellenistic and Hebraic assumptions.

Patrick Madrid's Follow-up:

The Catholic position doesn't entail *non sequiturs* or an infinite regress. Scripture is infallible, yes, but it cannot box our ears, rap our knuckles, or cry out, "Hold on! You've misunderstood!" But the Church can.

The infallibility of the Church derives from the fact that she is a living organism, the bride of Christ, teaching and sanctifying with his authority and guidance (see Luke 10:16 again). She explains, clarifies, and answers questions in her councils, for example. When an Arius or a Pelagius pops up with heterodox interpretations of Scripture, the Church can point out where he went wrong. Scripture can't. There is no regress of infallible interpreters.

It's understandable that Doug would wish to shift the focus away from the nature of Scripture to the nature of the Church; doing so will avoid having to deal with thorny issues like the canon and defining what exactly he means by the "church." His response didn't really answer the question "how does Scripture infallibly interpret itself?" We were told it "missed the heart of the debate." Not so.

The *WCF's* expression of *sola Scriptura* (certainly a "classical" Protestant statement) pivots on this assertion. I don't see where Doug has made a case for this.

His appeal to the Fathers actually worsens matters for him. The quote he cites from Chrysostom, for example, makes my point, *a fortiori,* regarding the serious doctrinal divisions among Protestants who adhere to *sola Scriptura.* Chrysostom's writings brim with doctrines such as baptismal regeneration, the Real Presence of Christ in the Eucharist, and the sacrificial character of the Catholic priesthood—doctrines Doug vehemently disagrees with.

Was Chrysostom a bad exegete? Or is it possible that Doug's understanding of Scripture is incorrect on those matters? And if it is, what good does *sola Scriptura* do him?

And then there was the claim that the infallibility of the Church is a "dangerous Roman novelty." How does he account for the teaching of Cyril of Jerusalem in A.D. 350 (among others) that the Catholic Church "teaches universally and infallibly"?

Doug Jones is a man of good will, and I admire the vigor with which he presents his position. But in spite of his considerable talent, the position he defends (*sola Scriptura*) remains untenable, as all errors are. Patristic testimony, logic, and, ironically, Scripture itself, demonstrate this. I invite our readers to study the evidence carefully, prayerfully, and without prejudice.

Regeneration Quarterly, *1997*

Comparative Religions

How many Hindus do you know? Not many, probably. But it's likely you know plenty of folks, including Catholics, who've been influenced by Hinduism or another eastern religion. But it's not just eastern religions that are making their presence felt more and more in western culture.

Islam is on the rise; Judaism, in its various forms, is alive and well; and several large pseudo-Christian religions such as the Jehovah's Witnesses and Mormons are picking up steam (and converts) at a rapid pace. The one thing these major religious ideologies have in common, with the exception of Judaism, is that they're working hard to make converts in the United States and Europe.

Sadly, due to poor catechesis and other such problems, many Catholics today are susceptible to the claims and theologies proposed by these groups and wind up leaving the Church to embrace a new religion or, if they remain in the Church, their faith is permeated and reshaped by non-Catholic influences.

Either option is bad. Therefore, it's crucial that Catholics understand the distinctions between Christianity and the other major religions first, so they can remain strong in their faith in and love for Christ and the Church, and second, so they'll be prepared to heed the Holy Father's call for a "New Evangelization" of the world. This section will offer a basic overview of several major religions and explain where and why they are incompatible with the Catholic Church.

Two will examine Judaism and Hinduism. The former is monotheistic and close to Catholicism in certain respects; the latter is polytheistic (worshipping many gods) and is quite alien to Catholicism. Subsequent articles will examine aspects of the Jehovah's Witnesses and Mormonism.

First, let's take a moment to rehearse what we as Catholics believe. The basic elements are found in the Nicene Creed: Monotheism ("We believe in one God"), the Trinity ("The Father almighty...Jesus Christ, his only Son, Our Lord...and the Holy Spirit, the Lord and Giver of life Who proceeds from the Father and the Son"), the Incarnation of God the Son and his mission of redemption ("For us men and for our salvation He came down from heaven... and for our sake He was crucified"), Christ's Resurrection and conquest of death ("On the third day He rose again in fulfillment of the Scriptures and is seated at the right hand of the Father"), the existence of heaven and hell ("He will come again to judge the living and the dead"), and the Church and the sacraments ("We believe in one, holy, Catholic, and apostolic Church. We acknowledge one baptism for the forgiveness of sins"). We could add to this list of core doctrines other distinctively Catholic doctrines on issues such as the communion of saints, Our Blessed Lady's role in the Church and in Christ's mission of redemption, purgatory, the Mass as a sacrifice, and the entire economy of sacraments.

These Catholic distinctives will be important when we consider the challenge of Protestantism in another article, but for now, let's look at how Catholicism compares with the world's other major religions.

The adage "Enthusiasm is a great engine, but it needs knowledge for fuel" is demonstrably true when it comes to doing apologetics. I am thankful to have learned and relearned this lesson multiple times in the past twenty-five years. For example, as I discuss in my article "Modern Art and Muslims," I had for many years assumed that I understood the deeper theology of the Catholic doctrine of the Trinity until one day in the mid-1980s when I read *Theology and Sanity,* a truly mind-blowing book by master Catholic apologist Frank Sheed (for more about him, see my essay "The Prophet of Hyde Park" elsewhere in this book). That book opened a door for me into a vast new area of knowledge about God that I didn't even know existed. You might say that, before reading that book, I didn't know what I didn't know.

And this is why, as I say, it is a lesson we must learn and relearn our whole lives. Striving to know God requires a great deal of effort, to be sure, but it is effort that comes with a gigantic payoff. It's just common sense: The more you know about God, the more effectively you can speak and write about him, and the better you can explain the truth to others. What's even better, the more you know about God, the more likely it is that you will truly come to know him—something utterly indispensable for any aspiring apologist. As I like to say often, "You can't give what you don't have." As I trace the arc of trajectory of my career, I see a corresponding arc of knowledge that was building, widening, and deepening as I sought to amass as much learning as possible. Along the way, an even more important thing happened: The more I learned, the more I saw how much I needed to learn.

Mormonism has long been a subject of great fascination for me. Twenty-five years ago, when I started in apologetics full-time, I focused a great deal of time and energy studying this religion, its history and teachings, its missionary tactics, and its efforts to portray itself as really just another form of mainstream Christianity—which it definitely is not. Here again, the more I studied, the more compelled I became to go deeper and learn as much as I could so that I would be as well-prepared as possible to help Catholics avoid the errors and misrepresentations of Christian history that are rampant in Mormonism. The two Mormonism-related essays you will read in this book are just "the tip of the iceberg" of my writings and lectures on this subject over the years, especially between 1988 and 1996.

Of all the subjects I think Catholics need to concentrate on when talking with Mormons, their doctrine of a "total apostasy" of the Church is the most important and beneficial for it is, I am convinced, the weakest of the weak links in the Mormon "chain" of doctrines. If it goes down, everything else goes down with it. And that's what I sought to do in the article "In Search of the

Great Apostasy." I wanted to show the average Catholic with no background at all in the history and teachings of Mormonism exactly how to dismantle this pivotal argument of theirs. I have used information I present in this article many times over the years in discussions with Mormons and I encourage Catholics to do so as well.

Modern Art and Muslims

I AM NOT A LOVER OF MODERN art. Perhaps I'm artistically handicapped, but I don't see much to get excited about when I look at a perfectly good piece of canvas that's had paint slopped, splattered, or smeared on it. I find it hard to appreciate what I don't understand.

I'm beginning to wonder, though, if God in his wisdom didn't give me this artistic blind spot to help me in my work as an apologist. My inability to perceive beauty in most modern art has actually helped me explain difficult theological concepts such as the Trinity.

I've always believed in the Trinity, of course, and I guess I've flattered myself thinking I understood it. But it wasn't until I read Frank Sheed's *Theology and Sanity* that I realized I had never remotely grasped the rudiments of the doctrine. Don't get me wrong. I claim no handle on the mystery of the Trinity now, but I'm closer to understanding it than I was.

It wasn't until a recent discussion I had with a Muslim friend of mine that I realized how the Trinity and modern art are related. Ahmed, a devout practitioner of his faith, was arguing against the Christian doctrine of God as being three persons sharing one divine nature (i.e., One God in Three Persons). I tried to explain the Trinity to him, but with little success.

Muslims worship the same God as do Jews and Christians; they refer to him as Allah (Arabic for "God"), but they abhor the Christian doctrine of the Trinity. To them, this is a division of God, a sort of divine partnership, and thus heresy. They can't get beyond the seeming mathematical paradox, the three-equals-one equation.

Islam is correct in its teaching that "there is no God but God, and he is one." But it misses the deeper theological insight, the mystery of the Trinity. Islam teaches that to think of God as more than one, as having "associates," is the supreme blasphemy, and to that extent it's correct. Muslims look at Christians as "polytheists." Our worship of Jesus Christ is, to them, the ultimate slap in God's face.

Muslims are unable to perceive a triune God, much the same as some folks (like myself) are unable to see much beauty in modern art. They don't integrate the idea of the Trinity with their belief in God's utter uniqueness. This is the single greatest obstacle for Christians seeking to evangelize Muslims.

In discussing the Trinity with Ahmed, I took the following tack. I told him about an incident that happened when I was in the eighth grade. My teacher, Sister Carol, brought an unusual piece of art into the classroom. It was white poster board covered with hundreds of black splotches, with no apparent order. We stared at it blankly, having no idea what it might be. Sister Carol told us there was a picture hidden somewhere in that jumbled, incoherent mass of dots and that we would see it only if we looked hard enough.

I stared intently but saw nothing. Then one of the girls squealed and raised her hand. Sister Carol ignored her and waited in amused silence. Soon others saw the hidden picture. After two or three minutes of bewilderment, *I* saw it. It was as though my eyes had suddenly focused. The black dots actually formed a likeness of Jesus. There were his hair, eyes, mouth, and nose. I could no longer see just random splotches even when I tried to. In that instant when I perceived the hidden order, I ceased being able to see what had before been only disorder.

Others had the same experience, but not everyone. Out of thirty children, five couldn't see what the rest saw. Sister Carol walked over to the picture and traced with her hand the outline of Jesus's features. Then three of the five children immediately saw the face. The other two couldn't see it, even with her help. As far as I know, they never did see it. What happened next was odd.

One of the two "blind" kids resigned himself to not being able to see the picture. He wasn't happy about it, but he was resigned. It was the other kid's reaction that surprised me. He told the rest of us he didn't believe there was a picture at all. He was sure that, if he couldn't see it, it couldn't be there. This was all an elaborate hoax by the rest of us to get him to say he saw something that wasn't really there—and then we'd all have a good laugh at his expense.

The memory of this incident helped me explain to Ahmed how Christians can believe that there is only one God, but a God with a triune nature. He had accused me of believing in a "Trinity that doesn't exist." He felt that I was attributing a characteristic to God that God doesn't possess.

I said I was seeing the same God as he, but I was seeing a deeper facet of God, one Ahmed couldn't perceive. When I told him the story about the picture of Jesus, he still wouldn't agree with me about the Trinity (and I didn't expect him to), but I'm sure he got a better insight into Christian thinking, and maybe he even went away thinking that he needed to consider the Christian doctrine of God from another angle. He needed, in other words, a fresh look at it.

The story of the picture, or one like it, can be used to help explain many things that seem at first "impossible," such as the Eucharist, the infinite perfection of God, the very existence of God, or the problem of evil. The key is to note that we often don't see something that's right in front of us.

Catholic Answers, *1988*

Mormon Missionaries: My First Encounter

LET ME TELL YOU ABOUT THE FIRST time I got cornered by a pair of Mormon missionaries. I learned some valuable lessons about how and how not to engage them in debate. It all started with an innocuous comment I made to a neighbor who had a Book of Mormon lying on her kitchen table. I had heard of the work before, but never had seen it, and I asked her what it was about. I should have realized something was astir when I saw the gleam in her eyes as she started to tell me about the book.

After she gave me a synopsis, I figured I'd better save her some time by telling her I was a Catholic, thereby putting to rest any hopes she might have. I thought I had made it plain I was curious about just the book, not the religion. I was wrong.

A few Saturdays later, I heard it—that inevitable knock on the door. Outside stood two sharply dressed guys with name badges emblazoned with the impressive title "Elder." One of them, probably the more senior missionary, shook my hand and informed me that they were representatives of the Church of Jesus Christ of Latter-day Saints and that my neighbor had suggested they visit me and answer any questions I might have about the Book of Mormon.

I was on the spot. I wasn't sure how to handle a discussion of Mormonism with one missionary, let alone with two. The problem was that I knew virtually nothing about that religion. After a few awkward moments of small talk on the porch, I decided to invite them in. We sat down, and the conversation quickly turned to the Book of Mormon. I let them give their spiel uninterrupted, until they made comments about a complete apostasy of the true Church Christ had founded.

As a Catholic, I'd been raised believing the Catholic Church was the true Church. I still am convinced of that fact, but at the time of this encounter I didn't know much about the Church of Jesus Christ of Latter-day Saints.

My Mistakes

For a novice apologist who knew quite a bit about his own faith but next to nothing about theirs, I have to say I didn't do as badly as I could have. That's not to say I didn't make mistakes—I did, plenty of them.

First of all, I let them lead the discussion. Looking back on it, it's easy to see that they had a prepared delivery, and they tried to keep to it. They knew what they were there to accomplish. I didn't. The second failing was that I tried to refute every argument they had against Catholicism with a Bible verse. It was a game of Scriptural badminton. They informed me there was an apostasy in which the Church founded by Christ was distorted until its authority was removed from the Earth by the time of Constantine. I countered with Matthew 16:18 ("and the gates of hell shall not prevail against it"). They brushed this aside and fired off another salvo of verses that seemed to contradict mine. And so it went, back and forth, for half an hour.

To be brutally honest here, I have to admit that if the Mormon authorities had sent a more experienced pair of missionaries, I would have been buffaloed. One mistake these fellows made was to get off the track of their canned presentation. I started to see some chinks in their defenses, and I knew I should try to take advantage of them. Remember, I wasn't winning this debate, but neither were they, and they knew it. After I saw the badminton technique was getting me nowhere, I wised up. I changed my tactics and started to force an issue as far as it would go. For example, we returned to the subject of the apostasy.

Although I didn't know the history or doctrines of the Mormon Church, I knew something about Catholic history. The missionaries and I started to look at what the Bible had to say about Christ's Church. My thesis was that Christ either was lying, miscalculating, or telling the truth in Matthew 16:18.

An Unbroken Chain

They had no satisfactory answer for that one. When I brought up the fact that history and tradition point to an unbroken line of continuity from the apostolic Church to the present day Church, they couldn't refute that. Again and again they left ecclesiastical history and the Bible and appealed to the Book of Mormon. They "testified" to me that they "knew" there had been an apostasy and that the Mormon claims were legitimate. Theirs was the only true gospel, they said. The rest of the conversation centered on their testimony.

They asked me to pray about the "truths" they had told me, and they assured me I would receive a "testimony" from the Holy Ghost (Mormons use "Holy Ghost" instead of "Holy Spirit") that the Mormon gospel is true, and so on. I countered with this line: "How do you explain the fact that I have a strong testimony that's diametrically opposed to yours? What if..." I asked them to consider for a moment the Catholic Church is the true Church and that Catholic doctrines are correct. If so, then their prayers were being heard by my God.

Then, I said, we could assume the reverse, that the Mormons were right and my prayers were heard by their God. Either way, only one God could be the recipient of the prayers. The argument, I said, boiled down to one issue: How is it that we are being heard by the same God, but that we receive drastically different testimonies? How could God testify to you that the Mormon Church is the one true Church, but to me that the Catholic Church is? That doesn't make any sense, but it does show the weakness of a personal testimony as the proof of a religion.

The badminton game was over. We had moved into a more stimulating and more profitable area of debate. The key to getting there was being ruthless in pursuing a subject until it had been examined to the point of impasse. I stumbled on this insight too late in the game, but I learned a lesson. By now the missionaries were uncomfortable. They couldn't give any answer to the question about Christ's promise to his Church in Matthew 16:18. They couldn't offer any logical or historical evidence to show there ever had been an apostasy. They were cornered, and they knew it.

"You're in Bondage to Satan!"

Our conversation ended on a strained note. I demanded more explanations from them on these subjects, but they couldn't produce them. They offered to check with their stake president (a "stake" is like a large Catholic parish) and get answers for me. Their final remark was this: "It's obvious that Satan has clouded your heart and mind so that you're unable to see the truth of the Gospel." That's where they left it. We said our good-byes, and they mounted their ten-speeds and rode off. I hadn't won the debate, at least not in the way I would have liked. And they never gave me a rematch.

Not only didn't I get a return visit from them, I got the cold shoulder from my neighbor after that. But that's okay. I did learn important lessons on how not to debate Mormons. No more Scriptural badminton for me. I knew I'd have to stick with a subject until it had been exhausted, and I had to keep myself from being intimidated through double-teaming. I knew I had to do two things in preparation for that next knock on the door.

First, I had to become more familiar with the facts about the Catholic Church's history. I resolved not to sit still for any of that Emperor Constantine jazz. Second, I had to study up on Mormonism—just the basics, please. I knew that I wouldn't have to do extensive research, and I got what I needed out of a few pamphlets the Mormons put out. I studied them and thought about how to answer the pamphlets' arguments.

That encounter with the missionaries whet my appetite. I realized that I didn't have to be afraid or nervous, just persistent. The same goes for you. Every time there's a knock on the door, it could be another opportunity for you to say, with a big smile, "Hi, elders! I'm glad you're here! I've been waiting for you!"

Catholic Answers, *1988*

In Search of the Great Apostasy

SINCE ITS BEGINNING IN 1830, THE MORMON Church has denied any continuous historical connection with Christianity. Mormonism's founder, Joseph Smith, claimed that in 1820 God the Father and Jesus Christ appeared to him in the woods near his home in Palmyra, New York. Jesus said that for the proceeding seventeen hundred years (give or take a century—Mormonism can't say exactly) the world had been living in the darkness of a total apostasy from the gospel.

This was the answer to a question the young Smith had been pondering. "My object in going to inquire of the Lord was to know which of these sects was right, that I might know which to join.... I asked the personages who stood above me in the light, which of all these sects was right (for at this time it had never entered into my heart that all were wrong), and which I should join. I was answered that I must join none of them for they were all wrong; and the Personage who addressed me [Jesus] said that all their creeds were an abomination in his sight; that their professors were all corrupt."

Smith convinced his credulous followers, most of them simple rural folk, that he'd been chosen, in what Mormons have come to call the First Vision, to be the first post-apostasy prophet—God's handpicked agent charged with restoring the true gospel.

Over the next several years Smith purported to have received additional revelations from "heavenly personages." He claimed that after establishing his church in Palestine, the resurrected Jesus appeared in South America to the

Nephites (Jews who, Smith said, had migrated to the New World between 600 and 592 B.C.) and organized a parallel church there (3 Nephi 11–28).

The new prophet seized on Jesus's words in John 10:16 ("I have other sheep that do not belong to this fold. These also I must lead, and they hear my voice, and there will be one flock, one shepherd") as proof of the Lord's impending South American travel plans. The exegesis might impress one unfamiliar with the New Testament, but the usual understanding is that the "other sheep" Jesus referred to were the Gentiles, to whom the gospel also was extended.

Smith claimed the Nephite church had the same hierarchy and ordinances as its sister church in Palestine—living prophets, twelve apostles, seventy disciples—but things didn't go well for either church. Both collapsed under the weight of pagan influences, dissolving into complete apostasy.

The late Bruce McConkie, a Mormon apostle and, during his life, perhaps Mormonism's leading theologian, explained things this way: "This universal apostasy began in the days of the ancient apostles themselves; and it was known to and foretold by them....With the loss of the Gospel, the nations of the earth went into moral eclipse called the Dark Ages. Apostasy was universal. ...[T]his darkness still prevails except among those who have come to a knowledge of the restored Gospel."[53]

Mormons believe the church Jesus established in Palestine, before its disintegration, was identical to the Mormon Church of today, with ceremonies such as baptism for the dead, a polytheistic concept of God (including eternal progression, the notion that God was a man who evolved into a god and that worthy Mormon males can also evolve into gods), and other peculiar Mormon beliefs. The fact that no historical evidence exists to corroborate this position doesn't put much of a dent in the average Mormon's mental armor.

A chief reason is the devotion Mormons have for Joseph Smith. They hold he was God's mouthpiece. His "revelations" came directly from God. This belief points to Mormonism's weak point. If you can demonstrate to a Mormon that Smith was wrong about the great apostasy, Mormonism crashes down in a heap. If Smith was wrong about this point, he could not have been a true prophet of

God, and Mormonism loses its basis (The Bible has strong words to say about false prophets in Deuteronomy 13:2–6 and 18:20–22.)

If Smith were right about apostasy, then Jesus was a pathetic failure when it came to establishing his Church. After all, what are we to think of his promises? If there really was a complete apostasy, how do we explain our Lord's claim that his Church never would be overcome, "Upon this rock I will build my Church, and the gates of hell shall not prevail against it" (see Matthew 16:19)? What about his promise that he would be with his Church until the end of time (see Matthew 28:20)? What about his promise to send the Holy Spirit as a guide who would abide with the Church (see John 14:16, 26)? What about the Holy Spirit guiding the Church into all truth (see John 16:13)?

A key difficulty for Mormons is that they can't say exactly when the apostasy took place nor can they point to any definitive historical event of it. Other than Smith's claims there is only an interior feeling or testimony on which Mormons can base their beliefs, but such subjective proof proves nothing. There are only a few choices: (1) Jesus's words in the passages just cited were misreported; (2) Jesus did in fact say these things but didn't really mean them—at least not in the way they had been understood by Christians for the first eighteen centuries; (3) Jesus was a liar, or (4) Joseph Smith was wrong and Jesus meant what he said.

Mormonism's claim to be the "restored" church hangs upon there having been a complete apostasy. The late James E. Talmadge, prolific Mormon writer and member of the Quorum of the Twelve Apostles, wrote:

> The Church of Jesus Christ of Latter-Day Saints proclaims the restoration of the Gospel, and re-establishment of the Church as of old, in this, the dispensation of the fullness of times. Such restoration and re-establishment, with the modern bestowal of the holy priesthood, would be unnecessary and indeed impossible had the Church of Christ continued among men with unbroken succession of priesthood and power, since the meridian of time [the time of Christ].
>
> The restored Church affirms that a general apostasy developed during and after the apostolic period, and that the primitive Church lost its

power, authority, and graces as a divine institution, and degenerated into an earthly organization only. The significance and importance of this apostasy, as a condition precedent to the re-establishment of the Church in modern times, is obvious (emphasis added).[54]

Talmadge is correct in evaluating the consequences, of course: if no apostasy, no restoration, and if no restoration, no Mormonism.

Mormons misconstrue the biblical passages that do refer to a "great apostasy" from the Christian Church. They read into the text a complete apostasy. Scripture mentions an apostasy in Matthew 24:4–12; Mark 13:21–23; Luke 21:7–8; Acts 20:29–30; 2 Thessalonians 2:1–12; 2 Timothy 3:1–7, 4:1–4; 2 Peter 2:1–3; and Jude 17–19. Most of these verses say "many" will fall away, and not one mentions a complete apostasy of the Church. Another complication for Mormons is that these verses say the apostasy will take place at the end times, the "latter days" as the King James renders it. The second and third centuries were not the "latter days."

The next time you encounter the apostasy argument, ask the Mormon to read the entire context of whatever verse he's quoting and show you where the writer mentions a complete apostasy. Usually he'll claim a complete apostasy was the intent of the writer and that it's at least implicitly taught in the Bible.

The best way to refute this charge is to have the Mormon read Jesus's promises regarding the doctrinal integrity and the temporal perpetuity of his Church:

"On this rock I will build my Church, and the gates of hell shall not prevail against it" (Matthew 16:18); "Behold, I will be with you always, even until the end of the world" (Matthew 28:20); "The Father. . . will give you another Advocate to be with you always" (John 14:16); "The Advocate, the Holy Spirit that the Father will send in my name, he will teach you everything and remind you of all I have told you" (John 14:26); "But when he comes, the Spirit of truth, he will guide you to all truth" (John 16:13). Go through each of these texts, pointing out that they deny the possibility of a complete apostasy.

Look also at the many New Testament verses which speak of the Church as Christ's own body, such as Romans 12:1–5; 1 Corinthians 12:12–27; Ephesians

3:4–6; 5:21–32; and Colossians 1:18. Since Christ is the mind and head of his Church (Ephesians 4:15–16), animating the body, the members enjoy and organic spiritual union with him (John 15:1–8). It's inconceivable that he would permit his body to disintegrate under the attacks of Satan. The apostle John reminds us that Jesus is greater than Satan (1 John 4:4).[55]

Although, tragically, the gates of hell can and do prevail over individual Christians who succumb to mortal sin and cut themselves off from life-giving union with Christ (Romans 11:22; Galatians 5:4; 2 Peter 2:20–22; 1 John 5:16–17), they can't prevail against the Church Jesus built on the rock of Peter.[56] If they could—if they did—Jesus is made to look foolish for having taught, "Which of you wishing to construct a tower does not first sit down and calculate the cost to see if there is enough for its completion? Otherwise, after laying the foundation and finding himself unable to finish the work the onlookers should laugh at him and say, 'This one began to build but did not have the resources to finish'" (Luke 15:28–30).

Consider another of Jesus's promises: "I will ask the Father and he will send you another Advocate to be with you always, the Spirit of the truth, which the world cannot accept, because it neither sees nor knows it. But you know it because it remains with you, and will be in you. I will not leave you orphans" (John 14:16–18). If Mormons are right about a complete apostasy, Jesus did leave us as orphans—for 1700 years!

One thing Catholics should never do is to try to avoid the fact that there have been immoral and heterodox members in the Church. Jesus didn't promise that the Church wouldn't be menaced by immorality and heterodoxy. Rather, he promised that the wheat and the chaff (good and evil) would be side by side in the Church until the end (see Matthew 13:24–43, 47–50).

In a recent written exchange,[57] Mormon apologist Robert Starling, attempting to prove the divine origin of the Mormon Church, cited the chief Rabbi Gamaliel's prediction regarding the New Testament Church: "[I]f this endeavor or this activity is of human origin, it will destroy itself. If it comes from God, you will not be able to destroy them; you may even find yourselves fighting against God" (Acts 5:38–39). Starling unwittingly undercut his own claim of a great apostasy. Gamaliel was right. The Church Jesus built could not be destroyed.[58]

In refuting Mormonism's theory of a complete apostasy (and in the process Mormonism itself), Catholics should be able to explain how the integrity of the Church was preserved. The answer: apostolic succession, the unbroken continuum of apostolic authority transmitted via the office of bishop.[59] This doctrine is the logical and Scriptural alternative to the Mormon concept of an apostasy and restoration.

Jesus bestowed a unique authority on the twelve apostles. He conferred on them his power to bind and loose in heaven and on earth (Matthew 18:18). He gave them his authority to forgive sins (see John 20:21–23; 2 Corinthians 5:18–20). He designated Peter as his vicar, giving him a special authority to govern the Church (see Matthew 16:18–19; John 21:15–17). He promised the apostles that when they taught, he spoke through them, and that whoever rejected their teachings rejected Jesus himself (see Matthew 10:40; Luke 10:16).

As the Church got off the ground, the apostles transmitted this authority to their successors (Acts 1:15–26). Paul exhorted a newly ordained bishop, "Do not neglect the gift you have, which was conferred on you by the prophetic words with the imposition of hands [ordination] of the presbyterate" (1 Timothy 4:14). Later Paul reminded Timothy that the conferral of apostolic authority was not to be handed on to others without prudent consideration of a candidate's qualifications: "As for the imposition of hands, do not bestow it inconsiderably" (1 Timothy 5:22).

Apostolic succession can be seen clearly in early Christian writings outside the New Testament. Around A.D. 80 Clement, a disciple of Peter and his third successor as bishop of Rome, in his letter to the Corinthians, expounded on many doctrines, including auricular confession, monotheism (Mormons claim the early Church believed in a "plurality of gods" and eternal progression), the ordained priesthood, and apostolic succession.

One of Clement's most telling lines is this: "Our apostles too were given to understand by Our Lord Jesus Christ that the office of bishop would give rise to intrigues. For this reason, equipped as they were with perfect foreknowledge, they appointed the men mentioned before and afterward and laid down a rule once for all to this effect: When these men [bishops] die, other approved men shall succeed to their sacred ministry."[60]

In A.D. 110, Ignatius, bishop of Antioch and disciple of the apostle John, while on his way in chains to Rome to be martyred for the faith, composed letters to six major centers of Catholicism, along the route (Ephesus, Magnesia, Tralles, Philadelphia, Smyrna, Rome). Ignatius provides us with valuable insights into doctrines and practices of the Christian Church at the close of the first century—only one generation removed from the time of Christ. His writings make it clear that the early Church was thoroughly Catholic. His letters contain a recurring exhortation to remain in communion with the bishops who are successors to the apostles:

> Be eager, therefore, to be firmly grounded in the precepts of the Lord and the apostles, in order that whatever you do you may prosper, physically and spiritually in faith and love, in the Son and the Father and in the Spirit...together with your most distinguished bishop and that beautifully woven spiritual crown which is your presbytery and the godly deacons. Be subject to the bishop and to one another.[61]

> Another Church Father, Irenaeus, bishop of Lyons, explained in A.D. 180, "It is possible, then, for everyone to know the truth, to contemplate the tradition of the apostles which has been made known throughout the whole world. And we are in a position to enumerate those who were instituted bishops by the apostles and their successors [down] to our own times; men who neither taught anything like these heretics rave about.

> Since it would be too long to enumerate in such a volume at this the succession of all the churches, we shall confound all those who, in whatever manner, whether through blindness and wicked opinion,

assemble other than where it is proper, by pointing out here the succession of the bishops of the greatest and most ancient church known to all, founded and organized at Rome by the two most glorious apostles, Peter and Paul, that Church which has the tradition and the faith which come down to us after having been announced to men by the apostles. With this Church, because of its superior origin, all churches must agree—all the faithful in the whole world—and it is in her that the faithful everywhere have maintained the apostolic tradition.[62]

The Mormon Church simply has no convincing answer to the ocean of the biblical and historical evidence of which this is just a drop. All of it contradicts the complete apostasy theory. Yet there's another problem with the theory: the problem of silence. There's no evidence of any outcry from the first or second century "Mormons" denouncing the introduction of "Catholic heresies."

Mormons might respond that, since Catholics gained the upper hand in the struggle for control of the true Church, they simply expunged any trace of the Mormons—a comfortable but inviable argument. We have records of many controversies that raged in the early days of the Church (we know in great detail what turmoil the early Church passed through as it fought off various threats to its existence), and there just is no evidence—none at all—that Mormonism existed prior to the 1830s.

It's unreasonable to assume the Catholic Church would allow the survival of copious records chronicling the history, teachings, and proponents of dozens of other heresies, but would entirely destroy only the records of early Mormonism.

If Mormons want their claim of a complete apostasy as to be taken seriously, they must evince biblical and historical evidence supporting it. So far they've come up empty-handed. Honest investigators will see the unavoidable truth: The Mormon "great apostasy" doctrine is a myth. There never has been—nor will there ever be—a complete apostasy. Jesus Christ promised that his Church, established on the rock of Peter, will remain forever. We have his Word on it.

This Rock, July 1991

The Iconoclast Heresy

"ICONOCLASM" (FROM THE GREEK WORD MEANING "IMAGE-BREAKING") is a heresy that opposes the use of religious images, which are called "icons" in the Eastern Church. Iconoclasm manifests itself in virtually all Protestant denominations as well as in religions as diverse as Islam, Mormonism, and the Jehovah's Witnesses. Modern-day iconoclasts condemn the Catholic custom of venerating religious statues, pictures, and crucifixes as "idolatry."

There have been a number of outbreaks of iconoclasm over the centuries, but the most severe came in the eighth century; the Church acted most decisively to condemn it. During the first seven centuries, those who opposed the use of icons were relatively ineffective in their efforts to sway the Church to their position. By about 720 the iconoclasts had gained ascendancy in political and ecclesiastical circles. Iconoclastic bishops such as Constantine of Nacolia, Theodosius of Ephesus, and Thomas of Claudiopolis were able to persuade Emperor Leo III to accept their position. They achieved this in part by reminding the monarch that the Muslims were enjoying intolerable success in their efforts to overrun Catholic regions in North Africa and Asia Minor. They convinced him that Islam's efforts at hegemony could be blunted if the Church could convert large numbers of Muslims.

More than anything else, the bishops argued, icons were an insurmountable obstacle to potential Muslim converts. "Abolish icons," they reasoned, "and the Empire will be swimming in converts. Once that's done, you won't have to worry about those pesky Islamic incursions on the frontier." The Emperor bought the argument and initiated a widespread persecution of Catholics who venerated icons. Churches and basilicas were ransacked of all statues, laws were enacted forbidding the possession of icons, and many bishops, priests, religious, and lay people were put to the sword for refusing to comply. The result? The empire was wracked with misery and unrest for decades, and there was no increase in conversions from Islam.

For sixty years iconoclasm gripped the Empire during the reigns of Leo III, Constantine V, and Leo IV. But in 787 the new ruler, the Empress Irene (who opposed the iconoclasts), urged Pope Adrian I to deal with the crisis. Heeding her advice, the Pope convened the Second Nicaean Council at which three hundred bishops assembled to examine the details of the controversy. After considering the biblical, patristic, and theological arguments for both sides, the bishops reaffirmed and formally encouraged the ancient Catholic custom of venerating religious images while steadfastly denouncing "icon worship." The Council fathers drew a distinction between adoration (*latría*), which is reserved to God alone, and veneration (*dulía*), which is honor bestowed on God's saints. Although it is proper to reverence icons because of what they represent, adoring them was expressly forbidden. Like all heresies, iconoclasm does have some truth to it: All Christians should abhor idol worship. Iconoclasts rightly condemn the worship of images—worship belongs to God alone—but they err in seeking to eliminate any use of religious images.

To defend their intolerance of images iconoclasts appeal to a variety of Bible verses and argue that God has forbidden the fashioning of images for religious purposes. Exodus 20:3–6 seems, at least at first glance, to make their case watertight: "You shall not have other gods besides me. You shall not carve idols for yourselves in the shape of anything in the sky above or on the earth below or in the waters beneath the earth; you shall not bow down before them." Other passages cited are Deuteronomy 5:8, Isaiah 44:9–20 and 45:20, Jeremiah 7:30, John 4:24, and Romans 1:23–24. Such verses, when read in context, really do nothing but reiterate the constant Catholic position that idol worship is gravely sinful.

Iconoclasts have no easy time reconciling their arguments with the many other biblical verses in which God permits and even commands the carving of statues and other images for religious purposes. Consider Exodus 25:18–22, 28:33–34, and 37:7–9; Numbers 21:8–9; 1 Kings 6:23–28 and 7:23–29; and 2 Chronicles chapters 3—5.

This Rock, January 1991

A Short Course on Judaism

THE DRAMATIC HISTORY OF THE JEWS, FROM the time of Jacob to the birth of the Catholic Church in the first century, is recounted best in the pages of Sacred Scripture. Judaism as a religion, with its specific code of doctrines and liturgical rituals, became a reality when Moses led the People of God out of the bondage of slavery in Egypt (see Exodus 12 ff.). Prior to this point, true religion consisted of the simple worship of the One True God (i.e., the period from Adam to Moses). There were no Ten Commandments, no ceremonies, no systematic theology of any sort. When Moses followed God's command to lead the Hebrews to the Promised Land, all of that changed. God fashioned Judaism with an elaborate system of animal sacrifice, a priesthood, doctrines, and commandments.

Over the centuries, the Jewish religion became more elaborate and complicated, but the Temple rituals of sacrificial holocausts were always at the center. The essence of Judaism is in its worship of the One True God, Yahweh—the God of Abraham, Isaac, and Jacob. This central belief is crystallized in the *Shema*: "Hear O Israel, the Lord your God is One God!" (Deuteronomy 6:4).

Circumcision, kosher food laws, observing the Sabbath, and the entire economy of ritual animal sacrifice were focused upon the worship of Yahweh. Christianity inherits much from Judaism, so it's no surprise that many elements of Christian liturgy, sacramental theology, and Scripture can be traced to Judaism. In fact, when Our Lord proclaimed his divinity and his saving mission of redemption, he emphasized his fulfillment of Judaism, rather than its abrogation: "I have not come to destroy the Law but to fulfill it."

This is why the Catholic Church sees itself as having an organic theological unity in many respects with Judaism. The New Covenant of Christ the Messiah, subsisting in the Catholic Church, his Body, is the literal fulfillment and perfection of the imperfect covenants the Lord made with the Jews. Today there are about fourteen million Jews in the world, about five million of whom live in the U.S. Judaism is often called the "Religion of the Book," in that Jewish life and worship revolve around God's revelation in Scripture.

What Christians call the "Old Testament," Orthodox and other Jews call the "Written Torah." It's composed of the *Torah* (Hebrew = "the Law": Genesis, Exodus, Leviticus, Numbers, and Deuteronomy); the *Neviim* (Hebrew = "the Prophets": Isaiah, Jeremiah, Ezekiel, etc.), and the *Kethuvim* (Hebrew = "the writings": Psalms, Proverbs, Lamentations, Daniel, etc.). Alongside the Written Torah exists the authoritative "Oral Torah"—the Jewish oral tradition of rabbinic interpretation of Scripture. The Jews believe that this oral tradition of how to understand the written revelation was promulgated by Moses and handed down through the ages by the rabbis. This sacred tradition continued in only oral form until the second century A.D., when it was committed to writing and compiled in a document called the *Mishnah*. Over the next several centuries, additional commentaries on the Torah and the *Mishnah* were added by the rabbis of Jerusalem and Babylon, and that collection is called the *Gemara*. In the fifth century, the *Gemara* and the *Mishnah* were combined to form what we know today as the *Talmud*.

Finally, another body of sacred (but not inspired) writings is the *Midrash*. This is another collection of rabbinic lore in which various biblical stories are embellished to make a moral or theological point. The rabbis added details not contained in the Scriptural account. For example, one tractate tells the story of Abraham, after his first encounter with the One True God, going to his father's home and destroying all the idols except for one large one.

When his father later asked him how this happened, Abraham blamed the big idol, saying it had destroyed the smaller ones. This was his way of showing how absurd idol worship is. Contemporary Judaism can be divided into three main movements: Orthodox, Conservative, and Reform. Orthodox Jews are those who hold a strict interpretation of the Torah and the Talmud. They observe the Halakhah (kosher) dietary laws and they strive to fulfill all the moral commandments laid down by God through Moses.

Perhaps the best-known group of Orthodox Judaism is the Hasidim. Hasidic men are identifiable by their long beards and *peyos* (ear locks), and black suits and hats. Jewish author Chaim Potok wrote a series of highly instructive novels depicting life in twentieth century Hasidic Judaism such as *The Chosen, The Promise*, and *In the Beginning*.

The next movement, known among Jews as being "liberal" in its theology is, ironically, called Conservative Judaism. It retains many of the forms and liturgical customs of Orthodox Judaism, along with an emphasis on the Torah, but it's not rigorous in observing such things as kosher food laws and Sabbath restrictions.

The third movement is Reform, which some would say is really not Judaism at all, at least not in a theological sense. Reform congregations typically condone abortion, contraception, homosexuality, divorce, and permit women rabbis. In short, this movement denies or deletes practically all significant doctrines of Judaism, and so is viewed by Orthodox Jews as not Jewish in any traditionally theological sense. For our purposes, though, Orthodox Judaism is the movement that embodies the doctrinal content, traditions, history, and essence of the Judaism we read about in the Old Testament.

The better we understand our Jewish roots, as shown forth in the Old Testament, the better we will appreciate the riches of the new and everlasting covenant of grace and friendship with God that Christ enacted with his shed blood on the cross. Judaism is not a religion that is theologically "wrong" *per se*; rather, it's obsolete now that Christ has come. Once Christ came as savior, the "One Mediator between God and Man" (1 Timothy 2:5), He provided the means of salvation that Judaism could only point to and yearn for.

The Jewish religion is based on the observance of the Law, the striving to please God through propitiatory sacrifices and strict observance of laws. This was good, but imperfect. In Christ Jesus, the ancient promises are kept, God's covenants are perfected and fulfilled, and we can rejoice that, "In times past, God spoke in partial and various ways to our ancestors through the prophets; but in these last days he spoke to us through a Son, whom he made heir of all things..." (Hebrews 1:1–2).

Spes Nostra, *March/April 1997*

A Short Course on Hinduism

THIS ANCIENT EASTERN RELIGION IS GAINING GROUND in the West, not because of proselytizing, but because its philosophy is seeping steadily into the fabric of our culture. While Judaism is theologically very close to Christianity, Hinduism is far away. For one thing, Hindus obviously do not recognize the God of Israel as the One True God. Rather, they are polytheists, worshipping a myriad of gods, the major ones in their pantheon including the divinities Shiva, Vishnu, Ganesha, Shakti, Surya, and Brahma. There are many lesser gods and goddesses, and countless flower-strewn, incense-wreathed shrines and temples in honor of these greater and lesser divinities dot the landscape of India.

Some Hindus will tell you that Hinduism is not so much a religion as a moral philosophy. Its moral and theological precepts are few, and all of them are based on the Hindu Scripture, called Vedas. In Sanskrit, the ancient written language that predominated in the Indian subcontinent, Veda means "knowledge," and these ancient writings (and other later writings Hindus regard as sacred, such as the *Vedangas, Upavedas, Agamas, Brahmanas,* and *Upanishads*) convey the theological insights of a Hindu Sage Vyasadeva, believed to have been an incarnation of the god Krishna. He is credited with systematizing Hindu thought into four *Vedas, Rg* (prayers), *Yajur* (hymns used when offering sacrifice), *Sama* (more hymns and prayers), and *Atharva* (philosophy about the maintenance and destruction of the body and the world and of casting spells and appeasing devils).

The *Rg Veda,* probably composed around 1000 B.C., is composed of hundreds of mantras (religious hymns) that are presented in ten chapters called "circles." Perhaps the best known of the Hindu scriptures is the Bhagavad Gita (Song of the Blessed One). It's a lengthy epic poem that contains practical advice, proverbs, Hindu history, and admonitions to seek spiritual purity and eventually join with the ultimate Divine Mind. The school of philosophy and interpretation that is drawn from the Vedas and the other Hindu holy books is known as Vedanta or "vedic knowledge."

All of this information comes from the "Divine Mind," an amorphous divine consciousness that is essentially impersonal, though it has been expressed in various gods, such as Rama and Krishna. As more scriptures were composed, we can see a metamorphosis of Hindu philosophy, moving from a simple religion to a more complex one. In fact, the most ancient form of Hinduism involved the worship of a single unknown god. The Hinduism of today, though, is saturated with polytheism and idol worship.

Over the centuries, two major sects within Hinduism grew out of popular devotion to the gods Shiva and Vishnu. Each god's followers sought to make him the chief god. And then there were the devotees of the god Brahma who felt he should be the head god. In Hinduism, the gods, although more or less good, are actually more like the supermen of Greek and Roman mythology. They are sensual and subject to passions like jealousy and rage. This makes it hard for Hindus to conceive of their gods being morally offended by human sin. Rather, these gods are *placated*, their egos and appetites sated, by the offering of incense, flowers, food, and drink in their honor. The gods are believed to aid and protect the pious Hindus who adorn their shrines, offer litanies to them, and pay them off with material goods.

Hindus select their own favorite god from among the "thirty three times ten million" gods, and spend their lives offering sacrifices and prayers as a petition to that god for protection and assistance. Although Hinduism remains alien and strange to most westerners, certain elements of Hindu belief have crept into Western culture and jargon. Karma, for example, is the Hindu concept of influencing the universe by exact performance of rituals combined with the right intention. Many misunderstand karma to mean pure fatalism (*que será será*). This is inaccurate.

In fact, karma is essentially the Hindu analog of the Christian heresy of Pelagianism: the belief that through his own natural abilities, man is capable of surmounting his spiritual weaknesses and sinfulness and achieving a state of supernatural perfection. Karma is at the heart of Hindu piety: man is seen as relying solely upon his natural powers to appease the gods (at least the ones he wishes to worship or those whom he fears might harm him), fulfill exactly the rituals laid down by Hindu custom and in the Vedas, do good to others, conquer personal sin and weakness, and, in so doing, arrive at a state of spiritual perfection. This is where the Hindu doctrine of reincarnation enters in. Human beings are almost never capable of achieving in a single lifetime the self-purification required to reach spiritual perfection.

Thus, the cycle of the soul transmigrating from one body to another repeatedly—living, dying, living again, dying, living again, etc.—is the solution. Karma dictates that one's own actions, not blind fate, are responsible for life's mishaps or joys. Lessons learned or left unlearned in one life will cause the soul to go to a higher or lower level in its subsequent reincarnation. The Hindu caste system flows from this belief.

The uppermost level, the Brahmans, have a right to their status, not due mainly to their actions in this life, but for the goodness they have accumulated in past lives. The lower castes, especially the Sudras (untouchables), are also not to be pitied or helped. Their own actions produced the karma that brought them to that misery. If they work at it, they can move to a higher level in their next reincarnation. This is another feature of Hinduism that makes it incompatible with Christianity.

While karma is the denial of man's need for a redeemer who alone is capable of bridging the chasm of sin separating us from God, reincarnation gives that denial flesh and bones, so to speak. Hinduism offers no solution for life's ultimate questions: Who am I? Who made me? What is my purpose in this life? How can I be truly happy? All Hinduism can do is tell you, "If you work hard enough and are reincarnated enough times to learn all the lessons life has to offer, some day, eons in the future, you'll reach the 'happiness' of being absorbed into the impersonal Divine Mind." Not a very pleasant prospect, if you ask me.

Spes Nostra, *May/June 1997*

Picking Fruit and Petting Animals

THE JEHOVAH'S WITNESS DOCTRINE OF PARADISE EARTH isn't all it's cracked up to be. The other day, two well-dressed, middle-aged women came to my home. As they passed by my office window heading for our doorbell, their modest leather satchels told me they were Witnesses of Jehovah. I wasn't surprised that they wanted to talk with me about all the "signs" that indicate that the end of the world—which they began calling "Armageddon," as soon as they realized I was a Bible-reading Christian—is right around the corner.

"How do you feel about all the wars and diseases and murders that are going on around the world these days?" the older of the two asked sweetly, eyebrows raised slightly, her smile expectant. "Wouldn't you like to know what God's Word, the Bible, has to say about his plans for ending all the strife and bloodshed?" she pressed.

By then her Bible was out of the satchel and she had begun a patter of verse-quoting that bounced from Old to New Testament, and back again. She spent a couple of minutes crisscrossing Scripture with proof texts that, she told me, prove that the end of the world and the destruction of all wicked folk, is very near.

These two pleasant Jehovah's Witness ladies were deadly in earnest about their message. They told me that Jehovah God will soon—very soon—push his celestial button from on high and initiate Armageddon, the final, fiery struggle between good and evil that will expunge his enemies from the face of the earth, once and for all. After that cataclysm, all living Jehovah's Witnesses will be transformed into immortals, and all Jehovah's Witnesses who have died over the years will be resurrected and will fan out to populate a renewed, wonderful, "paradise earth." That new terrestrial life of unmitigated bliss will be eternal.

Watchtower literature such as the twin magazines, *Awake!* and *The Watchtower*, incessantly portray the soon-to-come "heaven on earth" (for JWs only) with scenes of deliriously happy men, women, and children of all races enjoying the endless, carefree leisure of picking fruit and petting wild animals. Lions, tigers, and bears are often shown in Watchtower books and pamphlets cavorting playfully and harmlessly with their human, fruit-laden, friends. (By the way, it seems that all "paradise earth" inhabitants will be strict vegetarians. There is no JW depiction that I know of that has ever shown these blissful folks slaughtering and eating any of the playful animals that cavort around them).

By this point in the conversation, I couldn't hold back any longer, and I began asking some pointed questions about the false prophecies concerning Armageddon and the end of the world that have been issued repeatedly by the Watchtower Bible and Tract Society, the Brooklyn-based "governing body" of the Jehovah's Witness religion.

Hearing this, the smiles faded from these ladies' faces, the corners of their mouths tensed slightly, and, after a few uncomfortable moments of silence after one of my questions, their Bibles were slipped quickly back into the satchels.

They stood. "It looks as though our discussion has reached a point where we should stop for now," the younger one said, smiling stiffly as she walked toward the door. I asked them to come back next week to discuss the issue further, and they offered a wan, noncommittal "That would be nice" as they headed out the front door and down the walk.

They haven't come back.

Jehovah's Witnesses are very eager to speak with you about one of their pet subjects: Armageddon. They want you to take their word for it that the end is very near and that the only way you and your loved ones can avoid being slain in the melee is to become a Jehovah's Witness and join them in the urgent task of going door to door with the message of imminent destruction.

If you haven't had this dire message delivered, piping hot, to your doorstep, don't worry. You will. Assuming you don't live in Antarctica, your home will soon be visited by friendly, sincere, and badly mistaken Jehovah's Witnesses whose aim is to scare you out of the Catholic Church and into the arms of the Watchtower.

Don't let that happen, and by all means, take steps to make sure you can help any of your friends or family who may be troubled by these scary predictions of Armageddon. How to prepare? Read *Envoy Magazine*'s articles on the Watchtower's beliefs and tactics.[63] You'll learn about the many flaws in the Jehovah's Witnesses reasoning about such things as Armageddon, the end of the world, the divinity of Christ, the Trinity, and the version of "paradise earth" they claim awaits all faithful Jehovah's Witnesses (but not anyone else— according to Watchtower theology, all non-Jehovah's Witnesses who are alive when Armageddon occurs will be annihilated, body and soul).

Unless they really, *really* love fruit and animals, paradise earth will not be nearly as rosy a scenario as the Jehovah's Witnesses might think.

Envoy, July/August 1999

Saturday or Sunday?

"I COULDN'T HELP NOTICING THAT BOOK YOU'RE reading. Are you a Catholic?"

"Yes, that's right. Why?"

"Well, I used to be a Catholic myself—now I'm a Seventh-Day Adventist—and I was wondering if you could tell me why the Catholic Church continues to violate the biblical command to keep the Sabbath holy."

"I'm glad you brought up the subject."

"You are?"

"Of course. You see, a few years ago my brother left the Catholic Church to become a Seventh-Day Adventist for that very reason. He came to believe that the Bible commanded Christians to worship on the Sabbath. He also picked up a lot of anti-Catholicism along the way."

"Well, I'm glad to know your brother became a Christian, but I'd still like to know your answer to my question."

"No problem. First of all, why don't you begin by showing me in the Bible your basis for Sabbath worship."

"All right. In Exodus 20:8–10 the Lord says: 'Remember the sabbath day, to keep it holy. Six days shalt thou labor, and do all thy work: But the seventh day [is] the sabbath of the LORD thy God: Remember the sabbath day, to keep it holy. Six days shalt thou labor, and do all thy work: But the seventh day [is] the sabbath of the LORD thy God. . . .' And in verse 11 he says, 'In six days the

Lord made the heavens and the earth, the sea and all that is in them, but on the seventh day he rested. That is why the Lord has blessed the Sabbath day and made it holy.'"

"Okay. Now, what else?"

"Actually, that's the main text. But remember that the people of God . . ."

". . . you mean the Jews, right?"

"Right—the Jews continued to honor God's commandment by keeping the Sabbath day holy, not Sunday."

"Well, first of all, you're right. God did command the Jews to keep holy the seventh day of the week, the Sabbath. But he also commanded them to do a whole bunch of other things. Does the Seventh-Day Adventist Church require circumcision?"

"No."

"Why not? That was a commandment of God, which he gave to the Jews at about the same time he mentioned the Sabbath."

"Well, that's different. But getting back to the Sabbath, God doesn't change! If he once demanded that worship take place on the seventh day, he's not going to change his mind about it now."

"First of all, it's not different. In fact, if you read the New Testament you'll see that eventually the practice of circumcision was abrogated, for example in Galatians 5:1–6, and replaced the by the sacrament of baptism. Second, your reasoning is faulty. God did change a number of precepts between the Old and New Testaments. The Old Law changed to the New."

"But in Matthew 5 Jesus said, 'Think not that I am come to destroy the law, or the prophets: I am not come to destroy, but to fulfill. For verily I say unto you, Till heaven and earth pass, one jot or one tittle shall in no wise pass from the law, till all be fulfilled. Whosoever therefore shall break one of these least commandments, and shall teach men so, he shall be called the least in the kingdom of heaven: but whosoever shall do and teach [them], the same shall be called great in the kingdom of heaven.'"

"I understand that, but remember that Jesus also defended his disciples when they were accused by the Jews of not observing the Sabbath in the traditional sense. That's in Matthew 12. And in Luke 13 and John 5 Jesus rebuked the Jews for too strict and legalistic an observance of the Sabbath. Most importantly, in Mark 2:27–28 Jesus demonstrated his authority to do as he pleased with the interpretation of the Sabbath law."

"Oh."

"Remember that in the New Testament Sunday played a significant role in the life of the Church. Jesus rose from the dead and appeared to his apostles on a Sunday, and he chose the Sunday following his resurrection to appear to them when Thomas was present. Pentecost was on a Sunday too."

"But that that doesn't mean that the Lord's Day could be changed."

"The Bible disagrees with you. In Acts 20:7 and Colossians 2:16–17, and Revelation 1:10 we're told that 'On the first day of the week' the Christians assembled to break bread. And in Galatians 4 Paul chastises Christians specifically for trying to return to a strict observance of Jewish customs."

"Well, you're just trying to bury me with out-of-context verses. I know what the Bible really means. It's the Catholic Church that distorted everything. The first Christians got together on Saturday, not Sunday."

"Is that so? Why don't you read 1 Corinthians 16:1–2?"

Catholic Answers, *July 1989*

What's New About the "New Atheism"?

The Archdiocese of Sydney interviewed Patrick Madrid on the pressing issue of the "New Atheism" and what Christians can do to effectively counter the phenomenon

What Is "New" About the New Atheism?

As my coauthor, Kenneth Hensley, and I point out in our book *The Godless Delusion: A Catholic Challenge to Modern Atheism,*[64] the "New Atheism" is much more "openly aggressive" and offensive than previous manifestations of atheism. Whereas past atheists were content to simply challenge widespread belief in God through debates and publications, more recent proponents of atheism wish to eradicate belief in God from the public realm altogether. In other words, they view religious belief as a positive "evil" (although ironically, as we argue in our book, the term "evil" is rendered devoid of any meaning in an atheistic worldview) and have even asserted that it is "child abuse" to teach children to believe in a Creator-God. There is little doubt that the number of atheists has risen in recent decades in western societies (including, of course, Australia) and that atheists are now making use of sympathetic media and the Internet to promote their beliefs and are arranging rallies (such as "The Reason Rally" held in the USA in March 2012) and conferences to make themselves heard, fortify themselves, and spur each other on to spread the message of atheism.

The increase in offense has been directly proportional to a decrease in the quality of the arguments put forward by New Atheists for the nonexistence in God or gods. While there still are more sophisticated atheists (normally philosophers), who recognize the force of the arguments for the existence of God, the New Atheists tend to write in areas out of their fields of expertise and therefore underestimate the strength of the theistic worldview. Unfortunately, most of us have not been trained in philosophy and are therefore unable to detect the flaws in their arguments. This is not helped by the fact that many books written by popular atheists (such as Richard Dawkins, Sam Harris, Daniel Dennett, and the late Christopher Hitchens—may God rest his soul) tend to be distributed widely, whereas books responding to their arguments are not as well known. In addition to books, we now see the production of videos, television programs, articles, lectures, and even billboards calling for the end of religious belief (or, at the very least, the end to its influence in the public sphere). Often these popular atheists tend to present their arguments in a very attractive way, urging people to abandon "superstition" and embrace the tenets of Reason. On its face, this is a very appealing offer; very few people like to think of themselves as irrational!

Is the New Atheism a Phenomenon That Christians Should Be Concerned About?

As Kenneth and I noted in our book, Christians, in general, have not adequately prepared themselves to deal with and respond to the arguments raised by atheists in the increasingly aggressive manner in which atheism is being promoted. The rise of this more militant version of atheism has been reasonably rapid and has caught many believers off-guard. Furthermore, most Christians, for various reasons, have either not studied or not had the opportunity to study the reasons for their belief in a Creator-God and can therefore become easily rattled when presented with forceful atheistic arguments by apparently confident people who dismiss theism as though nothing could be said in its favor. In worst-case scenarios, people can fall away from the Christian Faith altogether or, at least, practice it with less conviction and joy. In turn, this makes the proclamation of the Gospel and the call to conversion much more difficult for Christians, as the central message of Christianity cannot even gain a fair hearing. As we are sadly seeing in more recent times, as atheism or naturalism (the belief that matter is all there is) gains a greater hearing in the public sphere, legislation is being put in place which is aimed at preventing believers from practicing their Christian Faith in its totality.

There have been a number of cases where Protestant pastors or Catholic priests have been accused of "discrimination" or "vilification" for speaking out against homosexual practice and the like. As we argue, views about morality are directly linked to views about what the human person is, which, in turn, is linked to one's worldview: whether theistic or atheistic. We are seeing but the tip of the iceberg of the consequences of the abandonment of belief in God. It is quite ironic that Christians, who are being accused of discrimination, are now the objects of discrimination themselves!

Is the Rise of the New Atheism Something That Western Society Generally Should Be Concerned About? What Are The Possible Consequences?

In our book, we estimate that, in the USA at least, approximately thirty million Americans doubt or deny the existence of God. That is a lot of people who could do a great deal of damage to society were they to live out consistently their atheism. While the numbers are doubtless a lot less in Australia, any increase in numbers should be cause for concern and positive action on the part of Christians.

It was, of course, Friedrich Nietzsche (1844–1900) who understood that atheism logically leads to, not merely the relativity of the moral law, but the death of morality. As we note in our book, Nietzsche laid this out in his well-known work, *Thus Spake Zarathustra,* in which the main character (Zarathustra) comes to the realization that if God does not exist, then morality does not exist either. Nietzsche understood man to be in the process of evolving into a sort of "superman"—a race of people freed from the shackles of religion, belief in God, and morality. This "Super Race" would employ their intelligence and will to create their own world devoid of "pathetic ideals" espoused by Christianity. In fact, Nietzsche once wrote that his "basic law" was that "there are no ethical phenomena...." Both his views and ideas, drawn from naturalist sources such as Charles Darwin's works, paved the way for moving Europe, and, in particular, Germany towards the worst period of violence in its long history. It is no great secret that Adolf Hitler was a man firmly committed to an essentially Nietzschean and Darwinian worldview and a great admirer of Nietzsche. He saw himself as implementing the "law of nature" which would, time permitting, result in the elimination of those unfit for existence and the eventual emergence of a "master race." As history records, these ideas were implemented with ruthless consistency and devastating consequences.

Possibly the most convincing evidence for the need to be concerned is the appalling immorality, or rather, amorality, promulgated and practiced in the twentieth century by some of the most repressive and totalitarian regimes in human history. Need I mention—to cite just a portion of the instances of this practice—avowed atheists such as Joseph Stalin, Mao Tse Tung, and Pol Pot, who have all contributed, in one way or another, to the culture of death? Stalin and Mao alone were responsible for the mass of murder over one hundred million men, women, and children.

Think this is too farfetched for modern western society? Think again. Our total acceptance of abortion and contraception and increasing acceptance of euthanasia, the overpopulation myth, homosexual "marriage," and the endless pursuit of scientific efficiency and pleasure at the expense of hitherto held moral principles is simply the logical outcome of our acceptance of an atheistic, naturalistic worldview. Stay tuned for further (horrific) developments in the near future.

How Is Your Approach—Specifically That Outlined in Your Book—Different From Previous Responses to Atheism?

Many books written by Catholics and Protestants have not only decisively refuted atheism but have cogently put forward the case for belief in God in a way that, in my opinion, atheists simply have not been able to refute. For example, see *The Last Superstition: A Refutation of the New Atheism* by Dr. Edward Feser, *Handbook of Catholic Apologetics* by Professor Peter Kreeft and Fr. Ronald Tacelli, s.j., and *Theology and Sanity* by your own Frank Sheed (an Australian).

For this reason, in conceiving our book, we knew that it was not necessary to cover previous ground. What we did realize, however, was that atheists, and especially modern-day atheists, are used to being on the forefront and attacking the very tenets of belief in God. Unfortunately, we believers normally oblige them and assume that we should be defending our belief in God. We are easily intimidated by accusations of being "unscientific" and tend to fall back into a fideistic stance ("You just have to have faith!")

Kenneth Hensley and I decided that it was about time that positions were reversed. It was time that we believers went on the offensive and subjected the atheistic worldview and its underlying foundations to a rigorous scrutiny. For this reason, we adopted what is termed the *presuppositional* approach. It has the advantage of being very practical and one that can be understood and employed without many years of philosophical training. When done properly and consistently, we believe that the approach demonstrates that atheism is both replete with internal contradictions and inconsistencies and that the atheistic worldview is unable to account for immaterial realities that we all know and experience such as knowledge, memory, self-awareness, love, good, evil, human rights, personhood, and freewill, to name but a few examples. In sum, it seeks to show that while belief in God makes sense of human experience, atheism cannot and does not. As an example (and as I noted above), atheists who say that nothing exists but matter cannot make sense of the existence of right and wrong. In fact, an atheist must *presuppose God's existence* in order to make sense of this. Atheists often raise "the problem of evil" as evidence *against* God; however, we show that realities such as good or evil are inconsistent with a natural worldview and that the atheist must assume God's existence to raise "the problem of evil" in the first place!

In other words, we wanted to maintain the focus on whether atheism per se can "stand on its own two feet" so to speak. For this reason, we do not rely on evidence for the existence of God as found in divine revelation: Jesus Christ, the Scriptures, and the Catholic Church. We wanted to instill in people the conviction that atheism can be critiqued and refuted without ever having to directly present the cogent case for the existence of God.

What are two main areas in which atheistic premises lead to absurd conclusions?
Perhaps the most obvious one is the death of morality. As C.S. Lewis notes in his classic work *Mere Christianity,* everyone (even so-called relativists) believes in what Lewis terms "the law of morality." Not merely a description of their personal likes and dislikes but a real law that exists in the world, the law of morality is as real as the laws of physics. This law applies to all people regardless of age, sex, race, and religious belief (or lack thereof!). People may disagree about the particular nature of the law, but they agree that a law of some sort exists. Try taking a wallet from or breaking a promise to a relativist, and immediately the response will be, "That's stealing," or "That's not fair."

We cannot help but make assessments or judgments about right and wrong. All of this fits beautifully with the belief that God exists. In fact, moral laws reflect the very nature of who God is. "God," as St. Thomas said, "is the absolute good, from whom all things are called good by participation." Think of the concept in terms of a straight line: the only way you can discern just how straight a line is would be to know what a truly straight line looks like. Likewise, without an absolute standard of "good" (which is God), there is no way to know how near or how far something is in relation to that standard. Can atheism account for the existence of a real standard, a real law of morality? The answer is no. Are "right" or "wrong" material things? Are they natural objects like trees or animals? If so, where can we see them? How much do they weigh? What are their measurements? Are they natural properties like the color blue or the property of smoothness? The answer is, of course, no. Rather, they are immaterial properties that are at the same time very real. And yet, an atheistic world consisting only of matter has no means by which the existence of a law of morality can be accounted for. To be consistent, the atheist must say that right and wrong do not exist. As I have said above, ironically, the "problem of evil" used to deny God's existence turns out to be a nonexistent problem in a naturalistic worldview.

Furthermore, atheism is also inconsistent with knowledge and personhood. For the believer, God is the source of ideas, reason, and thought. He created us as a body-soul composite with inherent abilities to abstract, judge, and reason. How can the atheist account for these abilities? For the naturalist, the mind is no more than a product of brain chemistry. As we note in our book, the philosopher Pierre Cabanis stated that the human brain produces thoughts and ideas in the same way that "the stomach and the bowels are destined to produce digestion."[65] With this view, not only can we therefore not trust our thoughts, but our thoughts are determined. Our freedom turns out to be an illusion. Finally, such necessary tools necessary to thought as abstraction (such as "triangularity" as opposed to "a particular triangle") and the laws of logic are clearly not part of the material world, and yet the thoroughgoing atheist prides him or herself on their ability to reason! Next time you see, smell, or bump into a law of logic, please let me know....

What Can We as Christians Do to Challenge Our Family, Friends, and Colleagues Who Are Atheists to Reconsider Their Views?

There are three things necessary, I believe, if we are to effectively challenge atheism and conclusively demonstrate to atheists that their worldview is irrational and cannot account for the fundamental realities of their existence. First, of course, we must pray for them: no change of heart and mind leading to ultimate conversion will take place without God's grace. Second, we must develop our abilities to understand and explain the many reasons for believing in God—in other words, the positive case for God's existence. Finally, we must understand how to critique atheism on its own merits.

Inform *magazine, May 2012*

SECTION THREE

Saints and Holy People

THERE'S NO WAY AROUND IT. OUR LADY and the saints play a very important role in the doctrines and devotional life of the Catholic Church. So it stands to reason that Catholic apologetics must deal with answering questions and objections to this integral dimension of the Faith that is so often misunderstood by non-Catholics.

In this section, you'll read a series of essays I wrote on the general theme of the communion of saints, most of which are overtly apologetical in nature (for example, "Does Honoring Mary and the Saints Offend God?"), some which are descriptive of living people—that is, those members of the Church Militant, who teach us immense lessons by their own heroic personal examples of spreading and defending the Catholic faith (such as "Blessed Miguel Pro," "Frank Sheed," and "The Divine Word Missionaries"). I can say without exaggeration that I have learned a great deal from them.

Then there are apologetics articles about the Blessed Virgin Mary and her role in the life and teachings of the Catholic Church: "Mary, Ark of the New Covenant," and "Any Friend of God's." The latter article, I am pleased to say, evoked from Karl Keating (someone not given to effusive praise) a rare yet meaningful comment:

"Pat," he said, "I think this may be the very best article you have ever written."

I will admit that, coming from Karl, those words meant an awful lot to me as a young apologist and a fledgling writer. Buoyed by the strong positive reaction the article garnered from readers after it appeared in *This Rock* magazine (recently replaced by the new *Catholic Answers* magazine), I decided to expand the article into a full-length book by the same title.

Over the eight years that I worked at Catholic Answers, 1988 to 1996, I was blessed to have a job that not only required endless hours of barnstorming from parish to parish conducting apologetics seminars in both English and Spanish, but also equally endless (and often quite lively) Q&A sessions with the large audiences of Catholics and Protestants who flocked to our seminars. Fielding literally thousands of questions from audience members, some of whom were not the least bit pleased to see Catholics make a biblical case for their beliefs, was a huge advantage for me. Reminiscent to me of the hurly-burly of street-corner preaching that the great Australian apologist Frank Sheed engaged in earlier in the twentieth century, I found that the constant flow of public presentations on the Catholic Faith served to really hone my skills as an apologist.

The freewheeling Q&A sessions especially were hugely formative for me. I learned not only how to handle an audience that was not always sympathetic (some debate audiences, for example, were openly hostile to me and the Catholic Church I was there to defend), but also how to handle myself in tense, unpredictable, "under fire" situations.

I recall, for example, the evening I spoke at a parish in Los Angeles, delivering in Spanish an apologetics defense of Catholic teaching on Mary and the saints to a full church. About twenty minutes into my remarks, a middle-aged Mexican woman stood up, several pews back from the sanctuary, and started shouting denunciations at me, saying that I was a *"profeta falso,"* a *"guía de ciegos!"* (blind guide), and the like. It turned out that she claimed to be the wife of the late Alberto Rivera, a colorful character in the pantheon of Fundamentalist anti-Catholic propaganda. His lurid Chick comic book "Alberto" purported to reveal his story as a cradle Catholic in Spain who became a "Jesuit spy" and eventually had a dramatic "born again" experience after finally reading the

Bible. He then repented of his Romanist machinations against God's people and thereupon devoted the remainder of his life as a Bible-believing minister of the gospel whose sole mission was to rescue Catholics from the blindness of Romanism.

When Alberto's "wife" leapt to her feet and started haranguing me, I had no choice but to scrap my talk and debate her, then and there, toe to toe, in front of several hundred breathless and quite entertained Catholics. I knew I had no other choice. If I refused to engage her, many of the Catholics in attendance that evening would have understandably wondered if I avoided the confrontation because I had no good answers to her challenges. So, we debated, lively and spontaneously, both of us with our Bibles.

As things progressed, an older man stood up and also started heckling me in Spanish. He claimed to be a former Catholic bishop who had read the Bible, been born again, and immediately left the Church to pursue the life of a Protestant evangelist. Really? I had no way of knowing who he was, so I asked him politely to sit down and be quiet so I could discuss matters with Alberto's wife. To my surprise and relief, he did. The fiasco continued until the lady had run out of things to say and, gathering her Bible and several of her followers (including the putative ex-bishop) left the Church in something of a huff.

¡Caramba! Did I ever learn a lot about the mechanics of apologetics in those days. That particular evening was one of the best, most memorable experiences of my career as an apologist. When the lady and her Bible-toting posse had left the building, the Catholic audience shot to their feet and started clapping and singing (singing!). They were happy to see the Catholic Faith defended, and happier still, I was keenly aware, to discover to their immense relief, that the Catholic Church and her teachings could be defended from the Bible.

Blessed Miguel Pro, Modern Martyr

MY MOTHER'S FAMILY BACKGROUND IS IRISH AND Swedish, and my father's side of the family is 100 percent Hispanic, from Spain by way of Mexico—hence, my surname Madrid. Growing up in Southern California, I was very close to my paternal grandmother, Esperanza Madrid (née Molinar). From the time I was a young child, she handed down to me the rich and sometimes dramatic, even violent, history of her and my grandfather's side of my family from generations ago, starting in Spain, through many years in Mexico, until they emigrated in the late 1920s to the United States.

As a young girl, my grandmother came face-to-face with Pancho Villa and his gang of thugs when they raided her family hacienda near Ciudad Camargo in the state of Chihuahua. They showed up in force looking for my great grandfather, Manuel, magistrate of the City of Camargo. Tipped off at the very last minute, he had just enough time to doff his suit and tie, scramble into the coarse white pants and white shirt, sandals, and sombrero of a poor campesino worker, hop on a donkey and hightail it out into the desert to get away.

Pancho Villa and his men were there to capture or kill him because he was wealthy, a local mayor, and because he was allied with the federal government of the relatively benign dictator Porfirio Díaz. When the Díaz government fell in 1911, there ensued a chaotic span of ten years during which a series of increasingly anti-Catholic presidents were elected in Mexico, culminating in the accession to power of one particularly ruthless dictator, Plutarcho Elías Calles, who was the strongman president of Mexico from 1924 through 1928.

Why the mini-lesson in Mexican history, you ask? Well, the reason is that, under Calles, the Catholic Church suffered a bloody persecution at the hands of the Mexican government—at the hands of Calles—and one of the great martyrs of the twentieth century was one of Calles's victims, the heroic Father Miguel Pro, Jesuit. His life was a type of apologetics toward the atheistic, masonic, anti-Catholic brutality of the Calles regime, under which it was illegal to practice the Catholic Faith under pain of death.

As a young Mexican Jesuit priest, Father Pro ministered undercover to Mexico City's beleaguered Catholics who sought to weather the storm of persecution by the government. Along the way, he helped save countless souls even though, in the end, he was captured and killed. Many of my own family members, especially the relatives of my maternal grandmother Esperanza, had to flee Mexico to avoid being killed in the government's murderous rampage against the Catholic Church.

I wrote the following brief profile of the life and times of Father Miguel Pro in an effort to remind my readers that the Catholic Church may very well come under bloody persecution in the United States in our own lifetime (if current trends continue, I fear). We can look to his stalwart defense of the Faith as an encouraging example of fearless martyrdom that we ourselves may someday be called upon to emulate (may God forbid it!) rather than concede and cave in to a secular effort to destroy the Church—just as he proclaimed his faith in Jesus Christ and the Catholic Church with his dying breath, shouting "Viva Cristo Rey!" as the firing squad shot their deadly hail of bullets into his body.

• • •

Miguel Pro is an example of Christian heroism in the twentieth century. The indefatigable Jesuit was martyred by the Mexican government in 1927 for performing his priestly duties.

Born on January 13, 1891, Miguel Pro Juarez was the eldest son of Miguel Pro and Josefa Juarez. His birthplace, the humble central Mexican village of

Guadalupe, was especially fitting in view of his intense, lifelong devotion to Our Lady of Guadalupe, Patroness of the Americas.

Miguelito, as his doting family called him, was, from an early age, intensely spiritual and equally intense in his mischievousness. From the time he could speak he had the reputation of being a motor mouth, frequently exasperating his family with his humor and practical jokes, a trait that remained with him into adulthood.

As a child he had an unbridled precociousness that sometimes went too far, tossing him into near-death accidents and illnesses. On regaining consciousness after one of these episodes, young Miguel opened his eyes and blurted out to his frantic parents, "I want some *cócol*" (a colloquial term for his favorite sweet bread). *Cócol* became his nickname, which he would later adopt as a code name during his clandestine priestly ministry.

Pro developed a particularly strong relationship with his older sister, Maria Concepcion, whom he called "Conchita." Their spiritual bond was a key element in his developing an awareness of his priestly vocation. Most assumed he would follow in his father's footsteps and become a prominent businessman, but Conchita's entrance into the cloistered convent (a painful and momentous parting for both of them) galvanized Pro's thinking in the direction of the priesthood.

Although he was vastly popular with the senoritas and had prospects of a lucrative career managing his father's thriving business concerns, Pro renounced everything for the sake of Christ his King and entered the Jesuit novitiate in El Llano, Michoacan in 1911. He studied in Mexico until 1914, when a tidal wave of governmental anti-Catholicism crashed down upon Mexico, forcing the novitiate to disband and the order to flee to Los Gatos, California.

In 1915 Pro was sent to a seminary in Spain, where he remained until 1924. By the time he was ordained a priest in Belgium in 1925, the political situation in Mexico had deteriorated. The presidency had been held by a succession of socialist, bitterly anti-Catholic thugs who tried to exterminate Catholicism. All Catholic churches were closed, and bishops, priests, and religious were rounded up for deportation or imprisonment. Those caught trying to elude capture were shot. Celebration of the sacraments was punishable by imprisonment or death.

Because the Church had been driven underground, Pro received permission from his superiors to return to Mexico incognito and to carry on his ministry undercover. He slipped into Mexico City and immediately began celebrating Mass and distributing the sacraments, often under imminent threat of discovery by a police force charged with the task of ferreting out hidden pockets of Catholicism.

Fr. Pro had many narrow escapes. Once, after celebrating Mass in a home, he received just enough warning to be able to slip out a side door before the police surrounded the place. With characteristic bravado, Pro changed into a police inspector's uniform (one of the many disguises he made use of while eluding authorities) and went back to the very house where the police were busy hunting for him. Swaggering up to the policeman in charge, Pro demanded to know why they hadn't yet succeeded in capturing "that rascal Pro." None the wiser, the abashed officer promised to redouble the search efforts.

Another time, Pro was in a taxi being pursued through the streets of Mexico City by several police cars. Ordering the driver to slow down as he rounded a corner, Pro rolled out of the car, lit a cigar, and began strolling arm in arm with an attractive (and startled) young woman. When the police roared by, in hot pursuit of the now Pro-less taxi, they paid no attention to the romantic young couple on the sidewalk.

He became known throughout the city as the undercover priest who would show up in the middle of the night, dressed as a beggar or a street sweeper, to baptize infants, hear confessions, distribute Communion, or perform marriages. Several times, disguised as a policeman, he slipped unnoticed into the police headquarters itself to bring the sacraments to Catholic prisoners before their executions. Using clandestine meeting places, a wardrobe of disguises (including policeman, chauffeur, garage mechanic, farm laborer, and playboy), and coded messages to the underground Catholics who received his notes signed "Cocol," Pro carried on his priestly work for the Mexican faithful under his care.

Finally, though, he was caught. A car previously owned by his brother had been used in an assassination attempt on General Obregon. The license plate was traced to Pro's brother, and this led to an informant telling the police where the Pro brothers, who knew nothing about the plot, were lodging. They were put in jail and held without trial for ten days while the government trumped up charges falsely implicating Pro in the assassination attempt. On November 13, 1927 President Calles ordered Pro to be executed, ostensibly for his role in the assassination plot, but in reality for his defiance of the laws banning Catholicism.

When called from his cell, Fr. Miguel walked to the courtyard, blessed the firing squad, and approached a bullet-scarred adobe wall. He knelt and prayed silently for a few moments. Refusing a blindfold, he stood, faced the firing squad, and held his arms outstretched in the form of a cross, a crucifix in one hand and a rosary in the other. In a clear voice he cried out, "Viva Cristo Rey!"

A volley rang out, and Pro fell to the ground riddled with bullets. A soldier stepped up and discharged his rifle at point blank range into the priest's temple.

In 1988 Pope John Paul II beatified Miguel Pro.

Any Friend of God's Is a Friend of Mine

EVERY SUNDAY MILLIONS OF CHRISTIANS RECITE THE Apostles' Creed, professing their belief in the "communion of saints." Few realize the importance of this phrase, which is sandwiched between other deep mysteries of the Faith. The Catholic understanding is denounced by many Protestants as "unbiblical." It's a bitter irony that the very doctrine of Christian unity has itself become a barrier to unity. The controversy revolves around the question, "Is it biblical to ask the saints in heaven to pray (intercede) for us?"

Catholics say yes. Since Christians are united with each other through Christ, and are commanded to love and pray for one another, Christians on earth can ask Christians in heaven for their prayers. Protestants say no. They say that praying to saints undermines Christ's unique mediatorship, pointing to 1 Timothy 2:5: "There is one God and one mediator between God and man, the man Christ Jesus." They think asking the saints to intercede for us is in direct conflict with this verse. The Anglican Reformers, under the leadership of Thomas Cranmer, the archbishop of Canterbury, said, "The Romish doctrine concerning ...[the] invocation of saints is a fond thing, vainly invented, and grounded upon no warranty of Scripture, but is, rather, repugnant to the Word of God."[66]

Vatican II gave the Catholic position: "By the hidden and kindly mystery of God's will a supernatural solidarity reigns among men. A consequence of this is that the sin of one person harms other people just as one person's holiness helps others. In this way Christian believers help each other reach their supernatural destiny.... This is the very ancient dogma called the communion of saints. It means that the life of each individual son of God is joined in Christ and through Christ by a wonderful link to the life of all his other Christian brethren. Together they form the supernatural unity of Christ's Mystical Body so that, as it were, a single mystical person is formed.... The union of the living with their brethren who have fallen asleep in Christ is not broken; the Church has rather believed through the ages that it gains strength from the sharing of spiritual benefits. The great intimacy of the union of those in heaven with Christ gives extra steadiness in holiness to the whole Church and makes a manifold contribution to the extension of her building. Now that they are welcomed in their own country and are at home with the Lord, through him, with him, and in him they intercede unremittingly with the Father on our behalf."[67]

As Paul said, "We are one body in Christ and individually parts of one another" (Romans 12:5). Catholics believe membership in Christ's Body means a personal relationship with Jesus and, through him, with all Christians.

"Me and Jesus" Christianity

Although Protestants may agree with this in theory, in application most of them (this is especially true of Evangelicals and Fundamentalists) promote an individualistic "me and Jesus" version of Christianity, teaching that the only thing ultimately important is one's own relationship with Christ, independent of any relationship to anyone else. While it may pay lip service to the communion of saints, in reality most of Protestantism ignores the organic bond of unity between the Christian faithful, a bond that perdures beyond death. Since most Catholics and Protestants agree the Bible is God's inspired, inerrant Word (some believe it is neither), the Bible is our common ground for dialogue. To be effective in explaining the communion of saints to Protestants, Catholics must know how to present the biblical foundations of this doctrine.

A Protestant sometimes remains unmoved in his objections even in the face of a thoroughgoing biblical defense of a Catholic doctrine. What the Protestant really disagrees with is the Catholic interpretation of verses, thus moving the argument beyond the "It's not in the Bible" category to the subjective "I don't agree with your interpretation" category. This attitude stems from Protestantism's fatal flaw, *sola Scriptura*, the notion that the Bible is the sole rule of faith, independent of Tradition or the Magisterium.

Protestants demand that Catholics substantiate their beliefs in Scripture (the old "Show me where it says that in the Bible" routine), yet when the demanded biblical evidence is produced, the Catholic conclusion is nonetheless rejected as "unScriptural." Since they reject the concept of an infallible interpreter of Scripture, whether it be the Church or an individual, Protestants can only put forth their own opinions on what they think Scripture means. They have no way of knowing for certain if their interpretation of the Bible is correct.

The Catholic position rests on four pillars: (1) The Church is Christ's Body; (2) Christ has only one Body, not one on earth and one in heaven; (3) Christians are not separated from each other by death; (4) Christians must love and serve each other.

The Church Is Christ's Body

Paul's use of the body as an image to describe the unity Christians have with Christ and with each other is particularly vivid: "For as in one body we have many members, and all the members do not have the same function, so we, though many, are one body in Christ, and individually members one of another" (Romans 12:4–5). The Lord alluded to this unity when he prayed, "may [they] be one even as we are one, I in them and thou in me, that they may become perfectly one..." (John 17:22–23). He used the analogy of himself as a vine and Christians as its branches to illustrate the organic bond Christians share (John 15:1–5).[68] The bond of Christian unity, the relationship between Christians on earth and those in heaven remains intact.

Jesus Has Only One Body

Jesus has only one Body—not one on earth and another one in heaven (see Ephesians 4:4; Colossians 3:15). All Christians, including those in heaven, are members of that one body.

Christians Are Not Separated by Death

Because of Christ's victory over death, a victory in which all Christians share,[69] natural death can't separate Christians from Christ or from each other. That's why Paul exulted, "What will separate us from the love of Christ? ...I am convinced that neither death, nor life...will be able to separate us from the love of God in Jesus Christ our Lord" (Romans 8:35–39). Since death has no power to sever the bond of Christian unity, the relationship between Christians on earth and those in heaven remains intact. The Protestant animus toward the idea that saints in heaven can pray for us bespeaks a sort of "out of sight, out of mind" mentality: "Since I no longer can see and speak to departed Christians, they must no longer matter to me."

This myopic position is not Scriptural. It clashes with verses that Protestants know by heart. Paul chides Christians who think they don't need other Christians: "God placed the parts, each one of them, in the body as he intended. If they were all one part, where would the body be? But as it is, there are many parts, yet one body. The eye cannot say to the hand, 'I do not need you,' nor again the head [say] to the feet, 'I do not need you.'.... God has so constructed the body, so as to give greater honor to a part that is without it, so that there may be no division in the body, but that the parts may have the same concern for one another. If one part suffers, all the parts suffer with it; if one part is honored, all parts share its joy" (1 Corinthians 12:18–20, 24–26).

Christians Are Bound in Charity

The fourth pillar is Christ's law of charity. Jesus said that loving one another is second in importance only to loving God (see Matthew 22:38; Mark 12:30–31; 1 Corinthians 13). This law of charity is emphasized in the New Testament at every turn, especially in the form of intercessory prayer. Paul exhorts Christians to pray, supplicate, petition, and intercede for all people. He emphasizes that intercessory prayer "is good and pleasing to God our savior" (1 Timothy 2:1–4).

Similar exhortations permeate the New Testament: "I urge you, brothers, by our Lord Jesus Christ and by the love of the Spirit, to join me in the struggle by your prayers to God on my behalf" (Romans 15:30–32). "In [Jesus] we have put our hope that he will also rescue us again, as you help us with prayer" (2

Corinthians 1:10). "We always give thanks to God, the Father of our Lord Jesus Christ, when we pray for you,.... We do not cease praying for you and asking that you may be filled with the knowledge of his will through all spiritual wisdom and understanding to live in a manner worthy of the Lord" (Colossians 1:3, 9–10).[70]

If, while on earth, Paul could say, "My heart's desire and prayer to God on their behalf is for salvation" (Romans 10:1) and "I remember you constantly in my prayers, night and day. I yearn to see you again" (2 Timothy 1:3), is there any reason to imagine that upon entering heaven Paul's charity and desire for others' salvation would be quenched and his prayers for others cease? Not at all. The Bible's many exhortations to mutual charity apply to all Christians, so they must apply to Christians in heaven.

Consider these admonitions regarding charity: "Bear one anothers' burdens, and so you will fulfill the law of Christ" (Galatians 6:2). "Love one another with mutual affection; anticipate one another in showing honor....contribute to the needs of the saints" (Romans 12:9–10). "No one should seek his own advantage, but that of his neighbor" (1 Corinthians 10:24). "On the subject of mutual charity you have no need for anyone to write you, for you yourselves have been taught by God to love one another. Nevertheless, we urge you, brothers, to progress even more" (1 Thessalonians 4:9–10). "Encourage one another, and build one another up....We urge you, brothers, admonish the idle, cheer the fainthearted, support the weak, always seek what is good both for each other and for all" (1 Thessalonians 5:11, 14–15; see 2 Corinthians 1:10–11).

Only to Christians Here Below?

At this point, a Protestant might object, "These verses refer to Christians on earth only. They say nothing about those in heaven." But where in the Bible do Protestants get the notion that God's commandment of charity is restricted to those on earth? Aren't the commandments of the Lord eternal, established in heaven as well as on earth? Although the saints in heaven are not explicitly mentioned in these verses, their participation is implied.

The Book of Hebrews gives us a compelling vision of the communion of saints in action. Chapter 11 extols the heroism of Old Testament saints, mentioning Noah, Abraham, Sarah, Joseph, Moses, and even Rahab the harlot. Chapter 12 reminds us that it's now our turn to run the race toward salvation. The writer encourages us to observe and imitate the heroic virtue of our Old Testament brothers and sisters and follow in their footsteps: "Therefore, since we are surrounded by so great a cloud of witnesses, let us rid ourselves of every burden and sin that clings to us and persevere in running the race that lies before us, while keeping our eyes fixed on Jesus, the leader and perfecter of faith" (Hebrews 12:1–2). Notice the Old Testament saints are called witnesses who surround us, as though they're cheering us on to victory as we run the race, following in their footsteps. This metaphor is derived from the Hellenistic foot race, a popular first-century spectator sport. The writer likens mortal life to a spiritual race that we must run, striving to win the crown of salvation (see 1 Corinthians 9:24–27). His didactic purpose in extolling the virtues of those who have run the race before us is twofold: first, to remind us that the saints are spectators of our race and, second, to urge us to imitate their examples. "Remember your leaders who spoke the Word of God to you. Consider the outcome of their way of life and imitate their faith" (Hebrews 13:7).[71] The saints aren't mere bystanders, devoid of compassion for us their fellow Christians still struggling on earth. Because of their love for us they earnestly intercede on our behalf before the throne of God. (If they didn't intercede, could it be said they in fact love us?)

Jesus alludes to this fraternal compassion of departed Christians in his parable about Lazarus and the rich man (see Luke 16:19–30). Notice that, although the rich man was in a place of torment, he showed charity toward his brothers: "I beg you, Father [Abraham], send [Lazarus] to my father's house, for I have five brothers, so that he may warn them, lest they too come to this place of torment." Even in his fiery sufferings, his thoughts were turned lovingly toward his family on earth.[72] I believe this passage is very likely a glimpse of purgatory (see 1 Corinthians 3:12–15; 1 Peter 3:19, 4:6), since the damned are incapable of charity and the rich man was exhibiting charity (which suggests he was not in hell). Protestants will contest this interpretation, arguing that the rich man was not in purgatory (since, they believe, there is no purgatory), but in hell. But this argument actually strengthens the Catholic position on the communion of saints, because if even the damned can intercede for those on earth, it follows *a fortiori* that the blessed in heaven can.

Two Common Objections

Two other common Protestant objections are that there is no biblical evidence of the saints interceding for us and that those in heaven are oblivious to earthly affairs. These notions are biblically untenable. In Revelation (the book which gives the clearest view of what the saints in heaven are doing) we find cases of the saints' intercession, and we consistently see that they're very much aware of what's happening on earth. See Luke 15:7 and Revelation 19:1–4. Two such examples: In Revelation 5:8 (see also Revelation 8:3–4) the saints stand before the throne of the Lamb, before the gold altar in the heavenly sanctuary. They sing hymns of praise and offer up the prayers of the saints on earth, prayers that rise like billowing clouds of incense. In Revelation 6:9–10 the martyred saints are praying imprecatory prayers against their murderers, urging the Lord to avenge their deaths.

But apart from such explicit passages, one can deduce that saints pray for us because we know that in heaven the saints are perfected in the virtue of charity that we on earth strive imperfectly to practice. They can love us and intercede for us with a single-minded intensity and efficacy they never could have had on earth. John tells us that "God is love" and that "Whoever does not love a brother whom he has seen cannot love God.... This is the commandment we have from him: Whoever loves God must love his brother" (1 John 4:16, 20–21).

God's Friends Are Ours

Far from being excluded from John's teaching, Christians in heaven best exemplify it. Since they see God face-to-face and are eternally bathed by his burning love, they can't help but love all those whom God loves. They're imbued with God's passionate love for his people. How could they not be? Because they love God they love and intercede for us. In heaven they perfectly fulfill the biblical mandate: "Since you have purified yourselves by obedience to the truth for sincere mutual love, love one another intensely" (1 Peter 1:22). Heaven would be a very strange place indeed, and God a very strange Father, if Christians in heaven were prohibited from intercessory prayer. Protestants must grapple with the question, "Why would God command intercessory prayer by Christians on earth but prohibit it by Christians in heaven?"

Even Martin Luther, when preaching on 1 John 3:13–18, reasoned his way very close to the Catholic position: "Such is the right interpretation and understanding of John's expression, 'We know that we have passed out of death into life because we love the brethren.' Here, in clear, decisive words, the conclusion is expressed that no man may boast of life unless he has love....One who knows the wretchedness and misery of death from experience, but has entered upon life with its solace and joy, blessings he seeks to maintain, such a person will desire for others the same blessing."[73]

The "One Mediator" Argument

Now we must still deal with several other common Protestant objections, the first of which is the "one mediator" argument: "Since Christ is the one mediator between God and man, asking the saints to intercede for us constitutes a gross infringement on his unique role. This is impermissible. We should just pray to God directly, period."

Actually, Catholics do both—and so do Protestants. Catholics and Protestants both pray directly to God and also ask their fellow Christians to pray for them. The difference is that Catholics don't restrict the term "Christians" to mean "only Christians on earth." It must be made clear that the Catholic Church in no way teaches that the saints are mediators in the special sense used in 1 Timothy 2:5. Because of the Incarnation, Jesus has a unique role as mediator. Since he is the only one who is God and man, the only contact point between us and the Father, only he is capable of bridging the chasm of sin that separates us from God. No saint can take Christ's place as mediator. The Catholic Church teaches instead that all Christians are intercessors who, because of Christ's mediatorship, are able to pray for each other.[74]

If asking Christians in heaven to pray for us conflicts with Christ's mediatorship, asking Christians on earth to pray for us conflicts for the same reason. If 1 Timothy 2:5 eliminates intercession by the Christians in heaven, it eliminates intercession by Christians on earth. But this would be a serious misreading. Far from excluding Christians from a share in Christ's mediatorship, Paul is actually emphasizing that we share in it through intercessory prayers. Our intercessions are effectual precisely and only because Christ is the one mediator.

"Mini-Mediators"

When Paul commanded that "supplications, prayers, petitions, and thanksgivings be offered for everyone...for this is good and pleasing to God our savior" (1 Timothy 2:1, 3), he was calling all Christians to exercise a "mini-mediatorship" through and in Christ. After all, someone who prays, supplicates, and petitions is a go-between—a mediator who goes to God on behalf of someone else and who asks the Lord to grant blessings or healing or strength or forgiveness or salvation. Christian mediatorship through intercessory prayer is qualitatively different from the mediatorship of Jesus, and it is only possible because Jesus is the mediator between us and the Father. By his death on the cross we can go boldly into the presence of the Father and pray, intercede, petition, and supplicate on behalf of others (see Ephesians 2:18, 1 Timothy 2:1–4, Hebrews 4:16).

Another reason there's no conflict between asking fellow Christians for prayers and believing that Jesus is the one mediator between God and man is that Jesus shares his other unique roles in lesser ways with Christians. Jesus is the creator of all things (see John 1:1–3, Colossians 1:16–17, Hebrews 1:1–2), yet when it comes to creating human life Jesus shares this role with men and women, mediating his creatorship through us via sexual intercourse. The human soul is created by God, out of nothing, at the instant the marital union produces a new body. The Lord could have chosen to create human life, body and soul, directly and unilaterally, but he didn't, preferring instead to make his role as Creator dependent in a way on human action.

Jesus is the shepherd of his flock the Church (see John 10:16), yet he shares his shepherdhood in a subordinate way with others, beginning with Peter (see John 21:15–17) and extending it later to others (see Ephesians 4:11). After saying he's the Good Shepherd, Jesus says he's the only shepherd (see John 10:11–16), yet this seemingly exclusive statement doesn't conflict with him making Peter shepherd over the flock (see John 21:15–17) or with his calling others to be shepherds as well (see Ephesians 4:11). Peter emphasizes that Jesus shares his role as shepherd with others by calling Jesus the chief shepherd, thus implying lesser shepherds (see 1 Peter 5:4). Note also that the Greek construction of John 10:16 ([there is] one shepherd, *heispoimen*) is the same as 1 Timothy 2:5 ([there is] one mediator, *heis mesites)*. The apostles and their successors, the bishops, are truly shepherds also.

Jesus is the high priest of the New Covenant, eternally present before the Father, mediating his once-for-all sacrifice for our redemption (see Hebrews 3:1, 4:14–15, 5:5–10, 7:15–26, 8:1, 9:11). But the Bible also says Christians are called to share in Christ's priesthood (see 1 Peter 2:5–9; Revelation 1:6, 5:10, 20:6). Jesus is the supreme judge (see John 5:27, 9:39; Romans 14:10; 2 Corinthians 5:10; 2 Timothy 4:1), yet Christians are called to share in Christ's judgeship. They will be judges in heaven, even judging the angels (see Matthew 19:28, Luke 22:30, 1 Corinthians 6:2–3, Revelation 20:4). Jesus is the sovereign king of the universe (see Mark 15:32; 1 Timothy 6:15; Revelation 15:3, 17:14, 19:16), but he shares his kingship with all Christians, who in heaven will wear crowns, sit on thrones, and reign as kings alongside Jesus—but always subordinate to him. Our Lord says, "I will give the victor the right to sit with me on my throne, as I myself first won the victory and sit with my Father on his throne" (Revelation 3:21). (See also Matthew 19:23; Luke 22:30; and Revelation 1:6, 5:10).

Jesus forgives our sins and reconciles us to the Father (see 2 Corinthians 5:18–21), but he calls us to share in various ways in his ministry of forgiveness and reconciliation (Matthew 9:5–8, 18:18; John 20:21–22; Acts 2:38; 2 Corinthians 5:18–20; James 5:14–15). Clearly, no Christian can usurp Christ's unique roles as creator, shepherd, priest, king, judge, and reconciler, but each Christian is called to share in these roles in subordinate ways. The principle of sharing in Christ's roles extends, in the form of intercessory prayer, to Christ's mediatorship as well.

Praying Straight to God

Another common argument against prayers to saints is the objection, "Why pray to the saints when you can go straight to God?" Protestants argue that verses such as these imply we should go only to God for our needs: "Through [Jesus] we both have access in one Spirit to the Father" (Ephesians 2:18); "Let us confidently approach the throne of grace to receive mercy and to find grace for timely help" (Hebrews 4:16); "We have one who speaks to the Father in our defense, Jesus Christ, the righteous one" (1 John 2:1). They feel that asking the saints for prayer is superfluous since, through Jesus, we now have a direct line to God. No "helpers" are necessary.

Sometimes this argument takes the form of an analogy: "If you had complete, unrestricted access to the president of the United States and could see him whenever you had a complaint or needed a favor, why waste your time going to see the secretary of state or the chief of staff when you could go directly into the Oval Office and get what you want from the man who makes the decisions?" In other words, why ask the saints to pester God for you (as though they can convince him to do things and you can't), when God loves you and wants to give you good things if you just ask him?

This is an incredibly obtuse line of reasoning. Of course God wants us to ask him for things directly—and we do—but he also wants us to ask each other for prayers (see 1 Timothy 2:1–3). What Protestant, when asked for prayer by a fellow Christian, would whirl on his heel and snarl, "How unbiblical! Why ask me to pray for you when you can go directly to God and ask him yourself?" Protestants realize that sharing in Christ's mediatorship on earth by intercessory prayer is no more "unbiblical" than sharing in Christ's priesthood or kingship or judgeship.

Many Protestants delight in being asked for intercessory prayer; isn't it reasonable to imagine the saints are just as delighted when asked for their prayers? They actively encourage it in others, especially in those they consider "prayer warriors," righteous Christians renowned for the efficacy of their prayers. As James 5:16 says, "The fervent prayer of a righteous person is very powerful." Christians in heaven are perfected in righteousness. Should their prayers be discounted? To ignore their role as "prayer warriors" makes no Scriptural sense.

Boettner's Argument

Loraine Boettner, the godfather of modern anti-Catholicism, takes a different tack in his argument:

> How dishonoring it is to Christ to teach that he is lacking in pity and compassion for his people and that he must be persuaded to that end.... When he was on earth it was never necessary for anyone to persuade him to be compassionate.[75] His love for us is as great as when he was on earth; his heart is as tender; and we need no other intermediary, neither his mother after the flesh, nor any saint or angel, to entreat him on our behalf. Thus Christ, because he is both God and man, is the only Savior, the only Mediator, the only way to God. Not one word is said about Mary...or the saints as mediators. Yet Romanism teaches that there are many mediators.[76]

While Boettner's pseudo-scholarly brand of anti-Catholicism is an embarrassment to better-educated Evangelicals, *Roman Catholicism* is widely used as a source for anti-Catholic arguments. His arguments must be reckoned with. This argument is a feeble contrivance. Note that Boettner never engages the Catholic position. He argues against a straw man by insinuating that Catholics believe that God needs Mary or the saints to intercede for us or else he won't act. No Catholic believes it's "necessary" for anyone to persuade God about anything.

Boettner Ignores the Bible

Boettner conveniently ignores the fact that the Bible says God is pleased by intercessory prayer (see 1 Timothy 2:1–4) and that sometimes, for his own inscrutable reasons, the Lord intervenes only as a result of intercession. Paul emphasizes that God frequently grants gifts "through the prayers of many" (2 Corinthians 1:10–11). Boettner also neglects to mention the biblical example of Mary's intercession with Christ in the relatively mundane matter of the wedding at Cana (see John 2:1–10), nor does he deal with the fact that the martyrs in heaven intercede with God, beseeching him to avenge their deaths (see Revelation 6:9–11). The Bible is full of examples of angels and saints interceding with God on behalf of others. Abraham intercedes on behalf of Sodom and Gomorrah (see Genesis 18:16–32). Moses intercedes for the people of Israel, begging God not to destroy them, and God relents (see Exodus 32:7–14). An angel intercedes on behalf of Jerusalem (see Zechariah 1:12). Paul intercedes on behalf of the Church (see Colossians 1:9–12).

Not All Prayer Is Worship

There is a more fundamental reason Protestants object to the invocation of saints. Many of them, especially Evangelicals and Fundamentalists, have a poor understanding of prayer. Since the highest form of worship Protestants have is prayer (they make no distinction between prayer and worship), Catholic prayers to saints seem blasphemous. In fact, the highest form of worship is not prayer but the Mass—Christ's own sacrifice on Calvary, presented again for us in space and time. Although all worship is prayer, not all prayer is worship. Prayers to saints are no more worship than is asking a fellow Christian for prayer. There's no other way to ask those in heaven to intercede for us except by mental communication, and we call this communication "prayer," but it should not be confused with the prayer of worship given to God alone.

What About Multiple Prayers?

There's also the "multiple prayer" objection: "How can the saints hear all those millions of simultaneous prayers, in all those different languages? To be able to do that would require them to be omniscient and omnipresent, but only God is omniscient and omnipresent."

This is faulty reasoning on three levels. First, since the saints are living in eternity, they aren't limited by time and space—they are beyond both. One might say it takes no time at all to hear all those prayers because the saints have no time. Second, since there are only a finite number of people on earth, there are only a finite number of prayers at any one time. So, neither omniscience nor omnipresence is required to hear all the prayers ever prayed at one time, no matter how great their number. Third, it's silly to think that the abilities of the saints in heaven are as paltry as ours are. Our inability to understand how the saints hear so many prayers is hardly a reason to deny that they can hear them.

In their glorified state the saints are capable of doing things we can barely imagine: "Eye has not seen, and ear has not heard, [nor has it] entered the human heart, what God has prepared for those who love him" (1 Corinthians 2:9). Those in heaven rejoice over the repentance of even one sinner (see Luke 15:7, 10), but we have no details about how they can know about individual repentances. We know that in heaven we'll be transformed into the image of Christ's glorious, resurrected body. "We shall be like him," Paul assures us in Philippians 3:20–21. John says, "We are God's children now; what we shall be has not yet been revealed. We do know that we shall be like him, for we shall see him as he is" (1 John 3:2). In his resurrected, glorified body, Jesus did all sorts of incredible things, such as walk through walls (see John 20:19). "So also is the resurrection of the dead. [The body] is sown corruptible; it is raised incorruptible. It is sown dishonorable; it is raised glorious. It is sown weak; it is raised powerful" (1 Corinthians 15:42–43). Heaven is an amazing place filled with people who, by God's infinite grace, are capable of doing amazing things.

The Necromancy Argument

Some raise the "necromancy" objection: "The saints are dead, and the Bible forbids contact with the dead." This is a misunderstanding of terms. Necromancy is an attempt to harness diabolical powers in order to, among other things, communicate with "familiar spirits." The Bible condemns this occult practice, which includes attempting to communicate with spirits through trances, séances, and incantations (see Leviticus 19:26, 31; 20:6, 27; Deuteronomy 18:10–12; 1 Samuel 28:4–18; Isaiah 8:19; 47:12–14). Asking saints to pray for us is not necromancy. Aside from the method of communication, asking our fellow Christians in heaven to intercede on our behalf is no different from asking a fellow Christian here on earth to pray for us. Besides, the saints aren't really dead at all. They're far more alive than we are on earth. Jesus said, "Have you not read in the book of Moses, in the passage about the bush, how God told him, 'I am the God of Abraham, the God of Isaac, and the God of Jacob'? He is not the God of the dead but of the living. You are greatly misled" (Mark 12:26–27. See also Wisdom 3:1–3 and John 17:3).[77]

A final question: If Jesus didn't want any contact between saints on earth (as Paul anticipatorily calls Christians) and saints in heaven, why did our Lord make a special point of appearing to Peter, James, and John on the Mount of Transfiguration in the company of Moses and Elijah (see Matthew 17:1–8), two "dead" saints?

This Rock, *September 1992*

Mary, Ark of the New Covenant:
A Biblical Look at the Immaculate Conception
of the Blessed Virgin Mary

HIS FACE STIFFENED, AND HIS EYES NARROWED to slits. Until now the Calvary Chapel pastor had been calm as he "shared the gospel" with me, but when I mentioned my belief in Mary's Immaculate Conception, his attitude changed. "The problem with you Roman Catholics," he said, his thin forefinger stabbing the air a few inches from my face, "is that you've added extra baggage to the gospel. How can you call yourselves Christians when you cling to unbiblical traditions like the Immaculate Conception? It's not in the Bible—it was invented by the Roman Catholic system in 1854. Besides, Mary couldn't have been sinless; only God is sinless. If she were without sin, she would be God!"

At least the minister got the date right, 1854 being the year Pope Pius IX infallibly defined the doctrine of Mary's Immaculate Conception, but that's as far as his accuracy went. His reaction was typical of Evangelicals. He was adamant that the Catholic emphasis on Mary's sinlessness was an unbearable affront to the unique holiness of God, especially as manifested in Jesus Christ.

After we had examined the biblical evidence for the doctrine, the anti-Marianism he'd shown became muted, but it was clear that, at least emotionally if not biblically, Mary was a stumbling block for him. Like most Christians (Catholic and Protestant), the minister was unaware of the biblical support for the Church's teaching on the Immaculate Conception. But sometimes, even knowledge of these passages isn't enough. Many former Evangelicals who have converted to the Catholic Church relate how hard it was for them to put aside prejudices and embrace Marian doctrines even after they'd thoroughly satisfied themselves through prayer and Scripture study that such teachings are indeed biblical.

For Evangelicals who have investigated the issue and discovered, to their astonishment, the biblical support for Marian doctrines, there often lingers the suspicion that somehow, in a way they can't quite identify, the Catholic emphasis on Mary's sinlessness undermines the unique sinlessness of Christ.

To alleviate such suspicions, one must understand what the Church means (and doesn't mean) by the doctrine of the Immaculate Conception. Pope Pius IX, in his constitution *Ineffabilis Deus* (issued December 8, 1854), taught that Mary, "from the first instance of her conception, by a singular privilege and grace granted by God, in view of the merits of Jesus Christ, the Savior of the human race, was preserved exempt from all stain of original sin." The doctrine includes the assertion that Mary was perpetually free from all actual sin (willful disobedience of God, either venial or mortal).

Several Objections Raised by Protestants

First, if only God is sinless, Mary couldn't have been sinless or she would have been God.

Second, if Mary was sinless, why did she say, "My spirit rejoices in God my savior" (Luke 1:47)? If only sinners need a savior, why would Mary, if free from sin, include herself in the category of sinners? If she were sinless, she would have had no need of a savior, and her statement in Luke 1 would be incoherent.

Third, Paul says in Romans 3:10–12, 23, "There is no one just [righteous], not one, there is no one who understands, there is no one who seeks God, all have gone astray; all alike are worthless; there is not one who does good, not even one…all have sinned and are deprived [fallen short] of the glory of God." In Romans 5:12 he says, "Therefore, just as through one person sin entered the world, and through sin, death, and thus death came to all, inasmuch as all sinned… ". These verses seem to rule out any possibility that Mary was sinless.

The Immaculate Conception emphasizes four truths: (1) Mary *did* need a savior; (2) her savior was Jesus Christ; (3) Mary's salvation was accomplished by

Jesus through his work on the cross; and (4) Mary was saved from sin, but in a different and more glorious way than the rest of us are.

Let's consider the first and easiest of the three objections. The notion that God is the only being without sin is false—and even Protestants think so. Adam and Eve, before the fall, were free from sin, and they weren't gods, the serpent's assertions to the contrary notwithstanding. (One must remember that Mary was not the first immaculate human being, even if she was the first to be conceived immaculately.) The angels in heaven are not gods, but they were created sinless and have remained so ever since. The saints in heaven are not gods, although each of them is now completely sinless (Revelation 14:5; 21:27).

The second and third arguments are related. Mary needed Jesus as her savior. His death on the cross saved her, as it saves us, but its saving effects were applied to her (unlike to us) at the moment of her conception. (Keep in mind that the crucifixion is an eternal event and that the appropriation of salvation through Christ's death isn't impeded by time or space.)

Medieval theologians developed an analogy to explain how and why Mary needed Jesus as her savior. A man (each of us) is walking along a forest path, unaware of a large pit a few paces directly ahead of him. He falls headlong into the pit and is immersed in the mud (original sin) it contains. He cries out for help, and his rescuer (the Lord Jesus) lowers a rope down to him and hauls him back up to safety. The man says to his rescuer, "Thank you for saving me," recalling the words of the psalmist: The Lord "stooped toward me and heard my cry. He drew me out of the pit of destruction, out of the mud of the swamp; he set my feet upon a crag" (Psalm 40:2–4).

A woman (Mary) approaches the same pit, but as she begins to fall into the pit her rescuer reaches out and stops her from falling in. She cries out, "Thank you for saving me" (Luke 1:47). Like this woman, Mary was no less "saved" than any other human being has been saved. She was just saved anticipatorily, *before* contracting original sin. God has permitted each of us to become dirtied with original sin, but she was not. God hates sin, so this was a far better way.

St. Paul's statements in Romans chapters 3 and 5 (no one is righteous; no one seeks God; no one does good; all have sinned) should not be taken in a crassly literal and universal sense—if they are, irreconcilable contradictions will arise. Consider Luke 1:6. Common sense tells us whole groups of people are exempt from Paul's statement that "all have sinned." Aborted infants cannot sin, nor can young children or severely retarded people. But Paul didn't mention such obvious exceptions. He was writing to adults in our state of life.

If certain groups are exempt from the "all have sinned" rubric, then these verses can't be used to argue against Mary's Immaculate Conception, since hers would be an exceptional case too, one not needing mention given the purpose of Paul's discussion and his intended audience.

Now let's consider what the Bible has to say in favor of the Catholic position. It's important to recognize that neither the words "Immaculate Conception" nor the precise formula adopted by the Church to enunciate this truth are found in the Bible. This doesn't mean the doctrine isn't biblical, only that the truth of the Immaculate Conception, like the truths of the Trinity and Jesus's hypostatic union (that Jesus was incarnated as God and man, possessing completely and simultaneously two natures, divine and human, in one divine person), is mentioned either in other words or only indirectly.

Look first at two passages in Luke 1. In verse 28, the angel Gabriel greets Mary as "*kecharitomene*" ("full of grace" or "highly favored"). This is a recognition of her sinless state. In verse 42 Elizabeth greets Mary as "blessed among women." The original import of this phrase is lost in English translation. Since neither the Hebrew nor Aramaic languages have superlatives (best, highest, tallest, holiest), a speaker of those languages would have to say, "You are tall among men" or "You are wealthy among men" to mean "You are the tallest" or "You are the wealthiest." Elizabeth's words mean Mary was the holiest of all women.

The Church understands Mary to be the fulfillment of three Old Testament types: the cosmos, Eve, and the ark of the covenant. A type is a person, event, or thing in the Old Testament that foreshadows or symbolizes some future reality God brings to pass. (See these verses for Old Testament types fulfilled in the

New Testament: Colossians 2:17, Hebrews 1:1, 9:9, 9:24, 10:1; 1 Corinthians 15:45–49; Galatians 4:24–25.)

Some specific examples of types: Adam was a type of Christ (Romans 5:14); Noah's Ark and the Flood were types of the Church and baptism (1 Peter 3:19–21); Moses, who delivered Israel from the bondage of slavery in Egypt, was a type of Christ, who saves us from the bondage of slavery to sin and death; circumcision foreshadowed baptism; the slain Passover lamb in Exodus 12:21–28 was a symbol of Jesus, the Lamb of God, being slain on the cross to save sinners. The important thing to understand about a type is that its fulfillment is always more glorious, more profound, more "real" than the type itself.

Mary's Immaculate Conception is foreshadowed in Genesis 1, where God creates the universe in an immaculate state, free from any blemish or stain of sin or imperfection. This is borne out by the repeated mention in Genesis 1 of God beholding his creations and saying they were "very good." Out of pristine matter the Lord created Adam, the first immaculately created human being, forming him from the "womb" of the Earth. The immaculate elements from which the first Adam received his substance foreshadowed the immaculate mother from whom the second Adam (see Romans 5:14) took his human substance.

The second foreshadowing of Mary is Eve, the physical mother of our race, just as Mary is our spiritual mother through our membership in the Body of Christ (see Revelation 12:17). What Eve spoiled through disobedience and lack of faith (see Genesis 3), Mary set aright through faith and obedience (see Luke 1:38).

We see a crucial statement in Genesis 3:15: "*I will put enmity between you [Satan] and the woman, between your seed and her seed; he will crush your head, and you will strike at his heel.*" This passage is especially significant in that it refers to the "seed of the woman," a singular usage. The Bible, following normal biology, otherwise only refers to the seed of the man, the seed of the father, but never to the seed of the woman. Who is the woman mentioned here? The only possibility is Mary, the only woman to give birth to a child without the aid of a human father, a fact prophesied in Isaiah 7:14.

If Mary were not completely sinless, this prophesy becomes untenable. Why is that? The passage points to Mary's Immaculate Conception because it mentions a complete enmity between the woman and Satan. Such an enmity would have been impossible if Mary had been tainted by sin, original or actual (see 2 Corinthians 6:14). This line of thinking rules out Eve as the woman, since she clearly was under the influence of Satan in Genesis 3.

The third and most compelling type of Mary's Immaculate Conception is the ark of the covenant. In Exodus 20 Moses is given the ten commandments. In chapters 25 through 30 the Lord gives Moses a detailed plan for the construction of the ark, the special container that would carry the commandments. The surprising thing is that five chapters later, starting in chapter 35 and continuing to chapter 40, Moses repeats word for word each of the details of the ark's construction.

Why? It was a way of emphasizing how crucial it was for the Lord's exact specifications to be met (see Exodus 25:9, 39:42–43). God wanted the ark to be as perfect and unblemished as humanly possible so it would be worthy of the honor of bearing the written Word of God. How much more so would God want Mary, the ark of the new covenant, to be perfect and unblemished since she would carry within her womb the Word of God in flesh. When the ark was completed, "the cloud covered the meeting tent and the glory of the Lord filled the dwelling. Moses could not enter the meeting tent, because the cloud settled down upon it and the glory of the Lord filled the dwelling" (see Exodus 40:34–38). Compare this with the words of Gabriel to Mary in Luke 1:35.

There's another striking foreshadowing of Mary as the new ark of the covenant in 2 Samuel 6. The Israelites had lost the ark in a battle with their enemies, the Philistines, and had recently recaptured it. King David sees the ark being brought to him and, in his joy and awe, says, "Who am I that the ark of the Lord should come to me?" (1 Samuel 6:9). Compare this with Elizabeth's nearly identical words in Luke 1:43. Just as David leapt for joy before the ark when it was brought into Jerusalem (see 2 Samuel 6:14–16), so John the Baptist leapt for joy in Elizabeth's womb when Mary, the ark of the new covenant, came into her presence (see Luke 1:44). John's leap was for precisely the same reason as David's—not primarily because of the ark itself, but because of what the ark contained, the Word of God. Another parallel may be found in 2 Samuel 6:10–12, where we read that David ordered the ark diverted up into the hill country of Judea to remain with the household of Obededom for three months. This parallels the three-month visit Mary made at Elizabeth's home in the hill country of Judea (see Luke 1:39–45, 65). While the ark remained with Obededom, it "blessed his household." This is an Old Testament way of saying the fertility of women, crops, and livestock was increased. Notice that God worked this same miracle for Elizabeth and Zachariah in their old age as a prelude to the greater miracle he would work in Mary.

The Mary/ark imagery appears again in Revelation 11:19 and 12:1–17, where she is called the mother of all "those who keep God's commandments and bear witness to Jesus" (verse 17). The ark symbolism found in Luke 1 and Revelation 11 and 12 was not lost on the early Christians. They could see the parallels between the Old Testament's description of the ark and the New Testament's discussion of Mary's role.

Granted, none of these verses "proves" Mary's Immaculate Conception, but they all point to it. After all, the Bible nowhere says Mary committed any sin or languished under original sin. As far as explicit statements are concerned, the Bible is silent on most of the issue, yet all the biblical evidence supports the Catholic teaching.

A last thought: If you could have created your own mother, wouldn't you have made her the most beautiful, virtuous, perfect woman possible? Jesus, being God, *did* create his own mother (see Colossians 1:16; Hebrews 1:2), and he did just that—he created her immaculate and, in his mercy and generosity, kept her that way.

This Rock, *1991*

Does Honoring Mary and the Saints Offend God?

ɪɪ

"Although Catholics deny that they worship and adore Mary, they generally contradict that denial by their practice." This is how Eric Svendsen, a Protestant apologist begins his argument against the Catholic Church.[78]

Let's see if his "Mary worship" charge has any merit. Svendsen continues his attack: "There seems to be some confusion on the part of Catholics as to what worship is. They insist in their writings that Mary is to receive honor, not worship; but their explicit practice more resembles worship than honor—bowing to, praying to, and singing praises to anyone must be considered worship, not mere honor."[79]

This argument is without merit. First, let's recognize that in Scripture it's common to read of "singing praises" to God, something Catholics and Protestants would agree is an excellent and necessary thing to do. But what about the biblical examples of "singing praises" to humans? For example, it's interesting that God would inspire the following words to be written in Scripture, including the prophecy that there would be "bowing to" and "praising" of Judah, a mere human being: "Judah, your brothers shall praise you; your hand shall be on the neck of your enemies; your father's sons shall bow down before you" (Genesis 49:7). "[T]he Lord has declared this day concerning you that you are a people for his own possession as he has promised you, and that you are to keep all his commandments, that he will set you high above all nations that he has made, in praise and in fame and in honor, and that you shall be a people holy to the Lord your God, as he has spoken" (Deuteronomy 26:18–19). "Praise his people, O you nations; for he avenges the blood of his servants, and takes vengeance on his adversaries, and makes expiation for the land of his people" (Deuteronomy 32:43). You get the idea. The fact is, the Bible doesn't merely speak approvingly of men's rendering such legitimate praise to other human beings, it actually provides us with many examples of God himself praising faithful men and women.

This is a type of *a fortiori* argument against his position that seems to be lost on Svendsen. In other words, if Scripture shows us clear examples of an all-holy, all-perfect God praising his creatures for the good things they do, *a fortiori* (i.e., we can conclude even more strongly) that sinful, imperfect human beings can praise those who do good in God's service. "He is a Jew who is one inwardly, and real circumcision is a matter of the heart, spiritual and not literal. His praise is not from men but from God" (Romans 2:29). How is it that God praises human beings and we are not permitted to do so? Where does the Bible offer support for Svendsen's (that is, Protestantism's) view? It doesn't. This type of argumentation is clearly absurd, not to mention unbiblical.

For example, the Holy Spirit inspired St. Paul to write the following words to his fellow Christians: "Be imitators of me, as I am of Christ. I praise you because you remember me in everything and maintain the traditions even as I have delivered them to you" (1 Corinthians 11:1–2). As for "bowing," Svendsen's apparent "all or nothing" approach to Scripture simply doesn't pan out. He'd have a hard time, if he's to be consistent with his own argument ("bowing to anyone must be considered worship, not mere honor"), explaining how it is that the patriarch Isaac could utter these prophetic words to his son Jacob: "Let peoples serve you, and nations bow down to you. Be lord over your brothers, and may your mother's sons bow down to you" (Genesis 27:29). Joshua bowed down and paid homage to an angel, but committed no sin in doing so (see Joshua 5:14). Ruth bowed down to the ground before Boaz in gratitude (see Ruth 2:8–10), but she was not worshipping Boaz. The Shunammite woman bowed down before the prophet Elisha after he had raised her child from the dead (see 2 Kings 4:37), but she was not committing idolatry. Neither was Lot, when he "bowed down" before two angels of the Lord (see Genesis 19:1). Nor was David sinning against God's commandment when he "bowed down and did obeisance" before King Saul (1 Samuel 24:8). Bathsheba and Nathan the prophet were also blameless when they "bowed down in honor" before King David, while the monarch was on his deathbed (1 Kings 1:16, 25).[80]

When Jacob and Esau had their dramatic reconciliation, we read: "He himself went on before them, bowing himself to the ground seven times, until he came near to his brother" (Genesis 33:3). And then there are the words of Christ concerning the honor and glory due to faithful Christians: "I know your works. Behold, I have set before you an open door, which no one is able to shut; I know that you have but little power, and yet you have kept my word and have not denied my name. Behold, I will make those of the synagogue of Satan who say that they are Jews and are not, but lie—behold, I will make them come and bow down before your feet, and learn that I have loved you" (Revelation 3:8–9).

If, as Svendsen and other Protestants argue, "praising" and "bowing down" before a human being "must be considered worship, not mere honor," then the Bible indicts St. Paul and the Lord Jesus Christ himself, since they are caught in the act of praising and honoring human beings! Such argumentation against the Catholic Church, then, proves nothing. The Bible says that bowing, if it's done to show respect and honor to a friend of God, is not just tolerable, but admirable. It also shows us that honoring and praising God's friends is good and itself honors and glorifies God. Scripture tells us that if we persevere in fidelity to Christ, we will receive honor and praise. This is, of course, exactly what the Catholic Church teaches and does when it honors and praises Mary and the saints. "In this you rejoice, though now for a little while you may have to suffer various trials, so that the genuineness of your faith, more precious than gold which though perishable is tested by fire, may redound to praise and glory and honor at the revelation of Jesus Christ" (1 Peter 1:6–7).

When we recognize and proclaim the beauty God has wrought in a majestic mountain, or a dazzling sunset, no one would think that doing so somehow takes away any glory from God. God is glorified in his creation (e.g., angels, mountains, stars, sunsets, human beings), and when we praise the beauty of his creation we are praising him. This principle is at the heart of the Catholic teaching on honoring Mary and the saints. We recognize the great beauty and the graces God has bestowed on these men and women (see Romans 8:30), and praising them redounds to God's greater honor and glory. On the other hand, bowing before anything or anyone in an act of worship is, of course, idolatry (see *CCC,* 2122–2124). The Catholic Church has always made this distinction clear. The Bible makes this clear too (see Judges 2:17, 16:30; Romans 11:4).

The Hebrew word for "bow down," *shachah,* means "to lie prostrate." The same word is used both in the passages that prohibit bowing (e.g., Exodus 20:5) and in some of those that show bowing as legitimate (e.g., Genesis 27:29). In fact, we're told the saints are worthy of praise and emulation. St. Paul said: "Our gospel came to you not only in word, but also in power and in the Holy Spirit and with full conviction. You know what kind of men we proved to be among you for your sake. And you became imitators of us and of the Lord, for you received the word in much affliction, with joy inspired by the Holy Spirit; so that you became an example to all the believers in Macedonia and in Achaia. For not only has the word of the Lord sounded forth from you in Macedonia and Achaia, but your faith in God has gone forth everywhere, so that we need not say anything" (1 Thessalonians 1:5–8).

Even Martin Luther, well after he had renounced the Catholic Church and became a Protestant, spoke of Mary in these glowing terms: "She, the lady above heaven and earth, must...have a heart so humble that she might have no shame in washing the swaddling clothes or preparing a bath for St. John the Baptist, like a servant girl. What humility! It would surely have been more just to have arranged for her a golden coach, pulled by 4,000 horses, and to cry and proclaim as the carriage proceeded, 'Here passes the woman who is raised above the whole human race!' ...She was not filled with pride by this praise...this immense praise: 'No woman is like unto thee! Thou art more than an empress or a queen...blessed above all nobility, wisdom, or saintliness!'"[81]

Statements of praise for Mary like these are sources of scandal and irritation for today's Evangelical Protestants. But in reality, they serve to show just how far Evangelicalism has drifted from its own roots. Today's Protestant antagonism against Catholic teachings on Mary and the saints arises not from any authentic, organic doctrinal system, but from five centuries of accreted hostility towards things Catholic.

Imitating the Saints

Not only is St. Paul pleased that the Thessalonian Christians imitated him and his apostolic companions, he also points out that they themselves had by then become objects of emulation for other Christians ("you became an example"). He speaks of their example as "going everywhere" and shows that it is good to recognize the holiness of God's saints (whether they're on earth or, by implication, in heaven) and imitate them. By such imitation we become saintly too, and this leads to our example being an encouragement to others.

Here's another key: "Brethren, join in imitating me, and mark those who so live as you have an example in us....Finally, brethren, whatever is true, whatever is honorable, whatever is just, whatever is pure, whatever is lovely, whatever is gracious, if there is any excellence, if there is anything worthy of praise, think about these things. What you have learned and received and heard and seen in me, do; and the God of peace will be with you" (Philippians 3:17, 4:8–9). The Protestant who objects that this conclusion involves a misapplication of this passage will have to explain why the saints should be excluded from those things that are "honorable," "just," and "worthy of praise."

Furthermore, there are several important components of these two passages from Philippians that we must consider. First, notice that we're told to think about honorable, pure, and just things. The Blessed Virgin Mary and the saints in heaven are the epitome of "honorable," "just," and "worthy of praise"—they have received from God the highest honor and praise possible, and they have been perfected in righteousness (see Hebrews 12:23). So, biblically speaking,

Christians are not just permitted to reflect on and speak about the saints, we are exhorted to do so.

Second, we see in Philippians 3:17 St. Paul's statement, "Join in imitating me." Protestants generally feel uncomfortable with the Catholic emphasis on the saints, suspecting that such focusing on them somehow robs Christ of attention. But nothing could be further from the truth. Here we see that St. Paul wants others to imitate him, just as he was striving to imitate Christ. It's not an "either or" approach here—either the saints or God—but a "both and" attitude. Imitate Christ and imitate those who were exemplary in imitating him. This, of course, is what the Catholic Church is doing when it encourages devotion to Mary and the saints. They are the model for us in Christian sanctity, heroism, and fidelity to Christ's Gospel. When we focus our attention on the saints, we are simply carrying out the excellent advice given to us by St. Paul.

Third, notice that St. Paul tells his readers that they (like we) should "do" (i.e., practice and believe) the things they saw and learned from him. What were these things? In the realm of "imitating virtue" (see 1 Corinthians 11:1), St. Paul showed himself to be zealous, diligent, brave, charitable, prayerful, kind, joyful, full of faith, a lover of Scripture and the Church, and above all, unswerving in his love for Christ. These are precisely the things each of us is called to be, and St. Paul holds himself out as an example.

Remember that he is not merely telling his first-century readers to meditate on his example and follow it. The Holy Spirit inspired those words and preserved them in the Church for us. This means that you and I are called to focus our thoughts on all the saints—God's friends—as models for us to follow: "Remember your leaders, those who spoke to you the word of God; consider the outcome of their life, and imitate their faith" (Hebrews 13:7). In the realm of "doing" the things St. Paul handed on,[82] we see the whole body of apostolic doctrine and practice that he received from the Lord and handed on to the Church.

Part of the reason Catholics emphasize devotion to the saints is that we see in them a profound understanding of and fidelity to the doctrines of the Faith, doctrines handed down to them from Christ and the apostles and which they, in turn, handed down to us in their writings, preaching, and exemplary lives. Scripture is clear that honoring the Blessed Virgin Mary and the saints is good and pleasing to God. But it's equally clear that God is displeased when someone goes beyond the proper honor due the Blessed Virgin Mary (*hyperdulía*) and the saints (*dulía*) and crosses into the idolatry of worshipping them as gods. To see how to admonish those who fall into this error, consider the case of the angel who rebuked John for his temptation to idolatry: "At this I fell at his feet to worship him. But he said to me, "Do not do it! I am a fellow servant with you and with your brothers who hold to the testimony of Jesus. Worship God!" (Revelation 19:10). The Catholic Church emphasizes at every turn that Our Lady herself would admonish with the same words anyone who would attempt to worship her: "Do not do it! I am a fellow servant with you and with your brothers who hold to the testimony of Jesus. Worship God!"

Rapid City's Straight-Talking Bishop

I FIRST MET (THEN) BISHOP CHARLES CHAPUT in early 1990, when he was the young (forty-seven) and virtually unknown bishop of Rapid City, South Dakota, and I was a wet-behind-the-ears young (twenty-nine) and utterly unknown Catholic apologist working at Catholic Answers. I had been invited to conduct a weekend series of apologetics seminars at the Rushmore Plaza Civic Center in "downtown" Rapid City. (If you have ever been to Rapid City, you will understand why I put quote marks around "downtown.") The evening I arrived, I had dinner with Bishop Chaput and a local Catholic couple at a small, mom-and-pop Chinese restaurant in town. It was a great opportunity to get to know him, and I was immediately impressed by his warmth, keen intellect, and easy approachability.

The following day, Saturday, as I stepped out onto the stage to face an audience of three or four hundred people, I was disconcerted to see the bishop sitting in the front row. As I recall, he remained there listening to my talks until early afternoon. On the one hand, I was flattered that a bishop (a bishop!) would spend that much time listening to what I had to say (which, of course, was nowhere near as compelling as whatever he might have said had he been the speaker instead of me). On the other hand, I am not ashamed to admit that it was quite nerve-racking for me to have a bishop (a bishop!), the teacher of the Faith for that diocese, doing quality control that day. Happily, my talks apparently passed muster. Not only, at the end of that day, did Bishop Chaput thank me for presenting, he told me he thought my talks were helpful. Best of all, that first visit to Rapid City marked the beginning of a friendship I have had with him ever since.

On a subsequent visit, he invited me to his house for dinner and even challenged me to a game of racquetball (his favorite sport, I discovered, at which he was rather formidable in those days, from what others told me). I wasn't able to accept that challenge, but I did get a good chuckle out of the fact that, when I chatted with him briefly at a conference we were both at in Orlando a couple of years ago, I reminded him that I was still holding a rain check for that racquetball game offer.

"Anytime!" he exclaimed with a twinkle in his eye. "I could still whip you, young man!" And even though he is now sixty-eight, I am quite sure he could.

In the twenty-two years since I first met him, now *Archbishop* Charles Chaput served as the widely beloved archbishop of Denver (1997–2007) and is now the archbishop of Philadelphia, a tough and challenging assignment if ever there was one, what with the raw wounds of the priest scandal debacle he inherited and is tasked by the pope with healing.

As I reread this interview with him back in 1994, I have no difficulty seeing the gentle but fearless and Christlike shepherd of souls he has continually proven himself to be ever since.

• • •

Charles Chaput, O.F.M., CAP., was ordained a priest in 1970 and bishop of Rapid City, South Dakota in 1988. Born in 1944, he is one of the youngest bishops in the country. He has been active in the National Conference of Catholic Bishops' deliberations about inclusive language in the liturgy, as these pages demonstrate. This interview, conducted by Patrick Madrid of the Catholic Answers staff, took place before the promulgation of *Ordinatio Sacerdotalis,* the Holy Father's letter on priestly ordination of women.

MADRID: What is your opinion of radical feminism in the Church? How do you assess this challenge?

CHAPUT: The role of women and how Church life and teaching are and should be affected by women are central issues of our time. It's important that the Church clearly enunciate its teaching about the value of women and their role in the Church. At the bishops' conference meetings, when we talk about this issue, we're not sure what language to use because some women who are very committed to promoting the role of women in the Church (such as women's ordination, for example) claim that we bishops "dismiss" their views when we use the term "radical feminism" in reference to their position. There is a good type of feminism, you know, in which women embrace their femininity in the fullest sense of the word, and the duty of men to respect and value that wonderful gift from God is obvious. The way some try to distinguish between Christian feminism and the kind that looks dangerous is to use the term "radical feminism," but many feminists reject using that language. So it's difficult to even know what language to use. I think in some ways that is one of the most important issues that I'll ever face as a bishop and one that we need to give close and careful attention to.

MADRID: If they don't like the title "radical feminism," just what do they like?

CHAPUT: I just don't know, Pat. I really don't. It's very difficult even to talk because the term "radical feminism" is shorthand for everything that I would object to in the feminist movement.

MADRID: What do you see as the long-range objective of the "radical feminists"?

CHAPUT: Well, I think that, on the positive side, there are some feminists who want to do all they can to emphasize the authentic Christian heritage of women and promote women in society and in the Church. I embrace that goal, and I think anyone who is a Christian should. But the agenda, the ultimate goal, of some who support "radical feminism" is ordination into the priesthood, and for those of us who believe it is not possible for the Church to ordain women and at the same time be faithful to the teachings of Christ, this is a totally unacceptable goal. The role of a bishop is to conserve the teachings of Christ. That's my essential responsibility, to do all I can to pass on, unchanged, the teachings of Christ and the apostles. It is not possible to be faithful to the apostolic teaching and ordain women.

MADRID: Is women's ordination the only goal? What about the clamor about abortion, contraception, and sometimes even lesbianism among "radical feminists"? Do "radical feminists" themselves know exactly what it is they want?

CHAPUT: I would not want to paint the entire feminist movement with all of the issues of abortion, contraception, and the like. Many people enthusiastically embrace part of the feminist agenda, but don't embrace all of it, so I think it's unfair to lump them all together. For example, I know many people who are faithful to the Church's moral teachings, regarding sexual morality, but who also favor the ordination of women. The two issues that most concern me are the questions of inclusive language and the ordination of women. There are those who believe that "patriarchy" has tainted all of the Church: Scripture, moral teachings, etc. Because they want the Church to change its teaching regarding the ordination of women, they are actually changing Scripture. They claim that Scripture is tainted by a patriarchal mentality and that by relying on it "as is" women are going to be subjected to the manipulation of men.

MADRID: How do you respond to such a claim?

CHAPUT: The answer is that Scripture is the Word of God, and the "patriarchal" elements that are certainly there are part of God's Word, God's way of dealing with his people. We must always understand Scripture in the light of the living tradition of the Church, and we don't go around changing things in Scripture to fit the philosophical movements that happen to be in vogue.

MADRID: What about the feminists who say that response "begs the question"? You say "we" shouldn't change things, but the "we," they argue, is men. The hierarchy obviously does not want to see those "patriarchal" things changed because it has a vested interest in retaining the status quo.

CHAPUT: If we really do believe that the Holy Spirit guides the Church, then the Holy Spirit guides the Church regardless of whether men are the ones making the decisions or not. It is Catholic teaching, and really the distinguishing issue that makes us Catholics, that the magisterium of the Church is guided by the Holy Spirit and cannot lead the Church into error in matters of faith and morals. That includes in a very special way the magisterium's interpretation of Scripture.

MADRID: What about feminists who say, "Well, that very claim plays into our hands. Here we are, a 'prophetic witness' to the direction the Holy Spirit is leading the Church, and you're stifling the movement of the Holy Spirit, who wants to move the Church into opening the priesthood to women." How should we reply?

CHAPUT: I've heard that argument innumerable times, and it's not convincing. They say I can't teach correctly because I'm a man, that I can't understand the movement of the Spirit because I'm a man. The point is, it's not *my* teaching that I'm defending. It's not *my* teaching that I'm responsible for. As a bishop, I am responsible for faithfully and accurately teaching what was taught by Jesus Christ and the Apostles. The argument that we should abandon "male-dominated" apostolic tradition and ordain women is a sham. God breaks through all of that. Jesus, when he chose his apostles, wasn't constrained by the cultural limitations of his time, as radical feminists like to argue. I deny this strongly. Jesus was not "historically conditioned," and he absolutely did not make mistakes. Scripture is not historically conditioned in that sense. The gospel message is not historically conditioned in that sense, though some of the forms of proclaiming the gospel surely are. Jesus Christ taught the truth that came from the Father without any diminishment or distortion of the gift that the Father wanted to give us.

MADRID: In other words, whenever Christ's teachings clashed with the culture and social mores of his day, the culture and mores gave way.

CHAPUT: Yes. They have to give way. And they will continue to, just as "radical feminism" will have to give way. It all boils down to this: We have to submit to the gospel. We are called by Christ to believe and trust and have confidence in his promise of the presence of the Holy Spirit to guide the Church. And where is that guidance found? The apostolic magisterium.

MADRID: I don't mean to put you on the spot with this next question...

CHAPUT: You're not putting me on the spot at all. I'm happy to answer all these questions.

MADRID: This may be a more sensitive question because it involves your brother bishops. As we all know, there are a handful of bishops in the United States, perhaps more than we realize, who are openly agitating for women's ordination. From your vantage point as a bishop, what course of action do you counsel lay Catholics to take in view of the conflicting opinions coming from within the body of bishops on the issue of women's ordination?

CHAPUT: Well, as for making judgments about my brother bishops, I have to start at the point of having confidence that they are doing what they think is appropriate and right. Some bishops, in fact, do feel that this is open for dialogue and requires the ongoing reflection of the Church. But I must remind them that the Holy See, in the past and recently, has told us—the bishops, clergy, and all the faithful in the Church—that this issue is not open for discussion and that a male-only priesthood is now and has always been the clear and confident teaching of the Church. When it comes to bishops who support women's ordination, we should remonstrate with them in a friendly, charitable, and Christian way, as their brothers—not attack them, but express disagreement and concern in a fraternal way. That's the way I try to do it. When I discuss this issue with bishops who have a very different opinion on this matter than I do, I tell them they're wrong, but hopefully in a way that doesn't belittle or make fun or diminish them as persons, but challenges them with the teaching of the Church.

MADRID: The view from the pew is often one of consternation and bewilderment. Many lay people sense that what they learned growing up as Catholics is now being thrown to the side and supplanted with what individual priests and bishops think is the "better way" to go and which they present as their own version of the Catholic Church. But since most lay people want and have a right to continuity in the faith, what do you counsel them to do? What should their attitude be?

CHAPUT: Well, I think it's important for all of us, whether we're bishops, priests, or lay people, to find support groups. I don't mean psychological support groups; I mean support groups where we can go for Scriptural insights, or for theological information, or just a group of Catholics with whom we find consolation and friendship. I think that's a good beginning point.

MADRID: You mean a group like Catholic Answers?

CHAPUT: Yes.

MADRID: How should lay people deal with bishops who publicly go against the teaching of the Church, for example, those who continue to agitate for women's ordination?

CHAPUT: Charitably, always charitably. We should avoid ways of communicating that take an "us against them" approach. That's damaging. A good way is to write friendly, respectful letters to bishops asking them for clarification of their opinions in light of Church teaching. I myself especially welcome letters like that. I think they're the most important letters I receive, and as a bishop my answers to these letters are the most important things that I write. It's a good way to pass on and reflect upon together the solid, ever-the-same teaching of the Catholic Church—like reading good magazines like yours. I think that's a very important thing for us to do. Reading and educating ourselves in the faith help us to have confidence in the midst of all this commotion—that this is Jesus Christ's Church, and, despite the sinfulness of its members and the confusion that is sometimes a part of our life together, Jesus Christ is leading us. It's his Church.

MADRID: Given your background as a mendicant friar, a Capuchin, can you say a few words about the spiritual dimension of the challenges we face? How should we meet these challenges at a spiritual level?

CHAPUT: You know, Francis of Assisi, my personal hero and also the founder of my religious community, lived in a time which, in some ways, was much more difficult than our own. The Church in his day was torn apart by the sins of the clergy in a way far beyond what we see in our own time. It's hard for us to imagine anything worse than what we see now, but in medieval Europe there was profound corruption in the Church. The way Francis dealt with that is the way we should deal with the issues of our own time. He decided that in the midst of all the scandal he would trust in God's providential care, and that led him to see all people as his sisters and brothers. This childlike trust led him in a "naive," radical kind of way to trust the Church. He took quite literally Jesus's words about entrusting the Church to Peter (John 21:15–17), and he required that his fellow Franciscans give themselves wholly in trust to the Church.

MADRID: How did that affect you?

CHAPUT: When I became bishop of Rapid City, I chose as my episcopal motto a line from St. Paul's letter to the Ephesians (5:25): "As Christ loved the Church." That's how I need to function as bishop. I think it's how all of us as Christians need to approach these troubling issues. We have to love the Church as Christ loved the Church and gave himself up for her. Francis changed the Church and he changed Europe because of his simple confidence and simple faith, and I think that's the solution to the problems facing us today. I think that in some ways the "theological establishment" in our country and in other parts of the world has taken itself far too seriously, and it doesn't have that charity and simple trust in the Church and in the magisterium anymore. I used the word "naive" about St. Francis deliberately. I don't mean "naive" in a silly kind of way, but in a simple kind of way. It's true—the Church is our mother. The Church is guided by the Holy Spirit as she teaches us the truth, and we are to have confidence in her. We should always have more confidence in what the Church teaches than in our own theological opinions or the opinions of anyone else.

MADRID: Are you alluding to Christ's teaching about becoming like little children?

CHAPUT: Absolutely. That's exactly what I mean.

MADRID: Your calling as a bishop is to care for the Church the same way Christ does. But isn't it true that there were times when Jesus had to be forceful and vigorous and even sometimes angry with the Church—his apostles and followers? Is this aspect of his ministry also part of your job as a bishop?

CHAPUT: Oh, yes. I think that's very important. I am responsible to God for the way I carry out my ministry of apostolic teaching. If my people are not faithful to the Church's teachings, I have a responsibility to call them back into line. When I visit my parishes I carry my crosier, the episcopal staff that is a symbol of my role as bishop and shepherd. The staff has two ends. One end is curved, and that's the end that I use to gently pull people to Christ. The other end is sharp. It's the one I sometimes have to use to prod people to be faithful to the gospel. We bishops have the job of drawing our people to Christ in a tender, loving way, but we also have to be able to be vigorous and challenge them to be faithful to the gospel when they're not.

MADRID: Do you see "radical feminism" as a passing challenge, or do you think that, like the Protestant Reformation, it's going to be a long-lived heresy?

CHAPUT: This is a lifelong challenge. I'm sure of it. And what scares me most about this challenge is that within the body of bishops there isn't a great deal of thoughtful discussion. The U.S. Bishops Conference has recently had some major struggles on the inclusive language translations of Scripture and liturgical books. We voted just recently on whether or not to approve the inclusive-language version of the Grail Psalter that's used by many women religious these days. Those bishops who are against this kind of inclusive language won the vote, but only because we barely defeated the two-thirds majority that was needed.

Understand the gravity of what I'm saying here: We didn't have a majority vote. We only won because those who favored it just couldn't get two-thirds. Within the body of bishops there is uncertainty and a lack of clarity and unity on some issues, such as inclusive language. It's a very theologically damaging issue, and in my six years as a bishop we really haven't had enough theological reflection together on it. We're always dealing with amending documents or approving or disapproving somebody's translation, but we have not done the basic theological reflection together as a group. I am very confident that if we do that in union with our Holy Father (and that's what is required of a bishop, to be in union with the Holy Father), then we will come to some common, clear, and strong positions. But we haven't had theological discussions as a body of bishops. We just don't have the forum to do that. We're always in the process of doing business rather than doing theology.

MADRID: Many lay Catholics have gotten the impression that American bishops have become more like bureaucrats than pastors. Do you see any validity in that perception?

CHAPUT: Well, I don't know about the American bishops as a group, but I can talk about myself. I know that I spend way too much time at my desk writing letters and doing business. But I am responsible as a bishop for the whole diocese: its financial aspects, its material aspects, as well as its spiritual aspects. For example, I'm trying to build a new high school. You know, we only have one Catholic high school in Rapid City, and we're renting space. I'm trying to build a building, and it's going to cost 3.5 million dollars—which isn't very much for some dioceses, but for this little diocese, it's a lot. So I spend a lot of time tending to things like that.

I want a Catholic high school because I think it's one of the best ways of proclaiming the gospel to the young people of our diocese, but I have to do a lot of legwork in terms of raising money and making sure it's done properly for that gospel goal to be accomplished.

So it's true that we are very bureaucratic. But if we don't do our job, we're also criticized for not taking care of the practical realities of the life of the diocese. I guess we'll always be criticized by some for anything we do. I think it should be one of our primary goals as bishops to free ourselves as much as possible from administration so that we can administer the Word of God, which is, after all, what the role of bishop is all about. The Church in the United States is very institutionalized, and as long as those institutions are the responsibility of the local bishop, he's going to have to spend time on those. I'm rather lucky in not having to deal with a lot of details some of my brother bishops have to deal with. The diocese of Rapid City has only 35,000 Catholics out of a total population of 200,000 people. It's quite small as dioceses go.

MADRID: You have taken a very active role in the fight against inclusive language during the bishops' conference deliberations on that issue. Where does it seem that we're headed with this?

CHAPUT: When I came into the bishops' conference six years ago, the first debate I was part of was on the principles of translation. You know, that's the best place to begin when you're deliberating on whether to accept a given translation. You must first determine what are the acceptable principles that underlie the translation, and I was rather concerned about some of the principles that we did approve because, although they sounded good in theory, I was worried about how they would be applied in practice. I have become more and more convinced that those principles that were adopted by the bishops' conference are very inadequate.

MADRID: What are some of those principles?

CHAPUT: Well, I don't have them in front of me, but they have been well-documented and could be found by reviewing the bishops' minutes of these discussions as far back as 1989. Anyone interested can contact the bishops' conference offices in Washington, D.C.

MADRID: Do you think that some day we'll see an approved inclusive language sacramentary?

CHAPUT: We do have inclusive language lectionaries approved. The American bishops have approved the New Revised Standard Version of Scripture, which is very "inclusive" in its language, and our own bishops' conference translation of the New American Bible will be an inclusive language translation. Now, I'm all for "inclusive" language if the language is an accurate rendering of the text. But I'm very much opposed to reading into the text one's own biases. You know, deleting words or adding words that aren't there. We have to take the Word of God as it is. In translation, even the very literal translation is one step removed from the original Word of God, which is written either in Hebrew or Greek. To accommodate the text to philosophical principles of inclusiveness leads to a paraphrase rather than a translation, and I don't want to paraphrase Scripture. I want a translation of Scripture. That's what's been done, actually, in some parts of the New Revised Standard Version. And I'm very concerned that this has been approved for liturgical use. I'm actually very frightened by it.

MADRID: What about the Vatican's recent statement regarding permission to use altar girls? That seems to be similar in nature to what you're describing with inclusive language. It's something that in and of itself is not doctrinal in nature, but it creates an atmosphere of confusion and fosters among some the hope that doctrines themselves will change. If that happened with inclusive language by the bishops allowing the NRSV, and now it seems to have happened with altar girls, where do you see this leading, and what would you say to the person who says, "Well, inclusive language has changed, altar girls has changed. It's only a matter of time until women in the priesthood changes"?

CHAPUT: First of all, if we bishops had closely studied these translations and not relied on "experts" to do them for us, we would be better off. We need to approve the translations, and we need to do it as a body. We can't entrust it to somebody else. If it might take years to do, then we should take years to do it rather than let it be done by others. This touches on the essence of what we do as bishops.

Regarding altar girls, I don't think it's the same kind of issue at all quite honestly, because it doesn't touch on doctrine the same kind of way. You know, I personally was hoping that the Holy Father would not approve the use of altar girls. I made that clear in my own diocese. And I have always spoken about this matter as clearly as I could because I'm quite convinced of it. The problem is that many ministries in the Church are feminized now. Most of the lay ministries of the Church are done preponderantly by women, and we all know that it's been much harder to attract men to ministries in the Church, not only to the priesthood, but to other lay ministries. I favored altar boys rather than both boys and girls because I felt it was necessary to have what might be called "affirmative action" toward men in this special case in the Church. I'm really afraid that once we have altar girls (and this has been proven to be the case where it has been done) that young men will quit serving.

Young boys establish their masculine identity in part by distancing themselves from things feminine, and once the ministry of altar server is identified as feminine, I think boys, especially very masculine boys, will stay away. I think many aspects of the Church have become too strongly feminine already. We need to do all we can to promote participation by men in the life of the Church. This affects the whole question of priestly vocations. Being an altar boy is a role in which young men can reflect and imagine themselves as being priests, and if we have fewer and fewer young men serving, we'll have fewer and fewer young men thinking about the priesthood.

Also, I think female altar servers gives false hope to people who think women should be priests, and, as one might expect, there will be many young girls who will imagine themselves as being priests. I think it will lead to great frustration, because women's ordination will never happen.

MADRID: What do you say to those who say, "Women in the priesthood is just a matter of time"?

CHAPUT: No, it's not. The Holy Father made that very clear, and I think all the official reflections on this matter have made it very clear that granting this permission for female altar servers is not a step in any way toward the ordination of women, any more than allowing women to read Scripture or distribute the Eucharist as extraordinary ministers of the Eucharist indicates that women will be priests. The Holy Father has approved the interpretation of the law that says that all those ministries, including altar server, are open to both genders. If this is what the Holy Father says, this is what the Holy Father says, and it's important for us who believe that we should give ourselves in confident trust to the decisions of the Holy Father to trust him here too.

Of course, the Holy Father hasn't told us that bishops have to do this. I personally don't know yet what I'll be doing here because I haven't heard from the bishops of our conference yet. Some people feel this permission is too much of a test of their faith in the Church. I think they've invested too much in the question. I personally would not have made the decision, but I know the Holy Father has a wisdom beyond mine and the guidance of the Holy Spirit beyond mine, and so I think that those of us who have taken other positions should not carry on as though disaster has struck.

I understand the disappointment people feel. When I first heard the decision, I was disappointed too. But I'm less disappointed today because of my great confidence in the Holy Spirit's guidance of the Church. I call all those who are concerned about this matter to have that same trust because trust is an important part of what it means to be a faithful Catholic.

MADRID: Obviously, we don't want an obedience that's divorced from our reason, so what happy balance should we be trying to strike?

CHAPUT: The essence of Jesus's life was obedience. He was obedient to the Father. He came into the world by the command of the Father. His ministry to us was the gift of the Father. His gift of himself on the cross was in response to the will of the Father. Understanding this joins us to him in an act of self-offering, primarily through our reception of the Eucharist. With Christ as my example, I see obedience as an essential aspect of membership in the Roman Catholic Church. But when we have concerns, we should ask for clarification and not be naive in a bad sense. We must also fight strongly and clearly for the truth as it has always been taught.

MADRID: What distinguishes what you just said from dissent on, for example, Church teaching on birth control and other issues? Some might respond to you, "That's what we're doing. We're simply giving the same type of witness to what we believe is the truth." Where is the distinction?

CHAPUT: If people who said that would, at the same time, say, "I will obey what the Holy Father teaches," I would have more confidence in their judgment, but I have never seen that happen, quite honestly. But those who say, "no matter what the Holy Father says, no matter what the bishops say, I am right," are in grave danger. The word "dissent" is related to the word "protest." The difference between being a Catholic and being a "Protest"-ant is that the Catholic believes that the Church is guided by the Holy Spirit and assents to the Church's teachings, even when it is difficult to do so. You cannot be a Catholic and dissent from Church teaching. You cannot be a Catholic and a protester against Catholic teaching at the same time. The two are incompatible. We must be willing to use our intellects and grapple with these difficult issues, doing our best to understand them, but, more importantly, we must have a joyful willingness to submit when the Church teaches, even when it is difficult to do so. This is a gift that comes from God. It's something outside ourselves that we have to constantly pray for. Let's remember: The truth is a gift. We cannot reject the gift of truth that the Father wants to give us through Christ and his Church. Dissent is the rejection of that gift.

MADRID: There's a phrase that's often used and, I think, misused: the Church's "position" on things. People talk about the Church's "positions" on birth control or on women in the priesthood as though they're political decisions. Would you share in the opinion that that phrase gives the wrong implication, because of the nature of the word "positions," that the Church's doctrinal teaching is something changeable?

CHAPUT: I favor the term "teaching" of the Church. What most Catholics mean when they say the teaching of the Church is the doctrinal teachings of the apostolic magisterium, the teaching office of bishops. Because they come from God, Catholic doctrines cannot change. Period. We can't be ambiguous about that. Some theologians like to talk about a sort of "dual magisterium," one made up of the bishops and the other made up of theologians. That's totally wrong. When I say "apostolic magisterium," I don't mean to imply that there's some other kind. There is no "theological magisterium." There is just one magisterium, and that's the apostolic magisterium, and I use the word "apostolic," you know, just to remind us that the magisterium is a matter of being faithful to the teachings of the apostles. There are many theologians in our country who see themselves in the role that properly belongs to bishops, that is, to be teachers of the faith. I think theologians assist the bishops and are certainly a gift to the Church, but they are not the teachers of the faith.

MADRID: You're familiar, I think, with James Hitchcock, professor of history at St. Louis University.

CHAPUT: Oh, yes.

MADRID: He theorizes that the Church is right now, especially in the West and in particular in the United States, in a de facto state of schism. He says that even though it's not formal schism, by gradually moving away from the authentic apostolic teaching of the Church, many people have moved into a state of schism even though they remain in the pews on Sundays. They dissent from so many Catholic teachings. Hitchcock thinks that the schism comes not so much from the level of bishops, but from vast groups of lay people who are simply no longer part of the Catholic Church. Is this a reasonable thesis?

CHAPUT: I think it is a very reasonable thesis, and that's why I think it is so important for the bishops in the Church in this country to be active teachers. As bishop, my first duty is to be faithful to my ministry of apostolic teaching. If there is a fault of the bishops, it is that we've focused on trying to unify our Church instead of taking firm, clear positions. We try to be moderators who come to some kind of compromise between various factions, and that's not our role. It certainly is the role of the bishop to bring unity to the Church, but only the unity of Christ's teachings—not the "unity" of feelings or agreement based on compromises. It's to bring ourselves into the unity of God and the teachings of Christ.

MADRID: What's your philosophy when it comes to dissent in your own diocese? What do you as a bishop most want to tell lay people?

CHAPUT: First of all, my philosophy is to engage the issue immediately. It won't get better. It won't get easier later on. If someone teaches something I know is wrong, I tell him he is wrong. I say that with great charity, I hope, but also with great clarity and great vigor because things don't get better by waiting and hoping he will take care of himself. So, first of all, immediate engagement. I think we need to do that across the board. I was very disappointed when the National Conference of Catholic Bishops did not approve the document about concerns of women in the Church a year and a half ago. The final draft contained unambiguous teaching on the fact that women cannot be ordained to the priesthood and that God has made us male and female—equal, but not the same. We're different from one another, but both genders have incredible gifts that have to be appreciated and embraced and respected. Some of my brother bishops are saying that it's better not to speak about that at this time; they say that sometimes it's more prudent not to say anything than to teach forcefully. I don't think that's ever the case. I think it's always important to teach clearly and to teach plainly and immediately, not with arrogance, but with conviction and love.

MADRID: And how do you do that in your diocese?

CHAPUT: If I'm in a group of people who have questions, I think I'm approachable enough that they raise the questions directly with me. For example, altar servers. If I came to a parish where there were girl altar servers, I'd ask them to quit. I mean, I know it would be difficult, and the people who suffer most are the young girls and their families. The ones who suffer for it aren't those who gave false permission. We bishops must teach clearly on all the difficult issues of our time, whether it's homosexuality, or contraception, or capital punishment, or whatever. It's important that the priests present the total teachings of our Church and proclaim them clearly, even if it means that they're not going to be popular.

MADRID: What message do you as a bishop want to tell your flock?

CHAPUT: I just want them to love the Church as Christ loved the Church.

Frank Sheed: The Prophet of Hyde Park

ONE BRISK, GRAY AFTERNOON IN LONDON, I stood on a corner of Hyde Park with one of Frank Sheed's old friends. "That's the spot where he used to stand and preach," she said with a wistful smile. Now an elderly widow, in the 1940s and 1950s she had worked in the London Catholic Evidence Guild with Frank and his wife, Maisie.

It was easy to imagine the scene: a portly, smiling, middle-aged fellow, who looked a lot like W.C. Fields, evangelizing anyone who stopped in front of his speaker's platform.

Over afternoon tea, Sheed's friend described what it was like to watch Frank manage the crowd. He worked on hecklers and skeptics and scoffers the way a chiropractor works on a bad back—probing, searching for the tensed-up muscle, finding it, and going to work on it with precision. He massaged the minds of his audiences, breaking down hardened prejudices against Catholicism, kneading the "God does not exist!" arguments until they crumbled, and showing atheists the folly of their denials. He made countless converts on the stump.

Frank Sheed was one of the twentieth-century's greatest apologists. Some—especially those who knew him personally and saw him in action—say he was the greatest Catholic apologist of the last hundred years, maybe longer. One thing is certain: Few people of any era have been endowed with his unique, powerful combination of gifts—including a rare talent for expressing complex theological concepts, such as the Trinity or the Hypostatic Union, in words that were understandable and compelling to the average reader. His style was clear and luminous; it had the power to persuade as well as to inform.

Sheed was also an accomplished speaker. He preached the Catholic faith under the open sky to any and all who would listen—often in unforgiving and even hostile locations, such as New York's Time Square and London's Hyde Park (stomping ground of Communist firebrands, Protestant preachers, and agitators for every kind of cause and "ism").

He believed the Catholic Faith to his core, and that belief impelled him to share the gospel with all those around him. For many of us, his "taking it to the streets" approach to Christianity might seem extreme or fanatical. It shouldn't. Frank Sheed understood that for Christians, public testimony about Christ should be the norm. "You are the light of the world," Christ told us. "A city set on a hill cannot be hid. Nor do men light a lamp and put it under a bushel basket, but on a stand, and it gives light to all in the house. Let your light so shine before men, that they may see your good works and give glory to your Father who is in Heaven" (Matthew 5:14–16).

Can Anything Good Come From Sydney?

Francis Joseph Sheed was born on March 20, 1897, in Sydney, Australia. His father, John Sheed, sprang from a long line of Scottish Presbyterians. John was a blue-collar worker with a bottomless thirst for ale. Frank's mother, the former Mary Maloney, was an Irish Catholic. By all accounts, she was a loving and devoted mother to her two sons, Jack and Frank. The religious issue between her and John remained always at a stalemate. His antipathy toward Rome never abated, while she remained a loyal, devout Catholic. John insisted the boys be raised Protestant.

At the turn of the century, Sydney was an exciting place. With the striking natural beauty of the city's harbor and the gentle, verdant hills that ring it, the metropolis was Australia's New York City. It was here that Frank began to make his way in the world. His family moved around a lot, largely because of his father's drinking problem. Frank's son, Wilfrid, recalls his father saying the family had lived in thirty-three homes by the time Frank was thirteen.

John Sheed, like many otherwise good men who suffer from alcoholism, drank himself into a sullen middle age, mired in the quicksand of dead-end, low-paying jobs. The daily combination of drink and drudgery brought out the bully in him, and he often beat his two sons. At the age of sixteen, Frank's brother died suddenly of a rare heart condition. It was around this time that Frank began spending most of his days out of the house, preferring the company of his aunts and cousins at their nearby home—out of the reach of his father's belt.

Growing up in the company of his Protestant and decidedly anti-Catholic aunts and uncles, Sheed learned the ways of anti-Catholicism firsthand. But he himself never bought into the anti-Roman line, quickly recognizing it as a kind of bigotry. The more anti-Catholic tracts, books, and comments were heaped upon him by his Calvinist relations, the more Frank was attracted to Rome.

Although raised as a Methodist by his Protestant relatives, Frank developed early on a private sympathy for Catholicism, sacraments and all. Then one day, he openly declared himself a Catholic. Naturally, this pleased his Irish-Catholic mother immensely and horrified his Protestant aunts and cousins.

Sheed's understanding of Protestantism and its biases against Rome would serve him well over the years. He had no antagonism toward Protestants, but he soon recognized the Reformation's inherent biblical and historical contradictions and was able to point them out with uncanny precision.

He did well in his studies and went on to earn a bachelor's degree from Sydney University. After graduation, there followed a stint at Sydney Law School, where he received a degree in law. Along the way he did extra study and acquired a deep knowledge of history and philosophy, as well as learning Latin, French, and Greek. While at the university, Sheed earned money by teaching at a Sydney high school. As a newly minted lawyer, he surveyed the Australian landscape to see what challenges awaited. Whatever he saw there wasn't enough to hold him; he decided to try his luck in a different direction. He boarded a ship and sailed for England.

That proved to be an important decision.

The House That Frank Built

They met at a Catholic Evidence Guild talk. He was working with the guild to make ends meet while he decided what to do with his life. Maisie Ward was a speaker one afternoon at the center where he was helping out.

Their encounter was the start of the famous Sheed and Ward publishing career that would catapult many now-legendary Catholic writers to prominence.

Maisie was as different from Sheed as one could imagine. He, although now a Catholic, had been raised a Protestant. The Wards were an ardently Catholic family that had converted to the faith in the 1860s. Maisie was born in 1889, when the English faithful were still severely tested by their country's oppressive anti-Romanism. Frank was an Australian with a broad, suntanned brogue and a taste for adventure and action.

Maisie was English, Edwardian, proper, upper crust, ferociously Catholic, witty, likable, and incredibly intelligent. Born into a family of writers and editors, Maisie's mind was as keen and expansive as Frank's, and she was steeped in centuries of tough-as-nails English Catholicism. His family was poor; hers had money. For years, the Wards had rubbed shoulders with the major figures in the English Church. This heady atmosphere, cloudy with incense and ringing with Latin and chant and the glorious echoes of generations of recusant English Catholics, was immensely attractive to Sheed. He gravitated immediately to Maisie and her live-wire Catholic world.

Once Frank and Maisie had married, they plunged into the work of Catholic apologetics with gusto. Soon children came: Rosemary in 1919 and Wilfrid in 1930. Frank's writing career began as he discovered his facility for conveying with the written word the same clarity and force he was able to muster on the stump. Books explaining the Faith poured forth in a steady stream: *A Map of Life, Theology and Sanity, What Difference Does Jesus Make?, Christ in Eclipse, The Instructed Heart, To Know Christ Jesus*. Frank Sheed had found his vocation as a Catholic apologist.

Along the way, he and Maisie decided that in addition to writing their own books, they would help fledgling Catholic authors launch their careers. And so they formed a publishing house: Sheed and Ward. Frank and Maisie worked with many of the great names of twentieth-century Catholic literature: Fulton Sheen, G.K. Chesterton, Hilaire Belloc, John Hugo, Arnold Lunn, Dorothy Day, Ronald Knox, Caryll Houselander, Clare Luce, and Evelyn Waugh. They moved easily among these writers with an amiable self-effacement that won many admirers.

In his apologetic writings, his lectures, his street-corner preaching, his countless open-air public debates about the Catholic faith with atheists, fundamentalists, Communists, freethinkers, and anti-Catholics of every stripe, Frank Sheed was a formidable contender in the age-old battle for truth. He had a gift for oratory—especially in the unpredictable hurly-burly of live debate— and a razor-sharp mind that cut through fuzzy thinking like a surgeon's scalpel. No faulty argument, no cleverly worded fallacy hurled from the mob that pressed around his speaker's platform could get past his guard. He shredded the arguments of atheist hecklers with a smile on his face. What made him so effective was his unflagging and unfeigned courtesy (a quality all too rare among professional apologists). He loved people in the way Christ asks us to love them, and that is part of what made him so successful in opening their minds and hearts to the gospel.

Sheed could spot bogus arguments in a flash and squash them flat, but he never left his opponent himself feeling squashed. This aspect of his personality was described to me over and over again by people who worked closely with him. Stories about Sheed often revolve around his good-natured disposition and the sunny approach he invariably took to the stormy world of theological debate.

This also explains why his writings are so attractive: They're amazingly free of polemic. He simply had no use for it. His approach to apologetics and evangelization was to explain the issue—whether it was the Trinity, spirit and matter, or the Eucharist—with such clarity that the truth stood on its own, naked in its beauty. That was his secret.

The Everyman's Catechist

Invariably, Sheed started his guided tour of the faith with a preliminary discussion about reality itself. For him, there was no point in tackling issues such as the papacy or infant baptism unless one had first laid the proper groundwork. He approached apologetics the way a builder approaches a project: Start with the foundation, build the first floor, and then raise the building from there. If the foundation was laid properly, a structure of any height could be built upon it.

As far as Sheed was concerned, no one was more insane than the man who ignored or denied the existence of God. He argued that if a man denies God's existence, he misunderstands the very nature of the universe and therefore is incapable of truly understanding anything—the laws of nature and natural law (two very different things), even himself. In *Theology and Sanity*, Sheed wrote:

> If we see anything at all—ourselves or some other man, or the universe as a whole or any part of it—without at the same time seeing God holding it there, then we are seeing it all wrong. If we saw a coat hanging on a wall and did not realize that it was held there by a hook, we should not be living in the real world at all, but in some fantastic world of our own in which coats defied the law of gravity and hung on walls by their own power. Similarly if we see things in existence and do not in the same act see that they are held in existence by God, then equally we are living in a fantastic world, not the real world. Seeing God everywhere and all things upheld by Him is not a matter of sanctity, but of plain sanity, because God is everywhere and all things are upheld by Him. What we do about it may be sanctity; but merely seeing it is sanity. To overlook God's presence is not simply to be irreligious; it is a kind of insanity, like overlooking everything else that is actually there.[83]

In order to "see" things the way they really are, one needs to exercise the mind, to dust off the intellect and apply it to the world around us. Many of Sheed's apologetic writings begin with an explanation of the human intellect: what it is and what it does. He points out how it is different from the imagination and warns that many people these days rely almost entirely on their imaginations, not on their intellects.

But he also understood the inherent limitations of human intellect: It's an indispensable instrument for navigating our journey through life, but it isn't the only tool God has given us. Divine revelation is God's gift to the human mind.

It provides information that, left to its own powers, even the keenest human intellect could never discover. And it further illuminates those areas man's mind has reached through its own natural powers.

Revelation leads the mind to the proper conclusions. It's not enough simply to have a welter of raw facts at one's disposal—like a bucket of nuts and bolts and other parts dumped on the table before you. Divine revelation acts as the "schematic" that tells us what to do with that mass of individual parts.

Many Catholics use the expression "It's a mystery" as an escape hatch. They really mean, "I'm too lazy to be bothered trying to understand this or that doctrine." Intellectual and spiritual laziness are a lethal combination for the person who claims to love the Lord. Sheed showed how to avoid the lazy way out by seeing a divine "mystery" for what it is: not something we can know nothing about, but something we can't know everything about.

Natural law was another key concept in Sheed's apologetics. His books, especially *Theology and Sanity,* provide a crash course on natural law: the rules of the road for successful living in the cosmos. He typically started by reminding his audience that there are plenty of laws, natural and supernatural, that surround us and govern reality. To deny or ignore them is foolishness. It leads, inexorably, into the jaws of that two-headed monster: suffering and death. The terms good and evil mean nothing, he explained, if they're divorced from the reality that God exists and has determined a moral system for his creation.

A Man of Action

Sheed had his faults. One of them was his ability to lacerate someone verbally. Sheed's son, Wilfrid, said that his father learned to be sarcastic from his grandfather and that he "reject[ed] this as he was absorbing it, and this was to be a lifelong struggle for him. His tongue could be rough enough as it was, and it was best to handle him with care in certain moods. (Since he worked hard at his equanimity, he might be surprised to hear that at times he reminded me of a hard-nosed Irish monsignor.) Unbridled, his tongue would have been a deadly weapon, equipped with nuclear capacity and he would never have made a single convert from his soapbox."[84]

And Sheed was no different from any of us when it came to wrestling with the human inclination to slough off one's duty to evangelize. There were times he'd much rather have worked on a crossword puzzle or read in his easy chair than preach the faith. Wilfrid remembers from his childhood:

> [W]henever they were in England, Frank Sheed and Maisie Ward trudged off every single Sunday afternoon—my father moaning to beat the band and praying for rain—to preach the Faith from soapboxes; and not just in glamour spots like Hyde Park, but in backwaters like Clapham and Pimlico and other places that properly belong in English comic monologues.
>
> At first, the only thing that really struck me as strange was the sound of a man praying for rain in England: then again perhaps he was the cause of it all, and was doing a bang-up job. What does one know at five?
>
> Only slowly did I begin to realize that other people thought my parents were a little crazy. Soapbox oratory is by definition crazy. And when I attended my first meetings I saw little to shake the definition. A group of city strays would gather in front of the rickety platform and hurl tipsy taunts or village-atheist challenges at my parents, who would answer with a gravity worthy of a lecture hall.
>
> My first thought was that they were going to get killed up there by some loudmouthed bully, and to this day I myself suffer from incurable stage fright. But on the way home, they might well complain about the blandness of the meeting: "If only a good drunk had come along," my father would sigh—surely as strange a wish as for rain on Sunday.[69]

That wish reminds us that it's normal and natural to shrink from the demands of sharing the Catholic faith in the blunt ordinariness of everyday life. Glorious martyrdom? Yes. Humdrum daily evangelism? No. It's so common—so Catholic—to secretly thrill at the daydream of dying for Christ in some glorious and vaguely well-publicized way. But we yawn and reach for the TV remote control when the opportunity actually presents itself to open the front door and share the faith with a couple of Jehovah's Witnesses. Few of us will ever be called to shed our blood for Christ. But everyone is called to be a witness for Christ (the Greek word for witness is martyr). Sheed knew this. Over the course of their long career, Frank and Maisie used their books, lectures, and work with the guild to engage people in a conversation about the God who loves them. In so doing, they blazed a trail for apologists to follow.

The Sheed and Ward publishing empire has faded dramatically from its former glory. As old age caught up with Frank and Maisie, it was no longer possible for them to manage the company. Around the time of Maisie's death in 1975, the company split into two Sheed and Ward houses (one in London, the other in Kansas City) and passed out of Frank's hands. He pressed on for the next several years and died in his sleep on November 20, 1982, from complications following a stroke. He and Maisie are buried in the Jersey City Cemetery.

Given the spiritual, moral, and cultural obstacles arrayed before us, Catholics need all the resources available to them to navigate the hazards they face in the twenty-first century. As Scripture tells us, we have a race to run, a finish line to cross, and a prize to win (see Hebrews 12:1–2; Philippians 3:14). Most important, there is the ancient baton of the Catholic faith that must be handed on to the generation of Catholics that will follow us. To do this well, we must limber up our minds, learn to think clearly and carefully, and stretch our hearts and souls with the expansive, invigorating truths of the Catholic faith.

The story of Frank Sheed's life continues to be an example and an encouragement for those who would undertake this project. Over the course of his sixty years as a teacher and defender of the Catholic faith, he discovered, tested, and marked out for us virtually all the lines of apologetics. He showed us the parameters of dialogue with the world and the answers to critics' most common objections. He ran the race himself, ran it well, and won it in style.

Crisis Magazine, *March 2002*

Divine Word Missionaries in the American South

THE TRAIN CHUGGED TO A WHEEZING HALT in front of the shed that served as a depot. Hot, rumpled, and exhausted after his six-hundred-mile trip from Chicago, Fr. Aloysius Heick, S.V.D., stepped down off the platform and turned to view his new home: the little town of Merigold, Mississippi.

What he saw of his new assignment did little to relieve the weary priest. Aside from the ramshackle train "depot," he saw only a scattering of houses, a general store, a commissary and blacksmith's shop. Beyond that meager smattering of structures he could see numerous cotton fields. Beyond those stretched the tangled, untamed vegetation of the rural Mississippi countryside.

It was the sweltering summer of 1905. Fr. Heick, born forty-one years earlier in Germany, had been sent to Merigold for a challenging task. His religious community, the Divine Word Missionary Fathers, had decided to send missionaries to work full-time among impoverished blacks in the South. Heick was the first priest chosen for the difficult new work.

Fr. Charles Boykins, the order's current South provincial, explains, "For a white priest to live among and work exclusively with blacks was a particularly unusual and unpopular thing in turn-of-the-century America. Many who did were ostracized."

In light of the prevailing racism, Fr. John Reid, S.V.D., provincial in 1905, had to select the right man or the work would surely founder. He needed a zealous, stouthearted missionary priest whose devotion and tact would win the trust of all he encountered. In Fr. Heick he made a wise choice because of the young German's dynamic energy, ingenuity and tremendous missionary zeal.

At the time, neither priest imagined how crucial his ingenuity would become in just a few short months. Although the Merigold project was the first of what would later become a fruitful missionary apostolate of Divine Word Missionary activity in the South, it wasn't the first time Catholics had been sent to extend the Faith across this isolated Mississippi territory.

In 1904, forty Catholic families came to Merigold as part of an experiment conceived by David Bremner, a Chicago Catholic businessman. He planned to introduce Catholicism into the region by transplanting Catholic communities there. King Cotton reigned in Merigold, and the locals, including the poor field hands and sharecroppers, scratched a simple, hardscrabble living from farming it. The transplanted Catholic families intended to do likewise, planting cotton on five thousand acres that had been purchased and dedicated to this project. But this plan wasn't destined to go smoothly.

The spring of 1905 brought torrential rain and flooding to the area. The Mississippi River, fourteen miles west of Merigold, overflowed its banks and destroyed the fledgling cotton crop. For weeks the townsfolk were stranded indoors, their fields inundated, their homes surrounded by an impassable quagmire of knee-deep mud.

To make matters worse, billowing clouds of mosquitoes flourished, hatching from pools of stagnant water left by the rains. Besides being tormented by itchy mosquito bites, the Catholic newcomers were decimated by malaria, dysentery, and other mosquito-borne miseries.

Finally, the demoralized families had reached their limit. They packed up and headed back to Chicago, abandoning Merigold forever. But Bremner remained undaunted in his desire to see a Catholic presence there. With help from Archbishop Quigley of Chicago, he was able to convince the Divine Word Missionaries to extend their apostolic efforts into the South.

Starting from scratch, Fr. Heick made amazing progress in short time. He went door-to-door to visit with the people in their homes. And he daily braved oppressive heat, humidity and anti-Catholic taunts, as he trudged from cotton field to cotton field to spend time with the field hands during their breaks. Fr. Heick's methods of evangelizing back then were unpretentious but effective.

Radiating charity, he would chat with the field hands. Telling humorous stories, distributing water and snacks when he had them, he would watch for opportunities to speak of Jesus's love for them. In a simple, non-intimidating way, he instructed the people in the basics of the Faith.

A Narrow Escape

Fr. Heick built a church for the field hands, a modest grammar school and a vocational school. While the African American community grew to love their new friend, some of the townspeople most heartily did not.

Their initial suspicion of this foreign "Romanist" blossomed into hatred as they witnessed his popularity and success. In time, Fr. Heick's very presence had become perceived as an unbearable, unspoken taunt to those locals who opposed any effort to educate blacks.

Today, Fr. Joseph Guidry, S.V.D., a black pastor of St. Paul the Apostle parish in Baton Rouge, Louisiana, points out the tragic irony of such bigotry. "If blacks really were mentally inferior, then why did some whites worry about blacks learning to read and write? It simply doesn't make sense when you think about it." And yet, Fr. Heick's schools were vandalized, and blacks who attended his classes were browbeaten, sometimes just verbally, sometimes with fists or sticks.

The situation was rapidly changing from difficult to dangerous. Death threats were now being sent to the priest who, uncowed by the virulent anti-black racism that infested many of the people around him, vowed to stay on until the last possible moment.

When Fr. Heick received word from a trusted friend in the community that his enemies were planning to kill him the next day, he realized he had no choice but to plan an escape. Since his movements beyond the rectory were by now being carefully watched, the priest needed his ingenuity now more than ever. He couldn't simply leave, or he would be stopped and "dealt with" by the local men who wanted him dead.

Finally, after prayer and racking his mind for a solution to his predicament, he hit upon the one ploy that seemed to have a chance of succeeding. He clambered into a coffin after instructing a trusted assistant to announce to the town that "Father had died suddenly and his body would be returned to Chicago immediately."

Caught by surprise, the would-be assassins were fooled by the ruse (which included a mock funeral service) and even looked on foolishly as his coffin was loaded on the train. The mortal danger he had so narrowly escaped hardly intimidated Fr. Heick. Instead of retreating to the safety of Chicago, he simply moved to Vicksburg, a mere hundred miles to the south. If he had anything to say about it, the Divine Word Missionaries and the Catholic Church were in Mississippi to stay.

With an African American population of 8,000 out of 15,000 inhabitants, Vicksburg was an ideal headquarters for the s.v.d. priests. More priests were sent from the provincial house in Techny, Illinois, and work among poor blacks began with gusto. By 1913, the Divine Word Missionaries opened a mission in Greenville and soon extended into Jackson, Meridian, Bay St. Louis, Yazoo City, and further west into the Arkansas cities of Little Rock and Pine Bluff.

Overcoming Obstacles

Wherever they went in the South, the priests encountered a certain amount of anti-Catholicism and suspicion. In the grand style of Fr. Heick, however, they overcame these obstacles. Another difficulty in evangelizing African Americans in the South, however, was the policy of American seminaries not to accept black students. For this reason, there were virtually no black priests then serving in the United States.

The Divine Word Missionaries knew this had to change and opened the nation's first all-black seminary in Greenville, Mississippi, in 1920. In just one year this minor seminary had seventy-one students and living space was crowded, so the new St. Augustine's Seminary was built in Bay St. Louis, Mississippi, in 1923.

The first four black s.v.d. priests were ordained from there in 1934. Black vocations increased as the Divine Word Fathers nurtured converts throughout the South. Although the order has recently experienced a decline in black vocations, Fr. Charles Boykins, provincial, explains that they are working to attract black men to the priesthood through vocation videotapes, pamphlets, and other literature.

"Virtually all our American-trained black priests and bishops received all or part of their seminary training in Bay St. Louis," said Fr. Boykins, "but we need more vocations." The Divine Word Fathers closed the major seminary at St. Augustine in the late 1960s—a reflection of a nationwide vocations decrease, said Fr. Boykins.

"To continue reaching out to black Americans as we have been for these last ninety years or so, we need more vocations." Meanwhile, both white and African American S.V.D. missionaries continue working throughout the South. Since the beginning of this century, the Divine Word order has worked steadily among the Black community in southern cities such as Biloxi and Jackson, Mississippi, and Lake Charles, Lafayette, and Alexandria, Louisiana. "I think the future is positive for our work among blacks," says Fr. Guidry. "But the work is never easy, especially in the mission field."

A century ago, Fr. Heick blazed a trail for the Faith through the tangled brambles of racism and anti-Catholicism. It's a trail that ever since his day has been well worn by faithful Catholic missionaries.

But there's no guarantee that the work of these Catholic men and women will remain permanently in place. Without our renewed commitment today to the task of evangelizing in the South among Whites, Blacks, and all races, Fr. Heick's achievements may simply fade into obscurity. And then whole regions, once won over to the cause of Christ, would fade into the gray oblivion of secularism and estrangement from the Church.

Let's pray that the Lord will send a new cadre of dedicated apostles into his vineyard; men and women who will radiate the love and saving power of Jesus Christ, the way Fr. Aloysius Heick did.

Extension Magazine, *October 1991*

SECTION FOUR
All Things Catholic

THE INTERVIEW I DID IN THE CONSERVATIVE Catholic newspaper *The Wanderer* was, I am pretty sure, the first real interview I had done in any periodical up to that point in my career as an apologist. As I reread that interview, which appeared shortly before my first book, *Surprised by Truth,* was released and two years before I would launch my own Catholic periodical, *Envoy* magazine, I am struck by a certain pugnacious tone in my answers, one which I am hopeful I am no longer afflicted with. Age does that to you. Most men, at thirty-four, feel they have to prove themselves, test their mettle, and show by the dents in their battle armor that they have what it takes to compete. Now, upon reaching fifty-two, I can honestly say that I no longer need (much less desire) any of that. But it is instructive to me, and if it is for you, then so much the better, to look back from this remove of nearly twenty years and take stock of how I have mellowed and matured in my approach to apologetics. While I don't think I was ever abrasive or impolite in any of my writings and lectures in my younger years, I can detect, nonetheless, an unfortunate edge to some things I wrote and can hear, at times, a subtle undertone of aggressiveness that I wish today had not been there.

To whatever extent my work as an apologist has helped people, I am quite certain that if only I had known then what I know now about the importance of humility and gentleness my efforts would have been that much more helpful.

I wrote some of these essays, such as "Common Sense Checked at the Door," to document experiences of mine that I wanted to share with others, in hopes that they would be useful to them when they got into similar situations. "Sects and Sin in Manila" was the first travelogue-style article I had written, but it seemed to work well as a way to inform and energize Catholics who wanted to help promote the Faith during World Youth Day in January 1995. The juxtaposed ambiguity of "sects" and "sin" (referring to the late Cardinal Jaime Sin) in the headline was intended to pique the reader's interest with a phrase that seemed somehow naughty. I was in Manila for World Youth Day, overseeing the distribution of about 200,000 copies of *Pillar of Fire, Pillar of Truth*—the thirty-page Catholic Answers evangelization booklet I coauthored with Karl Keating in mid-1992, in advance of the 1993 WYD in Denver.

Karl asked me to compose a succinct explanation of the basics of the Catholic Faith that could be printed up in booklet form and disseminated far and wide at events such as World Youth Day. A week or so later, I submitted my first draft. Karl had chosen *Pillar of Fire, Pillar of Truth* for the title and, while I wasn't crazy about that, I did agree with Karl's rationale that the Catholic Faith is indeed our God-given guide in this life, in a way analogous to the way God guided his people during the time they wandered in the Desert of Sinai—with a massive column of fire at night and one of smoke during the day.

After several rounds of careful proofreading and copyediting, the final version of *Pillar* was sufficiently polished. Karl wrote a couple of introductory pages and the concluding page, and off it went to press. Catholic Answers distributed well over 300,000 copies in Denver during Blessed Pope John Paul II's visit there in August of 1993. For WYD in Manila, we had to use a local printer and distribute a version translated into Tagalog. It truly boggles my mind that, in the twenty years since I wrote the first draft of this booklet, it has been translated into approximately a dozen languages and seen many millions of copies printed and distributed around the world. Looking back on it, I wish now that Karl and

I had put our names on the front cover.

The other essays in this section reflect aspects of particular apologetics controversies I was either a party to (e.g., "More Vicarius Thrills") or challenges and questions that often came up during the countless parish seminars I conducted over the past two and a half decades (such as "Pope Fiction" and "Purgatory: God's Emergency Room for Sinners"). And one, "When Opportunity Knocks," was a mini-reflection on a real-life experience of having unsuspecting Mormon missionaries knock on my front door.

An Interview With *The Wanderer* Newspaper

Q. First could you assess—generally—the state of the relationship between Catholics and Protestants after nearly thirty years of "ecumenism"? Has there been progress? Is there more mutual respect and less antagonism?

A. At an institutional level, the situation is better in the sense that there is a dialog reaching a conclusion. That area is important, but not the most important because these dialog committees usually never go beyond producing a common statement of agreement. In terms of the practical effects of apologetics as it affects individual Protestants, the situation is now much better than it was thirty years ago. The reason, I believe, is that God has seen the need for apologetics and has raised up men like Scott Hahn who can conduct genuine ecumenism—I say genuine because Catholic apologetics in the pure, classical sense, is designed to convert people to the Catholic Church. That is the purpose of true ecumenism. It is not to bring Catholics to a greater understanding of Protestantism.

Q. In your opinion, have Catholics generally done what was expected of them by Vatican II in dialoguing with Protestants?

A. No, we've done a horrible job. That's why we see so many ex-Catholics who are Protestant. There are Protestant churches that are 80 percent ex-Catholic. The vanguard of anti-Catholicism is led by ex-Catholics. That is a dismal testimony. But that is changing.

Q. There is some continuing evidence of the old barb, "Scratch a Protestant, find an anti-Catholic bigot." For example, many Catholics were outraged recently when Dr. James Dobson aired the testimony of a former Catholic who was weaned away from the Church by her local parish janitor. How do you account for or explain such continuing Catholic-baiting?

A. I have a lot of respect for Dobson, and over the years I have found him very irenic. I would hope he did this as an oversight and not as an intentional tactic. I have not seen him use that tactic before.

Q. *This Rock*, it seems, is answering Protestant critiques of the Church as often as it is answering complaints from Catholics about Church teaching. Does this mean Catholics have been Protestantized?

A. In some cases, yes. I think that the deadly combination of poor catechesis and the relentless efforts on the part of Protestants makes Catholics who do not know the faith and do not know how to explain it to others. But, I see the tide turning on this, as evidenced by the many wonderful works of apologetics that have come out in recent years, for example, those of Scott Hahn, Steve Wood, Peter Kreeft, Tom Howard, and others, and, of course, Catholic Answers, as an organization.

Q. As a Catholic 100 percent involved in the field of apologetics, how do you view the phenomenon of Catholic bishops inviting evangelist Billy Graham into their dioceses, using parish resources to guarantee a packed stadium, and encouraging Catholics to attend his revivals?

A. I understand the reasoning that goes into it. Bishops think Billy Graham is going to draw a large audience, and they think it would be good for Catholics to hear his message preached in the powerful way he preaches it. It's good PR for them to be seen as cooperating with Protestants—but therein lies the problem. This problem is multifaceted. The Council of Trent formally condemned those elements of Protestant teaching which are in conflict with Scripture and the Catholic faith—for, example, errors such as justification by faith alone *(sola Scriptura)*, and the denial of the efficacy of the sacraments and the authority of the hierarchy. So, the first problem arises when you have a bishop assisting a Protestant to broadcast error that the Catholic Church has officially condemned. The second problem is that the bishops of the Catholic Church themselves are charged with teaching the faith. And so it is highly incongruous that the bishops relegate this task to a non-Catholic instead of doing it themselves. Why don't we see stadiums filled with people hungry to hear our bishops preaching the faith in all its beauty? It's no surprise that Catholics flock to events such as the Billy Graham Crusade; after all, they are starved for authentic and authoritative teaching, and they seek it out wherever they think they can find it.

That said, there are bishops in this country who are doing tremendous work in the area of teaching and evangelization. Bishop Donald Wuerl must be given credit for his stalwart efforts at teaching the Catholic faith to his flock—his weekly television program on the doctrines of the faith, his catechism, his book on the Church Fathers. Bishop Charles Chaput of Rapid City, South Dakota, Bishop Sean O'Malley of Fall River, Massachusetts, formerly of the U.S. Virgin Islands, Bishop John J. Myers of Peoria, Illinois, and Bishop Robert Brom of San Diego, among others, are also doing great work.

But what's so crucial is that these lay people unite their enthusiasm for evangelization with a sound knowledge of the teachings of the Catholic faith. Much damage can be done by an enthusiastic Catholic inadvertently misrepresenting the faith and leaving his Protestant listener with a false understanding of what the Church teaches. The old adage is true: You can't give what you don't have, so every Catholic, regardless of age or gender, should be studying the Catholic faith on an ongoing basis so he is able to share it with others. Without that study, he won't have the data to articulate the message.

Q. How much of your readership is made up of Protestants who want to know what the Catholic Church really teaches? How much of your audience is made up of converts?

A. I don't have a numerical figure. I would say the majority is Catholic, but a substantial minority is Protestant. Of those Protestants, there are a number who read us just to monitor our activities.

Q. One of the most obvious signs that we are living in a post-Christian culture is the spread of New Age beliefs. Can the New Age be opposed with traditional Catholic apologetics, or is a new form of response needed?

A. The truth of the Catholic faith is eternal and so is its appeal. People in all ages have gravitated toward Catholic truth when it is presented. When I see the multiplication of sects and the proliferation of New Age ideologies, I think we Catholics must take the blame for this. It's our fault in large measure for this phenomenon because we have ceased proclaiming and living our Catholic faith in all its beauty. We've become placaters, compromisers, appeasers, afraid to preach the Catholic message for what it is.

Q. But how do you convince people who believe vegetarianism and environmentalism have brought them to a higher plane of reality which makes them superior to meat-eating Christians and their religion, especially since so many of the New Agers are formerly Catholic?

A. I would exert my energies to showing that everybody, including them, is in danger of going to hell, and they need Christ and his Church as much as everyone else does.

Q. Do you mention hell when you're on a speaking engagement?

A. When it's appropriate, yes. Words such as hell, sin, and forgiveness are socially gauche because they are so infrequently heard. When was the last time you heard the word hell in a sermon? I don't want to give the impression that I'm morbid or obsessed with the Last Things, but we should all remember that heaven is not guaranteed for any of us, and if there is a possibility we may not get to heaven, then there is the danger we will go to hell, unless we have faith in Christ and are obedient to him.

Q. How does doing apologetics with New Agers differ from apologetics directed at Mormons or Jehovah's Witnesses?

A. The difference is that with Protestants, Jehovah's Witnesses, and Mormons, you have a common respect for the Bible. Even though they misuse it and misunderstand it, they are willing to regard what it teaches as authoritative. Our job as Catholic apologists is to show them the proper interpretation of Scripture according to the teaching of the Church. When dealing with those who do not regard the Bible as authoritative, we have to use other tools, primarily logic and philosophy. Pascal's Wager, for example, is a good logical exercise to use to get someone to consider the possibility of God.

Q. What about apologetics directed at Jews? If Catholics can no longer seek to evangelize or proselytize Jews, what in your view constitutes a purpose for Jewish–Catholic dialogue?

A. The basis for any dialogue is to bring people into the fullness of Christianity, which is to bring people into the Catholic Church. It's important to remember that the Jews as a people have a special relationship with God, but Jesus told the apostles in Matthew 28:19, "Go and baptize all nations in the name of the Father, Son, and Holy Spirit." The mission of the Church extends to all people. If this were not true, we would have a hard time explaining why Paul and the other apostles spent so much time evangelizing the Jews as well as the Gentiles. We should always remember, though, that Judaism is the foundation of our Catholic Faith, and as Pope Pius XI said, all Catholics are "spiritual Semites"— we are all children of Abraham. Vatican II teaches that we must regard Jews with respect and charity whenever we engage in dialogue with them. We should also remember that Catholicism is the fulfillment of Judaism, not a repudiation of Judaism.

Q. How do you view the recent document written principally by Fr. Richard John Neuhaus and Charles Colson, *Evangelicals and Catholics Together,* which said it is "not prudent" for evangelicals and Catholics to proselytize among active adherents of another Christian community?

A. I was recently invited to be on an evangelical radio program that is broadcast nationally, and this document was a subject of discussion. The Evangelicals and I agreed on one thing: This document is seriously flawed and does more harm than good. Now, I understand the laudable motivation that Chuck Colson and Fr. Neuhaus and the other signers had in mind, and I applaud them for their efforts to bring about unity in Christ.

The problem is that this document unintentionally misrepresents the nature of the Church, giving the impression that Catholics and Protestants belong to the same visible Church, and we do not. Protestants do not belong to Christ's visible Church. By virtue of Baptism, which is the initial Catholic sacrament, those baptized Protestants are made members of the Mystical Body of Christ, but this document makes it appear that Catholics and Protestants belong to the same Church.

Another problem is that it asserts that Catholics should not evangelize Protestants. That's ridiculous. Vatican II, among other Church councils, made it clear that the Catholic Church has the duty of evangelizing all those who are outside the Church, and this includes Protestants.

Q. Obviously, *This Rock* is filling a need. Do you sense that the number of Catholics who want to be apologists for the faith is increasing?

A. Yes—definitely yes. But I want to rephrase the question to say that more and more Catholics want to be good Catholics in every sense of the word, and this includes—but is not limited to—being an apologist. Vatican II in its Decree on the Apostolate of the Laity made it clear that lay people have the obligation to evangelize in whatever capacity they are able, and since we are experiencing a shortage of priests and religious, the lay faithful are needed more than ever to teach the faith and evangelize.

Q. You have a new book to be published soon on conversion stories. Can you give *Wanderer* readers a preview of some of the stories?

A. The name of the book is *Surprised by Truth*. This is a conversion story anthology unlike any you have ever read. These eleven accounts give you the biblical and historical reasons for becoming Catholic. Besides being a great read with an inspirational message, *Surprised by Truth* will help Catholics share the Faith with others. These personal testimonies from eleven recent converts will help Catholics explain the faith and will help non-Catholics see the Catholic Church for what it is—the one true Church established by Christ. Besides the personal accounts, Scott Hahn wrote the foreword.

The Wanderer, *1994*

Wine or Whine?

|||||||||||||||||||||||||||||||||||||||||||||||||||||||||||||||||

Jehovah's Witnesses, Fundamentalists, Mormons, and many Evangelicals share an aversion to the drinking of wine. Many of them, at their communion services, substitute grape juice or even water (in the case of Mormons). They claim that at the Last Supper Jesus didn't use wine, but grape juice, and that—in a more general context—drinking wine, or any sort of alcoholic beverage, is proscribed by the Bible.

Jimmy Swaggart, in his book *Questions and Answers,* tackles the issue like this:

"Question: Did the Savior use intoxicating wine in the Lord's Supper? Answer: Personally, I do not think that he did." In the description of the Lord's Supper, the Bible never uses the word wine. We are told, 'He took the cup and gave thanks and gave it to them, saying, 'take ye all of it' (Matthew 26:27). Mark says, 'He took the cup and when he had given thanks he gave it to them' (Mark 14:23). Luke says, 'He took the cup...' (Luke 22:17). Jesus called this drink 'the fruit of the vine' in Matthew 26:29 and also in Mark 14:25 and Luke 22:18.

"It seems the Holy Spirit carried this directive right on through even into the early Church. The apostle Paul said, 'After the same manner also, he took the cup, and when he had supped, saying, this is the new testament in my blood' (1 Corinthians 11:25). Then, following, he mentioned 'this cup' and then later on, 'that cup.' It becomes clear, when these passages are read consecutively, that God intended for us to use grape juice. I also think the Holy Spirit took particular pains not to use any words that could be construed as referring to any kind of intoxicating beverage. There is not a single reference in the Word of God that a person should use intoxicating wine for the Lord's Supper."

Swaggart might be asked how "the fruit of the vine" could mean grape juice, not wine, given that grape juice spoils rapidly in the absence of refrigeration. (There were few refrigerators in ancient Palestine.) If the phrase meant grape juice, then, when grapes were not in season, which is to say much of the year, no one could have had "the fruit of the vine," but we know the ancients drank it all year long, which implies it must have been wine.

Two of several verses cited against any wine drinking are Proverbs 20:1, "Wine is a mocker, strong drink is raging, and whosoever is deceived thereby is not wise," and Ephesians 5:18, "And do not get drunk on wine, in which lies debauchery." Notice that Paul doesn't say, "Do not drink wine," which would be a complete proscription. Rather, he commands the Ephesians not to drink wine to excess. Did Paul disapprove of wine drinking under all circumstances? No. He demonstrates this in 1 Timothy 5:23, "Stop drinking only water, but have a little wine for the sake of your stomach and your frequent illnesses." It may be argued that he was only allowing wine for medicinal purposes, but at the very least we know that Paul didn't completely forbid drinking wine.

What was the Bible's general attitude toward wine drinking? Jesus' parable of the new wine in old skins in Matthew 9:17 sheds light on this question. It was a common practice for the Jews to pour freshly pressed grape juice into goatskins for fermentation when the more customary clay jars were not at hand. If the skin was old or had been used previously to store wine, it couldn't expand as the gases were given off by the fermentation and would burst. If Jesus had eschewed wine as some people claim, why did he so frequently make use of it in his parables and activities?

Because he didn't disapprove of drinking wine, so long as it conformed to the biblical guidelines of moderation. The Church teaches, and common sense corroborates, that wine—like food, sex, laughter, and dancing—is a good thing when enjoyed in its proper time and context. To abuse any good thing is a sin; the thing abused is not sinful in itself. The Old Testament contains examples of the goodness of wine when used correctly.

Deuteronomy 14:22–25 tells us that if one lived too far from the Temple to deliver the prescribed wine tithe, he should sell it and use the proceeds to buy a thanks offering for God. "You may then exchange the money for whatever you desire, oxen or sheep, wine or strong drink, or anything else you would enjoy, and there before the Lord your God, you shall partake of it and make merry with your family" (verse 26). This is hardly the sort of command God would give if he disapproved of wine drinking. The Bible tells us that wine had good uses (Genesis 14:18; Psalms 104:15; Ecclesiastes 10:19) and wicked uses (Genesis 9:21; Isaiah 5:11; 28:7).

Sirach (Ecclesiasticus) 31:12–31 is a discourse on the virtue of moderation and explains that the sin of gluttony includes both food and drink. Just as food is a wonderful thing (what Witness or Fundamentalist would forswear eating simply because the danger of gluttony exists?), so also is wine.

Wine taken in excess is not only gluttony, but also the door to other sins— remember what happened to Noah in Genesis 9:20–24 and to Lot in Genesis 19:30–38. "Let not wine-drinking be the proof of your strength, for wine has been the ruin of many. As the furnace probes the work of the smith, so does wine the hearts of the insolent" (Sirach 31:25–26).

These stern words might seem to imply that it's better all around to avoid wine lest one be ruined by it, but the next verses disprove this notion and put wine and wine drinking into proper perspective: "Wine is very life to man if taken in moderation. Does he really live who lacks wine which was created for his joy? Joy of heart, good cheer, and merriment are wine drunk freely at the proper time. Headache, bitterness, and disgrace is wine drunk amid anger and strife" (Sirach 31:27–29).

The Talmud's tractate Kethuboth (writings) has many wine drinking stories, including this exchange between two zealous wine drinkers: "'As for me,' said one man, 'each of my bunches produces a whole barrel.' Said the other, 'I have pressed so much that for several stadia all around you walk in a sea of wine up to your ankles.'" These men, good Jews both, were not teetotalers. Our Lord himself certainly drank wine. Indeed, his first recorded miracle was to turn water into wine at the wedding feast at Cana (John 2:1–11). This point is a source of irritation for the anti-wine crowd.

They invariably counter this passage, as did Swaggart, with the assertion that Jesus, like all observant Jews of his time, drank grape juice, not wine. This is simply not the case. The eminent French historian Henri Daniel-Rops, in his magnificent Daily Life in the Time of Jesus, explains, "It was certainly red wine they drank. The Old Testament speaks of the redness of wine many times (Genesis 49:11–12; Deuteronomy 32:14), and there is no mention of white. Some kinds were better than others, and the account of the marriage at Cana in the Gospel shows that the best was served at the beginning of the meal and the inferior wine later, when the guests had already drunk a great deal.

Generally speaking it was a very full-bodied deep purple wine, rich in both alcohol and tannin, and it was drunk mixed with water, not neat" (page 205). After reading the account of the wedding at Cana, one might ask, "If John knew Jesus really turned water into grape juice, why did he go out of his way to quote the headwaiter's remarks: 'Everyone serves good wine first, and then when people have drunk freely, an inferior one,'?" At the Last Supper Jesus chose wine, "fruit of the vine and work of human hands," to become his blood.

Jesus certainly drank wine and was even accused of being a drunkard (Luke 7:34). It's unlikely that, had he disapproved of wine drinking, Jesus would have referred to it and made use of it so prominently in his public ministry. Daniel-Rops adds a final bit of clarity to the biblical understanding of the place and dignity of wine: "The vine was the symbol of Israel, and since a golden vine was to be seen in the Temple, was not wine a holy drink? Therefore, it had ritual laws. Like meat, it had to be kosher, and it had to be made entirely by Jewish hands.

When Jesus spoke of himself as the vine, and when he consecrated wine to the point of saying, 'this is my blood,' he was speaking like a son of Israel. He was entirely in the tradition of his people" (page 205).

Catholic Answers, *September 1989*

Pope Fiction: Answers to Five Myths and Misconceptions About the Papacy

||||||||||||||||||||||||||||||||||||||||||||||||||||||||||||||||||||||||||||||||||||||||||||||||||||||||||

RITA, ONE OF MY WIFE'S FRIENDS, described an incident that happened to her recently. She was driving to our house and wasn't sure which street to turn on, so she pulled over to the side of the road to check a map. She noticed that the car that had been behind her for the last mile or so had also stopped and pulled alongside her. Thinking the middle-aged woman in the other car had stopped to offer assistance, Rita rolled down her window and smiled. "Could you help me with some directions, please?" she asked through the rolled up window of the other car.

The woman couldn't hear her through the glass, but she understood the question. Staring hard at Rita, she shook her head and scowled. Perplexed, Rita asked, "Could you roll down your window, please?" pantomiming the motion of turning the window handle. The woman shook her head again and her scowl deepened. Then, leaning across the front seat of her car, her face inches from the window, she mouthed slowly and clearly: "I HATE THE POPE." Then she made an obscene gesture with her finger, pulled back onto the road, and drove off.

Rita was dazed and wondered what could have provoked such a bizarre expression of hostility. Then it dawned on her: The bumper sticker on her minivan read "Follow me, I'm behind the pope!" and included a picture of a smiling Pope John Paul II. Apparently it so offended the woman that she had to go out of her way to let Rita know. Was she an anti-Catholic Evangelical Protestant? A Jehovah's Witness on her way home from a meeting at the Kingdom Hall? A secularist of no particular religion? Perhaps she was a "pro-choice Catholic" who hated the pope because his efforts to defend the sanctity of unborn life clash with her agenda to "Keep Abortion Legal." Maybe she's mad that he won't compromise Catholic teaching that the sacrament of holy orders is reserved to men.

Who knows? There is one thing we do know. A lot of people dislike, even hate, Pope John Paul II, not because of his personality or ethnicity or whatever, but because they don't like the Catholic Church. The pope is the flesh-and-blood reminder of that Church and its teachings—he personifies Catholicism—and for some this is particularly offensive. Some make their dislike for the papacy felt in articles, tracts, and videos, calculated not merely to refute Catholic teaching, but to undermine the trust Catholics have in the Church and the pope. Millions believe myths and legends and historical inaccuracies about the papacy, almost all of which were concocted centuries ago by critics of the Church. Many labor under the twin burden of ignorance and an unwillingness to be shown the truth, heirs of a generations-old anti-Catholicism handed down from family, friends, social circles, and nearly three hundred years of subtle American, Protestant propaganda.

But there's hope. John Henry Newman, a Protestant scholar who converted to Catholicism in 1845 and became a leading apologist and later a cardinal, said in his book *Apologia Pro Vita Sua,* "When I was young…I thought the pope to be the antichrist. At Christmas 1824–5 I preached a sermon to that effect." If Newman could be brought to see the truth, so can that angry woman driver who HATES THE POPE. As apostles for Christ, we have work to do. The myths and misconceptions that form the vast body of "Pope Fiction" are widespread and pernicious—but like other ills, they can be counteracted and cured with a healthy dose of the facts. Let's examine five of the more common ones.

Fiction #1

Peter was not the first "pope." He didn't have any special primacy or jurisdiction over the other apostles or other early Christians. In fact, he denies this by referring to himself as merely a "fellow presbyter" (1 Peter 5:1)—an office lower than an overseer (bishop). If anything, Paul had a greater authority than Peter.

Although St. Peter never called himself "pope" in Scripture, he did indeed have a special apostolic primacy and jurisdiction. The Scriptural evidence for this is substantial and explicit. Of the twelve apostles, St. Peter is by far the one mentioned most often in Scripture. He appears 195 times. The next most often mentioned apostle was St. John, who comes in at a whopping twenty-nine times. St. James the Greater is mentioned nineteen times, St. Philip fifteen, and the numbers dwindle rapidly for the others. Does this in itself prove St. Peter's primacy? No, but it does shed considerable light on his importance. What does that light reveal? Among other things, we see that when the twelve apostles are listed by name (see Matthew 10:2–5; Mark 3:16–19; Luke 6:14–17; and Acts 1:13), St. Peter's name is always first—and Judas Iscariot is always listed dead last. Far more commonly, though, the New Testament refers to simply "Peter and the Twelve," as if to say that the tempestuous fisherman signified in himself the unity of the whole apostolic college.

There are many other biblical signs of St. Peter's preeminence among the apostles. He is the only one who receives a name change from Christ. He was Simon, but Christ calls him "Rock" (Matthew 16:18). Name changes given by God that we read about in Scripture have huge significance and imply an elevation in importance and a special mission given to that person by God (e.g., Abraham, Jacob). He is also singled out by Christ to receive the keys of the kingdom of heaven and is promised, "[W]hatever you (singular) bind on earth will be bound in heaven, and whatever you (singular) loose on earth will be loosed in heaven" (Matthew 16:19). St. Peter is the lone Apostle Christ calls out of the boat to walk on water (see Matthew 1:28–29). At the tomb of Christ, St. John waits to allow St. Peter to enter ahead of him (see John 20:6). It was to him among the apostles that God first revealed the Resurrection (see

Mark 16:7). The risen Christ appears to him first, before the other apostles (see Luke 24:34). Christ preached the Gospel to the crowds from St. Peter's fishing boat (see Luke 5:3). St. Peter is told by Christ, "Simon, Simon, behold Satan has demanded to sift all of you like wheat, but I have prayed that your (singular) faith may not fail. And once you (singular) have turned back, you (singular) must strengthen your brethren" (Luke 22:31–32). Christ makes St. Peter the shepherd of his Church (see John 21:15–17). In Acts 1:13–26, St. Peter leads the other apostles in choosing Matthias as successor to Judas, and he leads the apostles in preaching on the day of Pentecost (see Acts 2:14). He performed the first Pentecost miracle (see Acts 3). He spoke in the name of all the apostles and for the whole Church when the twelve were brought before the Sanhedrin for a trial (see Acts 4). It is to St. Peter alone that God sent the revelation that Gentiles are to be allowed into the Church (see Acts 10), and he is the apostle who first welcomes them into the Church (see Acts 11). St. Peter's dogmatic pronouncement was accepted and caused all disputes to cease at the Council of Jerusalem (see Acts 15). After his conversion and healing from blindness, St. Paul went to visit St. Peter to have his teachings confirmed by him (see Galatians 1:18).

Having said that, what should we make of St. Peter's reference to himself in 1 Peter 5:1 as a "fellow presbyter"? Does this signal that he was unaware of his special role as chief of the apostles? The answer is found the same passage. "Clothe yourselves in humility in your dealings with one another," he says, "for God opposes the proud but bestows favor on the humble. So humble yourselves under the mighty hand of God, that he may exalt you in due time" (1 Peter 5:5). Since he was cautioning his Christian audience to be humble, it makes perfect sense that he would take his own advice and, setting an example for them, speak of himself in humble terms. And in doing so, he was following Christ's command, "Whoever wishes to be great among you shall be your servant, whoever wishes to be first among you shall be your slave" (Matthew 20:26–27). But this humility shouldn't blind us to the substantial body of biblical evidence showing that he did receive a special apostolic preeminence and authority—

evidence that critics of the papacy often ignore or strain to explain away.

St. Paul, like St. Peter, was also humble when referring to himself. He was by far the most prominent and prolific New Testament writer, responsible for about half of the New Testament, but he said, "I am the least of the apostles, not fit to be called an apostle, because I persecuted the Church of God" (1 Corinthians 15:10), and "To me the very least of all the holy ones, this grace was given" (Ephesians 3:8). On numerous occasions he called himself a mere deacon, the very lowest level of ordained ministry in the Church (see 1 Corinthians 3:5, 4:1; 2 Corinthians 3:6, 6:4, 11:23; Ephesians 3:7; Colossians 1:23, 25). But clearly, St. Paul had an authority far greater than that of a deacon. As with St. Peter, these examples of St. Paul's humility are balanced by statements of his authority: "Although I have the full right to order you to do what is proper, I rather urge you out of love" (Philemon 8–9), and 1 Thessalonians 2:7: "[A]lthough we were able to impose our weight as apostles of Christ. Rather, we were gentle among you, as a nursing mother cares for her children." St. Peter's calling himself a "fellow presbyter" doesn't disprove his primacy any more than St. Paul's habit of calling himself a "deacon," proves he had no authority greater than a deacon's.

Fiction #2

The bishop of Rome can't be the "successor to Peter," since Peter was never in Rome. The Bible nowhere says he went there, and Paul, who did go there, never mentions Peter being in Rome. If Peter were the "pope," he certainly would have mentioned it.

Trying to prove that St. Peter did not go to Rome and die there is a lot like trying to prove that St. Matthew didn't write the Gospel of Matthew. True, the Bible doesn't explicitly say he went to Rome, but the surrounding historical evidence is more than sufficient to prove that he did. But first, we should ask, "If St. Peter didn't go to Rome, where did he go? Where did he die?" We'd expect to find plenty of evidence in the writings of the early Church telling us where this prominent apostle carried out his final years of ministry, if it were some place other than Rome. The historical record contains no hint that he ended his days anywhere else but Rome. No other city except Rome ever claimed to possess the site of his martyrdom or his tomb (and early Christians were extraordinarily diligent about making and proving such claims). No other city—not even Antioch, where he resided for a time during his apostolate—claimed he ended his days among them. No Church Father or Council or any other early Church record indicates that he finished his days anywhere else but in Rome. That's the lack of evidence side of the coin. The flip side is the mountain of evidence proving he did go to Rome. Everyone everywhere in the early Church agreed that St. Peter went to Rome, ministered there for over two decades, and suffered martyrdom by inverted crucifixion in A.D. 65, under the persecution of Emperor Nero.

Given the grave danger to the early Church from a hostile Roman government, it makes perfect sense that St. Paul would not mention St. Peter's whereabouts in his letters. He didn't want to draw unfriendly attention. It's also quite possible that St. Peter had not yet arrived in Rome when St. Paul was writing. We even see St. Peter himself making what seems to be a cryptic reference to his presence in Rome when he says "The chosen one at Babylon sends you greetings, as does Mark, my son" (1 Peter 5:13). "Babylon" was a commonly used code word for Rome among Christians, because its pagan decadence and opposition to Christ were reminiscent of the idolatrous wickedness associated with ancient Babylon. But once St. Peter had been martyred, the testimonies of his sojourn in Rome with St. Paul poured forth in a flood from the early Christian writers. Perhaps the most detailed of these early accounts came from St. Irenaeus of Lyons (d. 200) in his apologetics work *Against Heresies*. He gave a detailed account of succession of the bishops of Rome, from St. Peter down to his own day. He referred to Rome as the city "where Peter and Paul proclaimed the gospel and founded the Church." Other notable early examples were St. Ignatius of Antioch (d. 107) who referred to the Church at Rome as "the Church of Peter and Paul" (Letter to the Romans); St. Cyprian (d. 251), who described Rome as "The place of Peter" (Epistle 52); and St. Jerome (d. 420), who called Rome "the See of Peter" (Epistle 15, to Pope Damasus).

Around A.D. 166 Bishop Dionysius of Corinth wrote to Pope Soter, "You have also, by your very admonition, brought together the planting that was made by Peter and Paul at Rome...."[86] Besides the vast amount of historical evidence showing that St. Peter went to Rome, modern archaeology has cinched the case even tighter by a definitive scientific demonstration that his bones (studies showed that they are of a powerfully built elderly man who died of crucifixion) are interred directly beneath the high altar in St. Peter's Basilica in Rome, several levels down, where the original first century Vatican hill sloped away toward the Tiber River. This was just outside the walls of what was once Nero's Circus—precisely where all the early Christian and even non-Christian records say St. Peter was crucified and buried.

Fiction #3

The papacy is a medieval Roman invention. The early Church knew nothing of a "supreme pontiff." Other bishops didn't regard the bishop of Rome as having special authority to operate the way modern popes do.

Archbishop Fulton Sheen once said, "It is easy to find truth; it is hard to face it, and harder still to follow it." This is certainly true for someone when it comes to facing the historical evidence for the papacy in the early Church. The hardcore purveyors of pope fiction refuse to believe that the papacy was established by Christ. But if the equivalent of the modern papacy was merely a Roman invention of the eighth or ninth century, how do we explain the fact that for the preceding seven hundred years, the bishops of Rome were regarded (and regarded themselves) as having a special, unique authority and responsibility for the whole Church?

Here are a few of the hundreds of examples that could be given. The earliest account we have of a bishop of Rome exercising authority in another diocese comes from the Epistle of St. Clement to the Corinthians. It was written by Clement, bishop of Rome, around the year A.D. 80. In it he responds to the Corinthians' plea for his intervention. The entire letter is written in a fatherly, kind way, but it is also clear that Clement was quite aware he had a special authority. Two key phrases stand out as testimony of this: "But if any disobey the words spoken by him [Christ] through us, let them know that they will involve themselves in sin and no small danger"; and "For you will give us joy and gladness if, obedient to what we have written through the Holy Spirit, you root out the lawless anger of your jealousy" (59, 63). Clearly, this early bishop of Rome wrote as one who expected his words to be obeyed. Pope Victor I (reigned 189–199) worked to settle a dispute among the bishops of the East and West over when to celebrate Easter—known as the Quartodeciman controversy.

The other bishops recognized his unique authority when they followed his directive to convene local and regional synods to deliberate on the issue. Most of the bishops decided to adopt his proposal that the whole Church celebrate Easter on the first Sunday after Passover. Those who didn't he threatened with excommunication. The fact that no bishop in the world—not a single one—disputed his authority as bishop of Rome to carry out such an excommunication is a powerful piece of evidence that the early Church recognized the unique authority of the bishop of Rome.

Shortly before his death in A.D. 200, St. Irenaeus of Lyons wrote to Pope Victor asking him to relent and allow the Eastern bishops to maintain their celebration of Easter according to the Hebrew lunar calendar, evidence that he recognized the pope's authority to threaten excommunication. After all, it was Irenaeus who wrote of the Church at Rome: "For with this church, because of its superior origin, all the churches must agree; that is, all the faithful in the whole world, for in her the apostolic tradition has always been preserved for the benefit of the faithful everywhere."[87]

Around the year 220, Pope Callistus wrote, "Callistus, archbishop of the Catholic Church in the city of Rome, to Benedictus, our brother and bishop, greeting in the Lord. By the love of the brotherhood we are bound, and by our apostolic rule we are constrained, to give answer to the inquiries of the brethren, according to what the Lord has given us, and to furnish them with the authority of the seal of the apostles."[88] Clearly he was well aware of his special role and authority in settling problems in the Church, even in other dioceses. Later, the same pope wrote a letter to all the bishops of Gaul, saying, "Callistus to our most dearly beloved brethren, all the bishops settled throughout Gaul.... We beg you not to permit anything to be done in those parts contrary to the apostolic statutes; but, supported by our authority, you should stop what is injurious, and prohibit what is unlawful.... Observe this law, which has been laid down by the apostles and fathers, and our predecessors, and has been ratified by us.... We have replied to your interrogations shortly, because your letter found us burdened overmuch, and preoccupied with other judgments."[89]

In the year 382, Pope Damasus wrote about his authority as bishop of Rome, anchoring it to the fact that he was the successor of St. Peter. He said the Church at Rome "has been placed at the forefront, not by the conciliar decision of other churches, but has received the primacy by the evangelistic voice of our Lord and Savior Who says, 'You are Peter, and upon this rock I will build My Church, and the gates of hell will not prevail against it; and I will give to you the keys of the kingdom of heaven, and whatever you shall have bound on earth will be bound in heaven, and whatever you shall have loosed on earth shall be loosed in heaven.'... The first See, therefore, is that of Peter the Apostle, that of the Roman Church, which has neither stain nor blemish."[90]

In A.D. 404, St. John Chrysostom wrote to Pope Innocent, "I beseech your Charity to rouse yourself and have compassion, and do everything so as to put a stop to the mischief at this point."[91] Note that Chrysostom, the archbishop of Constantinople, a powerful diocese, recognized the need to appeal to the bishop of Rome to resolve a controversy. Many other examples of the primacy of the bishop of Rome in the early Church could be added. Even from the earliest years, the bishop of Rome had—and everyone recognized that he had—a special authority in the Church. Anyone who says the papacy is a "medieval Roman invention," is either ignorant of history or dishonest. Either way, it's a sham argument.

Fiction #4

In the middle ages, there was a "Pope Joan," a woman who hid her gender and rose through the ranks of the Church, became a cardinal and was elected pope. No one knew she was a woman until, during a papal procession through the streets of Rome, she went into labor and gave birth to a child. She and the baby were killed on the spot by the mob, enraged at her imposture.

A lot of things are said about the alleged "Pope Joan." Depending on who is telling the story, she was a courageous feminist, a clever opportunist, a brilliant scholar who couldn't make it as a woman in a man's world. She is said to have been a wise ruler and an astute theologian, though, oddly, no decree or theological teaching purporting to have come from her has made its way down to our day. In any case, the fact is there was no Pope Joan. She exists only as pure legend, but one that makes for a sexy story.

And when it comes to sexy stories, you know Hollywood will try its hand at making a blockbuster out of this piece of pope fiction. New Line Cinema (that's right, the same good folks who produced *The Last Temptation of Christ*) has reportedly bought the movie rights to *Pope Joan*, the bestselling 1996 novel by Donna Woolfolk Cross. Her book is couched as an historical "novel"—embellishing on a grand scale the rather sparse details that have clung to the legend of a brilliant, plain girl who rises to the highest levels in Church service, culminating in her being elected pope by an unwitting college of cardinals. The way the book is written and the way it's being promoted support my concern that it will be seen by most of its historically ignorant readers, not as a novel, a fiction, but as a real biography of the one woman who "made it to the top." When the movie comes out, this problem will certainly grow in proportions.

It's important to remember that even if there had been a female impostor pope, this would just mean that an invalid election had taken place, nothing more. Other invalidly elected claimants to the papal office have come and gone over the centuries, and the fact that a woman made that list would simply mean that a woman made that list. She would not have been pope—no one invalidly elected would be. And nothing in the Church's teachings about the papacy would be injured or disproved.

But in reality, the "Pope Joan" story is all sizzle and no steak. The basic outline of the main legend (actually, there have been several competing legends over the centuries) has it that in the ninth or tenth century, a plain but extraordinarily brilliant young woman contrived to enter the university disguised as a man. Her intellect outstripped her male classmates and she shot to the top rank of students. Talk of her prowess in law, science, rhetoric, philosophy and languages was widespread. In another legend, popularized by several thirteenth century works such as the *Chronicle of Martin Polonus,* the *Universal Chronicle of Metz* and *Wonders of the City of Rome,* she traveled first to Greece with her boyfriend (why he wanted a girlfriend who disguised herself as a man is unknown), made a name for herself in the university there, and then traveled to Rome. Here all the legends converge into the main one that has come down to our day.

Once in Rome, Joan managed to enter religious life (although no legend is able to say which order she entered), she was ordained a priest, and earned a high reputation as a skilled notary in the papal court. Eventually, she was noticed by the pope and made a cardinal. You can guess what happens next. She is eventually elected pope, takes the name John, and sets about skillfully ruling the Church.

It's at this point that the most dramatic scenes of the story unfold. The legends vary as to how Joan's gender and identity were discovered. One holds that she was granted a vision by God in which she was shown two options for her fate, being discovered and disgraced by the world or roasting in hell for her crime. She chose the former. Another version says that she got pregnant by one of her curial advisors and worked to maintain the charade until she gave birth to the baby. At that point her secret was discovered and she was deposed as pope and sent to a convent to do penance for the rest of her life. In this legend, the child she bore went on to became the bishop of Ostia, about thirty miles southwest of Rome, and when she died, he had her body buried there.

Of course, no evidence exists to support that. The main detail these legends have in common is that Joan was discovered because her hanky-panky with a cardinal or secretary resulted in pregnancy, and the childbirth exposed her fraud. The main legend is most gory on this point. In it, Pope Joan goes into labor while riding in her *sedes gestiatoria*—the portable throne in which popes were carried—as her procession passed the Coliseum on its way from St. Peter's Basilica to St. John Lateran Cathedral. The procession halted, the baby was born, and the confused and angry onlookers killed Pope Joan and her baby on the spot. Most accounts say she was killed by stoning, another says she died in childbirth as the mob watching the spectacle shouted and insulted her. Still another says she was dragged to death behind a horse as punishment.

Either way, the legends agree that the Romans didn't appreciate the unpleasant discovery. Several odd historical details gave weight to the legend, including the fact that among the carved busts of the popes in the cathedral of Siena was one of an unnamed woman. No one knows who created it or how it was put there, but when Pope Clement VIII discovered it, he ordered it reworked enough to represent Pope Zacharias, whose image had not previously been included in the collection. This is not surprising, though, given the widespread belief in Europe in the Pope Joan legend during the thirteenth through eighteenth centuries. Versions abounded, and many credulous folks, Catholics included, were sincerely convinced that there had indeed been a female pope. But the facts of history show otherwise.

The primary proofs that this is all just a fable are these. First, the earliest point to which we can trace the legend is the mid-thirteenth century, but the legend didn't really gain wide currency until the late fourteenth century. No evidence of any kind exists from the ninth century (when Pope Joan was alleged to have reigned), nor do we see any in the tenth through twelfth centuries. None of the annals or acts of the popes that were written between the ninth and thirteenth centuries (and none after that, either) mention her.

Church historian J.P. Kirsch wrote "Not one contemporaneous historical source among the papal histories knows anything about her; also, no mention is made of her until the middle of the thirteenth century. Now it is incredible that the appearance of a 'popess,' if it was an historical fact, would be noticed by none of the numerous historians from the tenth to the thirteenth century. In the history of the popes, there is no place where this legendary figure will fit in. Between Leo IV and Benedict III, where Martinus Polonus places her, she cannot be inserted...."[92]

So where did the legend come from? There are two likely possibilities. The first is that the Roman population became disgusted with the corrupt influence wielded over Pope Sergius (reigned 904–911) by the powerful and wealthy Theodora Theophylact, and more specifically by her young daughter Morozia, a cunning and exceptionally attractive woman. It appears that Morozia was Sergius's mistress and bore him at least one son (the future Pope John XI).

The fabulously wealthy and prestigious Theophylact family wielded immense power in Rome during the tenth century, even, sadly, over several popes. This is a sorry episode in the history of the Church, one which displayed a decadence and immorality that even popes, at times, could fall prey to—a reminder to us all that men, even the holiest of men, are not invulnerable to temptation and personal weakness. Despite their sins, Christ's promise that the Church would be protected from error was not, nor has it ever been, broken. From the details of Sergius III's pontificate, it seems clear that he was a vain, violent and sensuous man. It's quite possible that the disgusted faithful took to mocking him or one of his immediate successors because he was perceived to have been under the influence of the Theophylact women.

Some historians trace the legend of a female pope to Morozia, saying that the people called her "Pope Joan" to mock the weak popes she controlled. Another possible explanation for the Pope Joan legend lies in the conduct of the much-maligned Pope John VIII (reigned 872–882). He appears to have had a very weak personality, even perhaps somewhat effeminate. Cardinal Baronius, in his Church history *Annals,* suggests that John VIII's reputation as effeminate gave rise to the legend. Indeed, it would seem that over time, the common folk added more lurid embellishments until the vulgar jokes about the hapless (and certainly male) pope ballooned and metamorphosed into a female "popessa."

Fiction #5

The pope is the Beast spoken of in Revelation 13. Verse 1 says that he wears crowns and has "blasphemous names" written on his head. Verse 18 says that the numerical value of his name adds up to 666. The pope's official title in Latin is Vicarius Filii Dei *(Vicar of the Son of God). If you add that up using Roman numerals, you get 666. The popes' tiara is emblazoned with this title, formed by diamonds and other jewels.*

I wasn't very good at math in school, but even I can follow this argument and run the numbers well enough to show it's bogus. (Besides, answering this question is apologetics at its most fun!) The charge that the pope is the beast of Revelation 13, because his title adds up to 666, is especially popular with Seventh-Day Adventists, but it's also widely repeated in some Protestant circles. *Vicarius Filii Dei* does have the mathematical value of 666 in Latin. Here's how it works. Like many ancient languages, such as Greek and Hebrew, some Latin letters are also used for numbers: I = 1, V = 5, X = 10, L = 50, C = 100, D = 500 and M = 1000. The letter "u" is rendered as V and the letter "w," which doesn't exist in the Latin alphabet, would be rendered as VV. So this title would read in Latin as VICARIVS FILII DEI. When calculating the value of a name or word, letters that don't have a numerical value are ignored. For example, drop out the no-value letters in my name, PATRICK MADRID, and you come up with 2102—1 (I) + 100 (C) + 1000 (M) + 500 (D) + 1 (I) + 500 (D) = 2102. (By the way, this is one reason why, as far as I know, no one has yet accused me of being in league with the antichrist. The numbers just don't add up.) But in the case of VICARIVS FILII DEI, they do add up to 666. Isolate the numbers and this is what you get: 5 (V) + 1 (I) + 100 (C) + 1 (I) + 5 (V) + 1 (I) + 50 (L) + 1 (I) + 1 (I) + 500 (D) + 1 (I) = 666.

But there are problems with this. The first is that *Vicarius Filii Dei*, or "vicar of the Son of God," is not now, nor has it ever been, an official title of the bishop of Rome. The second problem is that virtually no one, including many unsuspecting lay Catholics, knows that this papal "title" is a fabrication. To an untrained ear, it sounds enough like one of the pope's real titles, *Vicarius Christi* (Vicar of Christ), to pass the test. Unfortunately for those who traffic in this particular piece of pope fiction, the real title, *Vicarius Christi*, adds up only to a measly 214, not the infernal 666. In fact, none of the pope's official titles, such as *Servus Servorum Dei* (Servant of the Servants of God), *Pontifex Maximus* (Supreme Pontiff), or *Successor Petri* (Successor of Peter), will add up to 666. That's why you never see any of them used by anti-Catholics.

If the person making this claim disputes these facts, ask him to furnish even one example of a papal decree, ecclesiastical letter, conciliar statement, or any other authentic Catholic document in which the pope calls himself or is referred to as the "vicar of the Son of God." He won't be able to find one, because none exist. *Vicarius Filii Dei* has never been an official title of the pope. Poof! [93]

That part was easy, but some people, especially Seventh-Day Adventists, will ignore the evidence (or lack of it) and hold tenaciously to the notion that "Vicar of the Son of God" is an official papal title and therefore identifies the pope as the Beast of Revelation. What else can be said in response? Using the same math exercise we did above, point out that the name of the woman who started the Seventh-Day Adventist church, Ellen Gould White, also adds up to 666 in Latin. (L + L + V + D + V + V + I = 666). Then ask if this proves that she is the Beast. I can assure you the answer won't be "yes." If the answer is "no," ask how this numbers game could possibly prove the pope or anyone else is the Beast. If you're answered with silence, it's a good bet that you've made some progress with the person. The main fact to impress on someone who uses this argument is that a papal title had to be invented, one that could produce the magic number, in order to give this argument legs.

But we're not quite finished cutting it off at the knees. The charge that the pope is the Beast because he wears a crown, because Revelation 13:1 says the Beast wears crowns and has "blasphemous names" written on his head, must also be answered. This we can do more quickly. Since about the year 708, many popes have worn at non-liturgical ceremonial events a special papal crown called a tiara, but the stylized beehive shaped papal crown of three diadems that we have come to know as a tiara emerged only after the fourteenth century. Although it was customary for these tiaras to be encrusted with jewels and precious ornaments, there is no evidence—no statue, bust, painting, drawing, or even written description of any of the many tiaras that were crafted—that any papal tiara ever had the name or a title of a pope emblazoned on it.[94] This is significant, because there have been medieval and Renaissance popes whose extravagant vanity prodded them to have lavishly ornamented, jewel-encrusted tiaras made for themselves. And we possess paintings and statues and other representations of them produced during their lifetimes that show these tiaras. If any popes in history would have been tempted to succumb to the bad taste of spelling out "*Vicarius Filii Dei*" in diamonds across the front of their tiaras, these men would have—but they didn't. No pope did. One particular anti-Catholic tract I've seen shows a plain metal tiara with *Vicarius Filii Dei* written in diamonds across it. But it was a drawing—not a photograph of a museum piece or even a photo of a painting of a tiara. It had to be drawn, of course, because the "666 papal crown" has only ever existed in the minds of those who perpetuate this fantasy.

Envoy, *2000*

More *Vicarius* Thrills: The Numbers of the "Beast" and the Men Who Flub Them

Do we need any more proof that apologetics is fun? Well, here's more. When I wrote my article "Pope Fiction," I knew it might rile some people, and it did. Shortly after it appeared, I received a letter from a Mr. Allan Drisko. He didn't care for my piece, especially my refutation of the 666 nonsense sometimes used against the papacy. He wrote:

> In regard to Mr. Madrid's zealous efforts to eradicate 'papal fictions' from the cobwebs of our minds, I was not impressed. To begin with, the attempt to locate an ecclesiastical colossus headed by the papacy at Rome as demonstrated in the New Testament, is an exercise in futility. We Protestants never cease to be amazed at your tireless armchair theological gymnastics to persuade us in the opposite, though not unreasonable direction.
>
> If the Lord Jesus Christ had intended to establish the supreme authority of Peter perpetuated in a dynastic line of popes who would enjoy absolute episcopal jurisdiction over the entire world, all logic demands that he would have categorically and intentionally informed his followers in no uncertain terms! But he did not. Other sacred offices of the church are set forth in Holy Writ, yet strange silence prevails with regard to that which is supposedly the highest of them

all! The silence of the inspired writers in omitting to mention such a high office is equivalent to Napoleon's biographer failing to use the title of emperor.

Now Mr. Madrid takes great glee in swinging the wrecking ball at those who would entertain the thought that the pope fits the description of the beast in Revelation 13. May I say that the allusions to Catholicism in the book of Revelation are quite intriguing, and many have concluded what Mr. Madrid rejects, but certainly not without reason. Besides, we are told that wisdom is needed here: "Let him that has understanding count the number...for it is the number of a man; and his number is 666." I noticed no attempt whatsoever on the part of the author to display any understanding in offering an alternative explanation. Hence, it is obvious he is only interested in bashing a popular Protestant position and is content to congratulate himself for doing so.

Mr. Madrid triumphantly concludes that the title *Vicarius Filii Dei* is not now, nor has it ever been, a title of the bishops of Rome, and insinuates that Protestants are merely dumb bunnies pulling this "rabbit" out of a hat. Unfortunately, the author is not being entirely forthright with his readers. He says, "If the person making this claim dispute these facts, let him produce...any official Catholic document in which the pope calls himself or is referred to as, "Vicar of the Son of God"...none exist." Drum roll please.

In the early collection of canon law, the *Decretum* of Gratian, first published in 1148, we read, (Latin) "*Beatus Petrus in terris vicarius Filii Dei videtur esse constitutus.*" Translated into English, it means, "Blessed Peter is seen to have been constituted vicar of the Son of God on earth." Furthermore, in the revised Corpus of Canon [*sic*], published by order of Pope Gregory XIII, it was to be corrected by, "the plenitude of apostolic power," so that it is, "entirely freed from faults." Therein we find the same statement as above. And I go on, when Lucius Ferraris wrote, *Prompta Bibliotheca* in 1755, he gave under the article "Papa," the title, *Vicarius Filii Dei*, and cited the revised canon law as his authority. When his work was revised and published in Rome in 1890, the document and aforementioned title were retained! Moreover, the *Catholic Encyclopedia* says his work, "will ever remain a precious mine of information."[95]

In conclusion, a subscriber to *Our Sunday Visitor*, a Catholic weekly periodical, wrote a letter to the editor, wherein he asked, "What are the letters supposed to be in the pope's crown, and what do they signify, if anything?" The answer given was, "The letters inscribed on the pope's miter are these: *Vicarius Filii Dei*, which is Latin for, Vicar of the Son of God."[96]

Some weeks later, Mr. Drisko sent me a follow-up letter:

> I wrote to you a couple of months ago [*sic*] in regard to your inaccurate article relating to papal fictions. I thought perhaps you might drop me a line as to where it was I erred, or maybe print a response in your letters section…neither of which you chose to do, and I quite understand why. You were wrong and you would look like a fool.

Clearly, Mr. Drisko was expecting to pull out the history books and have himself a wonderful time, but I'm going to have to disappoint him. As I'll show in a moment, there's a lot less to his argument than meets the eye. But first, I should point out that Mr. Drisko was not completely on the level with me in his first e-mail. He plagiarized a significant chunk of his argument, word for word, from *The Prophecies of Daniel and the Revelation*, a book written by a Seventh-day Adventist named Uriah Smith. Evidently, he didn't think I'd be familiar with the book, and thought he could get away with passing off Mr. Smith's work as his own.

Not long after receiving Mr. Drisko's letters, I received an e-mail from Michael Scheifler, an Adventist apologist and creator of the Bible Light Homepage. Note the striking similarity between Mr. Scheifler's arguments, and those of Mr. Drisko:

"In your cover story, 'Pope Fiction,'" he writes, "...you issue a challenge for the critics of Catholicism to furnish one example of an official Catholic document in which the pope is referred to as *Vicarius Filii Dei*. I accept your challenge." He continues:

I personally have Lucius Ferraris's *Prompta Bibliotheca*, 1858 Paris edition, a Catholic theological encyclopedia, in which the title *Vicarius Filii Dei* appears in volume 5, column 1828, under "Papa," article 2. I have scanned the item and it appears in an article on my Bible Light website. *Prompta Bibliotheca*, according to the 1913 *Catholic Encyclopedia,* is "a veritable encyclopedia of religious knowledge," and "will ever remain a precious mine of information" and is quoted frequently as an authoritative Catholic source.

Vicarius Filii Dei also appeared repeatedly in Catholic canon law for hundreds of years (Anselm's, Cardinal Deusdedit's, and Gratian's *Decretum*, also known as *Concordia Discordantium Canonum*), in quotes of the Donation of Constantine, which contained the title and was considered authentic by the Church for many hundreds of years, having been cited by as many as 10 popes as proof of their temporal authority. One is the 1879 edition of *Corpus Juris Canonici* containing *Vicarius Filii Dei* is presented in my article.

In *Crossing the Threshold of Hope*, by Pope John Paul II, in the first chapter, page 3, you will find that, "The pope is considered the man on earth who represents the Son of God, who 'takes the place' of the Second Person of the omnipotent God of the Trinity." If you directly translate "represents the Son of God" into Latin, the official language of the Church, you get *Vicarius Filii Dei*.

I am a Seventh-day Adventist, and wish to dispel the notion that Adventists ignore "the evidence" as you claim. You may still claim that it is not today, nor ever has been an officially recognized papal title, but since the association with 666 apparently first surfaced in 1612, it is no real surprise that Catholics are ignorant of the facts on this matter today, or that the title is denied by Catholic apologists.

The lack of official recognition today, however, does not in any way, prove that *Vicarius Filii Dei* is a fantasy or fabrication concocted by Protestantism. The documented evidence I present shows beyond any doubt that *Vicarius Filii Dei* is not, as your article suggests, merely a groundless anti-Catholic invention. On the contrary, it has a very long history of use by the Catholic Church, having appeared in print in the Catholic Canon Law, a respected Catholic encyclopedia and Catholic newspapers. Those are the hard facts, which the Adventists, at least, choose not to ignore.

Hard facts? Mmm...no. I don't think so. But I will say this much for Mr. Scheifler: He obviously thought about this matter long and hard before coming up with the wrong answer. In fact, the "hard facts" indicate that Mr. Scheifler also seems to have plagiarized from the same book out of which Mr. Drisko took his arguments. Perhaps Seventh-day Adventists have only a single anti-Catholic sourcebook to filch from. In any case, at least Mr. Scheifler, unlike Mr. Drisko, had the good taste not to copy Uriah Smith word for word. Even so, the remarkable similarity between his "essay" and the corresponding section in Mr. Uriah Smith's book is unmistakable—the kind of similarity that would get him into hot water, perhaps even expelled, if he tried something like this in a university setting.

But enough. With that unpleasantness aside, I'll now respond to the arguments raised in these letters, most of which (thanks to Mr. Drisko and Mr. Scheifler's, ahem...borrowing from a common source) are shared by all three writers.

1. First, Mr. Drisko remarks about me that, "[I]t is obvious he is only interested in bashing a popular Protestant position and is content to congratulate himself for doing so." How ironic! If anyone is "bashing," isn't it the Seventh-day Adventists? After all, they are the ones who conjured up the *Vicarius Filii Dei* canard in the first place to attack the Catholic Church. My article responded to this charge. Mr. Drisko's equating this with "bashing" is astonishing.

2. Mr. Drisko claims that if Jesus meant to found the papacy, "all logic demands that he would have categorically and intentionally informed his followers in no uncertain terms!" Very well. Let's apply this same principle to the Trinity.

If Jesus meant for Christians to believe in the Trinity (the most fundamental tenet of the Christian Faith), logic demands that he would have categorically and intentionally informed His followers in no uncertain terms.

Perhaps Mr. Drisko could show us in Scripture where, "in no uncertain terms," Jesus Christ teaches that God exists in three co-equal, co-eternal, consubstantial persons.

Obviously, he nowhere does this. The Trinity doctrine is certainly Scriptural, but any systematic biblical defense of it must be assembled from many verses. So, if even as bedrock a doctrine as the Trinity is neither mentioned by name nor categorically explained "in no uncertain terms" in Scripture, it's inconsistent and incorrect to demand the same of the papacy.

Mr. Drisko also argues that "the attempt to locate an ecclesiastical colossus headed by the papacy at Rome as demonstrated in the New Testament, is an exercise in futility." Here I agree with him, but not for the reason he might think.

He's right. We shouldn't (and don't) expect to find the full-blown, developed papacy, colossal or otherwise, in the New Testament. Why not? Because the New Testament shows us a picture of the primitive Church, the Church as it was in its infancy, the Church in "mustard seed" form. And Christ himself promised that His Church, "The Kingdom of God," is an organic entity, one that would grow and develop until it became tree-like.

The mustard seed bears no resemblance whatsoever to its mature form. Surely Mr. Drisko must recognize this. Christ's teaching about development is true, of course, with the Church's teachings, such as the Trinity and the papacy. So while it would indeed be futile to attempt to find a fully developed papacy in the pages of the New Testament, it is equally futile for Mr. Drisko to claim that this somehow undermines the Catholic position on the papacy. It doesn't.

3. Both Mr. Drisko and Mr. Scheifler cite the *Decretum* of Gratian and the Corpus of Canon Law as evidence that *Vicarius Filii Dei* is contained in "official" Catholic documents. What they don't seem to realize is that those sections of the *Decretum* and the Corpus are actually from the *Donation of Constantine,* a famous

forgery (anyone familiar with medieval Church history could have told them that). Obviously, a forged document is not an "official Catholic document," even though it may have been regarded by many as authentic.

Mr. Drisko and Mr. Sheifler should have read "Pope Fiction" more carefully, for they seem to have entirely missed the point here. My claim centered on the twin facts that *Vicarius Filii Dei* is not an official papal title and that it is never used as such in actual, official ecclesiastical documents—not forged documents, not civil documents, not unofficial documents. Since these two are fond of quoting the *Catholic Encyclopedia* when it suits them, I should point out that they didn't bother to quote from the "Pope: Primacy of Honor: Titles and Insignia" article in the same 1913 Encyclopedia. Actually, they wouldn't have been able to quote from it, since, under the section of "official titles," *Vicarius Filii Dei* is nowhere to be found. But we shouldn't be surprised that this escaped the notice of these two men. It seems they relied heavily (and in Mr. Drisko's case, entirely) on the flawed "evidence" contained in Mr. Smith's book, without bothering to check the accuracy of his charges.

The fact that the *Donation of Constantine* was, at one time, wrongly assumed to be legitimate is irrelevant. What makes the Donation even more irrelevant to this issue is that even if it were not a forgery, it still wouldn't qualify as an official Catholic document. At best, it would have been an official state document, emanating from the Roman imperial government. That's because whoever forged it purported to be the Emperor Constantine, decreeing a series of land grants and various other temporal advantages to the bishop of Rome. So, unfortunately for Mr. Drisko and Mr. Scheifler's argument, the forged Donation of Constantine cannot qualify, on two counts: A) it's bogus and B) even if it weren't, it would only be a civil document.

4. Next, both Mr. Drisko and Mr. Scheifler cite Lucius Ferraris's *Prompta Bibliotheca* as further evidence that *Vicarius Filii Dei* is an official title of the pope. But here again, both men seem to be lost in a maze of historical details they don't understand.

The section of *Prompta Bibliotheca* Mr. Scheifler refers to is also a quote from the *Donation of Constantine* forgery. Naturally, Fr. Ferraris, a Franciscan ecclesiastical historian, could have been considerably more careful in his use of sources, given the fact that for fully 300 years before he compiled the *Prompta Bibliotheca*, it was widely known that the *Donation of Constantine* was a forgery. But again, his injudicious inclusion of the forgery hardly constitutes evidence of *Vicarius Filii Dei* being used as an official title of the pope. In fact, regarding Ferraris's scholarship, the *Catholic Encyclopedia* passage Scheifler and Drisko quote incompletely reads in full, "This supplement serves to keep up to date the work of Ferraris, which will ever remain a precious mine of information, although it is sometimes possible to reproach the author with laxism." His use of the *Donation of Constantine* is certainly one such instance.[97] Not surprisingly, Mr. Scheifler and Mr. Drisko both failed to include the italicized portion of this Encyclopedia quote. Why? Because it undercuts their argument, and they apparently don't wish the unsuspecting reader to know that.

5. Mr. Drisko offers a quote from a 1915 edition of *Our Sunday Visitor* newspaper, to the effect that the papal miter is inscribed with diamonds with the title *Vicarius Filii Dei*. I contacted Robert Lockwood, the president of Our Sunday Visitor, about this. He had personally gone through the *OSV* archives and reported that he had found no evidence that this quote ever appeared in any issue of the paper.

Evidently, it had been removed from the archive. The error on the part of a newspaper staffer (and let's remember, the Catholic Church does not claim infallibility for journalists) was caught only after it had slipped into print, but the editor was obviously concerned about the incorrect answer being perpetuated, so he expunged that issue from the archives. Not surprisingly, those who perpetuate the *Vicarius Filii Dei* myth never mention the strong disavowals of this issue made by the *Our Sunday Visitor* newspaper over the years. For example, in the August 3, 1941, issue, a reader posed this question: "A pamphlet has come to me entitled Mark of the Beast. It identifies the pope with the mark (i.e., 666) referred to in Revelation 13:16–18."

The editor responded: "The question you ask has been answered many times, although not in recent years, in this paper. If we have recourse to the best biblical scholars or exegetes, we find them applying the text from Revelations to Nero, the arch-persecutor of Christianity in the first century. To give color to their accusation, enemies of the Church publicize something that is not at all true, and that is that the pope's tiara is inscribed with the words '*VICARIUS FILII DEI*,' and that if the letters in that title were translated into Roman numerals, the sum would equal 666. As a matter of fact, the tiara of the pope bears no inscription whatsoever."

Robert Lockwood has written a letter on behalf of *Our Sunday Visitor* explaining that the 1915 remark regarding the alleged inscription on the pope's miter was an unintentional and unfortunate error that should not be used as "evidence" to support the *Vicarius Filii Dei* argument. A copy of this letter is being sent to the Seventh-Day Adventist headquarters, demanding that they stop using this episode as some sort of "proof" to prop up their argument. Let's hope that honesty and a desire to know the truth will compel Seventh-Day Adventists to stop using the illegitimate *OSV* quote.

So, if the very best our Adventist friends can do is point to an obscure passage from a newspaper printed nearly a century ago, this demonstrates further the fact that *Vicarius Filii Dei* is not an official title of the pope. If it were, why would Adventists have to go through such gyrations to find an example of it? If it were an official papal title, examples would be strewn everywhere (as are occurrences of *Vicarius Christi, Servus Servorum Dei,* etc.). In spite of his strenuous efforts at historical sleuthing, the "evidence" Mr. Drisko presents is hardly the smoking gun he imagines it to be.

6. Finally, Mr. Scheifler claims that the phrase "represents the Son of God," quoted from Pope John Paul II's *Crossing the Threshold of Hope,* if translated directly into Latin, comes out to *Vicarius Filii Dei.*

Alas, if only Mr. Scheifler's Latin were as good as his imagination. In fact, the phrase, "Represents the Son of God," translated directly into Latin, yields "*Filium Dei repraesentat,*" not *Vicarius Filii Dei.* Oh, well. It should suffice to point out that "represents" is a verb. "Vicar" is a noun. But let's not belabor the obvious.

To sum up, the errors in both Mr. Scheifler's and Mr. Drisko's letters are based on three fundamentally flawed premises. The first is that the Latin form of Vicar of the Son of God is a title (not an actual title, of course, but a made-up one), and the book of Revelation identifies the number of the Beast as a name, not a title (Revelation 13:17–18). So all this talk about titles is irrelevant anyway.

Second, they erroneously assume that simply because the pope has been called *Vicarius Filii Dei*, or described in a roundabout way as such, that it must necessarily be an official title of the pope.

Think about that. Office workers often call their supervisor "the boss." While that's an apt description, it's nevertheless not an official title. You might also refer to the boss as "the Big Cheese," or "the Big Kahuna." While these may be apt descriptions of the individual, they're nevertheless not official titles. Similarly, the pope can indeed be described as the Vicar of the Son of God, even in official documents, for that is exactly what he is, yet this is not an official title. In my article, I stated that *Vicarius Filii Dei* has never been an "official title" of the pope. I didn't claim that no one in the two-thousand-year history of the Church has ever described him that way.

I am at fault, though, for not having been more precise when I wrote, "If the person making this claim disputes these facts, let him produce…any official Catholic document in which the pope calls himself or is referred to as, 'Vicar of the Son of God.'" I assumed the reader would understand that the mere fact that if a pope had been described as the vicar of the Son of God, which, as I mentioned, is a theologically accurate description, that would not be the same as an example of an official title. If I had left out the phrase "referred to as," I could have saved Mr. Drisko and Mr. Scheifler all their trouble. *Mea culpa.* (By the way, that adds up to 1155.)

Back to the matter at hand: The third fatal flaw in the Seventh-day Adventist argument is its arbitrary selection of the Latin "title" *Vicarius Filii Dei*. Why not use a real title of the pope? I listed several in my original article (e.g., *Servus*

Servorum Dei, Pontifex Maximus, and *Successor Petri*). The reason our Adventist friends neglect to mention, much less deal with, these actual papal titles is because they refute their claim. None adds up to 666, the number they so badly want to pin on the pope.

And another question: Why do Seventh-day Adventists and other papal critics insist on using a Latin phrase to arrive at 666, when Revelation was written, not in Latin, but in Greek? The numeric identification of the Beast as "666" in Revelation is tied to the values of Greek letters, not Latin ones. Adventists like Mr. Scheifler ignore this basic fact for an obvious reason: The Greek form of *Vicarius Filii Dei* doesn't add up to 666.

Notice too that Mr. Drisko and Mr. Scheifler ignored the fact that, as I pointed out in "Pope Fiction," the name of Ellen Gould White, the founder of their religion, adds up to 666 in Latin. The same is true of Martin Luther and of other figures they hold dear. Allow me to demonstrate how this technique works:

First we begin with a title. Since he started the ball rolling, let's assign one to Allan Drisko. How about, Drisko Vicar of Scheifler? Translate that into Latin, and we have *Drisko Vicarius Scheifleri,* which produces a hefty 760. Not quite 666. But in the true spirit of Seventh-day Adventist scholarship, let's get a little bit more creative:

I ran the numbers on MICHAEL SCHEIFLER. In Latin that comes to 1302—way too much to get him into any biblical trouble. But then I noticed that 666 x 2 = 1332, a mere 30 away from double trouble! So then I made up a Latin title for Mr. Scheifler, to reflect his use of Mr. Smith's work: *Scheifler Vicarius Smithi.* That yields 1265, and since Mr. Scheifler can only claim half the credit for his work, we reduce that figure by half and get 632. So close, yet so far. Unfortunately, this tack seemed to lead nowhere, luckily for Mr. Schiefler. So I turned again to Mr. Drisko.

First, I converted ALLAN DRISKO into Greek and Hebrew (the two languages of the Bible). His name in Greek adds up to 1246, while the Hebrew gives us 634. When we put the two together (just as the Hebrew Old Testament was joined with the Greek New Testament) we get 1880. We divide this by three (the three persons of the Trinity being at the center of the Old and New Testaments) and get 626.6666666667.

The first number is an obvious hint as to our next action. 626 can also be understood as saying "6 to 6." So, keeping the Scriptures at the center of all our calculations (to keep Mr. Drisko happy), we count the number of books between the sixth book of the Protestant Old Testament (Joshua) to the sixth book of the New Testament (Romans). The number we get is forty, which is then added to our previous number. The result is a frightening 666.6666666667. Since seven is the Biblical number indicating perfection or completion, we know we're finished with our calculations. So, it seems that Mr. Allan Drisko bears the number of the Beast not once, not twice, but four times over!

Needless to say, I'll be sending my findings to the Vatican.

Guess What, Mom

IN THE LATE 1980s, I TRIED MY hand at writing dialogue articles such as "Guess What, Mom." They were an attempt to capture the parlance and cadences of the arguments against the Catholic Church I was personally encountering at that time from non-Catholics and former Catholics. I wanted to distill in print the phraseologies and emphases that people had been voicing to me during the Q&A sessions at my parish seminars, the reasons for abandoning the Catholic Church that folks were giving me (often vehemently) in one-on-one conversations, and the various arguments against the Catholic Church that I was hearing every day on the Protestant call-in apologetics radio programs, such as *The Bible Answer Man*, that I listened to so avidly back then.

As I wrote this dialogue, I pictured in my mind's eye an earnest young married woman in her late twenties "breaking the news" to her Catholic mom that she had left the Church for a true "Bible-believing" church. What ensues is the mom's unflappable response to her daughter's challenges. Of course, few of us Catholic parents would, in real life, have the imperturbable, well-prepared, and quick-witted poise that this mom shows. I sought, rather, to voice her character more as an ideal to be emulated.

• • •

"Hello."

"Hi, Mom, it's me."

"Hi, honey. How's everything going? Are the kids all right? It's been a long time since you've called."

"We're all fine. No problems. In fact I've got some great news, and I wanted to share it with you and Dad."

"You sound a little nervous."

"Well, I am a little, I guess. I've wanted to tell you this for a while, but I didn't know how to do it—how to say it, I mean. Mom, something wonderful has happened. I've been saved."

"Saved from what?"

"No, not saved from what—saved *by* what. I've accepted Jesus as my Lord and Savior. That's what I mean. I've been saved now that I have a personal relationship with Jesus."

"What do you mean a 'personal' relationship? You're a Catholic! You were baptized and confirmed and you made your First Communion. You've been raised in a personal relationship with God since the day of your birth."

"No. That's just it. I never made a commitment to the Lord. I guess I always just accepted things as true because you and Dad and the Church said they were. I never checked things out for myself in the Bible. Now that I'm saved, I read the Bible every day. I never did that as a Catholic."

"'As a Catholic'? What does that mean? That now you're not a Catholic? Have you left the Church?"

"Don't get mad. Yes, I've left the Catholic Church, but I've joined the true church of Jesus."

"Oh? And what is the true church of Jesus?"

"It's not any particular denomination. It's the community of all believers in Christ who worship him in spirit and in truth using the Bible—God's precious Word—as the only authority, not relying on any popes or bishops or priests or manmade traditions. *That's* the true church, the church of Bible-believing Christians who have a personal relationship with Jesus, not with some denomination."

Well, *my* relationship is with Jesus."

"In a way it is, but not the way that I'm talking about, not in the way that counts. See, Catholics think they have to experience Jesus through the Catholic Church."

"Are you saying you think I worship the Catholic Church?"

"No. But you put too much emphasis on it. The Bible says, 'There is only one mediator between God and Man, the man Christ Jesus.' That means that you won't be saved by being a Catholic or by going to Mass or by saying rosaries. As a born-again Christian, I experience the Lord directly. I don't need priests or sacraments or the pope to be intermediaries for me. I go to God directly."

"Listen, you said that this was a wonderful thing, but I'm not so sure it is. It sounds to me like your enthusiasm has blinded you to what the Bible really says about the Church."

"I go to a Bible study every Wednesday night. Our pastor teaches straight from the Bible every Sunday. For the first time in my life I know what the Bible says. You and Dad don't read the Bible, and you never taught me to read it."

"Every Sunday at Mass you heard the Bible read—Old and New Testaments. Didn't you notice?"

"Mass was so boring I couldn't pay attention. That's the reason why I stopped going when we moved here. I wasn't getting anything out of it. The Bible-believing church I go to now is great. We have fellowship and song and lots of time in the Word."

"So you think you understand what the Bible really means, right?"

"Right. For the first time."

"I've been studying the Bible a lot lately myself, and…"

"You…you read the Bible, and you're still *Catholic?*"

"I sure do, and I sure am. Why does that surprise you?"

"Well, the Catholic Church teaches non-biblical doctrines—traditions of men. Catholics pray to saints, and that's not in the Bible. You can't be a Bible-believing Christian and a Catholic at the same time."

"I believe the Bible *and* I'm a Catholic. In fact, since I've started attending the weekly Bible study at the parish, I've become more interested in my religion, and I really feel like my relationship with the Lord has grown."

"But Catholic teachings contradict what the Bible says."

"*Oh?* Give me an example."

"How about purgatory? You won't find it anywhere in the Bible. Paul says that to be absent from the body means to be present with the Lord. He doesn't say a word about purgatory—in fact, the word purgatory isn't anywhere in the Bible. It's a manmade tradition."

"Do you have your Bible handy? Take a look at Luke 16:22–26."

"Just a second…. Okay, here it is. It's where the rich man goes to hell for his selfishness and the poor man, Lazarus, goes to heaven. So what?"

"How could Lazarus have gone to heaven when Jesus hadn't died yet and heaven was still closed to men?"

"What do you mean?"

"I mean that Jesus described the destinations of two people after death. They didn't go to the same place, and neither one went to heaven. One of them went to hell. Where did the other one go? This is an example of Jesus referring to a third place—not heaven or hell—which means he's talking about purgatory."

"If Jesus had meant purgatory he'd have used the word purgatory. It's not really clear what he meant by that parable, but we know that he wasn't talking about purgatory."

"Do you believe in the Trinity?"

"Yes, of course, but what does that have to do with it?"

"Where in the Bible do you find the word 'Trinity'?"

"Well…the Bible doesn't use that *exact* word, but the teaching is clear from all the references."

"So what you're saying is that you believe in the Trinity even though the Bible doesn't use the word, right?"

"Yes, but the Trinity is a biblical doctrine."

"How do you know that it is? Just what is your authority for interpreting the verses that may refer to it? Where did your infallibility come from?"

"Now you're being sarcastic, Mom. You don't need to be infallible to understand the Bible. Its message is plain."

"But other people who claim to use only the Bible as their authority differ with you on this very subject. Jehovah's Witnesses and United Pentecostals are two examples. They don't believe in the Trinity and claim the Bible doesn't teach it."

"They're misinterpreting Scripture."

"How do you know? What's your authority for interpreting the Bible?"

"The Bible alone is my authority. That's all I need."

"Where does it say that in the Bible?"

"I don't know the exact verse, but I know the verse is there. The Bible is all we need."

"No, the Bible is not all we need. And the verse isn't there. The Bible doesn't claim to be the sole authority. We also have to listen to the Church. Remember that Jesus founded a specific Church—*his* Church—and in Matthew 16:19 he promised it would never be overcome. At the end of Matthew's Gospel he promised to be with his Church even to the end of time. And in John 14:16 he promised the Holy Spirit would abide with the Church forever."

"Where did you learn that?"

"At our parish Bible study. We covered purgatory a few weeks ago, and I'm looking at my notes right now."

"Let me get back to what I asked earlier, Mom. Do you have a personal relationship with the Lord Jesus?"

"I sure do! Every morning at Mass I receive him in the Eucharist, body and blood, soul and divinity. You can't get much more personal than that! If you want to know what the Bible says about the Eucharist, take a look at the sixth chapter of John's Gospel."

"Yes, I know all about that—but you see, Jesus is speaking metaphorically there, not *literally*."

"That's incorrect, honey. Read the chapter again Jesus says that if you don't eat his body and drink his blood you won't have life within you—that means you'll be spiritually dead if you refuse the Eucharist."

"I don't believe that's what Jesus meant."

"Okay, so I ask you again: What's your authority for knowing what he meant? We both read the same words, but interpret them differently. Other people have still different interpretations. How can the Bible be the final authority when so many people disagree on exactly what the Bible means?"

"Mom, I know in my heart that I'm right. The Lord has shown me."

"Well, I can say the same thing, and we'd both agree that the Lord isn't going to lead us in two different directions. We can't both be right. And that's where the Church comes in. Jesus promised the Holy Spirit would guide his Church into all truth."

"What are you driving at?"

"What I mean is that the Church was teaching the gospel for decades before a single word of the New Testament had been written—before the Bible as we know it was in existence. We had the authority of the Church to guide believers before the Bible hit the scene. Now, I certainly don't mean that the Bible is somehow unimportant. The entire New Testament was written by Catholics, for Catholics, and about Catholics."

"Come on, Mom. That's crazy!"

"Then how do you explain the fact that the earliest Christians, the men and women who knew the apostles and the authors of the New Testament, believed in things like the Eucharist, the Mass, and purgatory?"

"I don't believe they did."

"The proof is there if you're willing to check it out. The Catholic Church's teachings on things like these aren't manmade traditions. Now, I know you have to run. I just want to say that I want you to know the truth—God's truth."

"I have that truth now, Mom, in a way I never did in the Catholic Church."

"Tell you what—think about what I said and pray about it. I'll send you a book I think you'll find interesting. It explains these things better that I can. Will you read it?"

"Um...sure."

"You read it using your Bible as a guide, and call me back when you're done so we can talk about it. Okay?"

"Okay. You know, I really thought you'd explode when I told you I'd become a Christian. I still disagree with you, and I think Catholicism's wrong, but I'm willing to read up on it to prove its errors both to myself and to you."

"I can't ask for more than that. Call again soon, honey, okay?"

Catholic Answers, *1989*

Purgatory: God's Emergency Room for Sinners

The doctrine of purgatory is prominent among those Catholic teachings that are particularly repellent to Protestants. This, I have found, is due chiefly to a profound misunderstanding of the Catholic doctrine of purgatory. Countless people have serious misconceptions about it and, in this 1999 article, my goal was to explain both what purgatory is and what it's not. Along the way, I wanted to show from the Bible that, because "nothing unclean can enter heaven" (Revelation 21:27), those who die in the state of grace but who are still sullied and weighed down by the temporal effects of sin must undergo some kind of purification before they enter heaven. Beyond that, my goal was to show why an all-loving God would allow us to suffer as part of our healing. A bloody childhood incident involving my son Timothy was useful in helping me discuss that dimension of purgatory.

• • •

I had never heard of a "papoose board" before the day I watched my three-year-old son, Timothy, being strapped onto one. My wife and I had rushed him to the emergency room with a large gash above his eye. A neighbor kid had been swinging a toy around and accidentally smacked Tim in the face with it, opening a deep wound. This wasn't something a Band-Aid could fix. It was clear that Tim was going to need several stitches to close the gash. We scrambled to get him into the car and bolted for the hospital.

The blood, the pain, and the look of deep worry on his parents' faces were enough to keep Tim whimpering all the way to the emergency room. But once we got there, and my wife handed him to the nurses, his whimpering spiked into a wail of fright and pain as they laid his twisting little body on the board and tightly laced its cloth flaps in place, immobilizing him.

Within moments, the doctor had arrived and began to work on repairing Tim's wounded eye. "Mommmmy!" our little boy shrieked, red-faced and wide-eyed, as he writhed within the confines of the papoose board. "Help me, Mommy! It hurts," he screamed. We stood by in anguish, helpless to do anything for him, watching the doctor clean and stitch the wound. It hurt us terribly to see him hurting like this, but there was nothing we could do. We knew we had to let our son undergo this painful and frightening procedure; we were actually doing what was best for him.

The doctor could cure him, but only at the price of the pain involved in stitching the wound. (The doctor did a good job. After the wound healed, there wasn't much of a scar to show for it.) And this fact is true of purgatory: that healing process of purification that many must endure before they enter into heaven. It's the temporary condition, after death, where any remaining temporal punishment due to sin—sins that have already been forgiven by God—is expiated and the soul is cleansed from the effects of sin.

Before we delve into the finer details of what this means, let's first step back and get a "big picture" look at what purgatory is (and isn't). You can think of purgatory as a kind of divine emergency room for souls; the process through which God, the Divine Physician, removes all traces of venial sins unrepented of before death and heals our self-inflicted wounds of serious sin that we accumulate in this life. In purgatory, our wounds are healed, the scars are erased, and our souls are scrubbed by God's fiery love, washed white as snow by the shed Blood of the Lamb, made ready to enter into the eternal wedding feast we call heaven.

Is Purgatory Biblical?

The doctrine of purgatory was part of the deposit of faith, once for all handed down to the holy ones (see Jude 3). It is part of the Sacred Tradition of the Church, taught by the councils and Fathers, and it is also discussed in Scripture. In chapter 12 of 2 Maccabees, there is an episode in which sacrifices are made in the temple on behalf of dead soldiers who were punished for a rather minor form of superstition. The passage concludes with the words: "In doing this [Judas Maccabeus] acted very well and honorably, taking account of the resurrection. For if he were not expecting that those who had fallen would rise again, it would have been superfluous and foolish to pray for the dead. But if he was looking to the splendid reward that is laid up for those who fall asleep in godliness, it was a holy and pious thought. Therefore he made atonement for the dead, that they might be delivered from their sin" (2 Maccabees 12:43–45).

Unfortunately, since many Protestants reject 2 Maccabees as not being part of the Old Testament canon, quoting this passage won't cut much ice with them. You may as well be quoting from the Yellow Pages. So let's consider the places in the New Testament where purgatory is mentioned. The most explicit of these is by St. Paul in 1 Corinthians 3. But before we examine that passage, let's look at a few other instances. In Luke 16, Christ mentions a third state after death—not heaven not hell—where he discussed the temporary fates of Lazarus and the rich man. The rich man may have been in purgatory, since he was praying for his brothers. This is an act of charity of which the damned in hell are incapable. In Matthew 12:32, the Lord mentions a sin that cannot be forgiven even "in the world to come," implying that there are some sins that will be forgiven after death.[98]

Similarly, in the parable about the Unforgiving Servant, Christ concludes with the fact that the Wicked Servant, even after his debt was canceled by the king, was thrown into prison for maltreating his fellow servant and told, "You wicked servant! I forgave you all that debt because you besought me; and should not you have had mercy on your fellow servant, as I had mercy on you?' And in anger his lord delivered him to the jailers, till he should pay all his debt"

(Matthew 18:32–34). Then Christ adds the warning to us: "So also my heavenly Father will do to every one of you, if you do not forgive your brother from your heart" (Matthew 18:35).

Echoing this theme, St. Peter speaks about the souls who are "in prison," awaiting their entrance into heaven (see 1 Peter 3:18–19, 4:6). The process of cleansing we Catholics call "purgatory" (from the Latin word *purgare* which means "to purify") involves pain, but it is necessary for God to make us pure and clean and whole, ready to meet him face- to-face in heaven. The *Catechism* says: "All who die in God's grace and friendship, but still imperfectly purified, are indeed assured of their eternal salvation; but after death they undergo purification, so as to achieve the holiness necessary to enter the joy of heaven" (*CCC,* 1030, emphasis added). This refers to the fact that, in heaven, "nothing unclean shall enter it, nor anyone who practices abomination or falsehood, but only those who are written in the Lamb's book of life" (Revelation 21:27). Why can nothing unclean enter heaven? The prophet Habakkuk says it's because God is all holy, and he will not allow anything in heaven with him to be less than holy and spotless: "Too pure are your eyes to look upon evil [O Lord], and the sight of misery you cannot endure" (Habakkuk 1:13).

"The Church gives the name purgatory to this final purification of the elect, which is entirely different from the punishment of the damned. The Church formulated her doctrine of faith on purgatory especially at the Councils of Florence and Trent. The tradition of the Church, by reference to certain texts of Scripture, speaks of a cleansing fire" (*CCC,* 1031; see 1 Corinthians 3:15; 1 Peter 1:7).

Ironically, for a doctrine that is so inextricably associated with Catholicism, the Catholic Church has not said all that much, "officially," about purgatory. The Council of Trent (1535–1548) was the setting for the Church's formal definition of the doctrine of purgatory. Here's what the Council said:

"Whereas the Catholic Church, instructed by the Holy Ghost, has, from the sacred writings and the ancient tradition of the Fathers, taught, in sacred councils, and very recently in this ecumenical Synod, that there is a Purgatory, and that the souls there detained are helped by the suffrages of the faithful, but principally by the acceptable sacrifice of the altar; the holy Synod enjoins on bishops that they diligently endeavor that the sound doctrine concerning Purgatory, transmitted by the holy Fathers and sacred councils, be believed, maintained, taught, and every where proclaimed by the faithful of Christ."[99]

Two Kinds of Punishment

Some people get mixed up at this point. They wonder why there should be a purgatory at all, given that Christ's work on the cross completed his mission of redemption. After all, Christ himself said, "It is finished" just before he died on the cross.

There are two issues at work here, and people often confuse them. The eternal penalty due to sin is hell, but that is distinct from the other, inevitable penalty that arises when we sin: the aftereffects that play out across space and time.

For example, let's say a married woman commits the sin of adultery. The eternal penalty incurred by her mortal (deadly) sin is the complete eradication of sanctifying grace from her soul. She renders herself spiritually dead, analogously, just as dead as if she had put a gun to her head and pulled the trigger. She has the promise of forgiveness from Christ if she repents of her sin, and the Lord will reestablish the life of sanctifying grace in her soul when she receives the sacrament of confession. She is forgiven, and she is back in a right relationship with God. The eternal penalty due to her sin (had she remained unrepentant and died in that state) would be the eternal death we call hell. But that penalty has been removed, washed away by the shed blood of Christ on the cross ("He was wounded for our transgressions, he was bruised for our iniquities; upon him was the chastisement that made us whole, and with his stripes we are healed"— Isaiah 53:5; "But God shows his love for us in that while we were yet sinners Christ died for us. Since, therefore, we are now justified by his blood, much more shall we be saved by him from the wrath of God"—Romans 5:8–9).

But the saga of the woman's adultery isn't over. There are the temporal effects due to sin that remain. Even though she is forgiven and back in the state of grace, those temporal effects remain. They are not eliminated by Christ's death on the cross. Perhaps she became pregnant. Perhaps she contracted a sexually transmitted disease. Perhaps her marriage was shattered as a result of her actions. There are many possible side effects that are due to sin, and anyone could happen, and those consequences are not expunged, even though the sinner has repented. And this is why purgatory exists. God permits this process of purification precisely because he wants the souls of his beloved sons and daughters to be perfect and clean, free of blemish or stain. And when we sin, this "wounds" the soul. The wound may be healed through the sacraments, but a scar remains. Those scars—the temporal effects due to sin—must also be expiated and removed. The *Catechism* then quotes the teaching of Pope St. Gregory the Great on purgatory: "As for certain lesser faults, we must believe that, before the Final Judgment there is a purifying fire. He who is truth says that whoever utters blasphemy against the Holy Spirit will be pardoned neither in this age nor in the age to come. From this sentence we understand that certain offenses can be forgiven in this age, but certain others in the age to come."[100]

To understand more clearly the need for purification from the temporal punishments due to sin, let's rewind back to the beginning of human history, back to the Garden of Eden. When Adam and Eve committed the "original sin" in the Garden (see Genesis 3:1–7), they disrupted their intimate friendship with the Lord. When they fell from grace, they lost their many supernatural gifts of grace and union with God, and they lost many of their natural gifts, such as freedom from their passions, control over their will, and a preternaturally enhanced human knowledge. Their gift of immortality was taken away. And with that loss came a series of other "temporal punishments," consequences of their sin, that continue, embedded in the human condition, down to our own day. Sadly, we all have a share in these punishments.

Earlier, before the Fall, God had warned Adam and Eve about the result of sin: "You may freely eat of every tree of the garden; but of the tree of the knowledge of good and evil you shall not eat, for in the day that you eat of it you shall die" (Genesis 2:17). This truth was echoed by St. Paul when he said,

"The wages of sin is death" (Romans 6:23). So death came for our first parents, but not all at once. Spiritually, it's true that they died that very day, because their life of grace and their union with God had vanished: "The man and his wife hid themselves from the presence of the Lord God among the trees of the garden. But the Lord God called to the man, and said to him, 'Where are you?' And he said, 'I heard the sound of thee in the garden, and I was afraid, because I was naked; and I hid myself' " (Genesis 3:7–10). But we also see that, following on the heels of their spiritual death came a series of natural consequences that also spelled death for humanity and all creation: Speaking first to the Serpent, God curses him for his wickedness in tempting Adam and Eve:

> Because you have done this, cursed are you above all cattle, and above all wild animals; upon your belly you shall go, and dust you shall eat all the days of your life. I will put enmity between you and the woman, and between your seed and her seed; he shall bruise your head, and you shall bruise his heel (Genesis 3:14–15).

> Then, turning to Eve and her husband, he said:

> I will greatly multiply your pain in childbearing; in pain you shall bring forth children, yet your desire shall be for your husband, and he shall rule over you." And to Adam he said, "Because you have listened to the voice of your wife, and have eaten of the tree of which I commanded you, 'You shall not eat of it,' cursed is the ground because of you; in toil you shall eat of it all the days of your life; thorns and thistles it shall bring forth to you; and you shall eat the plants of the field. In the sweat of your face you shall eat bread till you return to the ground, for out of it you were taken; you are dust, and to dust you shall return (Genesis 3:16–19).

Adam and Eve were forgiven of their sin, and the eternal penalties of that sin, for them and all the rest of humanity that repents and asks forgiveness, is eliminated by Christ's death on the cross. But the suffering and temporal effects due to sin—sickness, anguish, death—remain (see *CCC*, 1008, 1472, 1505).

This principle of a separate temporal punishment due to sin is seen throughout the Bible. A striking example is the tragic aftermath of King David's double-barreled sin of adultery and murder:

Nathan said to David, "You are the man." Thus says the Lord, the God of Israel, "I anointed you king over Israel…and gave you the house of Israel and of Judah; and if this were too little, I would add to you as much more. Why have you despised the word of the Lord, to do what is evil in his sight?"….David said to Nathan, "I have sinned against the Lord." And Nathan said to David, "The Lord also has put away your sin; you shall not die. Nevertheless, because by this deed you have utterly scorned the Lord, the child that is born to you shall die" (2 Samuel 12:7–14; see Numbers 12:1–15; 22:12; 27:12–14).

Restitution

Clearly, the penalty of physical death they incurred would come gradually. Toil, pain, difficulty, sickness, death—that was the declining arc of existence that Adam and Eve had set themselves on when they disobeyed God. And those penalties lie squarely in the category of what we Catholics call the "temporal effects due to sin." These are distinct from the "eternal penalty" due to sin, which is hell, eternal separation from God. In purgatory, we undergo a process of expiation and purification. Purification is the process whereby God removes the effects of sin on the soul, and expiation is what we sometimes call "restitution." It involves the repayment of a debt that is incurred by the sin.

Consider this analogy. Let's imagine you had figured out a clever way to steal a very expensive "big screen" television from your local electronics emporium without getting caught. You steal the TV, get it home, and immediately begin feeling remorse over your crime. This step equates with the sinner whose conscience torments him, prodding him to repent. Then, you feel so badly about what you've done, you go to the store, find the manager and confess that you stole the TV (this step equates with the sinner making a good act of contrition). The store manager thinks for a moment and says, "I'll tell you what. By law, you are guilty of a felony, regardless of the fact that you are here confessing to me. I could call the police and have you arrested. You would be tried in court and sentenced to a long, unpleasant prison term as punishment for your theft. You would forever have a felony on your record. You'd be barred from getting certain kinds of work, your life would be ruined as a result of this theft" (this equates with God's just punishment that the sinner deserves).

"But," the manager says with a smile, "since you've confessed this crime, I'm not going to call the police. I'm not going to have you arrested and tried. There will be no jail for you. I will treat this as if it had never happened." You are ready to faint with relief. You didn't deserve this forgiveness, but you're ecstatic. You're going to be let go without paying the penalty.

As you shake the store manager's hand gratefully, and turn to leave the store, he taps you on the shoulder. "Now, I'll expect you to bring the TV back to me today." That's restitution—the replacement of the stolen item. Clearly, even though you've avoided the legal penalty your crime deserved, you still are obligated to return the TV to the store. If you didn't, you would in effect be nullifying the store manager's kindness. You can't keep the TV. And if you had damaged or sold it, you would be expected—obligated as a matter of justice—to pay the sum equal to the value of the TV.

The Early Christians Believed in Purgatory

The most explicit extra-biblical evidence for the belief in the doctrine of purgatory in the ancient Church is found in its liturgies. Without exception, in the East and the West, the various Eucharistic liturgies contained at least one *memento mori,* "remembrance of the dead." There would have been no point in praying for the dead if they were in heaven, as they would have no need of prayers. If they were in hell, prayer could do them no good. But the Church knew then, as she does now, that there is a "middle state" where those who die in the state of grace and are assured of their salvation can benefit from our prayers. This "middle state" some souls pass through on their way to heaven is called purgatory. Catholic historical theologian, Edward J. Hanna, points out a significant piece of historical evidence for the antiquity of the Christian belief in purgatory:

"The teaching of the Fathers, and the formularies used in the Liturgy of the Church, found expression in the early Christian monuments, particularly those contained in the catacombs. On the tombs of the faithful were inscribed words of hope, words of petition for peace and for rest; and as the anniversaries came round the faithful gathered at the graves of the departed to make intercession for those who had gone before. At the bottom this is nothing else than the faith expressed by the Council of Trent (Session 25, "On Purgatory"), and to this faith the inscriptions in the catacombs are surely witnesses."[101]

The Fathers of the Church were adamant about the existence of purgatory. Many of them, such as St. Augustine, wrote lengthy treatises on the process of purification some souls undergo after death and before their entry into heaven.[102]

Writing at the middle of the fourth century, St. Ambrose of Milan remarked about the Old Testament's use of the "fire" image as the process of purifying one from evil speech: "Howbeit, now must I needs confess the Prophet Isaiah's confession, which he makes before declaring the word of the Lord: 'Woe is me, my heart is smitten, for I, a man of unclean lips, and living in the midst of a people of unclean lips, have seen the Lord of Hosts.' Now if Isaiah said 'Woe is me,' who looked upon the Lord of Hosts, what shall I say of myself, who, being 'a man of unclean lips,' am constrained to treat of the divine generation [i.e. explain the Trinitarian relationship of God the Son and God the Holy Spirit to God the Father]? How shall I break forth into speech of things whereof I am afraid, when David prays that a watch may be set over his mouth in the matter of things whereof he has knowledge? O that to me also one of the Seraphim would bring the burning coal from the celestial altar, taking it in the tongs of the two testaments, and with the fire thereof purge my unclean lips!"[103]

The reason Christians have always prayed for the dead is because they have known, having learned it from the apostles themselves, that for many, perhaps most, who die in a state of friendship with God, there is a process of purification that involves suffering. And prayers on behalf of our deceased brothers and sisters in the Lord can help alleviate and even shorten that suffering.[104]

Feel the Burn

No discussion of purgatory would be complete without mention of the ubiquitous image of fire. The fire imagery, so closely linked to the doctrine of purgatory, is not, as many imagine, a "medieval invention" of a sadistic Catholic Church, bent on frightening poor peasants into repentance. No. Throughout Scripture, fire is an image frequently used to explain God's wrath and punishment (as in the fires of hell; see Matthew 18:8–9; 25:41), but it also appears as a manifestation of his power and love and presence (as in the burning bush with Moses [Exodus 3:2] the pillar of fire guiding the Israelites in the desert [Exodus 13:21] and tongues of flame that appeared over the heads of Mary and the Apostles on the Day of Pentecost [Acts 2:3]). Scripture says, "Our God is a consuming fire!" (Hebrews 12:29; see 2 Thessalonians 1:17). The reason fire is so closely associated with the doctrine of purgatory is because St. Paul taught the doctrine using that image to show us how God purifies the soul:

"According to the grace of God given to me, like a skilled master builder I laid a foundation, and another man is building upon it. Let each man take care how he builds upon it. For no other foundation can any one lay than that which is laid, which is Jesus Christ. Now if any one builds on the foundation with gold, silver, precious stones, wood, hay, straw—each man's work will become manifest; for the Day will disclose it, because it will be revealed with fire, and the fire will test what sort of work each one has done. If the work which any man has built on the foundation survives, he will receive a reward. If any man's work is burned up, he will suffer loss, though he himself will be saved, but only as passing through fire" (1 Corinthians 3:10–15).

Let's break this teaching on purgatory down to its basic components:

(1) This passage deals with events taking place after death, on "the day" of a man's judgment (see Hebrews 9:27, "It is appointed for men to die once, and after that comes judgment").

(2) The metaphor of fire describes the way in which God tests the man's life and "burns away" the dross.

(3) This process involves loss and suffering.

(4) This process of purification is temporary and culminates in the release of the soul from this state and his entrance into heaven and the beatific vision: "he himself will be saved, but only as through fire." The *Catholic Encyclopedia* explains:

> At the Council of Florence [1431–1445], [Basilios] Bessarion [the Patriarch of Constantinople] argued against the existence of real purgatorial fire, and the Greeks were assured that the Roman Church had never issued any dogmatic decree on this subject. In the West the belief in the existence of real fire is common.…How this fire affects the souls of the departed the Doctors do not know, and in such matters it is well to heed the warning of the Council of Trent when it commands the bishops "to exclude from their preaching difficult and subtle questions which tend not to edification, and from the discussion of which there is no increase either in piety or devotion."[105]

As far as the fire goes, we can be content with saying that Scripture and the early Church Fathers used the image of fire to convey the reality of what happens in purgatory: a painful cleansing process of temporary duration that takes place after death and before one's entrance into heaven. Is it "real" fire? Probably not, at least not as we understand fire in a physical sense. Will this fiery process of purification hurt? Yes, as St. Paul says in 1 Corinthians 3: the soul in purgatory suffers and will enter heaven, "only as though passing through fire." Perhaps the most important lesson we can learn from these facts is that we can avoid purgatory altogether, or at least an extended stay there, by offering to the Lord our daily trials and pains. These sufferings are purgatorial in themselves, if they are offered to God with a loving and contrite heart. In this way, our suffering is purified and elevated. It becomes a participation in the redemptive sufferings of Christ (see Colossians 1:24).

Whether or not you or I will need to pass through the purifying flames of purgatory depends on decisions we make now. If we leave this world with clinging weeds of inordinate self-love, attachment to creatures, and venially sinful bad habits, we will need those weeds cut away and burned off before we can enter heaven. If our souls bear the scars of the self-inflicted wounds of mortal sin, we'll need those scars removed by the Divine Physician. It hurts, yes, but it hurts so good, because we know that the process is bringing us closer to Christ, closer to that moment when we can enter the wedding feast of the Lamb, spotless and pure.[106]

Envoy, *November/December 1999*

Common Sense Checked at the Door

I WROTE THIS ONE SOON AFTER A rather intense, real-life encounter I had at the home of a Catholic Filipino family in Southern California. Frantic because some of their family members had been siphoned off into the virulently anti-Catholic Iglesia ni Cristo sect, the couple had invited me to have an informal "living room debate" with the Iglesia ni Cristo minister who was on their trail. Living up to the legendary Filipino reputation for hospitality, this Catholic family first fed me bounteously on succulent native delicacies, such as Lumpia and Adobo, before the minister and his disciples arrived for the debate.

When I sat down to compose this article, the whole thing was still vivid in my mind, and this article is, if not a verbatim transcript of what was a much longer discussion, it captures, I think, both the essence of the arguments against the Catholic Church I had to deal with that evening, as well as the mutual snarkiness that pervaded our conversation. I don't recall that my defense of Catholic teaching had any discernible effect on any of the hardcore Iglesia folks who were there that evening (least of all the minister), but a week later I did receive a thank-you note from the man of the house, in which he informed me that not only had it helped his wavering Catholic family members who had been "on the fence" before that evening, but it also had given him and his wife the encouragement they needed to keep the dialogue open with their family members who had left the Catholic Church. More often than not, I have found, that is what makes all the difference in helping ex-Catholics come back to the Church.

• • •

In this dialogue, I am "Trent Lateran" and the Iglesia ni Cristo minister is "Felix Manalo."

"Ah, Mr. Manalo! I'm glad you were able to make it. Come on in. I see you've brought a few friends with you."

"Well, I'm sorry I didn't tell you earlier, but eighteen of the brethren wanted to be here tonight for our discussion. I hope you don't mind."

"No problem."

"Thanks, Mr. Lateran. We're looking..."

"Please, call me Trent. Let's not be formal around here."

"Okay, Trent. We're really looking forward to this discussion. In fact, since he was free this evening, I also invited our minister, Brother Felix. He's quite interested in speaking with you."

"Happy to meet you, Felix."

"Likewise. I notice your home has quite a number of idols. Did you know that the Word of God forbids men to worship such idols?"

"Oh yes, I'm quite aware of that. But if you're referring to things like these pictures of Jesus and Mary and that crucifix on the wall over there, then you've entirely missed the boat. They're not idols, and I don't worship them."

"Let's examine God's Word, shall we?"

"By all means. Tell me, what version of the Bible does the Filipino Church of Christ use?"

"The King James Bible is the *only* legitimate Bible, and we prefer to be called by our correct name—the Iglesia ni Cristo—which means 'Church of Christ' in Tagalog."

"I see."

"Now then, you Catholics worship idols, which is something the Bible expressly forbids. It says in Exodus 20:4–5: 'Thou shalt not make unto thee any graven image, or any likeness of anything that is in heaven above, or that is in the earth beneath, or that is in the water under the earth. Thou shalt not bow down to them, nor serve them for I the Lord thy God am a jealous God.' Catholic churches are filled with such idols! They're abominations in the sight of God!"

"Look. As a Catholic who owns quite a number of religious images, I agree completely with the passage you just read, but I still don't see your point."

"Well, the point is obvious to anyone who understands English—the Bible condemns the Catholic practice of idol worship!"

"Ah. Well, I'm sure you had no intention of offending me with that last remark, but I've always fancied myself a proficient speaker of English."

"Please show me the verse in the Bible that says it's okay to have and bow down to such idols."

"The Bible does condemn idol worship—you know that—but it does not condemn the ancient Catholic custom of venerating the saints and making use of statues and images to represent those saints."

"But..."

"Let me finish, please. You see, we Catholics have plenty of graven images in our churches and homes, but we don't *worship* them. That would be gravely sinful, not to mention gravely stupid."

"But you...!"

"A statue is merely a piece of wood or a hunk of plaster. Anyone dumb enough to do obeisance to an inanimate object, thinking all the while that it's a god, is simply fooling himself. Don't you agree?"

"Certainly. But God plainly says in verse 5 that you shouldn't bow down before any religious image. In the Philippines one can see all kinds of pagan processions in which people carry statues of the so-called saints and Mary. At these processions all the Catholics *bow down* to these-idols, and in God's eyes that's the same as worshiping them! Show me a verse in the Bible that allows Catholics to bow down to religious images."

"True, Catholics may bow down or even kneel in front of a statue, but they aren't worshiping either the statue or the person it represents. Let me explain. Do you have pictures of your wife and children in your wallet?"

"Yes."

"Well, those pictures are graven images. Did you know that?"

"Hmmm."

"Why do you carry around those pictures?"

"To remind me of my family. But that's not the point."

"That's *exactly* the point! You hit it on the head. Do you love the person a picture reminds you of or the picture itself?"

"Naturally, I couldn't care less for the picture. I love my family, not a piece of Kodak paper!"

"Precisely my point, It's the same with statues of saints. They merely remind us of the persons they represent."

"But the Bible says you shouldn't carve idols, and..."

"First of all, there's a big difference between a statue and an idol in the sense the Bible uses the word idol."

"No, there's *not*. A picture of my family is merely a casual thing and has no religious purpose, but any statue that's used for religious purposes is an idol in the sight of God. I'm not interested in what men have to say. I only believe what God says in the Holy Bible. You'll have to show me verses to support your position."

"All right. Tell me, what's Iglesia ni Cristo's final authority for its doctrines?"

"Why, the Bible, of course! But don't change the subject!"

"I'm not changing the subject, Felix. You'll see in a minute why I asked you that question. Look, since you claim the Bible as your sole authority and you keep demanding that I quote Bible verses as proof for everything, why don't you show me a Bible verse that says there's no difference in God's eyes between an idol and a statue that's used for religious purposes?"

"I just read it a minute ago—Exodus 20:4."

"Yes, but that verse simply prohibits the carving of images for the purpose of *worshiping* them."

"No! In God's eyes anyone who carves an image and bows down to it is worshiping it and that's idolatry!"

"Let me help you out on this one. I see where you're making your mistake. There is a difference in God's eyes between veneration given to a saint and worship that is given only to God. God can tell the difference between a person who honors Mary and uses a statue to remind himself of her when he prays and someone who actually worships the statue or Mary herself."

"No! As far as God is concerned it makes no difference what a man says in his heart. God doesn't care! To him it's all the same. Bowing down to religious images for whatever reason is idolatry in the eyes of God! It says so in Exodus 20:4."

"So you're saying that when God observes a man bowing down before a religious image he can't tell what's in the man's heart and he doesn't care if the man has no intention of worshiping the image? Do you mean to say that, no matter what the man's intention is, God just counts it as though he were really worshiping the image?"

"Yes. That's right."

"But wait. In your own King James Bible, 1 Chronicles 28:9 says, 'The Lord searcheth all hearts.' And in Proverbs 5:21 the Bible reminds us that 'the ways of man are before the eyes of the Lord, and he pondereth all his goings."

"Yes, but..."

"No buts about it, Felix. You're wrong, and the Bible—God's holy Word—proves you wrong. God can tell the difference, and he does make a distinction between honor and worship, between praying to saints and idolatry. God tells us in Ezekiel 11:5, 'I know the things that come into your mind, every one of them.' And in Luke 16:15 Jesus said, 'God knoweth your hearts.' "

"But that's different. God does know what's in a man's heart, but in Exodus he forbids both the bowing down to and the worshiping of statues. You Catholics do both. God did not say you can bow down to them only if you're not worshiping them."

"But see? The whole point of Exodus 20:4 is to forbid men from worshiping anything other than God. The seeming separation, between the words 'bow down to' and 'worship' is only semantics."

"Let me give you an analogy, Trent. If a man killed another man with a shotgun in cold blood—blew his head off—he could say: 'Lord, in my heart I didn't have the intention of killing that man. I really only intended to stop him from moving.' But God doesn't care what the man says. He only cares about what he did. It's the same thing with worshiping idols. God doesn't care what euphemisms you use. He only sees that you have bowed down before an image and committed the sin of idolatry."

"You drove right over the cliff with that analogy! Let's take your logic a little further, Felix. Consider the case of a man who, when an armed intruder breaks into his home, uses a shotgun to kill the intruder before he can harm the man or his family. He killed another human being just like the murderer in your example killed his innocent victim. Each man used a shotgun to kill another human being. We could even say both men killed with *premeditation*. But there's a difference here, wouldn't you say?"

"Well, yes, but that's a false analogy. Let's turn to Psalm..."

"No. We'll stay right here. In your scenario, did the murderer commit an action that broke a commandment of God?"

"Yes. He killed somebody."

"Okay. So the action of killing was present, but what about the *intention* to commit murder? Was that present also?"

"Well, yes, but..."

"Now then, in the case of the man defending his home against the intruder, was the action of killing present also?"

"Yes, but I don't see the point in all!"

"Wait a minute. You'll see the point in just a moment. So, in the second case the action of killing was present, but what about the intention of committing murder? Was that present?"

"Let's get back to Psalm..."

"Not yet! Answer my question. In the scenario I described, was the *intention* to commit murder present?"

"I don't see what you're driving at. It's a silly question."

"Silly or not, why won't you answer it?"

"I'd really like you to take a look at Psalm 95, where..."

"Felix, I'm sure you would, but the Psalms can wait for a minute. You're dodging my question, and you know it. You know quite well that your own analogy backfired on you and actually proves my point. And now you won't answer my question because you know that your faulty reasoning, when carried to its logical conclusion, refutes your argument. I ask you again: Did the man who killed the intruder while defending his family have the *intention* to commit murder?"

"No."

"Good. So, even though he killed someone, will he be condemned for *murder* by God?"

"No."

"Why not?"

"I guess because he didn't intend to commit murder."

"Precisely."

"But using religious images is different."

"Why?"

"Well, ummm, it's different because..."

"Felix, please show me in the Bible where it says there's a difference."

[Silence]

"You can't show me such a verse because it isn't there, and you know it. You also recognize, even if you won't admit it, that there's no difference between the First and Fifth Commandments when it comes to God discerning the motives in a person's heart. I just showed you that if God, despite each man's external actions, can tell the difference between murder and self-defense he can certainly tell the difference between idol worship and the valid and laudable veneration of his saints through the use a statues."

"No! The Bible says that if you make statues and bow down to them you are committing idolatry! Period. God forbids us to carve statues under any circumstances, and you Catholics are idol worshipers!"

"Why do you refuse to admit that you see my point? I can tell by the look on your face that you do."

"I go by the Word of God alone! I don't listen to the vain philosophizings of men."

"Not even when they're right?"

"As it says in 2 Timothy 2:16, we true Christians are to 'shun profane and vain babblings for they will increase unto more ungodliness.' You Catholics carve images for religious purposes, and that's idolatry. Nothing you can say—none of your clever philosophizings—will stand up against the Word of God!"

"Oh? Tell me, do you think the Bible can contradict itself? Could God contradict himself?"

"Of course not!"

"I see. Then, let's take a look at Exodus 25:18 and 20. Would you read them please?"

"Very well. 'Thou shalt make two cherubims....' "

"Who's speaking here?"

"God."

"Right, and who's he speaking to?"

"Moses and the Israelites."

"Correct. They are the very same people he just commanded not to make any kind of religious image. Right?"

"Uh, right."

"Continue, please."

"Thou shalt make two cherubims of gold, of beaten gold thou shalt make them, in the two ends of the mercy seat....And the cherubims shall stretch forth their wings on high, covering the mercy seat with their wings, and their faces shall look one to another.' So what?"

"So, here God—the same God who, five chapters earlier commanded the Israelites not to carve any images—commanded them to carve images of angels. And what's more, these images are to be used for religious purposes. In 1 Kings 6:23–25 God commanded two fifteen-foot high images of angels to be carved and covered in gold leaf. These were standing in the Holy of Holies of Solomon's Temple. In 1 Kings 7:23–29 we're told the Temple also contained carved images of lions, oxen, and more angels. In Numbers 21:8–9 God commanded Moses to fashion in bronze the image of a serpent and hold it up on a pole for the people to look upon and be healed. If you're right, and God really does prohibit any kind of religious statues, then how do you explain these verses?"

[Silence]

"It's quite simple really. Iglesia Ni Cristo makes a huge blunder by not realizing that God does allow and, as we've seen, even commands the use of religious images when they're used properly and not worshiped in place of him. The images of the angels in the Holy of Holies and on the Ark of the Covenant were put there to remind the Israelites of heaven."

"Well, they may have been permitted to carve such images, but they didn't bow down before them. That's what you Catholics do, and it is idolatry!"

"You say it's a sin to bow down before a religious image?"

"I don't say it. The Bible does."

"I see. Well, let's look at Joshua 7:6. Read it for us, please."

"'Joshua rent his clothes, and fell to the earth upon his face before the Ark of the Lord until the eventide.'"

"In other words, since the Ark of the Covenant had angels carved on it, Joshua bowed down before religious images, right? Doesn't that mean, at least the way you see things, that he was committing idolatry?"

"No, because Joshua wasn't worshiping the images, he was worshiping God."

"But how could God tell the difference? Joshua was bowing before carved religious images, and you yourself said a minute ago that, in God's eyes, it doesn't matter what's in a man's heart. If he bows down in front of religious images he's committing idolatry no matter what he may say to the contrary."

"Harrumph! I can see I'm getting nowhere with you, Mr. Lateran. You just don't understand the Word of God. I'd rather not waste any more of your time or mine. We'll all be leaving now. And we'll be praying for your soul."

"Come back any time, Felix."

Catholic Answers, *October 1989*

A Big Blast of Smells and Bells: Discovering the Catholic Church's Eastern Rite

I'LL NEVER FORGET THE SPASM OF NEGATIVE reaction this article provoked in the "Letters to the Editor" section of the *Latin Mass Magazine*. That wasn't even the magazine in which I had published it! Apparently, my praise for the Divine Liturgy of the Catholic Church's Eastern Rites was something up with which some Catholics would not put. Oddly, they misinterpreted my respectful salute to the East to entail a different sort of "salute" toward the Latin Rite of my upbringing, though nothing could have been further from the truth. One *Latin Mass Magazine* reader excoriated me, saying that she felt this article was tantamount to my "hurling insults over my shoulder" at the Traditional Latin Mass. I was truly nonplussed to read that.

The truth is, my real intention in writing what amounted to a pean to the Eastern Catholic Divine Liturgy was not to denigrate the Traditional Latin Mass (far from it!), but to extol it indirectly by way of contrasting the beauty I saw in the Eastern Liturgy with the banal and often arid distortions that had crept into many parish celebrations of the *Novus Ordo Missae*. My aim was to show that there is something ineffably beautiful in the traditional rites that speak to the soul in ways that should not go unnoticed or unappreciated.

• • •

My wife and I recently invited a young Catholic couple to attend our parish church one Sunday. Afterward, over coffee and donuts in the social hall, the wife leaned over and asked me in a stage whisper, "This is a *Catholic* church, right?"

Her question is typical of Roman Rite Catholics who attend their first Eastern Rite liturgy. It's the question I asked myself the first time I witnessed the exotically beautiful ritual. What Western Catholics call the Mass, Eastern Catholics call the Divine Liturgy. There's no ontological difference between the two. Both are the same thing: making present Christ's redemptive sacrifice on Calvary. Externally, however, there are many differences.

The typical Eastern Rite Divine Liturgy is long, about an hour and a half. The church interior is covered with icons of biblical scenes and the Fathers and Doctors of the early Church. The Blessed Virgin Mary, the saints, and angels—that "cloud of witnesses" who surround us, as spoken of in Hebrews 12:1—are depicted in a profusion of color. The sanctuary is separated from the body of the church by an iconostasis, each panel formed by a life-size icon of Christ, the Blessed Virgin Mary, angels, and saints. The altar is small and square, with an ornate tabernacle placed at the back center. The entire Liturgy is sung, with the hymns and antiphons alternating among priest, deacon, and congregation. The robust singing impressed and attracted me when I attended my first Liturgy. The people, led by a cantor, participated in prayer with gusto. The hymns are beautiful and theologically rich. The prayers, hymns, and actions are a vivid reflection of the early Church liturgy (the same is true, of course, of the Traditional Latin Mass). Then there is the heavy use of incense, bells, processions, bowing, and the custom of everyone making the sign of the cross every time the words "Father, Son, and Holy Spirit" are uttered.

All of these elements of the Divine Liturgy express the deepest sentiments and aspirations of the soul, and dispose the mind toward heaven. Most Roman Rite Catholics find it foreign and odd at first, but the oddness quickly fades as the Liturgy becomes familiar, and soon they revel in the signs and symbols. They drink in the ancient splendor of the Eastern Rite, an oasis of dignified worship (often in English) amidst the arid banality of many Roman Rite parishes. Their thirst for transcendent, aesthetically beautiful worship is slaked.

The Eastern Rites of the Catholic Church include the Antiochene, Chaldean, Armenian, Alexandrian, and Byzantine Rites, and the various "sub-Rites" contained within these groupings. Each of these rites is in full communion with the bishop of Rome. They are fully Catholic, though they preserve (fiercely, at times) the cultural heritage from which they sprang.

There are about 512,000 Eastern Rite Catholics in the U.S., compared with sixty million or so Roman Rite Catholics. The Eastern Rite has been called the "invisible" Catholic Rite. The onion domes that adorn the exteriors of many Eastern Rite churches are a striking sight as you drive past, but going into the church beneath the domes does not cross the minds of many Catholics.

But this is changing. Over the past decade, there has been a remarkable trend among Roman Rite Catholics to move Eastward, even if only temporarily. In the U.S., Eastern Rites took root and flourished mainly in the working-class sectors of the major cities of the Midwest and the East. Chicago, Toledo, Cleveland, Pittsburgh, New York, Philadelphia, Boston, and Newark have large populations of Eastern Catholics. Ethnic solidarity and a seemingly impenetrable tangle of Old World customs are the predominant causes of the insularity of Eastern Catholics in the U.S. Moreover, Eastern Catholics generally lack a missionary impetus. These factors have contributed to most Roman Rite Catholics' being oblivious to the existence of the Eastern Rites.

An increasing number of Catholics are discovering the riches of the East, not by leaving the Church for Eastern Orthodoxy, but by experiencing an Eastern Rite of the Catholic Church. My wife, Nancy, and I are examples. We were born and raised in the Roman Rite and have no intention of leaving it. We registered our family at the local Byzantine parish (all the magnificent prayers are in English) because we're captivated by the beauty and majesty of the Liturgy and because we want our nine children to experience this important dimension of the heritage of the Church. For certain Roman Rite Catholics, attending a Byzantine parish is a respite from the kookiness in some Roman Rite parishes.

As for me and my house, we're just visiting Byzantium, but some Roman Rite Catholics head there not as visitors but as immigrants. Some, sadly, go as refugees, contemporary Catholics displaced by their yearning for real Catholicism—no, not the "good old days" of Bing Crosby and Barry Fitzgerald, but a dynamic Catholic *present*. They hunger for a Catholicism with depth and vitality, resplendent in devotions and liturgies, images and icons, "smells and bells" that speak to the soul so eloquently about heavenly realities. They want to pray fervently and sing robustly. They want to know they have truly *worshiped* God. And, perhaps most urgently, they want their children to experience these things, too.

Many Catholics can't locate these primordial elements of the Faith in the local parish. So, questions are asked. "Do I grit my teeth and say nothing when the priest, like Houdini, wriggles his way out of practically every Mass rubric? What about my children? How can I form them in the Faith without any substantive Catholicism with which to form them? How long can I endure the shallow feminism that has overrun my parish?"

Answers vary. Some folks, tragically, jump ship. They dive over the side of the Barque of Peter (imagining, perhaps, that they've narrowly escaped the *Titanic*) and take up with a local schismatic Traditionalist chapel. Some stay home, boycotting the Church, as if their absence will somehow punish the ones who are to blame for the liturgical silliness that drove them away. Others cease struggling and allow themselves to be submerged in the bland heterodoxy that has swamped their parishes. Still others escape to those Evangelical churches where the preaching is good, the hymns actually mean something, and the pews are filled with people who are serious about seeking God's will for their lives (by the way, typically, more than half the people in those pews are ex-Catholics). There is a variety of other options, but you get the point: Many Catholics leave the Church out of sheer frustration at what's happening (or not happening) at their parishes.

Not everyone makes those defective choices. Many Catholics are finding warmth and encouragement in the *orientale lumen*, "the light of the East"—a light that illuminates a path that leads not away from the Church but deeper into her heart. The Eastern Rite is playing a quiet but important role in the renovation of the Church.

Pope John Paul II's frequent reminders that Roman Rite Catholics should recognize, venerate, and acquaint themselves with the Eastern heritage of the Church are having a positive if gradual effect. I see in his writings (*Orientale Lumen* and *Ut Unum Sint*) an exquisite pastoral balance between fidelity to and love for the Roman Rite, and proper affection and deference for the patrimony of the East.

Unfortunately, most Catholics don't read the pope's writings. With the startling decline in Mass attendance and reverence for the Eucharist over the past three decades (to name just two problems we face), the Eastern Rite's ancient expression of the Catholic Faith is attractive to Catholics who hunger for contact with the holy mysteries of the Faith. Many, perhaps most, of the Roman Rite Catholics I know who attend a Byzantine Rite parish do not seek to change rites canonically. Rather, they register at a Byzantine parish and remain in the Roman Rite. The numbers are still small, considering the Catholic population in the U.S., but the trend seems to be growing.

I was born in southern California in 1960 and was raised in a devout Catholic family. I grew up serving as an altar boy in the local Roman Rite parish, and even had the experience (unique for my age) of serving the pre-1962 Tridentine Mass during my grammar school years at the Mission San Juan Capistrano parish. The pastor had received a special indult from Pope Paul VI to continue using the Tridentine form of the sacraments in that parish. I have vivid memories of serving Holy Mass in the elaborate sanctuary, cloudy with incense, where Father Junipero Serra had celebrated Mass two centuries earlier: I on my knees, reciting the acolyte's responses in Latin, watching the priest's every motion. So many realities of the Faith were communicated to my young soul by the elements of that traditional Mass. I love the Roman Rite, and my current exploration of the riches of the East reminds me of the often hidden riches of the West.

Three years ago, when we moved to San Diego, our family registered in the local Ruthenian Byzantine parish. "Why?" our Roman Rite Catholic friends asked. The first answer is that Nancy and I want our children to experience

Sunday Mass powerfully. We want them to know the sense of the sacred—the solemnity, majesty, and beauty of the sacrifice of the Mass. We want them truly to worship and praise God, as he wants to be worshiped and praised. We want them to *swim* in the symbols and signs and words of the Catholic Faith. As parents, we will someday have to answer to God for the way in which we raised our children in the Faith. Neither of us wants to be in the position of trying to explain to the Lord why we didn't take full advantage of all the opportunities he afforded us.

The second answer is that I want to praise God in meaningful, reverent song. And I am moved by the liturgical prayers that flow from the heart of the ancient Eastern Church. I want my heart's deepest aspirations and urgent longings to soar heavenward.

This isn't easy to accomplish at many Roman Rite parishes, which are drab interiorly and architecturally, and have drifted away—sometimes far away—from their moorings in traditional Catholic orthodoxy. "Sacred," "majestic," and "beautiful" are not modifiers that leap to mind when one tries to describe the typical modern parish down the street.

How we got into this mess is another article in itself, but here's a synopsis: We have our *nouveaux* liturgists and their sycophantic groupies (lay and clerical) to thank. They gave us permission to do whatever we wanted at Mass and to omit whatever we didn't want to do. And now we basically don't do anything. We don't show reverence for the Eucharist. We don't engage in traditional Catholic devotions. We don't go to confession much anymore. And, worst of all, we are no longer bothered that we don't do these things. We've developed a massive, collective amnesia.

There are times I wonder how we've kept the Faith. The eggheadery masquerading as "liturgical renewal" has done far more damage to the average Catholic parish than the eighth-century iconoclasts ever did in their heyday. For the past thirty years, we've heard all the jiggery-pokery talk by those who want to make the Mass "relevant," "meaningful," and "inclusive." Well, they've jigged and poked the typical Roman Rite parish Mass into an intensely bland experience. The hymns stink, the sermons are lame, and the fire of faith is sputtering in the hearts of the people in the pews. It's no wonder that in such parishes, festooned with felt banners and awash in feminist sensibilities, Catholics starve for lack of authentic Catholicism. We've become anemic, sluggish, Tradition-deficient.

The Grand Liturgical Experiment has failed. Banishing the authentic Catholic forms and symbols and actions from the Mass and from the buildings in which the Mass is celebrated banishes the transcendent. The mind is no longer ordered to God. But this difficult season in the life of the Church has, ironically and providentially, paved the way for Roman Rite Catholics to discover the riches of the Eastern Rite without abandoning their own sacred heritage.

Moreover, the Holy Father and the growing number of excellent bishops and priests who are following his lead are working to reform the botched reform of the liturgy. It's a slow process, but it's happening. In the meantime, what Catholics want, whether they realize it or not, is solid food. They want the authentic, undiluted Faith.

Many Catholics go to the Byzantine Rite—I hate to break this to my Traditionalist Catholic friends—to find tradition. They are seeking honest-to-goodness Catholic piety, but a piety that's not tethered to anti–Vatican II agendas, elitist snobbery, or smoldering resentment of the *Novus Ordo Missae.* So far as I can tell, the Catholics who gravitate toward the Eastern Rites are not snubbing Rome. With one or two exceptions perhaps, the Roman Rite Catholics who attend my Byzantine parish are respectful and loyal to the Roman Rite. Many alternate between attending our Byzantine Rite parish and attending Mass at the local Roman Rite parish. They attend the Byzantine Rite to get, for themselves and their children, the "essential vitamins and minerals" of the Catholic Faith: reverent worship, untampered-with rubrics, the sense of the sacred, and a big blast of those "smells and bells."

The icons and incense, the celebrant and people facing east together, and the elaborate hymns and ceremonial pomp are not anachronisms, as some might charge, nor are they sops to retrograde "pre–Vatican II" sensibilities. They are consistent with Vatican II and its goals, and they speak to the soul about the eternal realities, just as the Roman Rite is supposed to do. One can see, for example, reverent and beautiful *Novus Ordo* Masses celebrated by some diocesan priests, priests of Opus Dei, priests who were formerly Anglicans, and others.

It's no coincidence that when the wrecking ball of liturgical deconstruction slammed into the Roman wing of the Church (completely contrary to the directives of Vatican II's decree on the reform of the liturgy, *Sacrosanctum Concilium*), vocations plummeted and fervor waned. So why didn't my family opt for a Traditional Latin Mass? Some Catholic acquaintances were perplexed, even dismayed, that we didn't join the local indult Tridentine Mass congregation. For some, our registering at the Byzantine parish smacked of a repudiation of the Tridentine Mass and even of the Roman Rite itself. But this is not so. I love and venerate the Tridentine Mass, just as we love and venerate and remain in the Roman Rite of the Church. One does sense at times a certain stultifying anger in some indult Tridentine Mass circles, and we didn't want to expose ourselves or our children to the subtle (and not so subtle) anti–*Novus Ordo* sentiments that often take up residence in those communities.

As new residents in a new town looking for a parish, we seemed to have discovered the Byzantine Rite by accident, but Divine providence was undoubtedly at work. I tell curious Catholic friends that our Father has opened for us the eastern wing of his mansion. We've inherited the whole house from him, but until recently we hadn't realized there was a vast, unexplored side. The books in the library, the paintings of long-forgotten relatives, and the family heirlooms scattered in profusion through the rooms all belong to us, but we never knew they were here.

Catholics who migrate East, and those (like me) who are respectful and grateful visitors, recognize that authentic Catholicism inhabits those incense-filled, icon-laden sanctuaries. The preeminent value of the *orientale lumen*, the light of the East, is that it helps illuminate the one path to Christ.

New Oxford Review, *October 1997*

When Opportunity Knocks...

SOME PEOPLE DREAD VISITS FROM DOOR-TO-DOOR missionaries. I think of them as laboratory experiments. Discussions with real live Jehovah's Witnesses and Mormons are the best way to hone your apologetics and evangelization skills.

One way to make use of their visits is to play dumb. Stalk them for a while before you get down to business (plenty of fun there). You'll learn a lot about how they approach a subject and the kinds of arguments they use.

Eventually you'll have to make your move and reveal that you know more than you were letting on—usually, that's when the conversation grinds to a halt. But in the meantime, you can test your arguments to see which ones work and which ones don't.

Remember that Jehovah's Witnesses and Mormons have received quite a bit of training in how to proselytize Catholics. So if you aren't confident you can handle whatever they throw at you, then direct the conversation to a subject you're prepared to talk about. Observe which of your arguments seem to be more effective and jot down the questions and Bible passages they bring up. This will help you prepare for the next time you hear that knock at the door.

Envoy, January/February 1997

Sects and Sin in Manila

THE SUN IS NINETY-THREE MILLION MILES from the earth, but in the Philippines it feels a lot closer. Never have I experienced heat like the heat I endured in Manila during a week's visit in May. I was there to make preparations for Catholic Answers's evangelization work during Pope John Paul II's visit to World Youth Day 1995 in January.

At World Youth Day 1993, held in Denver, Catholic Answers distributed 225,000 free copies of its evangelization booklet, *Pillar of Fire, Pillar of Truth*. We hope to give out as many as twice that number—some in English, some in Tagalog—in Manila, where up to a million people are expected to participate in the weeklong activities.

LAX, Monday, 10:00 A.M.

Two hundred of us were herded aboard the Northwest Airlines 747, and I settled into my seat for the thirteen-hour flight to Seoul, where, after a two-hour layover, I'd catch my connecting flight to Manila. Catholic apologetics is a no-frills occupation, and I had a no-frills coach-class ticket. I was seated in the no-smoking section, but my seat was close enough to the cigarette crowd that it should have been called the no-inhaling section.[107] For a moment I wondered why my row was empty, even though the rest of the coach seats were occupied. I discovered the reason when I tried to recline my seat—it wouldn't move. In fact, the entire row of seats wouldn't recline because of the bulkhead right behind them. "Oh well," I sighed. "At least I'll be able to lie down later and sleep." But I never could get to sleep, so I sat up straight and read.

Aquino International Airport, Manila, Tuesday, 11:09 P.M.

I cleared customs quickly—officials waved me through without even glancing at my bags—and headed across the concourse toward the exit that, even at that late hour, was jammed with travelers. By the time I exited the terminal I felt like I was wrapped in a soggy heating blanket—and that was the comfortable part. As I'd learn in a few hours, in the Philippines the evening's heat and humidity are mild compared to the day's.

My Catholic contacts, Rommel and Cocoy Garcia, sons of General Vic Garcia (retired from the Philippine National Police), were waiting for me at the curb in an air-conditioned Toyota. As we drove to their home in Angeles City, ninety minutes north of Manila, I asked lots of questions, and they filled me in on the state of the Church in the Philippines. They told me about the challenges the Catholics face: a government which promotes mass-distribution of contraceptives, a lack of solid Catholic books and tapes, a lack of funds, a lack of priests to minister to the islands' 56 million Catholics, and stiff competition from sects.

During the drive I counted at least a dozen Iglesia ni Cristo churches along the way. (Iglesia ni Cristo is a fast-growing, virulently anti-Catholic sect headquartered near Manila). Rommel and Cocoy were enthusiastic when I explained about Catholic Answers's evangelization efforts planned for Manila. They knew that the distribution of *Pillar of Fire, Pillar of Truth* would give a boost to the Church.

At about 12:30 a.m. I arrived at the home of Hermie and Cen Yusi, a couple active in the local prayer group. They offered to put me up in a spare room of their home for the entire week. I unpacked my bags and headed for the shower. My room had a large fan but no air-conditioner, and though the mercury was past the 90-degree mark, I was too exhausted to care about the heat. I set the fan on high, aimed it at the bed, and fell asleep.

Iglesia ni Cristo headquarters, Quezon City, Wednesday, 10:15 A.M.

I figured that since I was in Manila, I'd take the opportunity to rattle Iglesia ni Cristo's cage and put its leaders on notice that Catholic Answers is coming to town to explain and defend the true faith.

Iglesia teaches that at the Second Coming of Christ all true believers (Iglesia members in good standing) will be "caught up into heaven." But this isn't your usual rapture, according to a widespread and (alas!) probably false rumor. Iglesia members, having received advance warning, are to make their way to the local Iglesia church and await the rapture indoors. The entire building and all its occupants will be lifted up to heaven. This idea may have been inspired by Iglesia architecture: The buildings are aerodynamic, as though designed to fly better in the rapture.

Iglesia ni Cristo's sprawling headquarters reminded me of the Emerald City in the "Wizard of Oz," the difference being that these munchkins were anything but friendly once they found out what organization I represented. After persistent negotiations with the guards at the front gate I managed to wrangle a meeting with Bienvenido Santiago, the editor of Iglesia's monthly magazine, *Pasugo*. I was ushered into his office and shown to a seat. Also present was Samuel Paran, a minister on staff. Santiago handed me his no-nonsense business card. It read: "Bien C. Santiago, Minister of the Gospel."

I think these fellows were a little surprised, perhaps a little miffed, at my persistence in trying to see them, but after I was seated Santiago did his best to put me at ease with his gracious banter.

"So, Mr. Madrid. What do you want?"

"I just dropped by to say howdy, and to tell you that Catholic Answers is sending a team of apologists to Manila for World Youth Day '95 to help out with the Holy Father's visit."

He grimaced when I said "Holy Father."

"We are well aware of your pope's visit next year."

"Oh? And do you have special plans to mark the occasion?"

Santiago grinned. "Let us just say that Iglesia ni Cristo will be ready for his visit."

I knew what that meant. Iglesia ni Cristo hates the Catholic Church and attacks its teachings whenever the chance presents itself. Each issue of *Pasugo* is crammed with articles showing how "unbiblical" the Catholic Church is for teaching doctrines such as the Trinity, the divinity and Incarnation of Christ, the Mass, and purgatory.

As our chat progressed I gleaned that Iglesia was gearing up for an anti-Catholic proselytization push to coincide with World Youth Day. This push will include open-air preaching by Iglesia personnel, a barrage of anti-Catholic radio broadcasts throughout the Philippine islands, a massive tract distribution effort, and televised broadsides against the pope and the Catholic Church.

We sparred for fifteen minutes or so, and out of the corner of my eye I saw Paran jotting down notes. For all I knew, the whole thing was being videotaped through the two-way mirror behind Santiago's desk, and I was being weighed, measured, and CAT-scanned, all for some sinister use by Iglesia at a later date.

I smiled. "Look, Bien, do you think you Iglesia folks might have an interest in another debate with Catholic Answers when we're here in January?"

Karl Keating had accepted a challenge to debate one of their ministers a few years ago. Held in a high school gym, the debate drew an overflow crowd of 3,500 spectators, most of them Iglesia members bused in from throughout Southern California.[108] No doubt the videotapes of the debate had been studied carefully by Iglesia's high command, which knew all about Catholic Answers.

Santiago smirked. "Why would you want another debate? Are you admitting that your Keating lost the first debate and now you would like a chance to redeem yourself?"

"Oh no, Bien," I smiled even more broadly. "Whatever would give you that impression? Haven't you seen the video of the debate? Keating killed your guy in that debate. We'd like to whip you again."

"That debate was a great victory for Iglesia ni Cristo. Keating lost."

The barbs went back and forth for several minutes, each of us smiling. I left a copy of *Pillar of Fire, Pillar of Truth* and the issue of *This Rock* that contained a cover story about our work in Denver at last year's World Youth Day. We made no agreement about a debate, except to express mutual interest in debating either the divinity of Christ or the papacy.

Outside, I looked back at the odd, streamlined buildings. With ten million members, Iglesia ni Cristo is growing quickly—not just in the Philippines, but among Filipinos in America. Nearly all converts, of course, are former Catholics.

Iglesia ni Cristo, which in its evangelization activity and theology is like the Jehovah's Witnesses, is tenacious in challenging the Catholic Church. Come World Youth Day, even if no other anti-Catholic sects show up to harangue visiting youths, Iglesia alone will pose a stout challenge.

Makati, Wednesday, 3:00 P.M.

I finished a long and beneficial meeting with one of the printers who will produce *Pillar of Fire, Pillar of Truth*. His card gives his name as Felicito Abiva, but everyone calls him Toots. He is president of the Asian Catholic Publishers Consortium and owns Felta Publishing.

Printing as many as a half-million copies of the booklet in the Philippines will save us thousands. Plus, we'll have them on site and ready for distribution when our evangelization team arrives on January 9, the day before the first scheduled event.

Toots and I hammered out the details of the project—getting bids from other publishers, determining the booklet's paper and size specifications, figuring out printing and shipping logistics, and, most importantly, agreeing on a price. The booklets will be dropped off by the printers and stored at our hotel and distribution center at Manila's gigantic Rizal Park, the venue for the major World Youth Day events, including the Pope's Masses.

Catholic Answers's headquarters will be at the Hotel Manila, directly across from Rizal Park. From there, and from our main distribution point within the park itself and just across the street, our team will coordinate the efforts of two hundred volunteers who will see to it that copies of *Pillar of Fire, Pillar of Truth* get into the hands of the visiting young people.

Angeles City, Thursday, 2:15 P.M.

I had several objectives during my visit, so I had to move quickly. I had to meet with printers, arrange for the translation of the booklet into Tagalog (the Filipino national language) visit Cardinal Jaime Sin and other bishops to acquaint them with Catholic Answers and secure their blessing on our evangelization plans, reconnoiter the World Youth Day sites in Rizal Park, arrange lodging and transportation for our staff, and otherwise make as many contacts as possible. I spent the afternoon drinking coffee in an effort to shake off the jet lag and making phone calls to arrange meetings. Soon I had a full appointment book.

At 8:00 Hermie and I drove through driving rain to a chapel used by the Sacred Heart parish prayer group. The storm had knocked out the power, and as I stood in the darkened doorway of the small building I could see by candlelight the outlines of the fifty people inside, praying and singing.

It was easy to picture this as a scene from second- or third-century Rome, when Catholics had to gather in secret, lest they be rounded up by the authorities. Then another thought intruded: The need for catacombs and clandestine Masses could arise again. Our World Youth Day efforts may be helping to convert and equip the Church's future leaders and martyrs. (I had cause to recall this thought a few days later.)

Hermie introduced me to Fr. Larry, the youthful pastor. Speaking loudly so he could hear me over the crash of the lightning and the steady drone of the rain, I acquainted him with the work of Catholic Answers, explained our plans for World Youth Day, and summed up by asking him to help us organize a cadre of volunteers to pass out booklets.

He was pleased with the project and promised to help however he could, including by contacting his bishop, Most Rev. Anacleto Aniceto, to seek his support. Mass was about to start, so I said good-bye and gave him copies of *Pillar of Fire, Pillar of Truth* and *This Rock*. We shook hands, and I headed into the rain.

Angeles City, Friday

I spent the day talking with other printers, arranging for volunteers, and visiting parishes to get a feel for the level of activity as Catholics prepare for the Pope's visit. What struck me was the profound spirituality of the average Filipino Catholic. Everywhere I went, in all the people I met, I saw a deep and reverent love for Christ and his Church. The people, like Catholics anywhere, were not particularly well-catechized, but they loved the faith. Every church I entered, at any time of the day or night, had dozens of men, women, and children on their knees praying before the Blessed Sacrament.

Still, I was worried by the anti-Catholic challenge. Many Filipino Catholics abandon the faith. You can't walk a block, it seems, without seeing a newly constructed Iglesia ni Cristo church or Fundamentalist chapel or Kingdom Hall. The Philippines is a Catholic country now, perhaps, but the writing is on the wall, and it's not hard to read: The Philippines won't be Catholic in twenty-five years unless more is done to combat the spread of heresies.

I was cheered to find that everywhere I went, priests, nuns, bishops, and lay people were enthusiastically supportive of Catholic Answers's plan to blanket World Youth Day with copies of *Pillar of Fire, Pillar of Truth*. One delightful young nun beamed at me after thumbing through the booklet. "This is just what we need here! What a great shot in the arm this will be for our young people!"

Manila, Saturday, 2:30 P.M.

I was in the waiting area at the residence of Cardinal Jaime Sin, Archbishop of Manila. This was the only time during the whole week that I wore a suit. Sweat trickled down my back as I sat in a wicker chair and chatted with Sr. Amparo Sanchez, B.V.M., the Cardinal's secretary. She told me the history of the Catholic Church in the Philippines and how, lately, it was experiencing great strain because of the onslaught of the sects.

"That's why I'm here, Sister." I smiled. "Catholic Answers hopes to secure Cardinal Sin's approbation for our evangelization plans."

A seminarian directed me to the second floor of the old building where the Cardinal had his quarters. I stepped into a small, high-ceilinged office, and there was Cardinal Sin, seated behind a modest, book-laden desk (which was cleared off for our photograph).

He spoke with conviction about the need for evangelism and fidelity to the Church. For half an hour we discussed Catholic Answers's work. He was pleased with our efforts and kindly agreed to tape a brief message of greeting to Catholics in the U.S., inviting them to come to Manila for World Youth Day. At the close of our conversation, the Cardinal remarked, "We must not forget all those who have died for the Catholic faith, and we must be willing to live that faith."

Aquino International Airport, Tuesday, 9:45 A.M.

I passed through customs on my way to the terminal where I would catch a flight to Tokyo, and I spotted a young monk standing a few yards away, his back to a gaudy duty-free store that beckoned travelers to make last-minute purchases of jewelry, clothing, and liquor.

Bearded, tonsured, and clad in sandals and a rough habit, he was an unassuming witness to the message of the gospel in the face of the sensuality of the world. I thought of Matthew 19:21: "Jesus said to him, 'If you wish to be perfect, go, sell what you possess and give it to the poor, and you will have treasure in heaven; then come, follow me.'"

I introduced myself, and he said he was Fr. Paul Franois de Sulauze, a French priest of the Congregation of St. John the Apostle. He was returning to Taiwan, where he and his community minister to the spiritual and temporal needs of the inner-city poor. We chatted until I had to board my flight.

As I settled into my seat I reflected on the importance of the evangelism work Catholic Answers will be doing in Manila next year. Fr. Sulauze is a priest today because he was given a solid formation in the faith. But what if he had been badly catechized and then converted by the Jehovah's Witnesses? What if he became, not a Catholic priest, but a Fundamentalist proselytizer out to convert Catholics?

I thought about the hundreds of thousands of young men and women from around the world who will be in Manila for World Youth Day. I thought about them and about what Iglesia ni Cristo and other anti-Catholic groups have in store for them.

And I thought about the vocations to the priesthood and religious life that could be lost to the Church if Catholic Answers and other groups don't go to Manila to share the faith and take a stand against the menace of the sects.

This Rock, July/August 1994

SECTION FIVE

Life, Morality, and Scandals

THE TERM "CATHOLIC APOLOGETICS" IS TYPICALLY ASSOCIATED with explaining and defending the Faith in discussion with Protestants, Mormons, Jehovah's Witnesses, Muslims, etc. There are, however, other important connotations to the term, such as apologetics directed toward the particular claims and challenges posed by secular culture. This section reflects aspects of my thinking about societal problems such as pornography, abortion, and fractiousness within the Catholic Church—things that do require a kind of apologetics response, if only as an answer to the unique challenges they present to Catholics, but also because they agitate and disorient so many people. While these entries are not, strictly speaking, apologetics in nature, they do express my attempts to begin addressing the problems, even if only by identifying some of their causes.

In "The Five Most Pathetic Words," I am speaking both to a young Catholic woman who flaunted her embrace of the culture of death in *The National Catholic Reporter* and to those who are at a loss to know how to respond to others like her. Apologetics can take many different forms, and sometimes it's necessary to simply speak the truth in as logically compelling a way as you possibly can in an effort to get through to someone who is, quite literally, hell-bent on promoting error and immorality. There's no guarantee, of course, that the person you're trying to reach out to will have "eyes to see and ears to hear," but we have to try as best we can anyway. As I write this, I am reminded of the pertinent warning God gave about this in Ezekiel 3:18–21.

> If I say to the wicked, "You shall surely die," and you give him no warning, nor speak to warn the wicked from his wicked way, in order to save his life, that wicked man shall die in his iniquity; but his blood I will require at your hand. But if you warn the wicked, and he does not turn from his wickedness, or from his wicked way, he shall die in his iniquity; but you will have saved your life. Again, if a righteous man turns from his righteousness and commits iniquity, and I lay a stumbling block before him, he shall die; because you have not warned him, he shall die for his sin, and his righteous deeds which he has done shall not be remembered; but his blood I will require at your hand. Nevertheless, if you warn the righteous man not to sin, and he does not sin, he shall surely live, because he took warning; and you will have saved your life.

I wrote the "Porn Chickens" piece hastily early one morning in May of 2004, after being confronted on the Drudge Report by the shocking and disgusting breaking news about the depredations against Iraqi prisoners by their American guards. Like everyone else, I was indignant and outraged that this could have happened, and I wanted to express what I believed (and still do believe) are the underlying societal causes that permitted things to have degenerated to such a grotesque level. I'm not sure what other kind of apologetics could possibly be brought to bear effectively against the monstrosities of pornography and brutality other than a vigorous denunciation of their evil and an earnest appeal to people's innate sense of justice and goodness, even when those instincts have been beaten down and covered over with several decade's worth of the toxic cement of militant secularism.

Two other entries in this section deal with the sordid saga of Fr. Marcial Maciel (1920–2008), the disgraced founder of the Legion of Christ religious order. They represent about a dozen commentaries I wrote on this subject dating back to January 31, 2009, when I gave a heads-up with the headline "Some Bad News Coming Soon." I wrote:

> I'm sorry to tell you that some shocking, saddening news about a prominent figure in the Church will soon become publically known, perhaps as early as Monday or Tuesday. Don't worry. This is not about the Holy Father or any previous pope, nor does it have to do with a layperson. Let's start praying earnestly that God will bring some kind of good from this and, of course, offer prayers for those involved.

Once the news about Maciel's spectacularly debauched double life broke into public view, it went from bad to worse in an unremitting cascade of ever more shocking revelations of just how corrupt he had been. But Maciel's own actions were only part of the story. Since he was by then dead and gone and off to his eternal reward, the pressing issue at hand was the future, or lack of one, for the Legion of Christ and its tightly connected lay movement Regnum Christi. My rationale for writing commentaries on the whole thing stemmed in part from my own erstwhile affiliation with Regnum Christi as an ostensible member. Because I had been publicly associated with them for a couple of years, when Maciel's house of cards began to collapse and the defections of Legionary priests and lay members of Regnum Christi began in earnest, many people asked my opinion of what was happening. Another reason for my personal interest in the matter is the fact that three of my sons, Jonathon, Timothy, and Maximilian, were all Legionary seminarians for several years apiece. (They are all happily married now, I am glad to report.)

My association with this group began in late 1997, when then Legionary priest Fr. Richard Gill invited me to become involved as a lay member. At the time, it seemed like a fine idea, though I eventually began to see that, even though I attended the required "Encounter" meetings on just a handful of occasions, I just didn't feel called by God to be part of this group, though I did not at that time put any stock in the criticisms of elitism and obfuscation on the part of the order, nor the outright accusations of depravity and corruption that dogged Maciel. Like many other unwitting American Catholics, I too was duped by that charlatan's masquerade of pious, holy, "kingdom-building" for Christ.

When I stepped away from the group sometime in 2000–2001, I had no idea how precipitously things would unravel for the Legion, once the reality of its founder's duplicity became definitively known. I assumed they would continue growing in power and influence and in doing good for souls. But when that terrible reality began to force itself out into the open and I began to comprehend what this meant, the shiny, happy, *winning!* exterior of the Legion of Christ began to crumble, revealing hardly more than a Potemkin village.

When I wrote "This Is No Time for Happy Face Stickers," I figured it might be of some interest, *ad intra,* to those who were either members of the Legion of Christ or Regnum Christi, though I didn't then foresee that it and my other commentaries on this subject would be of interest to a far wider audience. Of all the things I have written professionally, those having to do with the Maciel saga have caused me the most sadness and chagrin.

The Five Most Pathetic Words:
"I Am a Pro-Choice Catholic"

||||||||||||||||||||||||||||||||||||||||||||||||||||||||||||||||||||||||||||||||||||||||||||||||||||||

HOW DOES A FORMERLY PRO-LIFE CATHOLIC college girl morph into a pro-abortion zealot who identifies the roots of her transformation as including attending the National March for Life?

You read that right.

As implausible as it might sound, Kate Childs Graham says that this happened to her, and the results are not pretty. In her recent article "I Am a Pro-Choice Catholic," which appears in that notorious bastion of contumacy, *The National Catholic Reporter*, Ms. Childs Graham reveals:

"I wasn't always a pro-choice Catholic. During college I attended the annual March for Life on more than one occasion. The first time my friends and I traveled to the event from Indianapolis, Indiana, was with a bus full of high-school students—most, seemingly, only going for the trip to Washington, D.C., with their friends, sans parental supervision. Needless to say, it was a noisy bus ride. After I transferred to Catholic University, I volunteered for the Mass for Life two years in a row, helping to herd all of those high school students into every crevice of the National Shrine of the Immaculate Conception."

One must wonder if Ms. Childs Graham herself was one of those young people who made the journey to Washington, not to protest the evil of legalized abortion, but simply because she wanted the freedom of a little road trip, "sans parental supervision."

She claims that, "Each time I attended the March for Life, I felt overwhelmingly conflicted. On one hand, it was moving to be among so many people, all energized by their faith around an issue. On the other hand, I sensed that I wasn't getting the complete picture—I wasn't being told the full story."

Hmm... unless this young woman was comatose during her high-school and college years, how could she not have been "told the full story"? The pro-abortion screamers have done nothing but tell their "story" in the most strident ways possible, including counter-demonstrating and handing out their propaganda to anyone who will take it at the Washington March for Life.

Their side of the story has thoroughly dominated the public consciousness through the sheer force and high-decibel volume of the pro-abortion diktat purveyed in the movies Ms. Childs Graham watched growing up, in the television programs she enjoyed during middle school and high school, and in the biased and often inaccurate coverage of the U.S. abortion debate with which the mainstream news outlets have persistently and perniciously inveigled their viewers and readers for the past thirty years.

But then, maybe Ms. Childs Graham never watched television growing up. And maybe she never saw any movies or watched the network news or read a mainstream secular newspaper or magazine. Maybe, but I doubt it. I'm pretty certain she got a great big dose, for years on end, of the pro-abortion crowd's side of the story.

If she was raised Catholic, as it appears, was she raised on a desert island somewhere, far away from any means of encountering Catholic teaching on the evil of abortion? Perhaps she never heard of Pope John Paul II nor listened to or read any of his many teachings on this subject?

Perhaps she attended parishes where the priests never preached on the evil of abortion, and she may never have visited any of the many Catholic pro-life websites or read the many Catholic periodicals that clearly proclaim what the Catholic Church has always and everywhere proclaimed, namely, that abortion is murder.

It's possible, I suppose, that Ms. Childs Graham never opened and read her Bible or the *Catechism of the Catholic Church*, both of which are as clear and forceful and unambiguous as can be about telling the other side of the story— you know, the side about how killing unborn babies through abortion is murder and how murder is always a mortal sin.

Maybe she never came into contact with any pro-life Catholics (who number in the tens of millions in this country, incidentally) and heard from them the other side of the story.

Maybe, but I doubt it. In fact, given her admission that she attended, at least a few times, the Washington, D.C., March for Life—as a participant, not a counter-protestor—I'm quite confident that Ms. Childs Graham heard both sides of the story and that, tragically, she has simply chosen to believe the lie, the fairy tale, the fable about how "protecting a woman's right to choose [i.e., to murder her unborn child]" is a good thing. How it "helps" women. And how illegal abortions are "unsafe." I wonder if it has ever dawned on this deeply misguided woman that, legal or illegal, abortions are always "unsafe" for the little child being killed in the procedure.

After reading her *NCR* article and the vacuous rationale she gives in defense of her ideology, I have to wonder.

I wonder if she has ever stopped to think about all the millions of unborn women who are being subjected to the un-safest of unsafe medical procedures when they are aborted.

During her trips to the Washington March for Life, did Ms. Childs Graham ever really listen to what was being said? Did she listen to any of the many eloquent speakers and teachers of the Catholic Faith—bishops, priests, religious, and laity—who travel there to explain to the March attendees the fundamental reasons why the Catholic Church teaches that abortion is murder and that murder may never, under any circumstances, be countenanced, much less promoted? Perhaps she was too busy herding all those high-school students into all those crevices of the National Shrine to pay attention to what was going on all around her. It's hard to say.

Ignorance of why life issues like abortion and contraception are inextricably linked and how both do incalculable damage to women and men, marriages, and society as a whole (prescinding for the moment from the wanton destruction of human life entailed in these two activities) seem to be the root problem here. Ms. Childs Graham assures her readers:

"[F]or me (and for many others), being pro-choice does not end at supporting the right to safe and legal abortion; it extends to discovering the best methods to prevent unintended pregnancies. Contraception promotion, comprehensive sexuality education, and access to affordable child care and healthcare are just some of the methods that are paramount to reducing the need for abortion."

One thing is for sure. If she never really heard the pro-abortion side of the story, as she alleges she didn't, since becoming a pro-abortion advocate, she sure has made up for lost time! She can parrot back with the best of them the vapid and long-discredited Planned Parenthood talking points that she spouts in her article. But you've got to give her credit for sheer persistence, if not for clear thinking. To borrow another writer's turn of a phrase, she is speaking from "a pinnacle of near-perfect ignorance."

"I am a pro-choice Catholic," she asseverates, because "my Catholic faith tells me I can be. The Catechism reads, '[Conscience] is man's most secret core and his sanctuary. There he is alone with God whose voice echoes in his depths.' Even St. Thomas Aquinas said it would be better to be excommunicated than to neglect your individual conscience. So really, I am just following his lead. After years of research, discernment and prayer, my conscience has been well informed. Being a pro-choice Catholic does not contradict my faith; rather, in following my well-informed conscience, I am adhering to the central tenet of Catholic teaching—the primacy of conscience."

Ms. Childs Graham claims to have a "well-informed conscience." Really? Perhaps she is being sincere when she says this (see *CCC,* 1790), but it appears that she completely missed that part in the *Catechism* where it declares:

"Moral conscience, present at the heart of the person, enjoins him at the appropriate moment to do good and to avoid evil. It also judges particular choices, approving those that are good and denouncing those that are evil. It bears witness to the authority of truth in reference to the supreme Good to which the human person is drawn, and it welcomes the commandments. When he listens to his conscience, the prudent man can hear God speaking" (*CCC*, 1777).

"Conscience must be informed and moral judgment enlightened. A well-formed conscience is upright and truthful. It formulates its judgments according to reason, in conformity with the true good willed by the wisdom of the Creator. The education of conscience is indispensable for human beings who are subjected to negative influences and tempted by sin to prefer their own judgment and to reject authoritative teachings" (*CCC* 1783).

"Conscience can remain in ignorance or make erroneous judgments. Such ignorance and errors are not always free of guilt" (*CCC*, 1801).

It's not necessary to explain here what St. Thomas actually said about man's duty to follow his conscience in observing the commandments and teachings of the Church, as that would simply be piling on and would be a further cause of embarrassment for Ms. Childs Graham. So, it will suffice to simply read the above statements from the *Catechism* about conscience in light of this other statement:

"Since the first century the Church has affirmed the moral evil of every procured abortion. This teaching has not changed and remains unchangeable. Direct abortion, that is to say, abortion willed either as an end or a means, is gravely contrary to the moral law: 'You shall not kill the embryo by abortion and shall not cause the newborn to perish.' 'God, the Lord of life, has entrusted to men the noble mission of safeguarding life, and men must carry it out in a manner worthy of themselves. Life must be protected with the utmost care from the moment of conception: abortion and infanticide are abominable crimes'" (*CCC*, 2271).

Ms. Childs Graham, please come to your senses. Wake up to the hideous realty of what you're saying and doing and supporting here. You have fallen for the wrong side of this story. You are wrong about what the Church teaches about conscience and human freedom. You are wrong in your opinion that, when it comes to being pro-abortion, "My Catholic faith tells me I can be." No, the Catholic Church tells you exactly the opposite.

I urge you take the time to honestly study what the Catholic Church really says on this issue. I call upon you in fraternal charity to be intellectually honest with yourself.

Please don't forget that, in due time, you, like the rest of us, will have to meet the Lord Jesus Christ face-to-face and be judged by him (see Hebrews 9:27). On that day, you will have to give an account for why you defied the clear teaching of his Church on the evil of abortion.

"I am a pro-abortion Catholic" are the five most pathetic words you could say.

For the sake of your own immortal soul and for the sake of the lives of the unborn children your ideology menaces, please rid yourself of this delusion.

New Oxford Review, *October 2009*

N.O.W., Hear This!

Some pro-abortionists are being won over to the truth, one heart at a time.

I was just a kid when, in 1973, the U.S. Supreme Court befouled itself and the nation with its ruling on the *Roe v. Wade* "abortion rights" case. From that moment forward, the forces of death have gathered strength.

Leering at us from behind the fig leaf of their newfound legal status, the abortionists and their many political quislings steamrolled ahead, grinding into the pavement of our national history the blood and torn flesh of millions of baby boys and girls. Their apologists have crowded the airwaves and print media for over two decades, jostling for our attention, screeching about a woman's right to choose, and shoveling scorn on anyone willing to stand up to their bullying rhetoric.

But those many men and women who have sought to protect the rights of unborn children have pressed doggedly onward. Although the pro-abortion screamers always seem to have the upper hand when it comes to dominating the media, the truth and goodness and beauty of the principle that unborn children have an absolute right to life is gradually seeping into the hearts of some of those who oppose this principle. For example, Carole Everett, who was the owner of two abortion clinics, is now a prominent pro-life speaker.

There's also Dr. Bernard Nathanson, a former abortion-performing doctor and foe of the pro-life movement, who not only turned his back on the "pro-choice" philosophy that fueled his lucrative abortion practice, he renounced all its pomps and funding when he experienced a profound change of heart. This journey eventually led him to become Catholic. Many other men and women who were once active in or sympathetic to the abortion industry have also been touched by God's grace and are finding their way into the light of reason and salvation, the light of Christ.

One of the refugees who managed to escape from the "pro-choice" nightmare is Norma McCorvey. You may not know her by her actual name, but you certainly have heard of the legal case that made her pseudonym, "Jane Roe," a household word. That's right, "Jane Roe"—the woman who, in 1973, stood at ground zero when this country officially declared war against the rights of unborn children—became pro-life, and now to complete her journey, has decided to become Catholic.

That's an unpleasant development for the members of pro-abortion groups like the National Organization for Women, as well as their governmental and media sycophants. Their main pro-choice, pro-abortion, pro-death icon has come to life.

Envoy, July/August 1998

Here Comes the Son

I GOT A CALL TODAY FROM A man who recently converted to the Church. He was concerned about the factions and bickering he was seeing among Catholics and wondered why there was such turmoil. After chatting for twenty minutes or so, I think we both felt that things weren't as bleak as it may have seemed to him before. We discussed the many great things taking place in the Church today: the rise in vocations in those orders and dioceses where orthodoxy and a joyful enthusiasm for Christ is present; the explosion of good, new Catholic magazines, publishing ventures, apostolates and apologetics radio programs; the consistent advances being made by Catholics in spreading the gospel through TV, the Internet, and short-wave radio. We talked about the many good bishops being named. Most of all, we reflected on Christ's promise that he would be with his Church "even until the end of the world" (Matthew 28:20).

Clearly, good things are happening in the Church, stalwart individuals and groups are rising all around us, willing and able, by God's grace and a holy generosity to shoulder the burden of the challenges that face us in the modern world. True, things are difficult and we face many dangers, but I rejoice in the evidence that Christ is always true to his promise: "I will not leave you orphans" (John 14:18).

Yes, we live in a tough time. Yes, being openly, unashamedly Catholic carries with it certain risks and costs. But this is nothing new. The Church has always lived in difficult times (epochs of peace have been relatively uncommon over the last two thousand years), and we shouldn't be surprised that our generation must face (and conquer) its own peculiar set of challenges. By the time my phone conversation with this new convert ended, I think we were both energized about our calling to be apostles for Christ. Rather than worry about how "bad" things might seem, our discussion prompted us both to a keener awareness that this is an exciting time, a wonderful time to be Catholic—ours is a moment of immense opportunities for grace.

But you and I, of course, must be willing to rouse ourselves to seize that moment. The New Testament is marked by the hopeful expectation of Christ's Second Coming, but it's also tempered by the reality that each generation of Christians, not knowing when he will return in Glory, must be busy about the Father's work, preparing for the coming of the kingdom.

Things are difficult today, yes, but I don't see darkness enveloping us. I see the light of Christ pushing back the darkness, slowly, inexorably, and not without a struggle on the part of each of us who loves him.

Envoy, *March/April 1998*

They Will Know We Aren't
Christians by Our Hate!

We, The greater concerned and anonymous warriors of the Christian Holocaust,
All humans concerned for liberation and justice for all humans,
All spirits wishing to be free in a world undestroyed by weakness,
DECLARE NIHILISTIC WAR, TOTAL HATE WAR UPON
CHRISTIANITY [sic]....Mayhem and destruction are all we can offer
for the deceptive and fascist order above us. This order is firmly rooted in the
tradition and philosophy of Christianity and must be exterminated through
WAR upon its ideology. At all levels it must be denied. [Sic, sic, sic]

THAT IS THE DELICATE INTRODUCTION THAT The Christian Holocaust website uses to begin its multi-page tirade against Christianity. (No, I'm not going to tell you their website address and in the process, help these knuckleheads gain what they most want: a wider audience).

These "greater concerned and anonymous warriors" are just some of the many anti-Catholic, anti-Christian websites that are springing up across the fruited plains of cyberspace. It's hard to know how to react to their yammering about "exterminating" Christians and their ideology. They obviously take themselves pretty seriously, but it's hard for me to do so.

After all...yawn...they're really not saying anything new. This "death to Christianity!" motif may shock some, but it's as old as the hills, having been the pet project of countless other groups that have come and gone over the last two thousand years. It's just that Joseph Stalin and the Emperor Diocletian didn't have flashy websites to tell the world about their aims.

"We will bury you Christians!" has been the boast of the Church's many persecutors. But we Christians have been burying them, one by one, praying for their souls, and hoping they have some good answers to the tough questions Christ the Judge no doubt asks them when they finally discover he is who Christians say he is.

No, I'm not worried that the folks behind most of these cheesy "kill the Christians" websites are themselves a real threat to the existence of the Faith once for all handed on to the holy ones. But I do see in them an important reminder that we can't take for granted our cushy situation here in the West. There are many Christians in other parts of the world who are being exterminated right now, as you read these words, because they love and profess Christ.

It could happen here too. We should never forget that. Nor should we forget that a real persecution of could break out in the West. Christ said: "If the world hates you, know that it has hated me before it hated you. If you were of the world, the world would love its own; but because you are not of the world, but I chose you out of the world, therefore the world hates you. Remember the word that I said to you, 'A servant is not greater than his master.' If they persecuted me, they will persecute you" (John 15:18–20).

Let's pray for the "greater concerned and anonymous warriors of the Christian Holocaust" and all those like them. They will know the truth in the end (and hopefully before that!). In the meantime, let's respond to their hate with the conquering power of Christ's love.

Envoy, *November/December 1998*

The Porn Chickens Are Coming Home to Roost

EARLY THIS MORNING, I LOGGED ONTO THE Internet news sites and saw the latest round of images of U.S. troops leering and mugging for the camera as they forced Iraqi men to stand naked and hooded, made them sprawl across one another on the floor in groups, simulating homosexual acts, and humiliated them in front of the cameras in other sexual ways, dragging a naked Iraqi man on the floor, a dog leash around his neck, and other atrocities.

It occurred to me that the reason this is happening, and the reason our country may be shocked—but shouldn't be in the least surprised—is the following: The pornography chickens are coming home to roost. Or to say it the way the Bible does, the American, indeed Western, fascination and enslavement to pornography has sown the wind and now we're reaping the whirlwind (see Hosea 8:7).

The U.S. (along with the rest of the West) has been in the steadily tightening grip of the pornography industry for the last forty years. It's a boa constrictor of lust that's not about to loosen its death embrace.

Hugh Hefner was the vanguard of the Porn Invasion, the tip of the spear, the first whiff of the rot that has steadily decayed our country and culture from within. The massive and steadily expanding availability of pornography, in all its forms (including, I'm sure, some that you and I would never even dream of), has become so widespread that it pervades every element of our culture: movies, TV, books, music, and beyond.

It's no longer just seedy men skulking around back alley bookstores and porn theaters in the bad part of town. These days, pornography is as common and as mainstream as cable TV (where much of it is easily available). It has a place in many, perhaps most, American homes—perhaps even in your own home.

Porn has metastasized across the Internet, and it's there in the mainstream neighborhood video rental places we all frequent. And when the thirty-something housewife stops by the video store after getting groceries, she picks up a Disney DVD for the kids and an X-rated DVD for herself and her hubby, to watch once the kiddos go to bed. Several Catholic priests I know have told me in recent years that the incidents of married women confessing sins involving porn (and related sexual sins) are skyrocketing. And that's just from those Catholic women who still go to confession. The actual number of women involved with pornography is, I fear, staggeringly high—much higher than we might imagine.

What once seemed to be a man's weakness has now become about as common among women as among men. Teens and even children are now being shaped and distorted by the steady diet of pornography that swirls all around them.

Hardly a week goes by without some new story involving grammar-school students getting busted for sexual antics (and sometimes crimes) on campus, in school buses, even in the classroom. Third-graders don't naturally know about this kind of behavior, much less act it out, unless they are learning it from somewhere. The multi-billion dollar porn industry is finding and forming eager consumers at every level. Its many tentacles slither across our culture, snaking their way into our homes through our computers, televisions, radios, and DVD players.

Which leads me to my thesis about the "bad apples" among our troops in Iraq. Of course it's only a small minority of Americans there who are acting out these macabre sexual impositions against their Iraqi captives, but it seems to me that it's a significant minority. They reflect the moral state of the nation. They are America. And though we recoil in shock and embarrassment when confronted with their stupid and shameful antics with the prisoners, we shouldn't be surprised by their behavior. They learned it here, stateside, on the Internet, in the movies, at their neighborhood video store, in their living rooms—remote control in hand to select that night's steamy fare from a variety of hard- and soft-core offerings served up on the platter of good ole satellite TV.

Is it any wonder that when, suddenly, these military "bad apples" (the blandly innocuous term so many people call them on talk radio these last few days since this story broke) are acting out the depraved images that litter the minds of people who are enslaved to porn? I don't think so. I think it's a perfect example of the old adage "garbage in, garbage out."

Or maybe it's more apropos to call it a good example of "monkey see, monkey do."

It's terrible to have to say such things about our fellow citizens, American men and women in uniform who are there in Iraq in our name, but what other conclusion can one draw from this? What else would explain their sexual, pornographic depredations against the Iraqis?

Yes, we're shocked by these pictures. We should be repulsed and horrified. But not surprised.

This Is No Time for Happy-Face Stickers

LAST NIGHT, AS MANY OF YOU ARE learning this morning, some very sad allegations about Fr. Marcial Maciel's duplicitous actions began seeping into the mainstream media. While a significant number of people knew ahead of time that this was coming down, no specifics were disclosed publicly until yesterday, and more details will come tumbling out soon in the mainstream press.

Predictably, the range of reactions to this bad news spans the gamut from outrage and stunned incredulity to something approaching despair to blasé "I-told-you-so" unconcern.

Regardless of how you react to this unfolding tragedy, be sure you look at it in perspective. Judging from what I've seen in the blogosphere in the past few days, it appears that some people just don't seem to understand what this deplorable situation really entails and what ramifications may arise from it.

Some have prattled on about how this really isn't bad news. It was long expected. And now that it's been proven and publicized, the temptation to lounge smugly in the worldly wise posture of "I-told-you-so" may be something too difficult for some to avoid. But we should avoid it, because this story is bigger than just the sum of the embarrassing details of sexual (and other) sins. Let's keep in mind a few important points.

First, this is indeed very bad news—the worst possible kind—for the thousands of good and faithful Catholics in the Legionaries of Christ religious order and its lay affiliate, the Regnum Christi Movement—the vast majority of whom have, over the years, steadfastly refused to believe any accusation against Fr. Maciel, however plausible and vehemently attested to by those who claim to have been witnesses.

Now, these faithful and dedicated Legionary priests and seminarians and good-hearted Regnum Christi folk are realizing that they have been duped. They are faced with the stunning, crushing, irrefutable evidence that their trust in this man was in vain, their unshakable faith in his goodness and innocence has finally been shaken to pieces. The gleaming giant of holiness they had admired for so long has been shown to have feet of clay (see Daniel 2:31–32).

Yes, many of Fr. Maciel's ardent followers have been naive in their refusal to consider that there may have been some truth to at least some of the myriad of accusations that mounted against him, but I believe theirs was a naiveté born of sincerity and love for Christ and the Church. This sincere love attached itself firmly (and now we know, undeservedly) to a man who, at least by outward appearances, seemed to merit their trust.

If nothing else, this sordid saga proves the powerful truth of Scripture's warning: "Put not your trust in princes, in man in whom there is no salvation. When his spirit departs, he returns to his earth, and on that day his plans perish" (Psalms 146:3).

Second, it is true, as some are saying, that, while painful, this bad news is actually a good thing, at least insofar as it entails light shining in a dark place. This may be exactly the necessary impetus—albeit a horrible one—that will lead to a purification and renewal of an organization that could do great good for souls in ways that go way beyond what many critics say was merely good work that had serving the Legion as its ulterior motive.

I make no judgment personally on that criticism, as to whether it is legitimate or not, but regardless, this new chapter in the Legionary saga can become the starting point for a very good thing in the Church. It may in fact be a bitter harbinger of a sweet and long-hoped-for outcome: a Legion of Christ that becomes free from the controversies and complaints that have dogged it for decades, a religious order that is seen by others to be truly at the service of the Church as a whole and not, as many of its critics allege, merely at the service of itself.

It could be that, by God's grace and the prudent courage and honesty of the group's leadership, there can be a good outcome—possibly a spectacularly good one. There may be a viable effort to undertake a thorough reform and reconstitution of the Legionaries of Christ and the Regnum Christi Movement, although there remain nagging reasons to wonder if that will really happen. It's too early to know. But we should be praying now for that to happen, if it be God's will. Time will tell.

One thing is for sure, though. If the Legionaries of Christ and the Regnum Christi movement are going to emerge from this crucible in one piece and remain in existence for the long haul, they cannot lapse into robot mode, they cannot don a happy-face mask and attempt to deny that this is a very serious problem for them. At this precise juncture, denial and dismissal of the clear and present danger that this situation poses to the Legion, will, I believe, sooner or later, prove fatal to its efforts at sustaining itself.

Again, we must keep this unfolding situation clearly in perspective and not succumb to the various myopic temptations that beckon: at one end, to shrug and simply ignore it as a nonissue, and at the other end, to join in a gleeful feeding-frenzy of morose delectation. Already, on the blogs, one can see people falling into both camps.

Third, let's be realistic. No matter what some of the Internet pundits and commentators may be saying, THIS IS BAD NEWS. To call it anything else is to badly misunderstand the import of what's taking place here. These salacious revelations (please God, may there be no more of them) have caused and will continue to cause serious damage, not only to the shell-shocked members of this group (many of whom have spent years in dogged defense of the holiness of Fr. Maciel and who now feel the sharp knives of betrayal and fraud sever the bonds of trust they once had in this man), but to the Catholic Church in general.

Watch and see. You'll soon notice certain people trying to use this scandal to malign Pope John Paul II (a long-time supporter of Fr. Maciel and the Legion), in a way similar to how some are right now attempting to exploit the recent SSPX Bishop Williamson Holocaust-debacle against Pope Benedict XVI.

As I've been saying all along on my blog, what we need to do is pray earnestly for all the people involved in this mess. They need our prayers, now more than ever. Pray for the soul of Fr. Maciel. Pray for the Catholic Church and also for those outside the Church who will be swayed or disoriented by this scandal, many of them seeing in it confirmation of their worst suspicions about Catholics and Catholicism. And let's not omit to pray for ourselves, that we might not fall from our own fidelity to Christ, however firm or tenuous it might be.

Now is a good time to contemplate the famous maxim, "There, but for the grace of God, go I." If nothing else, these revelations about Fr. Maciel should serve as a cautionary tale to hammer that point home for each one of us.

Finally, it's worth repeating: Don't lose your sense of perspective. Don't think that this bad news isn't bad news. Let's call it what it is and avoid the temptation to slap a happy-face sticker on it.

Prayer, Forgiveness, and Doing the Right Thing

ONE OF THE VITALLY IMPORTANT LESSONS THAT the Lord has impressed on my heart and mind over the years is how crucial a healthy prayer life is—for all Christians, yes, but in a particular way for those who seek to explain, defend, and share the Faith with others. Without prayer, your efforts to engage in apologetics become merely futile exercises in trying to give what you haven't got. How can you talk to others about Jesus Christ with clarity and conviction if you don't really know him yourself?

In my book *Search and Rescue: How to Help Your Family and Friends Come into (or Back into) the Catholic Church,* I wrote at length about how—without daily, heartfelt prayer—our "search and rescue" efforts to help others draw closer to the truth can quickly spiral out of control into "search and destroy" missions. The reason for this deplorable shift (as, I confess, I have at times discovered the hard way) is that when we don't pray much or we don't pray well or, worse, we don't pray at all, our otherwise laudable desire to defend the Faith quickly degenerates into a pride-filled expedition to conquer another person. Believe me, I've seen it happen. And as others before me have pointed out, when pride, not love, is the motive impulse behind apologetics, we are likely to do far more damage than good by driving others further away from the truth because of an obnoxious or supercilious attitude.

As Dom Chautard reminds us in his superb book *The Soul of the Apostolate* (a work I have avidly read and reread many times in the past quarter century):

Listen to St. John of the Cross. "Let the men eaten up with activity, and who think that they are shaking the world by their preaching or other exterior works, reflect here a moment. They...would be much more useful to the Church, and more pleasing to the Lord, not to mention the good example they would spread around them, if they gave more time to prayer and exercises of the interior life.

Under these conditions, by a single good work of theirs they would do far more good with far less trouble than they accomplish by a thousand others on which they waste their lives. Mental prayer would merit for them this grace and win for them the spiritual strength they need to produce such results.

Without prayer, all they do merely amounts to a great uproar; it is like the hammer falling on the anvil and making the neighboring echoes resound. They accomplish a little more than nothing, and sometimes they even cause harm. May God preserve a soul like that if it happens to get puffed up with pride! In vain will appearances be in its favor. The truth is that it will achieve nothing, for it is absolutely certain that no good work can be carried on without the grace of God....

Those who abandon the practice of the interior life...aspire to conspicuous good works in order to put themselves on a pedestal and make themselves the admired of all. Such people have no understanding of the source of living water and of the mysterious fountain which makes all fruit to grow."

I can attest to the truth of this teaching, both because I have observed it in others and because I have seen the difference in my own life between the "good fruit" that God's grace produces for others when I am attentive and faithful to prayer versus the din of a "clanging gong" that results, as St. Paul teaches in 1 Corinthians 13, when charity is absent due to my lack of prayer.

The entries in this section, then, represent my own attempts to remind myself every bit as much as my readers of how necessary prayer is. Rereading them now, in some cases many years after I wrote them, I am again struck by just how much we all need to be reminded of these things.

The piece on fatherhood was, for me, a kind of "apologetic" for a man's responsibility to be diligent and capable in his efforts to raise good children. There are so many men in the world today who have essentially abdicated their true, God-given role of the spiritual leader of their families, and though I am far from a perfect father myself, I know enough to know what to strive for, and this article on father was my attempt to crystalize my thinking on the subject.

How I Pray Now

I'M PRETTY SURE I SHOULDN'T BE WRITING this article. I definitely shouldn't be writing it if you're reading it in hopes of learning how to scale the heights of prayer.

Let me tell you right up front: I'm no paragon. Keeping my prayer life consistent and focused is a struggle. Distraction is my constant and noisy companion, laziness my Siamese twin. I don't pray as often as I should, as intensely as I should, or as generously as I should. In this I'm probably like many other Catholics who have the same struggles.

On the plus side, I do pray, and that, I know, is a good start. It's comforting to know that what God wants most of all from us in our prayer relationship with him is that we try, that we make an effort to converse with him, however unspectacular the results may seem.

When I was a kid, I prayed mostly because my folks told me I had to. I don't mean they were oppressive or overly demanding in regulating our family devotions—they were wise and kind in the ways they taught us the Faith. But they instilled in me a deep sense of prayer being a natural—no, an indispensable—facet of daily life.

Growing up, family rosary, prayers before meals, Advent-wreath devotions, Lenten Stations of the Cross and, of course, the prayers of the Mass were the very air we breathed. Sure, my childhood prayers before meals were usually mechanical and rattled off clickety-clack, but even so, I was aware that I couldn't even think of taking a bite into that baloney sandwich without first asking the Lord to bless his gift, which I was about to receive. It was like being taught to always wear your seat belt. That's a lesson that stuck. Just as I can't get into a car without instinctively reaching to fasten the belt, I can't pass the day without spending at least some time in prayer.

I've grown in my awareness that I need to pray. That awareness has a lot to do with how I pray now. My parents ingrained in me a need for the rhythm of prayer to order and mark the days and nights of my life. That sense of prayer being a vital necessity in my life has never left me. My prayer life, mediocre as it may be, is imbued with the realization that my prayers really matter.

My efforts to talk to God daily, to pour out to him my angers and fears, worries and joys, to open my heart to him in sorrow for the sins I've committed against him, to smile at him now and then throughout the day, to thank him and praise him for the wondrous gifts of my wife and children, have meaning to me precisely because I know they have meaning to him.

When I was a child, I figured that prayer was more of a duty, a chore I had to perform if I didn't want to make God angry. How wrong I was! I've learned that God is pleased by my efforts to talk with him. He's like a daddy who rejoices at even the slightest show of affection from his little child just learning to talk.

I'm still like that child. I find that my daily prayers mainly revolve around asking my daddy to teach me to grow up to be like him. "Teach me to walk. Teach me to know and love you. Catch me when I fall. I'm sorry for what I did." Perhaps this is what Our Lord meant when he said, "You must become like little children" (see Matthew 18:3).

Now that I am a father myself, I see my parent's wisdom in making regular family prayer non-negotiable. As my wife and I do our best to teach our children to pray, the wisdom comes back full circle. When I tell my children when, how and why they must pray, I'm looking in the mirror telling these things to myself.

My typical day's prayer regimen: brief morning prayer when I rise; prayers before meals, five decades of the rosary with the family after breakfast (we homeschool our children and that is the most convenient time); Mass at noon at least one weekday; twenty minutes or so reading Scripture or another spiritual book; a simple and brief examination of conscience; and several minutes of mental prayer before I go to sleep. That's the form. The content is a mix between rote prayers, such as the Our Father, Act of Contrition, and the *Memorare*, and moments of spontaneous prayer that well up from the soul. One of the most beautiful and helpful prayers I say is the Gloria.

I try to pray the Gloria to the Blessed Trinity once a day, just to remind the Lord (and myself) that I love and praise him simply for who he is. When I pray the Gloria, I'm not asking for anything—no petitions, requests, or expressions of sorrow. I can lift my mind and heart to God as I pray this ancient hymn of the Church: "Lord, God, heavenly King, almighty God and Father, we worship You, we give You thanks, we praise you for your Glory."

Another reason I love this prayer and have made it an integral part of my prayer routine is because my prayers can so easily get bogged down in my cramped little assortment of wants, needs, and apologies. The Gloria rises above all that, focusing my soul's gaze where it belongs: on the Blessed Trinity. And for my money, it's more "praise powerful" and theologically precise than any spontaneous prayer I could ever come up with. The Mass is the pinnacle of my prayer life.

No, I'm not transported with ecstasy as I sit there in the pew. Far from it! I struggle to stay focused, and I have to repeatedly fend off the inevitable gaggle of distractions that flutter and flit around the edges of my imagination. But the key is that I know what the Mass is: the once-for-all sacrifice of Christ on Calvary. I know I can be united with Christ most intimately at the Holy Sacrifice of the Mass.

At the moment of consecration, my single prayer is simply, "Lord, please save me." This plea encompasses everything. I'm the world's biggest panhandler when it comes to mooching prayers (Hey, I'm a realist—I know I need all the prayers I can get), so it's a matter of justice to make good on my promise to pray for others. I try to pray for folks by name, but that's not always possible, so to be safe I always tack on "Lord, I also pray especially for all those I've promised to pray for, but whose names I can't remember."

I also talk to God often about my family. There's a priestly dimension to fatherhood so I try to make this a focus of my night prayers and examination of conscience. I pray for my wife and for each of my children by name. I believe strongly that the father of the family should fulfill his special duty of praying for his children individually, interceding specifically for each child in turn.

The Lord has entrusted these souls to my care, and I must seek his blessing for them, and his guidance for me to be a good husband and father. Ironically, I find that my mental prayer at the end of the day is when I am best able to focus my mind and heart. I survey the day and its contents and speak to the Lord about how I think it went. And I try to remember to ask him how *he* thinks it went: "I know you've given me a limited number of days on this earth, Lord. Please help me make the best use of them I can."

Time is what I pray about most. The older I get, the more I appreciate the preciousness of time. I only have so much of it allotted to me, and there are no reruns. I have to be busy attending to my Father's work before the sand in my particular hourglass runs out.

So, Lord, please keep me focused.

Covenant, *March 1997*

Life Is Short. Pray Hard.

I'VE BEEN THINKING A LOT ABOUT PRAYER lately. Maybe it's because I turn forty next year and my personal appointment with middle age has arrived. This milestone arrived far faster than I ever imagined it would, and that turns my thoughts toward the strange reality of how time seems to speed up, the older we get.

Back when I was a pimply-faced high-schooler, the thought of turning forty was laughable—it wouldn't happen to me for a long time—and now it's almost here.

I'm not laughing. But I'm not crying either, nor am I freaking out over "getting older," or any of that sort of nonsense.

No. Getting older isn't the issue. It's the realization that, like it or not, I, you, we, are all getting closer to that moment when this life ends and the next one begins. At that point there are no more chances to improve or repent. That fact, combined with the realization of how fleeting life is, makes the importance of prayer more vivid than ever. After all, prayer is simply conversation with God.

The lovely Latin phrase *cor ad cor loquitur* (heart speaks to heart), expresses the true basis of the Christian life—not apologetics seminars or magazines or writing books, not classes or pilgrimages or radio programs—but prayer, talking to God and listening to him.

The problem, at least in my own life, is that I don't pray as often or as well as I should. Perhaps you're in the same boat. We want to pray, and we know we need to pray, but somehow in the midst of the hurly-burly of daily life, we forget to pray as we ought. Life is so very short. And our chances to pray for ourselves and others (to petition, repent, thank, and praise God) are not endless; someday, perhaps soon, they will run out.

And then comes death and judgment, and our eternal destiny—heaven or hell—is fixed forever. What really motivates me to pray more and better is the knowledge that my eternal destiny depends on how I love God *now*, while there's still time. Prayer is the foundation of that love.

Since we can all stand to be reminded of how important daily conversation with God is, allow me to share with you one of my favorite prayers, sometimes called the "Universal Prayer." Pope Clement XI seems to have been its author. I love this prayer because it so perfectly articulates the heart's yearning to be pure and trusting and pleasing to God, the desire to die in a state of friendship with him, and the petition that the Lord would give us the graces necessary to finish up our time on earth with maximum effectiveness for good.

Saying this prayer every day is a big help because it reminds me of all the things I have to be attentive to in my life. It's a kind of spiritual checklist that helps me regain my focus and commitment when the worries and distractions of everyday life conspire to blur that focus and weaken that commitment (for me that's a daily conspiracy, by the way, so that's why I try to say this prayer daily).

I hope this prayer helps you too.

The Universal Prayer

Lord, I believe in you: increase my faith. I trust in you: strengthen my trust. I love you: let me love you more and more. I am sorry for my sins: deepen my sorrow. I worship you as my first beginning, I long for you as my last end. I praise you as my constant helper, and call on you as my loving protector. Guide me by your wisdom, correct me with your justice, comfort me with your mercy, protect me with your power. I offer you, Lord, my thoughts: to be fixed on you; my words: to have you for their theme; my actions: to reflect my love for you; my sufferings: to be endured for your greater glory. I want to do what you ask of me: in the way you ask, for as long as you ask, because you ask it. Lord, enlighten my understanding, strengthen my will, purify my heart, and make me holy. Help me to repent of my past sins and to resist temptation in the future. Help me to rise above my human weaknesses and to grow stronger as a Christian. Let me love you, my Lord and my God, and see myself as I really am: a pilgrim in this world, a Christian called to respect and love all those lives I touch, those in authority over me or those under my authority, my friends and my enemies.

Help me to conquer anger with gentleness, greed by generosity, apathy by fervor. Help me to forget myself and reach out toward others. Make me prudent in planning, courageous in taking risks. Make me patient in suffering, unassuming in prosperity. Keep me, Lord, attentive at prayer, temperate in food and drink, diligent in my work, firm in my good intentions. Let my conscience be clear, my conduct without fault, my speech blameless, my life well-ordered. Put me on guard against my human weaknesses. Let me cherish your love for me, keep your law, and come at last to your salvation. Teach me to realize that this world is passing, that my true future is the happiness of heaven, that life on earth is short, and the life to come eternal. Help me to prepare for death with a proper fear of judgment, but a greater trust in your goodness. Lead me safely through death to the endless joy of heaven. Grant this through Christ our Lord. Amen.

Envoy, *September/October 1999*

Are Novenas No-Nos?

THIS IS, INTERESTINGLY, THE ONLY ONE OF my early articles about prayer that approaches the subject from a strictly apologetics perspective. Back in 1989 when I wrote this one, I had been interacting with Bart Brewer, a former Carmelite priest who abandoned the Catholic Church and became a Baptist minister and a professional anti-Catholic. I say "professional" only because that is how Bart made a living—he went around the country conducting seminars about the "evils" of the Catholic Church at Protestant churches where his audiences thrilled to his firsthand accounts of what the Catholic Church (which he called "Romanism") really taught. Bart was an aggressive character, who relentlessly attacked the Catholic Church and its teachings and practices, and I learned a lot about how to handle people like that from my different discussions with him.

In one of our conversations, probably in 1990, Bart harped on how "unbiblical" Catholic prayer practices are, such as novenas. So, with Bart's arguments ringing in my ears and a few of his vitriolic anti-Catholic tracts tucked into my Bible, I sat down one day in my office at Catholic Answers and wrote this article as a response to his arguments.

• • •

Novenas have a long history in Catholic spirituality, but recently the practice of this venerable and beautiful custom has fallen into decline. These days, many

285

Catholics are rather hazy on what novenas are and what they're for. Some even suspect novenas of being dangerously close to superstition in the category of the "vain repetitions" Jesus condemned in Matthew 6:7.

First, let's determine what a novena is. The *1989 Catholic Almanac* defines "novena" as "a term designating public or private devotional practices over a period of nine consecutive days; or, by extension, over a period of nine weeks, in which one day a week is set aside for the devotions."[109] The word comes from the Latin word *novem*, meaning "nine." Each particular novena (to different saints, angels, or our Lady) has its own special prayers.

Although, strictly speaking, a novena lasts nine days or nine weeks, the term can rightly be applied to intervals of prayer that are longer or shorter. For example, Jesus made a forty-day "novena" in the desert by fasting and praying in preparation for his public ministry. A biblical example of a novena is found in Acts 1:13–14 and Acts 2:1.

We're told the apostles, Mary, and other holy women gathered in Jerusalem and spent the nine days between the Ascension and Pentecost in intense prayer and contemplation. This first and greatest New Testament novena culminated on Pentecost with the descent of the Holy Spirit. In Acts 9:9, Paul made a post-conversion "mini-novena" (three days) at the home of Ananias. The Old Testament invests certain numbers (such as three, seven, twelve, and forty) with symbolic meaning. The "ninth hour" figures prominently in the New Testament. Jesus died at the ninth hour (Matthew 45–47; Mark 15:34) and the apostles frequently gathered to pray in the temple at the ninth hour (Acts 3:1). That prayer novenas were present in the early Church is evidenced by Augustine's caution against the practice for fear that some would be scandalized in thinking Christians were mimicking pagans.

The historian Durandus de Saint-Pourçain, in his *Rationale*, says that "some did not approve this, [in order] to avoid the appearance of aping pagan customs." Many Christian writers defended novenas, arguing that the mere potential for superstitious abuse and passing similarity to pagan practices doesn't mitigate the salutary effects of praying novenas. In the Middle Ages the most common form of novena was the novena of preparation. It included the recitation of special prayers on each of the nine days before Christmas in honor of the nine months our Lord spent in the womb of the Blessed Virgin Mary.

This practice flourished in Spain and France as early as the seventh century, but it was only in the seventeenth century that the pre-Christmas novena of preparation caught on in Italy (although novenas for deceased popes and cardinals had been celebrated there for centuries and, in Sicily, it was common for religious communities to observe novenas in the nine days prior to the feast day of their founder).

But what about the charge that novenas, which are simply formula prayers repeated at nine intervals, are condemned by Jesus in Matthew 6:7? The fact is that Jesus did not condemn formula prayers. This is demonstrated in the very next verse, where he gave us the best of all formula prayers, the Our Father. Neither is Matthew 6:7 a condemnation of the repetition of prayers. We know this because after teaching the formula prayer, Jesus, in Luke 18:21 and Luke 21:36, told us to pray always. St. Paul echoed this need for continual prayer in 1 Thessalonians 5:17 and in 2 Timothy 2:8.

The Old Testament also corroborates the concept of repeating formula prayers. The Psalms were written for the express purpose of being sung or prayed repeatedly, week after week, in the synagogues. It's important to keep in mind that the Holy Spirit—God himself—inspired these repetitious prayers in order that they be used by his people. In other words, God himself intended that these prayers be repeated, just as he inspired the writers to set them down on paper.

Examples of this kind of divinely inspired "repetitious prayer" are seen in passages such as Psalm 136:1–26 (where the refrain "for his mercy endures forever" repeats twenty six times in a row!) and Daniel 3:52–90 (where the refrains "Blessed are you...praiseworthy and exalted forever" and "Praise and exalt him above all forever" are repeated many times).

Let's focus on the meaning of Jesus's condemnation of "vain repetition." It pivots on his use of the word "vain"—not, as is commonly thought by

Protestants, on the word "repetition." At the time of Christ, pagans had a silly habit of running through a tiresome litany of titles when addressing their gods. They believed that if they didn't use the correct "title of the day" when invoking the god they were supplicating, the god, quite petulantly, would refuse to hear their prayers. In order to solve this dilemma, the pagans resorted to "scattershot" litanies of great length designed to mention any conceivable title the god might desire to be called by on that day.

Completely aside from the biblical condemnation of praying to false gods (see Exodus 20:4–5), Jesus condemned the uselessness (vainness) of the pagan prayer hoopla, complete with its elaborate titles and endless repetitions, precisely because the gods weren't up there to hear it. Pagan periods of special prayers bear nothing more than a passing resemblance to Catholic novenas. Those who condemn novenas as "pagan" should remember that by using the same logic, one could condemn fasting, hymn singing, meeting for worship on a particular day of the week, and even praying itself, simply because pagans also did all these things.

Catholic Answers, *December 1989*

Forgiveness

OVER THIS PAST YEAR, I'VE REFLECTED, AS Pope John Paul II has called on Catholics everywhere to reflect, on the new millennium that has been rising to meet us. And now it's finally here. The time for preparation has come and gone, and this new stage in our journey homeward is already starting to unfold. Forgiveness and reconciliation have been the twin themes at the center of the Holy Father's messages to the world these last several years. His message to Christians and non-Christians, to the head of state and to the man in the street, to everyone, has been: "Forgive one another. Seek forgiveness from those whom you have wronged, and offer forgiveness to those who have wronged you." In his message for the January 1, 2000, World Day of Peace, Pope John Paul said:

> The Great Jubilee is inseparably linked to this message of love and reconciliation, a message which gives voice to the truest aspirations of humanity today.... In the century we are leaving behind, humanity has been sorely tried by an endless and horrifying sequence of wars, conflicts, genocides and 'ethnic cleansings' which have caused unspeakable suffering: millions and millions of victims, families and countries destroyed, an ocean of refugees, misery, hunger, disease, underdevelopment and the loss of immense resources....
>
> To the young people who, unfortunately, have known the tragic experience of war and who harbor sentiments of hatred and

resentment I address this plea: make every effort to rediscover the path of reconciliation and forgiveness. It is a difficult path, but it is the only one which will enable you to look to the future with hope for yourselves, your children, your countries and all humanity.

This consistent call to forgiveness that the pope has given us has taken many forms. "Forgive debts," he has challenged governments, in many cases with surprisingly successful results. "Forgive your persecutors," he has gently encouraged the many millions of Christians who live under harsh, even deadly, circumstances in Asia, Africa, and elsewhere where oppression, violence, and death coil around them. "Forgive one another," he has asked Catholics and Orthodox, hoping that a wellspring of such mutual forgiveness will break forth in a fountain of genuine, permanent reconciliation for the two Churches. For years, the pope has been a modern-day John the Baptist, calling on each of us to prepare the way of the Lord, to make straight his path.

As we stand in the doorway of the new millennium, with a renewed mission of evangelization before us, let's take to heart the Holy Father's exhortation to forgive others and to seek forgiveness for sins we've committed against them. To help crystallize the reality of what it means to forgive, let me share with you a true story of a young woman's forgiveness and loving courage in the face of a personal catastrophe. It has been an object of reflection for me since I first read it. This letter she wrote, as she walked with Christ along that lonely road to Calvary, summarizes what the pope has been saying about the urgent need for us to forgive others, of the immense power of forgiveness.

Her name is Sister Lucy, a young nun from the former Yugoslavia. Her words, written just a few years ago during the war there between the Serbians and Bosnians, have taught me a lot about what it means to forgive the way Christ does. This is an excerpt from a letter she wrote to her superior. I think it is worth meditating upon as we search the dark corners of our own hearts where anger and jealousies and grudges make their nests. Her story can help us see the power of love.

I am Lucy, one of the young nuns raped by the Serbian soldiers. I am writing to you, Mother, after what happened to my sisters Tatiana, Sandria, and me. Allow me not to go into the details of the act. There are some experiences in life so atrocious that you cannot tell them to anyone but God, in whose service I had consecrated my life nearly a year ago. My drama is not so much the humiliation that I suffered as a woman, nor the incurable offense committed against my vocation as a religious, but the difficulty of having to incorporate into my faith an event that certainly forms part of the mysterious will of Him whom I have always considered my Divine Spouse.

Only a few days before, I had read *Dialogues of Carmelites* and spontaneously I asked Our Lord to grant me the grace of joining the ranks of those who died a martyr for Him. God took me at my word, but in such a horrid way! Now I find myself lost in the anguish of internal darkness. He has destroyed the plans of my life, which I considered definitive and uplifting for me, and He has set me all of a sudden in this new design of His that I feel incapable of grasping.... It was already daytime when I awoke and my first thought was the agony of Christ in the Garden. Inside of me a terrible battle unleashed. I asked myself why God had permitted me to be rent, destroyed precisely in what had been the meaning of my life; but also I asked myself to what new vocation He was calling me. I strained to get up, and helped by Sister Josefina, I managed to straighten myself out. Then the sound of the bell of the Augustinian convent, which was right next to ours, reached my ears. It was time for nine o'clock matins. I made the sign of the cross and began reciting in my head the liturgical hymn: At this hour upon Golgotha's heights, / Christ, the true Pascal Lamb, / paid the price of our salvation.

What is my suffering, Mother, and the offense I received compared to the suffering and the offense of the One for whom I had a thousand times sworn to give my life? I spoke these words slowly, very slowly:

May your will be done, above all now that I have nowhere to go and that I can only be sure of one thing: You are with me.

Mother, I am writing not in search of consolation, but so that you can help me give thanks to God for having associated me with the thousands of my fellow compatriots whose honor has been violated, and who are compelled to accept a maternity not wanted. My humiliation is added to theirs, and since I have nothing else to offer in expiation for the sin committed by those unnamed violators and for the reconciliation of the two embittered peoples, I accept this dishonor that I suffered and I entrust it to the mercy of God.

Do not be surprised, Mother, when I ask you to share with me my 'thank you' that can seem absurd. In these last months I have been crying a sea of tears for my two brothers who were assassinated by the same aggressors who go around terrorizing our towns, and I was thinking that it was not possible for me to suffer anything worse, so far from my imagination had been what was about to take place. Every day hundreds of hungering creatures used to knock at the doors of our convent, shivering from the cold, with despair in their eyes.

Some weeks ago a young boy about eighteen years old said to me: "How lucky you are to have chosen a refuge where no evil can catch you." Then he added: You will never know what it means to be dishonored. I pondered his words at length and convinced myself that there had been a hidden element to the sufferings of my people that had escaped me as I was almost ashamed to be so excluded. Now I am one of them, one of the many unknown women of my people, whose bodies have been devastated and hearts seared. The Lord has admitted me into his mystery of shame. What is more, for me, a religious, He has accorded me the privilege of being acquainted with evil in the depths of its diabolical force.

I know that from now on the words of encouragement and consolation that I can offer from my poor heart will be all the more credible, because my story is their story, and my resignation, sustained in faith, at least a reference, if not example for their moral and emotional responses. All it takes is a sign, a little voice, a fraternal gesture to set in motion the hopes of so many undiscovered creatures. God has chosen me—may He forgive my presumption—to guide the most humble of my people towards the dawn of redemption and freedom. They can no longer doubt the sincerity of my words, because I come, as they do, from the outskirts of revilement and profanation....That night, in which I was terrorized by the Serbs for hours and hours, I repeated to myself these verses, which I felt as balm for my soul, nearly mad with despair. And now, with everything having passed and looking back, I get the impression of having been made to swallow a terrible pill.

Everything has passed, Mother, but everything begins. In your telephone call, after your words of encouragement, for which I am grateful with all my life, you posed me a very direct question: What will you do with the life that has been forced into your womb? I heard your voice tremble as you asked me the question, a question I felt needed no immediate response; not because I had not yet considered the road I would have to follow, but so as not to disturb the plans you would eventually have to unveil before me.

I had already decided. I will be a mother. The child will be mine and no one else's. I know that I could entrust him to other people, but he—though I neither asked for him nor expected him—he has a right to my love as his mother. A plant should never be torn from its roots. The grain of wheat fallen in the furrow has to grow there, where the mysterious, though iniquitous sower threw it. I will fulfill my religious vocation in another way. I will ask nothing of my congregation, which has already given me everything. I am very grateful for the fraternal solidarity of the Sisters, who in these times have treated me with the utmost delicacy and kindness, especially for never having asked any uncareful questions.

I will go with my child. I do not know where but God, who broke all of a sudden my greatest joy, will indicate the path I must trod in order to do his will. I will be poor again, I will return to the old aprons and the wooden shoes that the women in the country use for working, and I will accompany my mother into the forest to collect the resin from the slits in the trees....

Someone has to begin to break the chain of hatred that has always destroyed our countries. And so, I will teach my child only one thing: love. This child, born of violence, will be a witness along with me that the only greatness that gives honor to a human being is forgiveness.

Envoy, *January/February 2000*

Do the Right Thing

||||||||||||||||||||||||||||||||||||||||||||||||||||||||||||||||||||||||||||

TEMPTATIONS COME IN DIFFERENT FORMS. SOME ARE brassy and exotic, hawking their wares so loudly that we can't easily ignore them. Others creep up quietly and, in whispers, coax us ever so gently toward a bad decision. We might hardly realize the temptation is there until, ZAP! we've given in, and it's too late.

Being human, we're all afflicted with temptations. Being Catholic, we have some powerful prayer and sacramental defenses against them.

I recently went through a moment of temptation that, as I look back on it, taught me an important lesson. I had been contacted by a Catholic publishing company with a request to rent my mailing list. (That kind of request is always nice, since it represents revenue. In this instance, the company wanted to rent the entire list.)

The request was accompanied by a sample of the mailing they intended to send to the list; a catalogue of books on spirituality and prayer written by a priest I was unfamiliar with. Although I had never read anything by the priest, something told me there might be a problem with his work. A little bell started ringing in the back of my mind, a warning that I should look more deeply into this before I allowed the list to be rented.

But no, I thought. I can just put this nagging question out of my mind and not ask any questions. Ignorance is bliss, right? Wrong. I knew that as tempting as it was to keep my mouth shut, not ask any questions that could bring answers I might not like, if I suppressed my conscience just long enough to make a few bucks, I'd kick myself later. It would be better to find out for sure if this writer was okay.

So, I got on the horn and called a priest I know from the same order as the priest whose books were listed in the catalogue.

"Father," I began, "What can you tell me about the writings of a priest named Fr. N?" His groan told the whole story. "No. His stuff isn't good at all. His books have a lot of problems with syncretism [i.e. mixing Catholicism with, in this particular case, Hinduism]," the priest said. "I'd stay away from it."

"That's what I needed to know," I said and hung up after thanking him for taking a moment to help me out.

But to be doubly sure, I called a second and then a third priest to get their corroboration. They, too, panned the books in the catalogue. So, armed with that information, I contacted the list rental agent and told him we couldn't approve the rental request from that publishing company.

The revenue from that rental would have been nice, but I knew I had an obligation to the folks on our list not to knowingly allow bad material to be sent to them. And this is where the temptation slithered into the picture.

I soon received a call from the director of the publishing company—a pleasant and well-spoken gentleman—asking me to reconsider. He did his best to reassure me that the writings in that catalogue were sound and that, although some had criticized the author, he really was a respected and important authority in spirituality. I have no doubt that the man was being sincere and that he really believed what he was saying was true. And, to be honest, I began to waver.

An image of the tidy check that would be sent in payment for that list rental floated up before my eyes. Mmm, yes. It really wasn't a big deal after all, *was* it? I mean, come on, his books were teaching people how to pray, and that's a good thing, right? What harm would there be in relenting and allowing the list to be rented?

I was lulled along in that way for a few moments, coming very close to giving in to the temptation, before I snapped out of it. No, it wouldn't be right to do this, I reminded myself, regardless of the money.

So, before I had a chance to change my mind and lapse back into my cowardly, greedy ways, I said a final "no" and thanked the director of the publishing company for calling to check, and hung up the phone.

About a week later I was stunned to read a story that went out on the religion wire services. It was about how the Vatican had formally, publicly condemned the writings of a priest—the exact same priest whose book catalogue I had declined. It was uncomfortable to think how close I had come to giving in and allowing the folks on the list to receive bad materials, all because I was tempted to take the money and look the other way.

Was this statement by the Vatican God's way of getting my attention? Perhaps, but regardless, he got it in a big way. If I had been stupid enough and greedy enough (and I hate to admit it, but I very nearly was) to suspend my ethics and look the other way on that list rental deal, I would have had a lot of people—those on the list who would have received the mailing—to apologize to. It was unsettling to realize how close I had come to letting that happen.

This lesson learned is simple but crucial: We have to do the right thing. If we don't we'll be miserable, and our bad choices will let other people down. Ultimately, our true happiness hinges on how readily we strive to do the right thing, rather than opt for the easy thing. And, ironically, it seems to be an axiomatic rule of the universe that doing what's right is usually not easy. Life is filled with opportunities to look the other way, to cheat just a bit here or there, to remain quiet when we should speak up about a mistake we made, to let money dictate the boundaries and test the elasticity of our business ethics.

The fact that we are Catholics is itself no guarantee that we will always behave as Catholics in our business dealings. That's why we have to stay close to Christ in the sacraments, especially confession. Any of us could fill volumes with examples from our own lives of temptations we encounter in the sphere of business, and we might take satisfaction in knowing we conquered (or at least ignored) most of them.

However, I do know this much: some temptations are overt and others are subtle, but all of them are dangerous. This is why St. Peter warned us, "Be sober and vigilant. Your opponent the devil is prowling around like a roaring lion looking for someone to devour. Resist him, steadfast in faith, knowing that your fellow believers throughout the world undergo the same sufferings" (1 Peter 5:8–9).

Let's not be discouraged or apprehensive. That dark thundercloud of warning has a silver lining: "The God of all grace who called you to his eternal glory through Christ will himself restore, confirm, strengthen and establish you after you have suffered a little. To him be dominion forever. Amen" (1 Peter 5:10–11). Amen.

Catholic Marketing Trade Journal, *May/June 1998*

Forgive From the Heart

ALEX KNEW HE WAS IN VERY SERIOUS trouble when he stepped into the kitchen and looked down at his shirt. Ten minutes earlier it had been white. Now it was covered with crimson stains. Blood, a lot of blood, had splashed on his shirt, his shoes, and his trousers. It was in his hair and on his face. He looked down at his hands and watched them tremble under the hideous weight of the red guilt that covered them. The butcher's knife slipped from his fingers and clattered to the floor. Behind him in another room, lying in a fetal position, was the child Alex had just stabbed fourteen times. She had rejected his attempted seduction and in a rage he pulled a knife and attacked her. The following day she died from her wounds, her little body wracked with pain. But her mind was lucid and her heart brimmed with Christlike love as she forgave from her heart and whispered, "For the love of Jesus I forgive him.… I want him to be with me in Paradise."

That girl's name was Maria Goretti. Her twenty-year-old murderer is better known as Alessandro Serenelli, the rapist who murdered Maria because she wouldn't go along with his unchaste demands. He was arrested, tried, and sentenced to thirty years in prison for his crime, a crime for which he showed absolutely no remorse. But God's grace is stronger than man's sin, and his forgiveness is stronger than the hardest of hearts. Alex's rebellion was no match for God's merciful love. Eight years into his prison term, St. Maria Goretti appeared to Alex in his cell to remind him of her forgiveness. He repented on the spot, turned his heart to Christ, and lived the next nineteen years of his prison term as a devout Catholic. When he was released from prison, Alex went straight to Maria's mother to beg her forgiveness. And he was present as a witness of the power of forgiveness in St. Peter's Basilica where, in 1950, Maria Goretti was canonized by the pope.

With Arms Outstretched

What caused this stupendous turnaround? What force penetrated his heart of iron? The greatest gift God can give his rebellious children: the grace of forgiveness. Through St. Maria Goretti's heroic martyrdom and forgiveness of her murderer, God the Father reenacted for us the profound drama of the Prodigal Son. He proved again how ready and eager he is to forgive and reconcile all sinners to himself. God loves us so passionately that he will spare no effort to extend his mercy and forgiveness. He loves us, no matter how enormous and vile our sins, and stands arms outstretched inviting us back to his table. Ponder the crucified Lord and you'll see in his broken, dying body the mystery of our merciful Father, his arms outstretched in the ultimate act of loving forgiveness—the ultimate "I Forgive You." The cross is proof that God's mercy is more powerful than our sin.

We, Too, Run From God

Alessandro Serenelli was a prodigal son. He left his Father's house, squandered the riches of grace that were given him in the sacraments, and lived in the mud with the swine as he committed his many sins. He was defiant and unrepentant. His life had become a seething cauldron of sin. Greed, lust, anger, sensuality, laziness, and murder boiled within him. Where once his soul had been adorned with virtue, shining with the sanctifying grace of God's infinite love, now there hung a tangle of writhing serpents and the razor wire of pride that the ego drapes around the soul.

Sadly, you and I play this role too. We may not commit murder, as Alex did, but to greater or lesser extents, we are all prodigal children in desperate need of mercy and forgiveness. We all commit sins—some grave, others less so—and we all at some point find ourselves on the run from God, guilty criminals on the lam. This sad reality has a long history. But so does the happy ending for those who return to God, and through repentance accept his infinite mercy. In the aftermath of Adam and Eve committing the original sin, we see this drama played out for the first time:

And they heard the sound of the Lord God walking in the garden in the cool of the day, and the man and his wife hid themselves from the presence of the Lord God among the trees of the garden. But the Lord God called to the man, and said to him, "Where are you?" And he said, "I heard the sound of thee in the garden, and I was afraid" (Genesis 3:8–9).

When we rebel against God through sin, we're right back there in the garden—naked, cowering and afraid of God's judgment. But God our Father wants to conquer our fear with his love. He wants to rescue us from where we're stranded in sin, prodigal children who wallow with the pigs, afraid to come home. He wants so much to heal our self-inflicted wounds of sin and restore our supernatural health. And, just as he promised Adam and Eve he would (see Genesis 3:15), he provided the way for this to happen, by Christ's sacrifice on the cross. The cross is the sign and seal, the official guarantee for all ages, of God the Father's mercy and forgiveness. No matter how big the sin, no matter how deep the shame we feel, he opens his arms to us and beckons "Come home!" I love you! Come home to me and I will throw my arms of forgiveness around you." As we're told in Scripture, we should never be afraid to turn from our sins, no matter how bad they may be, and come home to our Father: "The Lord is merciful and gracious, slow to anger and abounding in steadfast love.... As far as the east is from the west, so far does he remove our sins from us" (Psalm 103:8, 12).

Forgive Me, Father, the Way I Forgive Others

Mercy and forgiveness are gigantic themes in the Gospels. Christ constantly reminds us that the Father's Divine Mercy is not a one-way street. That mercy must permeate us and be lived out daily in the way we treat our neighbors. It's crucial to remember that just as God is always ready, waiting with open arms to forgive and forget our sins, he expects us to have the same exact attitude toward others. When St. Peter asked him, "Lord, how often shall my brother sin against me, and I forgive him? As many as seven times?" Jesus responded, "I do not say to you seven times, but seventy times seven" (Matthew 18:21–22). In other words, "Be always ready to forgive your brother, just as your Father in heaven is always ready to forgive you."

Let's not forget Christ's cautionary story of the unforgiving servant who was brought before the king because he owed him ten thousand talents; and he could not pay. The servant implored mercy and mercy was granted him. The king canceled the debt. But then the man did not extend the same mercy toward his fellow servant who owed him a small sum. He was not forgiving and he got into big trouble because of it. "You wicked servant!" the king rebuked him. "I forgave you all that debt because you besought me; and should not you have had mercy on your fellow servant, as I had mercy on you?" Then Christ adds, "And in anger his lord delivered him to the jailers, till he should pay all his debt. So also my heavenly Father will do to every one of you, if you do not forgive your brother from your heart" (Matthew 18:32–35).

This fact is embedded in the Our Father: "Forgive us our trespasses, as we forgive those who trespass against us." Happily, all is not doom and gloom here. The Lord's mercy and forgiveness are a silver lining of grace in the thundercloud of sin. They are the pledge and promise of our eternal reconciliation, our eternal homecoming. We must open our hearts, repent of our sins, and embrace that mercy. So too, we must follow Christ's example and forgive others. When the clouds of anger, bitterness, envy, and revenge pass overhead in life, the Holy Spirit wants to breathe His forgiveness through us. And he will, if we let him.

Forgive from the heart. What a powerful thing this is! When we prodigals repent and return to our Father's house of mercy, we receive from his loving heart the infinite riches of grace and peace. In the same way, when we forgive others from the heart, this torrent of merciful love—the very lifeblood of the Blessed Trinity—overflows our hearts and surges into the hearts of those around us.

Fatherhood

||||||||||||||||||||||||||||||||||||||||||

ON DECEMBER 8, 1989, A MASSIVE EARTHQUAKE struck a wide section of Soviet Armenia, toppling buildings, flattening villages, and killing over fifty thousand people in a few terrifying moments. When the shaking stopped, one father rushed from his home and headed toward the grammar school where his son had been in class. When he arrived at what was left of the school, the father found a massive heap of rubble and twisted metal—no signs of life, no survivors clambering out of the rubble. He raced to the corner of the building where he knew his son's classroom once was. He knew the boy would be somewhere underneath the tons of rubble in that corner.

He began clawing at the rubble, unfazed by those around him who tried to convince him that his efforts to save his son were futile. Other dazed parents milled around in confused panic, trying to comprehend the horror that their children were entombed within the ruined building.

"It's useless!" a fireman shouted. "They're all dead. Go home." But the father wouldn't stop. While other parents grieved, he dug. He dug for hours, for over a day, calling his son's name repeatedly in hopes he would find him alive.

Finally, after thirty-eight hours, the exhausted father removed a chunk of cement and heard a weak cry from the blackness below: "Dad? Is it you?" His father shouted in joy. His son was alive! Those near the hole could hear the boy tell his trapped friends, "See? I told you my father would find me. He promised he would always be there when I needed him."

Before long, over a dozen buried children had been hauled into the light, into the waiting arms of their parents, bruised and frightened, but alive. This true story (recounted by Mark Victor Hansen in the book *Chicken Soup for the Soul*) exemplifies the mission of fatherhood. The son's words, "See? I told you my father would come for me" were not a boast. They sprang from his loving confidence that his father would do anything within his power to save his son, no matter the cost to himself.

This story jolted me with the reality of how much God the Father loves us— loves you and me personally. As I reflect on how God the Father raises us, his children, I see how I, as a father, must strive to raise my own family. He wants what is best for me, even when I don't recognize it or want it or accept it. And like the Armenian father who drove himself to save his buried son, even when all seemed hopeless, I realize that God the Father pursues each of his children tirelessly, sparing no effort of grace and illumination to save us from the many tombs of sin and selfishness we so often bury ourselves within.

In his 1989 encyclical *Guardian of the Redeemer*, Pope John Paul II points us to St. Joseph as the perfect model of human fatherhood: "Through his complete self-sacrifice, Joseph expressed his generous love for the Mother of God, and gave her a husband's 'gift of self.'"[110] This giving of self is the key to God's fatherhood and the key to men being true fathers to their children. In the same way, St. Joseph gave himself to Christ and Mary without reserve. He fulfilled in his mission as father what Pope John Paul II has called "the practical demands of love." That translates to: doing what is right and good, even when it's hard and sacrificial to do so.

So what are these "practical demands of love" we fathers face, and how can we become better at fulfilling them? There are several virtues of a good father. We see them preeminently in God our Father and reflected in those many great fathers here on earth, starting with St. Joseph.

Heroic Generosity

Fatherhood means, more than anything else, giving oneself completely to the family. This takes many forms. A father's generosity with his time, being patient, and being willing to sacrifice his own needs for the sake of his family's are signs of authentic giving of self.

My dad was always a good example to me of this kind of fatherly generosity. For example, as I was growing up, our family lived on a pretty tight budget. We children never went without shoes or clothes when we needed them, but my dad often did.

Rather than spend money to buy a new pair of shoes for himself—even when his shoe had a hole in the sole—he would do without so we could have new ones. And there were the mornings I'd come downstairs for breakfast before school and find just enough cereal and milk there for me.

My mom explained later that my dad had gone to work on an empty stomach because if he had eaten, we kids wouldn't have. These sacrifices he made for us were small, yes, but not insignificant. They taught me about how a father should be generous with his family. The day-to-day acts of heroic generosity a father makes are almost always going to be quiet and unobtrusive, hidden even from his family, but they reveal the greatness of a man who is willing to sacrifice for his children.

In Christ's Incarnation, we see the depth of the Father's generosity toward us. Calvary is the proof that he would go to any length to bring us into his family.

A Spirit of Justice and Mercy

The father is an image of God to his family. I believe that more than from any other person, children will learn about who God is from their fathers. In the same way that God deals with us justly and mercifully, so too should fathers deal with their families. I have found that this area is crucial in teaching my children about their relationship with God.

A father's spirit of justice and mercy will have a profound impact on his children. If he is unjust in his dealings with them, or if he lacks mercy, his children will grow up with a warped view of God's love for them. Cynicism and a hardness toward others can set it early on. Conversely, if he is overly indulgent, his children lose a sense of being just in their dealings with others. But the father who is consistent and thoughtful in dispensing justice and quick to show mercy will not only raise happier, more virtuous children, his children will grow up with an authentic understanding of God's eternal justice and mercy.

We fathers must reflect often on Christ's admonitions about forgiveness and seek to live them out in the family, teaching by example about God's justice and mercy. Christ's teachings about the Prodigal Son (Luke 15:11–32), the Unforgiving Servant (Matthew 18:21–35), and the Good Shepherd (John 10:7–17) are wonderful tools for fathers. Not only are they sure guides for us in raising our children, they remind us of how God our Father deals with us.

A Father Must Be a Model of Holiness

Pope John Paul II related once how his encyclical letter on the Holy Spirit, *Dominus et Vivificantum,* arose from a conversation he once had with his father on the way home from church. Young Karol Wojtyla received a spiritual pep talk from his father, who didn't feel his son properly appreciated the role of the Holy Spirit.

Within a few short minutes, his father had imparted to him key principles and insights about the Holy Spirit that, decades later, formed the basis of an encyclical letter! This episode demonstrates the powerful influence a father's piety can have on his children. I believe that great fathers are those who personal efforts to grow in holiness are visible to their families—not in an ostentatious or self-conscious way, of course.

St. Joseph is the perfect example of this. His quiet devotion to the Holy Family, his willingness to do whatever God asked of him, his consistency in fulfilling his religious duties were all ways of showing forth his deep love of God. St. Joseph understood the mission of fatherhood. As fathers, our love for God should be visible (though not put on display) to our families, in particular to our children.

It's hard for a father to teach his children to pray or go to confession regularly if they never see him pray or go to confession. Why should they bother about going to Mass and attending to all those other Christian "duties" if their father doesn't bother about them? The "do as I say and not as I do" attitude, so common in our society, is a death sentence for a father's success in raising his children strong in their Catholic Faith. Rather, the much rarer "do as I say and see that I too do as I say" attitude is what works.

When our children see us loving God and taking our prayer commitments seriously, they are far more likely to do so themselves. I know from experience that my children look to me to set the tone of our family prayer life. If I as their father am lazy or distracted, they quickly follow suit. This principle extends to the way the father treats the mother. When children see their father loving, honoring and respecting her, they learn to treat her the same way. When they see sarcasm or bickering, they unconsciously learn from their father to treat mom the same way.

A Father's Unconditional Love for His Family

This fatherly virtue is the simplest to summarize: Be willing to do whatever is necessary to fulfill those "practical demands of love." Actually, all the other traits are bound up in this overriding attitude of loving and sacrificing for one's family, without limits.

God does nothing less for his universal family, and He asks us to do nothing less for the family he has entrusted to our care here on earth. Like that Armenian father who refused to give up hope for his son, God our Father refuses to give up on us. When we've buried ourselves in the self-created rubble of our sins, or when the trials of everyday life threaten to crush us, he comes searching for us. As St. Paul said, even "If we are unfaithful he remains faithful, for he cannot deny himself" (2 Timothy 2:13).

Our mission as human fathers is to seek what is best for our families, even when what is best isn't what is easiest. If we strive to cultivate a holy, unconditional, fatherly love for our families, what better reward could we ask for than to see in our children the attitude of, "See? I told you my father would find me. He promised he would always be there when I needed him."

Marian Helpers Bulletin, *June 1998*

An Embarrassing Case of Sacramental Mistaken Identity

ONE SATURDAY, SOME YEARS AGO, A FRIEND of mine visited from out of town. Looking for some prayerful encouragement and, probably, a kick in the rear to get himself to confession, he confided tearfully to me that he had fallen into a pattern of serious sexual sin, about which he was understandably distressed and embarrassed. (Let's just say that the particular sins burdening him went well beyond the solitary sort that many men are prone to these days.) During a frank conversation, in which my friend was searingly honest with himself, I offered some advice and encouragement, after which we clambered into my car and drove to a nearby parish so he could receive the sacrament of confession.

His discomfiture at having to confess these sins to another man was palpable. Promising him the meager benefit of my prayers for courage and trust in the Lord's mercy, I knelt in a pew at the back of the church while my friend approached the confessional. The red light above the door indicated that a priest was waiting for penitents. Aside from my friend and me, the church was completely empty.

Fifteen minutes passed. My friend exited the confessional and scuttled to a back pew in the shadows of the left transept, where he remained motionless in prayer, head bowed, his face covered by remorseful hands.

There were no other penitents.

Five more minutes went by. The priest exited the confessional and walked toward the back of the church…where I happened to be kneeling.

The priest did not notice my friend kneeling in the transept.

The priest did, however, notice me.

The closer he got, the more clearly I saw the abashed look on his face as he recognized me. Although this priest and I have only ever exchanged but a few words in passing, he knew who I was.

"Awkward" is not a sufficiently descriptive adjective to describe the look we exchanged as he passed by. Panicking, I realized that the priest thought he had just heard *my* confession.

"Oh, ho!" I imagined the good father thinking to himself. "What a fraud!"

Meanwhile, my friend remained conveniently engrossed in prayer for several minutes more, off in his wonderfully anonymous dark corner, unaware of the unpleasant little drama playing out as the priest whisked by me with that look on his face.

I admit, I was tempted to run after him and explain that he had it all wrong, that I am not that guy, that his newfound view of me is really just a case of mistaken identity. But I stayed put.

Why? Because, in a momentary flash of (albeit dim) understanding, I was painfully reminded of my own lifetime-constructed ziggurat of sin and my savior, Jesus Christ, was wrongly accused of crimes he did not commit but for which he willingly suffered the penalty—for my sake. For my countless sins he suffered so that by his stripes I might be healed.

In the years that have passed since that day, I occasionally see that priest. In truth, I have searched for but never detected even a hint of "that look" on his face when he sees me. Perhaps he forgot what he heard in the confessional minutes later (many priests have assured me that this happens to them—a kind of grace of state that enables them to blank out any lingering memories of what is unburdened to them by penitents). Or maybe he is just a kind and compassionate man who would never even think of betraying the thought that he had been scandalized. I don't know.

I do know this though: My sins may be different from my friend's, or yours, or that priest's, but I am a sinner in grievous need of God's grace and mercy, just like my friend. Just like you. And I am so grateful to the Lord for his gift of the sacrament of confession. He knows how much and how often I need it.

If You Love Them, Tell Them

JESUS SAID, "THIS IS MY COMMANDMENT: LOVE one another as I have loved you. No man has greater love than this, than to lay down his life for his friends" (John 15:12–13). Chances are, you and I won't ever be called to literally die for someone, but Christ's words still apply to us. We're called by name to live out our love for him by laying down our lives for the truth, to speak about him, even when it's uncomfortable or unpopular.

"Evangelization" means sharing the Good News of Christ and his Church. It's the supreme way to love others. Think of it: Jesus loves us so much that he died on the cross to save us from eternal death. He established his Church and its sacraments, and he gave us his own mother to be our mother. Now he asks us to return that love by spreading this Good News to everyone around us.

"But I can't do that," you might be saying to yourself. "I'm not prepared to evangelize."

Actually, you're better prepared than you may realize. First, you're prepared by virtue of your baptism. The Holy Spirit indwells your soul and floods it with the graces you need to be an apostle of his love. Call on him to strengthen you. He will answer you! Especially in the Eucharist and confession, he prepares you to evangelize.

Second, you have the benefit of Scripture and two thousand years of Catholic wisdom and experience to draw upon. The Church's countless saints and missionaries have already blazed the trail, showing us how to "go forth and make disciples of all nations" (Matthew 28:19). So there's no need for us to "reinvent the evangelization wheel." We just need to follow in their footsteps and work to extend the borders of Christ's Kingdom.

Third, you have powerful friends in high places! Our Lady and the saints are ready and willing to help you with their intercession. So ask for their help. Scripture says, "The fervent prayer of a righteous person is very powerful" (James 5:16). Whether you're a housewife, a teacher, a dentist, a factory worker, a student, or even retired, you can evangelize! God is calling you personally to go forth and share the Faith.

Don't worry if you feel unprepared. Rely on the Holy Spirit and begin anyway. The disciples were far from "ready" when Christ first sent them forth, midway through his public ministry, but He sent them anyway. He knows that we, like those disciples, will learn by doing. With the Blessed Virgin Mary as your model and the Holy Spirit as your guide, prayerfully speak to others about Christ and you'll see grace-filled results—we have his Word on it! "I am the vine, you are the branches. Whoever remains in Me and I in him will bear much fruit" (John 15:5).

Don't Make Excuses
We all make excuses for not evangelizing. Some common ones are: "I'm too old—I'll leave that to the younger people," "I'm too young—I'll leave that to the older people," "I'm too busy," "People will think I'm a fanatic," "It's not polite to talk about religion." Obviously, no excuse is a good excuse to avoid evangelization. Moses tried all sorts of them to avoid God's call to rescue His people. Happily, he stopped making excuses and said "yes" to God. You and I are like Moses. People need to hear the liberating message of Christ, and some can only be reached by us. Like Moses, we should put aside our excuses and say "yes" to evangelization.

Look for Opportunities and Use Them
Evangelization doesn't have to be a nerve-racking experience. If you're shy or become tongue-tied and nervous when religion comes up in conversation,

look for creative ways to share the Faith. For example, if you aren't up to a deep discussion, give a Catholic book or cassette tape to your non-Catholic friend and ask her to get back to you with her thoughts. It's easy to evangelize through good books and tapes. Lending a Catholic video to non-Catholic neighbors is a great way to break the ice and start a dialogue. Another handy method is to enclose inexpensive Catholic tracts or holy cards in your bill payment envelopes. You'd be amazed at how they can change lives. Invite non-Catholic friends to attend Mass with you or to come to your home for a rosary circle and coffee hour. There are many ways to evangelize your friends and family without changing your lifestyle one bit.

Each day, Christ puts people in your path for a reason. He wants you to share his love with them. So we must be willing to look for opportunities and act when we find them. This means talking about the Faith when opportunities arise—obviously, in a tactful and charitable way—and letting the light of Christ radiate from us, wherever we may be.

Listen to What the Person Is Saying (and Not Saying)

Evangelization involves listening as much as talking. We can easily fall into the trap of talking so much that we never really hear the other person's questions. Some people are alienated from Christ and his Church for reasons they don't mention verbally. Listen with your heart, and you'll pick up on things often said only through body language or facial expressions. Many lonely and hurting people need someone to listen to them before they can listen to Christ.

Recently, an elderly man told me that he left the Catholic Church in a huff over some aggravation and stayed away for over thirty-five bitter, angry years. "What brought you back after all that time?" I asked. His answer startled me. "I met a Catholic one day," he explained, "and started throwing anti-Catholic arguments at him. Rather than argue back, he just listened patiently. Then he put his hand on my shoulder and smiled, saying, 'I just want you to know you're always welcome to come home. The door to the Church is always open to you.'" That was all it took. The man's eyes got misty and his voice grew thick with emotion as he described that moment of grace. The Holy Spirit used that

Catholic's gentle response to pour out healing graces and bring a wayward son home to the Church and back to the sacraments. By listening—really listening, we can discover the best way to evangelize.

Prepare Through Study and Prayer

You know the old saying: "You can't give what you don't have." This is especially true when it comes to evangelization. We must know the Faith before we can teach others, and we must love Christ if we're to help others love him. This means we must prepare our heads and our hearts for the task. Mary is our model here. She prayed and studied constantly: "She kept all these things and pondered them in her heart" (Luke 2:19). We too should ponder and study the Faith. Spend fifteen minutes a day reading Scripture and pages of the Catechism— you'll be amazed at how this will build your knowledge and your confidence. Prayer is the other key. You can't help others love Christ if you yourself don't love him. And true love involves communication—spending time with Christ, listening to him, sharing your cares and plans with him. When he is your friend, it becomes easy and natural to introduce others to him.

Let God Do the Heavy Lifting

Evangelization is really the Holy Spirit's work, not ours. How liberating it is to realize that he is the Master of the harvest, not us. So don't be disturbed when you don't see instant results. He is working even when it seems your message isn't getting through. He is ready to do marvelous works of conversion, but he wants you to help him. The Lord is saying to you, "Be not afraid. I have a mission prepared just for you. Will you help me?" Let Our Lady's response be your response: "Behold the servant of the Lord. Let it be done to me according to your word."

Marian Helpers Bulletin, *September 1998*

EPILOGUE
"Pat-pourri"

IN A RECENT INTERVIEW A JOURNALIST ASKED me, "When did you begin to write?"

My response: "I started writing in kindergarten, but nothing significant came from those early efforts. In fact, everything from that phase of my career has been lost to posterity."

Cheeky, yes, but not entirely absurd, when you consider that nothing in my childhood and youth gave even the faintest indication that I might one day become an author. As my parents and teachers would have told you back then, while I definitely had the gift of gab (usually, to a fault), I did not have the gift of write—at least not until my mid-twenties, when the prospect of a career writing for a living gradually began to mysteriously materialize. If it weren't for the astonishingly fortuitous opportunity that God (and Karl Keating) offered me in working at Catholic Answers, I might well have never had the occasion to write a single word in an effort to publically explain, defend, and share the riches of the ancient Catholic Faith into which I was to be born. But, as the old adage goes, man proposes and God disposes. And I will be eternally grateful to God (and everyone else concerned) for the fact that he disposed things as he did.

The literary dimension of the last twenty-five years of my life, if "literary" can be considered an appropriate descriptor of my work, has been for me an ineffable, wholly unanticipated blessing. I can only pray that it may also have been a blessing for others.

As I mentioned in another interview during a recent Australian lecture tour, given the many ways in which I failed to serve God in my youth and young adulthood because of sin and selfishness,[111] I want to make up for that lost time by trying to help others as best I can. I'm overjoyed to be able to do this work and am constantly astonished each time it reoccurs to me that God is allowing me to participate in it when there are so many smarter, more talented, and holier people than I who could be doing it better than I can. But I'm not complaining! No, I am profoundly grateful to the Lord for allowing me to have had a small part to play in the Church's perennial work of always being "prepared to make a defense to anyone who calls you to account for the hope that is in you" (1 Peter 3:15).

Notes

|||||||||||||||||||||

1. Audio of both of these debates, the only ones ever held between a Catholic and an official Mormon spokesman, are available in their entirety at www.patrickmadrid.com/ store. They are titled, respectively, the "First" and "Second Mormon Dialogues."

2. Several devout Mormons have told me that this is unheard-of for a Catholic apologist.

3. MP3 audio and CDs of my debates are available at www.patrickmadrid.com.

4. Born 1932; cofounder of Southern Evangelical Seminary in Charlotte, N.C. The term "moderate Calvinist" is how Geisler describes his theological views.

5. Professor of theology at Christendom College.

6. Michael Horton is professor of theology at Westminster Seminary California; Robert Godfrey is resident of Westminster Seminary California.

7. Professor of theology at Concordia University, Irvine, California.

8. This claim forms the core of the Protestant principle of Scripture's formal sufficiency, as expressed in the 1646 Calvinist *Westminster Confession of Faith*.

9. I.e, the matador's final, lethal sword thrust between the shoulders of the bull.

10. Lutherans believe in baptismal regeneration. Calvinist deny that baptism regenerates.

11. The audio recording of the entire "What Still Divides Us?" debate, as well as my other debates including "Does the Bible Teach *Sola Scriptura*?" (Madrid vs. White) and "The Denver 'Bible Only?' Debate" (Madrid & Keating vs. Jackson & Nemec), are available in CD or downloadable MP3 format at www.patrickmadrid.com.

12. For example, his erroneous claim that the Second Person of the Trinity only "became the Son of God" at the Incarnation, thus denying that Christ is "eternally begotten of the Father," one of the major tenets of the Nicene Creed. See Walter R. Martin, *The Kingdom of the Cults* (Minneapolis: Bethany, 1985), pp. 117–118.

13. I.e., *Surprised by Truth* (San Diego: Basilica, 1994), *Surprised by Truth 2* (Manchester, N.H.: Sophia, 2000), and *Surprised by Truth 3* (Manchester, N.H.: Sophia, 2002).

14. EWTN's remarkable and grace-filled saga is chronicled by Raymond Arroyo in *Mother Angelica: The Remarkable Story of a Nun, Her Nerve, and a Network of Miracles* (New York: Doubleday, 2005).

15. President of the apostolates Living His Life Abundantly and Women of Grace.

16. This and many other of my debates with Protestant ministers, Mormon leaders, and other non-Catholic spokesmen are available in CD and downloadable MP3 audio format at www.patrickmadrid.com.

17. Basil of Caesarea, *The Westminster Confession of Faith*, 1646, p. 7.

18. Basil of Caesarea, *On the Holy Spirit*, 27.

19. Basil of Caesarea, *On the Holy Spirit*, 71.

20. St. Athanasius, *Contra Gentiles*, 1:1.

21. St. Athanasius, *39th Festal Letter.*

22. St. Athanasius, *Ad Afros*, 1.

23. St. Athanasius, *Ad Serapion*, 1:28.

24. Cyril of Jerusalem, *Catechetical Lectures*, 4:17.

25. *The Westminster Confession of Faith*, 7.

26. *The Thirty-Nine Articles of Religion*, 6.

27. For a discussion of the history of the material sufficiency position among Catholic theologians, see Patrick Madrid, *Scripture and Tradition in the Church* (Melbourne: Freedom, 2012) and George H. Tavard, *Holy Writ or Holy Church: The Crisis of the Protestant Reformation* (London: Burns & Oates, 1959).

28. Yves M.J. Congar, *Tradition and Traditions* (New York: MacMillan, 1967), pp. 23–85, 156–168, and especially 376–426.

29. So St. Thomas: *"Sacra Scriptura ad hoc divinitus est ordinate ut per eam nobis veritas manifestetur necessaria ad salutem"* (*Quodl.* 7, 14).

30. John Henry Newman, *Certain Difficulties Felt by Anglicans in Catholic Teaching, Considered in a Letter Addressed to the Rev. E. B. Pusey, D.D., on the Occasion of His Eirenicon of 1864*, Vol. 2, section 2, 2.

31. *Dei Verbum*, 9–10.

32. See Gerhard Delling's article on *téleios* in *Kittel's Theological Dictionary of the New Testament*, Gerhard Friedrich, ed. (Grand Rapids: Eerdmans, 1972), vol. 8, pp. 67–78, where he translates *téleios* as: "totality," "undivided," "complete," and "perfect."

33. Delling, vol. l, pp. 475–476.

34. St. Vincent of Lerins, *Commonitoria*, 25, 26, 25.

35. *The Westminster Confession of Faith*, 6, 7, 9.

36. John Calvin, *Commentary on 1 Corinthians 4:6*.

37. Loraine Boettner, *Roman Catholicism* (Phillipsburg, N.J.: Presbyterian and Reformed, 1962), p. 95.

38. St. Thomas More, *Dialogue Concerning Tyndale*.

39. St. Thomas More, *Dialogue Concerning Tyndale*.

40. Paul Stenhouse, *Catholic Answers to Bible Christians: A Light on Biblical Fundamentalism* (Kensington, NSW: Chevalier, 1988).

41. Quoted in Stenhouse.

42. *The Westminster Confession of Faith,* I, 9.

43. *Dei Verbum,* 10.

44. St. Athanasius, *Ad Afros.*

45. C. of Arm. & Sel.

46. *Homilies on Genesis, Homily 13* (13).

47. *Dei Verbum* 10.

48. *Ad Serapion* 1:28.

49. St. Cyril of Jerusalem, *Catechetical Lectures,* 18:23.

50. St. Augustine, *Letter 93,* A.D. 408.

51. Basil of Caesarea, *On the Holy Spirit,* 27.

52. *Commonotoria* 2:1–2 [A.D. 434].

53. Bruce McConkie, *Mormon Doctrine* (Salt Lake City: Bookcraft, 1966), pp. 43–44. McConkie, ever pugnacious when his religion was at stake, made it clear that the Catholic Church was the wholly corrupt phoenix that rose from the ashes of Christ's failed Church. "Iniquitous conditions in the various branches of the great and abominable church in the last days are powerfully described in the *Book of Mormon* (2 Nephi 28; Mormon 8:28–38; *Doctrine and Covenants* 10:56). It is also to the *Book of Mormon* to which we turn for *the plainest description of the Catholic Church as the great and abominable church.* Nephi saw this 'church was the most abominable above all other churches' in [his] vision. He 'saw the devil that he was the foundation of it,' and also the murders, wealth, harlotry, persecutions, and evil desires that historically have been part of this satanic organization. He saw that this most abominable of all churches was founded after the day of Christ and his apostles; that it took away from the gospel of the Lamb many covenants and many plain and precious parts; that it had perverted the right ways of the Lord; that it had deleted many teachings from the Bible; that his church was the mother of harlots; and that, finally, the Lord would again restore the gospel of salvation" (ibid., 1958 ed., pp. 314–315). In recent years the Mormon Church has engaged in a strenuous public relations program designed to garner for itself acceptance as a mainstream "Christian" denomination. Anti-Catholic comments such as McConkie's, although de rigueur among Mormon apologists in the past, are no longer allowed in official Mormon works. Emphasis added.

54. James E. Talmadge, *The Great Apostasy* (Salt Lake City: Desert, 1968), p. iii. For a discussion of apostolic succession see Warren H. Carroll, *The Founding of Christendom* and *The Building of Christendom* (Front Royal, Va.: Christendom College Press, 1985).

55. 1 Timothy 3:15 describes the Church as "The household of God...the pillar and foundation of truth." In light of this, we find additional assurance that the house that Jesus built will not be pillaged by Satan. "No one can enter a strong man's house

to plunder his property unless first he ties up the strong man. Then, he can plunder his house" (Mark 3:27; see Matthew 12:29). Jesus is the "strong man" guarding his household, the Church.

56. Jesus did not command his followers to do things he himself couldn't do. "Everyone who listens to these words of mine and acts on them will be like a wise man who built his house on a rock. The rain fell, the floods came, and the winds blew and buffeted the house. But it did not collapse; it had been set solidly on a rock" (Matthew 7:24–25). It was no coincidence that Jesus used the words, "on this rock I will build my Church and the gates of hell shall not prevail against it" (Matthew 16:18; Luke 6:46–49). See also Hebrews 11:10 and 1 Peter 2:6–8.

57. Robert Starling, *This Rock*, July 1991, p. 18.

58. For a full-length examination of this issue, see the recording of the debate, "A Catholic-Mormon Dialogue" (Patrick Madrid vs. Gary Coleman, 1989), available at www.patrickmadrid.com. This was the first-ever debate between a Catholic apologist and an official representative of the Church of Jesus Christ of Latter-day Saints. See also the debate between Patrick Madrid and Frank Bradshaw (LDS).

59. For a thorough treatment of early Church writings see William Jurgens's three-volume *Faith of the Early Fathers* (Collegeville, Minn.: Liturgical, 1970) and Johannes Quasten's four-volume *Patrology* (Westminster, Md.: Christian Classics, 1986). A helpful critique of Mormonism, including the First Vision, is found in Isaiah Bennett, *Inside Mormonism: What Mormons Really Believe* (San Diego: Catholic Answers, 1999).

60. *Epistle to the Corinthians,* 44

61. *Letter to the Magnesians,* 13:1–2.

62. Ignatius, *Against Heresies,* 3, 3:1–2.

63. Available at www.envoymagazine.com.

64. Patrick Madrid and Kenneth Hensley, *The Godless Delusion: A Catholic Challenge to Modern Atheism* (Huntington, Ind.: Our Sunday Visitor, 2010).

65. Quoted in Stanley L. Jaki, *Angels, Apes & Men* (Peru, Ill.: Sherwood Sugden, 2006), p. 45.

66. *Articles of Religion,* article 22.

67. *Sacrosanctum Concilium,* 4–5.

68. The teaching that the Church is Christ's Body is emphasized throughout the New Testament (see 1 Corinthians 10:16; 12:12–27; Galatians 3:28; Ephesians 1:22–23; 3:4–6; 4:4, 15, 25; 5:21–32; Colossians 1:18; 3:15; Hebrews 13:1–3).

69. See 1 Corinthians 15:25–26, 54–56; 2 Corinthians 2:14; 2 Timothy 1:10.

70. See Acts 8:24; 2 Corinthians 13:7; Philippians 1:9; Galatians 5:13; 6:2; Ephesians 4:32; 1 Thessalonians 3:10–12, 4:9–18; 5:14–15, 25; 2 Thessalonians 1:3; 3:1; 1 Timothy 2:1–4;

2 Timothy 1:3–4; Hebrews 3:19; 13:18; James 5:16; 1 Peter 1:22; 3:8; 1 John 4:7–21; 2 John 5.

71. See also: 1 Corinthians 11:1; Philippians 3:17; 4:19; 1 Thessalonians 1:6–7.

72. While it's true the rich man received a negative answer to his request, it can't be denied that he was interceding for his relatives on earth.

73. *Sermons of Martin Luther*, John Nicholas Lenker, ed. (Grand Rapids: Baker, 1988) vol. 8, pp. 52–54.

74. The official Catholic position on this issue appears in *Canons and Decrees of the Council of Trent* (Rockford: Tan, 1978), Session V ("Decree on Original Sin"), pp. 25–28, Session XXV ("Decree on the Invocation of Saints"), pp. 214–217.

75. This is untrue. There are a number of biblical cases in which Jesus was persuaded to be compassionate. A particularly striking example is the Canaanite woman who had to beg Jesus repeatedly for mercy (almost to the point of arguing with him) before he would agree to cure her daughter (see Matthew 15:21–28). Rather, when he saw the blind and the lame, the afflicted and hungry, he was moved with compassion for them and lifted them out of their distress. He had immediate mercy on the wicked but penitent thief on the cross, and there was no need for intercession by Mary although she was there present.

76. *Roman Catholicism* (Philadelphia: Presbyterian and Reformed, 1962), pp. 147–148.

77. When the Lord spoke these words to Moses on Mount Horeb, the three patriarchs had been "dead" for over five hundred years.

78. Eric Svendsen, *Protestant Answers: A Response to Recent Attacks Against Protestant Theology by Catholic Apologists* (Atlanta: New Testament Restoration Foundation, 1995), p. 90.

79. Svendsen, p. 90.

80. Other examples of legitimate bowing down in honor before human beings are found in Genesis 23:7–13; 33:4–7; 42:5; 43:26–29; 48:9; Numbers 22:31; 1 Samuel 20:41; 25:41.

81. *Luther's Works,* 21:327, 36:208, 45:107.

82. The term "handed on" is the English equivalent of the Greek verb used here, *pared⁻oka*, from which we get the English word *tradition*. St. Jerome rendered *pared⁻oka* into Latin as: *tradidi* ("what I traditioned [to you]"). See 1 Corinthians 11:1; 23–26; Galatians 1:24; 4:12; and Hebrews 11:1–40; 12:1–2.

83. *Theology and Sanity,* pp. ??

84. Wilfred Sheed, *Frank and Maisie: A Memoir With Parents* (Old Tappan, NJ..: Touchstone, 1986).

85. Sheed, *Frank and Maisie.*

86. Quoted in Eusebius, *Ecclesiastical History,* 2:25.

87. St. Irenaeus of Lyons, *Against Heresies*, 3:3.

88. Pope Callistus, *First Epistle*, 1.

89. Pope Callistus, *Second Epistle, To All the Bishops of Gaul*, 2, 6.

90. Pope Damasus, *Decree of Pope Damasus*, 2–3.

91. St. John Chrysostom, *First Epistle to Pope Innocent I*.

92. J.P. Kirsch, article on Pope Joan, *Catholic Encyclopedia*, (New York: Robert Appleton, 1911).

93. Subsequent to my article and no doubt in response to it, at least one industrious Seventh-Day Adventist apologist was able to locate examples of variants of the phrase Vicarius Filii Dei being used in certain official Church documents, such as Pope Paul VI's 1968 apostolic constitution Bafianae. I therefore stand corrected in my unduly exclusive assertion that "no" examples can be found of this phrase. Nonetheless, such counter-examples notwithstanding, the relatively rare instances of this usage not only do not rise to the level of being a formal title of the pope (remember that in the Catholic Encyclopedia's article on papal titles, Vicarius Filii Dei is conspicuously absent from the list), they do not vindicate the notion that this obscure and rarely used description of the pope's office equates with the "the name of the beast or the number of its name" (Revelation 13:18).

94. The one exception I have subsequently become aware of is an ornate tiara given as a gift to Pope Pius IX by members of the court of the King of Belgium in 1871. Known as the "Belgian Tiara," it has four small metal plates affixed to it containing the Latin words Christi, Vicario, In Terra, Regum. I have found no evidence that the pope ever wore this tiara.

95. *Catholic Encyclopedia*, 1913, vol. 6, p. 48.

96. *Our Sunday Visitor*, April 18, 1915, vol. 3, Number 51, p. 3.

97. Fr. John Hardon, S.J., defines "laxism" as "a theory in moral theology condemned by the Church. Laxism permits one to follow the opinion that favors liberty and against the law, even though the opinion is only slightly or even doubtfully probable. (Etym. Latin *laxus*, slack.) [*Modern Catholic Dictionary* (New York: Doubleday, 1980). The Merriam-Webster Dictionary defines laxism's broader, secondary meaning as: "a theory that certainty is impossible especially in the sciences and that probability suffices to govern belief and action."

98. St. Augustine interpreted this passage this way, with regard to purgatory, in *City of God*, 21:24:2.

99. The Council of Trent, Session 25, November 4, 1563.

100. St. Gregory the Great, *Dialogue*, 4:39.

101. *The Catholic Encyclopedia*, vol. 12, p. 577.

102. See St. Ambrose, *Sermon Twenty on Psalms*, 117; St. Jerome, *Commentary on Amos*, 100:4; St. Augustine, *Commentary on Psalms*, 37, and *On the Care that Should be Taken for the Dead*; St. Cyril of Jerusalem, *Catechetical Lectures* 5:9; Pope St. Gregory the Great, *Dialogue 4*, 39; Origen, *Homily Six on Exodus*; St. Gregory of Nyssa, *Sermon on the Dead* (A.D. 382); St. John Chrysostom, *Homilies on the Epistle to the Philippians 3:4–10* (A.D. 398); Serapion, *Prayer of the Eucharistic Sacrifice,* 13:1–27 (A.D. 350).

103. St. Ambrose of Milan, *On the Mysteries,* 132.

104. For a biblical examination of how our prayers can help the souls in purgatory, see my book *Any Friend of God's Is a Friend of Mine.*

105. *The Catholic Encyclopedia,* 1911, vol. 12, p. 578.

106. Originally from *Envoy Magazine,* November/December 1999.

107. Today in 2012, it seems weird to read about smoking in airplanes, but that was still (cough, cough) a reality back in 1994.

108. For Keating's account of this debate, see his article "Into the Maw of the Cult" in *This Rock* magazine; www.catholic.com.

109. Page 320.

110. Paragraph 20.

111. Discussed in tedious detail in my chapter "Conclusions of a Guilty Bystander" in *Surprised by Truth 2.*

Index

‖‖‖‖‖‖‖‖‖‖‖‖‖‖

Scripture Index

I||||||||||||||||||||||||||||||||||||||||||||||||||||||||

About the Author

PATRICK MADRID (www.patrickmadrid.com) is a lifelong Catholic. The director of the Envoy Institute, he has also authored or edited eighteen books on Catholic themes, including *Search and Rescue, Answer Me This, Does the Bible Really Say That?*, the acclaimed *Surprised by Truth* series, and *A Year With the Bible*. Patrick hosts the *Right Here, Right Now* radio broadcast, produced by Immaculate Heart Radio and carried across the EWTN Radio Network of over 200 AM & FM radio stations, on Sirius-XM Satellite Radio, and globally via shortwave (Monday through Friday from 4:00 to 5:00 pm ET). Patrick is also a frequent guest on the "Catholic Answers Live" radio program and he conducts parish seminars and speaks at conferences across the country and around the world. He earned a B.Phil. in philosophy and an M.A. in theology at the Pontifical College Josephinum, Columbus, Ohio. Patrick and his wife, Nancy, were married on February 7th, 1981, and have been blessed by the Lord with eleven children and twelve grandchildren. They reside in the Diocese of Columbus, Ohio.